Warman's® Antiques & Collectibles

52nd Edition

2019

NOAH FLEISHER

Published by

Krause Publications, a division of F+W Media, Inc.
700 East State Street • Iola, WI 54990-0001
715-445-2214 • 888-457-2873
www.krausebooks.com

To order books or other products call toll-free 1-800-258-0929
or visit us online at www.krausebooks.com

ISBN-13: 9781440248658
ISBN-10: 1440248656

Designed by Nicole MacMartin
Edited by Paul Kennedy

Printed in China

10 9 8 7 6 5 4 3 2 1

FRONT COVER: Tiffany Studios Favrile Glass and Bronze Acorn Table Lamp, circa 1910, 16 3/4" high, 12" diameter, $18,750. Image courtesy Heritage Auctions, www.ha.com

BACK COVER: Quezal Feather-Pulled Glass Floriform Vase, circa 1910, 6 1/2" high. $812. Image courtesy Heritage Auctions, www.ha.com

Contents

Introduction

Finding timeless beauty in things we love

By Noah Fleisher

Welcome to *Warman's Antiques & Collectibles 2019!* Can it already be time for our 2019 offering? It seems just a few weeks ago I was sitting at this very keyboard, typing the Introduction to the 2018 *Warman's Antiques & Collectibles* wondering what the year would bring.

It's safe to say that the year that just passed us brought us plenty. Let's put aside global chaos, political division and the myriad complications these things have wrought and focus on what really matters – the antiques and collectibles. All the rest are but just temporary distractions. What really matters are the things that we cherish, the things that tie us to our collective past and give us a tangible, lasting connection to years, decades and centuries past.

What's on our minds this year at *Warman's?* It's holding on to the precious things that bind us together with a common heritage, a mutual appreciation for the ideas and images that unite us, not drive us apart – that is, after all, our stock in trade. Yours, too, I hope.

The past year was a decidedly good year for antiques and collectibles, as the past decade or so has been, but it all seems to boil down to one spectacular piece for me – not the most expensive, or the shiniest, but one that reminded me of what I think is best about our collective memory, our shared pop culture history and the best of our insanely creative human brains: the $478,000 sale in August 2017 of an original, singular First Post-War Release Italian 4-Fogli movie poster for *Casablanca* (Warner Brother, 1946). You can admire it on the next page. It is, to be sure, a thing of mythical beauty.

This poster was unknown when it showed up at Heritage Auctions and set the collecting world abuzz. It doubled as an amazing piece of film memorabilia and a great piece of art. It hit me, and so many others, squarely in our guts and made us take notice.

Starring Humphrey Bogart and Ingrid Bergman as

Writer and author **NOAH FLEISHER** has 20 years of experience in the antiques and collectibles field. He is the author of *The Beatles: Fab Finds of the Fab Four, Warman's Modern Furniture,* and *Collecting Children's Books.*

Prized Italian movie poster for *Casablanca*.
Courtesy of Heritage Auctions, www.ha.com

star-crossed lovers in a war-torn world, *Casablanca* was, and still is, one of if not *the* greatest film of all time. It holds up today as well as it ever had throughout its almost 80 years of existence. It is a masterpiece of writing, acting, cinematography, dramatic tension and – as evidenced by this poster – art.

Time changes everything. It's trite but true. Fashions come and go. Tastes vary wildly from year to year. What's old is new. If you wait a minute or two, what's new seems old. And old in our culture, unfortunately is often viewed as antiquated, not antique. There's a difference. But then we are reminded that old can be timeless. In a singular moment we discover anew that art matters not for art's sake but for ours. And so here we are with a rare and wonderful poster of a great movie, *Casablanca*.

American versions of the *Casablanca* poster are highly sought-after and original posters in good condition always bring top dollar. This piece, however, having originated in Italy and having stayed carefully hidden and preserved across the decades, is a thing completely unto itself. It is a survivor, the only one of its kind and a piece of exceptional delicacy and beauty, much like the film itself. In its discovery, presentation and sale, it transcended its original purpose – a paper advertisement meant to draw people like you and I into a movie theater for a few hours of distraction – and has become a timeless piece of art. It is now a piece of our collective memory, something to be treasure.

It doesn't matter that an individual purchased it, or that it will likely hang in a private place in someone's house or gallery space. What matters, only, is that the poster exists.

The mere fact of its presence on the planet, just knowing this magnificent poster exists, is enough for me. It enters the common annals of our shared experience for all of us to hold dear because of its very essence of timelessness. It embodies the very best of this business of collecting antiques and collectibles that has drawn us all to this precise moment, holding this book in your hands and letting your heart fill with love for its continued existence. This shared affection, wherever the actual physical thing itself lives, bestows an immortality upon it and, by association and appreciation, on us all.

That, to me, is the very essence of why we collect, why things – great and small, priceless and worthless – matter.

Once more I welcome you to this year's edition of *Warman's*. The art, antiques and collectibles that populate the following pages are why you're here and I commend you all for that. Long after the writers, editors and all the other

Camera used to photograph
President Lincoln. **$66,725**

Courtesy of Heritage Auctions, ha.com

contributors to this guide have
faded into the dust of days past,
the things we love will still be
here, they will bear witness to
our collective memory and, in
so doing bestow upon each and
every one of us who love them
and shared immortality, even if
our names are not written upon it.

The love we hold for them,
so alive today in our hearts, and
passed on to posterity, assure it.

Special Thanks

There have been so many talented
and insightful people who have worked
on *Warman's* over the years that it
would take up far too much space to
thank them all here. They know who
they are and I hope they accept these
heartfelt thanks from me on behalf of
Krause Publications for all the work and
effort they have put into this title over
the years. I am honored to follow in
their footsteps.

For the 2019 edition in particular I
would be remiss in not thanking Paul
Kennedy, editorial director of this
book, for his continued guidance and
friendship. I would also like to thank
all the contributors whose brilliant
work makes up these pages. Last, but
certainly not least, I would like to thank
the great loves of my life, my wife and
daughter, Lauren Zittle and Fiona
Fleisher. As always, their patience and
love guide my every action.

In the Beginning

Edwin G. Warman was an
entrepreneur in Uniontown,
Pennsylvania. He dabbled in several
ventures, including ownership of a radio
station. He was also an avid antiques

collector who published his
price listings in response to
requests from friends and fellow
collectors. The first modest price guide
was published in 1948 as *Warman's
Antiques and Their Current Prices*. It was
a bold move. Until then, antiques were
sold primarily through dealers, antiques
shops, and at auctions. The buyers and
sellers negotiated prices and were forced
to do their own research to determine
fair values. Under Warman's care, the
price guide changed all that forever.
Warman also published some specialized
price guides for pattern glass and
milk glass, as well as his "Oddities and
Curiosities" editions, under the banner of
the E.G. Warman Publishing Co.

Although the name varied slightly
over the years, *Warman's Antiques
and Their Current Prices* covered such
collectible areas as mechanical banks,
furniture, and silver, just like the
Warman's of today. His pages consisted
of a brief statement about the topic,
either relating to the history or perhaps
the "collectibility" of the category. A

listing of current prices was included, often containing a black and white photograph.

E.G. Warman died in 1979. His widow, Pat Warman, continued the tradition and completed work on the 15th edition after his death. The estate sold the E.G. Warman Publishing Co. to Stanley and Katherine Greene of Elkins Park, Pennsylvania, in 1981. Chilton Books bought the Warman Publishing Co. in the fall of 1989. With the 24th edition, *Warman's* was published under the Wallace-Homestead imprint. Krause Publications purchased both the Warman's and Wallace-Homestead imprints in 1997.

We are proud to continue the rich tradition started 70 years ago by Mr. Warman, a man driven by his love of antiques and collectibles and by a thirst for sharing his knowledge.

The Warman's Advantage

The Warman's Advantage manifests itself in several important ways in the 2019 edition. As we reviewed past volumes, we wanted to make this book as easy to use as possible. To that end, we've consolidated and reorganized how we present several key categories. Our new mantra is, "What is it first?"

For instance, an antique clock may also have an advertising component, reflect a specific design theme (like Art Deco), and be made of cast iron. But first and foremost, it's a clock, and that's where you'll find it listed, even though there are other collecting areas involved.

There are a few categories that remain iconic in the collecting world. Coca-Cola collectibles cross many interests, as do folk art, Asian antiques, Tiffany and advertising, to name but a few. These still have their own broad sections.

Prices

The prices in this book have been established using the results of auction sales across the country, and by tapping the resources of knowledgeable dealers and collectors. These values reflect not only current collector trends, but also the wider economy. The adage that "an antique (or collectible) is worth what someone will pay for it" still holds. A price guide measures value, but it also captures a moment in time, and sometimes that moment can pass very quickly.

Beginners should follow the same advice that all seasoned collectors share: Make mistakes and learn from them; talk with other collectors and dealers; find reputable resources (including books and websites); and learn to invest wisely, buying the best examples you can afford.

Words of Thanks

This 52nd edition of *Warman's* would not be possible without the help of countless others. Dozens of auction houses have generously shared their resources, but a few deserve special recognition: Heritage Auctions, Dallas; Backstage Auctions, Houston; Woody Auction, Douglass, Kansas; Greg Belhorn, Belhorn Auction Services LLC, Columbus, Ohio; James D. Julia Auctioneers, Fairfield, Maine; Anthony Barnes at Rago Arts and Auctions, Lambertville, New Jersey; Karen Skinner at Skinner, Inc., Boston; Morphy Auctions, Denver, Pennsylvania; Susan Pinnell at Jeffrey S. Evans & Associates, Mount Crawford, Virginia; Rebecca Weiss at Swann Auction Galleries, New York; and Leslie Hindman Auctioneers, Chicago. And, as always, special thanks to Catherine Saunders-Watson for her many contributions and continued support.

Read All About It

There are many fine publications that collectors and dealers may consult about antiques and collectibles in general. Space does not permit listing all of the national and regional publications in the antiques and collectibles field; this is a sampling:

- *Antique Trader,* published by Krause Publications, 700 E. State St., Iola, WI, 54990 – *www.antiquetrader.com*
- *Antique & The Arts Weekly,* 5 Church Hill Road, Newton, CT 06470 – *www.antiquesandthearts.com*
- *AntiqueWeek,* P.O. Box 90, Knightstown, IN 46148 – *www.antiqueweek.com*
- *Maine Antique Digest,* P.O. Box 358, Waldoboro, ME 04572 – *www.maineantiquedigest.com*
- *New England Antiques Journal,* 24 Water St., Palmer, MA 01069 – *www.antiquesjournal.com*
- *The Journal of Antiques and Collectibles,* P.O. Box 950, Sturbridge, MA 01566 – *www.journalofantiques.com*
- *Southeastern Antiquing & Collecting Magazine,* P.O. Box 510, Acworth, GA 30101 – *www.go-star.com/antiquing*

Visit an Antiques Show

One of the best ways to enjoy the world of antiques and collectibles is to take the time to really explore an antiques show. Some areas, like Brimfield, Massachusetts, and Manchester, New Hampshire, turn into antiques meccas for a few days each summer when dealers and collectors come for both specialized and general antiques shows, plus auctions.

Here are a few of our favorites:
- *Brimfield, Massachusetts, shows,* held three times a year in May, July, and September, *www.brimfield.com*
- *Round Top, Texas, antique shows,* held spring, fall, and winter, *www.roundtoptexasantiques.com*
- *Antiques Week* in and around Manchester, New Hampshire, held every August, *www.antiquesweeknh.com*
- *Christine Palmer & Associates antiques and collectibles shows,* including the Portland, Oregon, Expos, *http://christinepalmer.net*
- *The Original Miami Beach Antique Show,* www.originalmiamibeachantiqueshow.com
- *Merchandise Mart International Antiques Fair,* Chicago, *www.merchandisemartantiques.com*
- *High Noon Western Americana Show and Auction,* Phoenix, *www.highnoon.com*

 ## LET US KNOW WHAT YOU THINK

We're always eager to hear what you think about this book and how we can improve it.

Contact:
Paul Kennedy
Editorial Director
Antiques & Collectibles Books
Krause Publications
700 E. State St.
Iola, WI 54990-0001
715-445-2214, Ext. 13470
Paul.Kennedy@fwmedia.com

Norman Rockwell's masterpiece, *Study for Triple Self-Portrait*, 1960, sold for **$1,332,500.**
Courtesy of Heritage Auctions, www.ha.com

Contributors

John Adams-Graf
Melody Amsel-Arieli
Eric Bradley
Brent Frankenhoff
Maggi McCormick
Gordon
Kyle Husfloen
Paul Kennedy

Karen Knapstein
Mark B. Ledenbach
Russell E. Lewis
Kristine Manty
Mark Moran
Allan Petretti
Michael Polak
Pat Prince

David Rago
Antoinette Rahn
Barry Sandoval
Ellen T. Schroy
Mary Sieber
Maggie Thompson
David Wagner
Martin Willis

Auction Houses

Sanford Alderfer Auction & Appraisal
501 Fairgrounds Rd.
Hatfield, PA 19440
800-577-8846
www.alderferauction.com
Full service

American Bottle Auctions
915 28th St.
Sacramento, CA 95816
800-806-7722
www.americanbottle.com
Antique bottles, jars

American Pottery Auction
Waasdorp, Inc.
P.O. Box 434
Clarence, NY 14031
716-983-2361
www.antiques-stoneware.com
Stoneware, redware

American Sampler/Cast Iron Online
P.O. 371
Barnesville, MD 20838
301-972-6250
www.castirononline.com
Cast iron bookends, doorstops

Antiques and Estate Auctioneers
861 W. Bagley Rd.
Berea, OH 44017
440-647-4007
Fax: 440-647-4006
www.estateauctioneers.com
Firearms/military, historical collections,
coins/currency

ATM Antiques & Auctions LLC
8915 US Hwy 19.
Homosassa, FL 34429
800-542-3877
www.charliefudge.com
Full service

Auctions Neapolitan
1100 First Ave. S.
Naples, FL 34102
239-262-7333
www.auctionsneapolitan.com
Full service

Belhorn Auction Services, LLC
2746 Wynnerock Ct.
Hilliard, Ohio 43026
614-921-9441
belhornauctions.com
Full service, American art pottery

Backstage Auctions
448 West 19th St., Suite 163
Houston, TX 77008
713-862-1200
www.backstageauctions.com
Rock 'n' roll collectibles and memorabilia

Bertoia Auctions
2141 DeMarco Dr.
Vineland, NJ 08360
856-692-1881
www.bertoiaauctions.com
Toys, banks, holiday, doorstops

Bonhams
101 New Bond St.
London, England W1S 1SR
44-20-7447-7447
www.bonhams.com
Fine art and antiques

Brian Lebel's Old West Auction
3201 Zafarano Dr., Suite C585
Santa Fe, NM 87507
480-779-WEST (9378)
www.codyoldwest.com
Western collectibles and memorabilia

Brunk Auctions
P.O. Box 2135
Asheville, NC 28802
828-254-6846
www.brunkauctions.com
Fine art and antiques

Caroline Ashleigh Associates, LLC
1000 S. Old Woodward, Suite 201
Birmingham, MI 48009-6734
248-792-2929
www.auctionyourart.com
Full service

Cedarburg Auction & Estate Sales, LLC
227 N. Main St.
Thiensville, WI 53092
262-238-5555
www.cedarburgauction.com
Full service

Christie's New York
20 Rockefeller Plaza
New York, NY 10020
www.christies.com
Full service

Clars Auction Gallery
5644 Telegraph Ave.
Oakland, CA 94609
888-339-7600
www.clars.com
Full service

Coeur d'Alene Art Auction
8836 N. Hess St., Suite B
Hayden, ID 83835
208-772-9009
www.cdaartauction.com
Western and American art

Cowan's
6270 Este Ave.
Cincinnati, OH 45232
513-871-1670
www.cowanauctions.com
Full service, historic Americana,
Native American objects

Doyle New York
175 E. 87th St.
New York, NY 10128
212-427-2730
www.doylenewyork.com
Fine art, jewelry, furniture

DuMouchelles Art Gallery
409 E. Jefferson Ave.
Detroit, MI 48226
313-963-6255
www.dumouchelle.com
Fine art and antiques, art glass

Early Auction Co., LLC.
123 Main St.
Milford, OH 45150
513-831-4833
www.earlyauctionco.com
Art glass

Elder's Antiques
901 S. Tamiami Trail
Nokomis, FL 34275
941-488-1005
www.eldersantiques.com
Asian, American and European antiques

Greg Martin Auctions
660 Third St., Suite 100
San Francisco, CA 94107
415-777-4867
Firearms, edged weapons, armor, Native
American objects

Great Gatsby's Auction Gallery
5180 Peachtree Industrial Blvd.
Atlanta, GA 30341
770-457-1903
www.greatgatsbys.com
Fine art, rare antiques, collectibles, classic cars

Grey Flannel Auctions
16411 N. 90th St., Suite #107
Scottsdale, AZ 85260
631-288-7800
www.greyflannel.com
Sports jerseys, memorabilia

Guernsey's
65 E. 93rd St.
New York, NY 10128
212-794-2280
www.guernseys.com
Art, historical items, pop culture

Guyette & Deeter, Inc.
24718 Beverly Rd.
P.O. Box 1170
St. Michaels, MD 21663
410-745-0485
www.guyetteandschmidt.com
Antique decoys

Hake's Americana & Collectibles
P.O. Box 12001
York, PA 17402
717-434-1600
www.hakes.com
Character collectibles, pop culture

Heritage Auctions
3500 Maple Ave., 17th Floor
Dallas, TX 75219
877-HERITAGE (437-4824)
ha.com
Full service, coins, pop culture

Humler & Nolan
225 E. Sixth St., 4th Floor
Cincinnati, OH 45202
513-381-2041
www.humlernolan.com
Antique American and European art pottery
and art glass

IGavel Auctions
887 Cross St.
New Braunfels, TX 78130
212-289-5588
igavelauctions.com
Online auction, arts, antiques and collectibles

Jackson's International Auctioneers and Appraisers
2229 Lincoln St.
Cedar Falls, IA 50613
319-277-2256
www.jacksonsauction.com
Full service, religious and Russian objects, postcards

James D. Julia, Inc.
203 Skowhegan Rd.
Fairfield, ME 04937
207-453-7125
www.juliaauctions.net
Full service, toys, glass, lighting, firearms

Jeffrey S. Evans & Associates, Inc.
P.O. Box 2638
Harrisonburg, VA 22801-2638
540-434-3939
www.jeffreysevans.com
Southern decorative arts, glass and lighting, ceramics, Americana

John Moran Auctioneers
145 E. Walnut Ave.
Monrovia, CA 91016
626-793-1833
www.johnmoran.com
Full service, California art

Julien's Auctions
8630 Hayden Place
Culver City, California 90232
310-836-1818
www.juliensauctions.com
High profile celebrity and entertainment

Keno Auctions
127 E. 69th St.
New York, NY 10021
212-734-2381
www.kenoauctions.com
Fine antiques, decorative arts

Lang's Auction, Inc.
663 Pleasant Valley Rd.
Waterville, NY 13480
315-841-4623
www.langsauction.com
Antique fishing tackle and memorabilia

Leland Little
620 Cornerstone Ct.
Hillsborough, NC 27278
919-644-1243
www.llauctions.com
Full service

Leslie Hindman Auctioneers
1338 W. Lake St.
Chicago, Il 60607
312-280-1212
www.lesliehindman.com
Full service

Litchfield County Auctions, Inc.
425 Bantam Rd. (Route 202)
Litchfield, CT 06759
860-567-4661
www.litchfieldcountyauctions.com
Full service

Louis J. Dianni, LLC Antiques Auctions
May 1-Oct. 10:
982 Main St., Suite 175
Fishkill, NY 12524
914-595-7013
Oct. 15-May 1:
11110 West Oakland Park Blvd., Suite 314
Sunrise, FL 33351
561-232-3620
louisjdianni.com
Full service

McMasters Harris Apple Tree Doll Auctions
1625 W. Church St.
Newark, OH 43055
800-842-3526
www.mcmastersharris.com
Dolls and accessories

Michaan's Auctions
2751 Todd St.
Alameda, CA 94501
800-380-9822
www.michaans.com
Full service, antiques, fine art

Michael Ivankovich Antiques & Auction Co.
P.O. Box 1536
Doylestown, PA 18901
215-345-6094
www.wnutting.com
Wallace Nutting objects

Morphy Auctions
2000 N. Reading Rd.
Denver, PA 17517
717-335-3435
morphyauctions.com

Mosby & Co. Auctions
905 W. 7th St., #228
Frederick, MD 21701
240-629-8139
www.mosbyauctions.com
Toys, advertising, Americana, Civil War, circus and carnival

Neal Auction Co.
4038 Magazine St.
New Orleans, LA 70115
504-899-5329
800-467-5329
www.nealauction.com
Art, furniture, pottery, silver, decorative arts

New Orleans Auction Galleries
333 St. Joseph St.
New Orleans, LA 70130
800-501-0277
www.neworleansauction.com
Full service

**Noel Barrett Antiques & Auctions, Ltd./
Pook & Pook**
463 E. Lancaster Ave.
Downingtown, PA 19335
215-297-5109
www.noelbarrett.com
www.pookandpook.com
Toys, banks, holiday, advertising

North American Auction Co.
34156 E. Frontage Rd.
Bozeman, MT 59715
800-686-4216
www.northamericanauctioncompany.com
Full service

Old Town Auctions
11 St. Paul St.
Boonsboro, MD 21713
240-291-0114
Toys, advertising, Americana; no Internet sales

Old Toy Soldier Auctions U.S.A.
P.O. Box 13324
Pittsburgh, PA 15243
Ray Haradin
412-343-8733
800-349-8009
www.oldtoysoldierauctions.com
Toy soldiers

Old World Auctions
4325 Cox Rd.
Glen Allen, VA 23060
804-290-8090
www.oldworldauctions.com
Maps, globes, charts, atlases, graphics

Past Tyme Pleasures
5424 Sunol Blvd., #10-242
Pleasanton, CA 94566
925-484-6442
www.pasttyme1.com
Advertising, collectibles

Philip Weiss Auctions
74 Morrick Rd.
Lynbrook, NY 11563
516-594-0731
www.weissauctions.com
Full service, comic art

Pook & Pook, Inc.
463 E. Lancaster Ave.
Downingtown, PA 19335
610-629-4040
www.pookandpook.com
Full service, Americana

**Quinn's Auction Galleries & Waverly
Auctions**
360 S. Washington St.
Falls Church, VA 22046
703-532-5632
www.quinnsauction.com
www.waverlyauctions.com
Full service, rare books and prints

Rago Arts and Auctions
333 N. Main St.
Lambertville, NJ 08530
609-397-9374
www.ragoarts.com
*Decorative ceramics and porcelain, Arts &
Crafts, modernism, fine art*

Red Baron's Antiques, Inc.
8655 Roswell Rd., Suite B
Sandy Springs, GA 30350
770-640-4604
www.rbantiques.com
Full service, Victorian, architectural objects

Rich Penn Auctions
P.O. Box 1355
Waterloo, IA 50704
319-291-6688
www.richpennauctions.com
Advertising, petroliana, and country-store objects

Richard D. Hatch & Associates
913 Upward Rd.
Flat Rock, NC 28731
828-696-3440
www.richardhatchauctions.com
Full service

Robert Edward Auctions, LLC
P.O. Box 430
Chester, NJ 07930
908-226-9900
908-888-2555
www.robertedwardauctions.com
Baseball, sports memorabilia

Rock Island Auction Co.
7819 42nd St. W.
Rock Island, IL 61201
800-238-8022
www.rockislandauction.com
Firearms, edged weapons and accessories

St. Charles Gallery, Inc.
1330 St. Charles Ave.
New Orleans, LA 70130
504-586-8733
Full service, Victorian

Freeman's
1808 Chestnut St.
Philadelphia, PA 19103
215-563-9275
www.freemansauction.com
Full service, Americana

Seeck Auctions
P.O. Box 377
Mason City, IA 50402
641-424-1116
www.seeckauction.com
Full service, carnival glass

Skinner, Inc.
63 Park Plaza
Boston, MA 02116
617-350-5400
www.skinnerinc.com
Full service, Americana

Sloans & Kenyon
7034 Wisconsin Ave.
Chevy Chase, MD 20815
301-634-2330
www.sloansandkenyon.com
Full service

Slotin Folk Art
5619 Ridgetop Dr.
Gainesville, GA 30504
770-532-1115
www.slotinfolkart.com
Naïve and outsider art

Sotheby's New York
1334 York Ave.
New York, NY 10021
212-606-7000
www.sothebys.com
Fine art, jewelry, historical items

Strawser Auction Group
P.O. Box 332, 200 N. Main St.
Wolcottville, IN 46795-0332
260-854-2859
www.strawserauctions.com
Full service, majolica, Fiesta

Susanin's Auctions
900 S. Clinton St.
Chicago, IL 60607
312-832-9800
www.susanins.com
Full service

Swann Auction Galleries, Inc.
104 E. 25th St.
New York, NY 10010
212-254-4710
www.swanngalleries.com
*Books, maps and atlases, prints and drawings,
posters, African-American fine art and
illustration art*

Ted Owen and Co.
Suite 71
2 Old Brompton Rd.
SW7 3DQ London, United Kingdom
www.tedowenandco.com
Eclectic collections

Theriault's
P.O. Box 151
Annapolis, MD 21404
800-638-0422
www.theriaults.com
Dolls and accessories

Tom Harris Auction Center
203 S. 18th Ave.
Marshalltown, IA 50158
641-754-4890
www.tomharrisauctions.com
Full service

John Toomey Gallery
818 North Blvd.
Oak Park, IL 60301
708-383-5234
www.treadwaygallery.com
Arts & Crafts, modernism, fine art

Tradewinds Antiques & Auctions
P.O. Box 249
24 Magnolia Ave.
Manchester-By-The-Sea, MA 01944-0249
978-526-4085
www.tradewindsantiques.com
Canes

Treadway Gallery
2029 Madison Rd.
Cincinnati, OH 45208
513-321-6742
www.treadwaygallery.com

Turkey Creek Auctions, Inc.
13939 N. Highway 441
Citra, FL 32113
352-622-4611
800-648-7523
antiqueauctionsfl.com
Full service

Victorian Casino Antiques/Morphy Auctions
4520 Arville St. #1
Las Vegas, NV 89103
702-382-2466
www.vcaauction.com
Full service

Waverly Auctions
360 S. Washington St.
Falls Church, VA 22046
703-532-5632
www.quinnsauction.com
www.waverlyauctions.com
Full service, rare books and prints

Woody Auction
P.O. Box 618
317 S. Forrest
Douglass, KS 67039
316-747-2694
www.woodyauction.com
Full service

Ride with Rose
Regular Gasoline
globe,13 1/2" single
lens in Capco body.
$2,750+

Advertising

By Noah Fleisher

The enduring appeal of antique advertising is not hard to understand. The graphics are great; they hearken back to a simpler time and a distinct American identity, and – perhaps best of all – are available across all price levels. That means buyers from all tax brackets and walks of life.

"It's like anything in collectibles and antiques," Dan Matthews, former president and owner of Matthews Auction in Moline, Illinois, and the author of *The Fine Art of Collecting and Displaying Petroliana*. "The best stuff, the very top, sells no matter what. Right now the medium-market is doing OK and the lower continues to drag a bit behind."

Seasoned collectors will warn, with good reason, that money should not be the motivating factor in the hobby. The true value of antique advertising signs, from gas stations to country stores to soda pop, lies in the context of their production and the nostalgia they evoke of that time.

The best antique advertising evokes the meat of the first half of the 20th century, when signs were the most effective ways to catch the eyes of car culture consumers. The signs and symbols evolved to reflect the values and styles of the regions where they were posted and the products they reflected. A sign with bold color, great graphics, and a catchy slogan can transport a collector back decades in an instant. Collectors feel a rapport with a piece; they don't see dollar signs.

"Buy it because you like it," said Matthews, "because you can live it with it and it means something to you. Never get into something because you think you'll make money."

Look at the market for one of the most collectible and popular markets: Coca-Cola. Twenty years ago the best Coke pieces in the middle market could reliably command several thousand dollars. Coca-Cola manufactured hundreds of thousands of signs and related ephemera, millions even, and they began to come

Writer and author
NOAH FLEISHER has 20 years of experience in the antiques and collectibles field. He is the author of *The Beatles: Fab Finds of the Fab Four*, *Warman's Modern Furniture*, and *Collecting Children's Books*.

▲ Embossed tin Luden's Cough Drops sign, excellent condition, framed 36 1/2" x 20 1/2". **$660**

Courtesy of Morphy Auctions, www.morphyauctions.com

Wooden Burma-Shave advertising sign, "Don't lose your head/to gain a minute/you need your head/your brains are in it." **$360**

Courtesy of Morphy Auctions, www.morphyauctions.com

Wooden Moon's Feeds sign, circa 1930s to 1940s, handmade, overall appearance is nice with proper crazing present on the lettering, construction is made of individual horizontal boards secured by metal straps on the back, mild to medium wear with slight weathering. **$420**

Courtesy of Morphy Auctions, www.morphyauctions.com

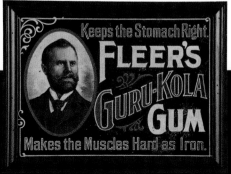

Tin Fleer's Guru-Kola Gum sign, circa 1905 to 1910, made by Sentenne & Green, great graphics and design, framed 15 1/4" x 11 1/2". **$1,800**

Courtesy of Morphy Auctions, www.morphyauctions.com

Tin Shoe Lace Service Station display, image of man driving a shoe on wheels, image on all three sides, excellent to near mint condition, 13 3/4" x 11 1/4" x 11". **$5,400**

Courtesy of Morphy Auctions, www. morphyauctions.com

out of the woodwork. There is little more evocative of classic Americana than the red and white of Coke, but as everybody sold their pieces and everybody acquired their bit of nostalgia, the market cooled and prices went down significantly. Pieces that had routinely brought $500-$1,000 could suddenly be had for significantly less, and people stopped selling.

Now, however, with several years of very quiet action in the books, the cycle seems to be turning around. New collectors have entered the market and older collectors are leaving. Those collections are finding new owners at a decent price.

As with any category, the best antique advertising will bring top dollar no matter what. It provides a tangible place for collectors to put real money. Top dollar can be had for the true rarities in the business, and the middle market provides a solid outlet for design-minded collectors as opposed to those who collect to amass a sizable grouping.

There are opportunities everywhere for the educated collector – from the country auction to the flea market. Going head to head with top collectors in the

business at top auctions may result in frustration. If you're just getting your feet wet, research online, email experts and ask for resources, do your due diligence in seeing what the market is bringing, and then take those skills to unlikely places and see what turns up.

"All the fields we deal in seem to be doing quite well right now," Matthews said. "The best thing to do is buy from reputable auction houses and dealers, from people who guarantee your product."

A lot of the steadiness in the market comes from the exposure antique advertising is getting in places like cable television, via shows like "American Pickers" and "Pawn Stars" where a premium is placed on supreme objects.

"These kinds of shows are only helping the hobby get bigger," Matthews added. Factor in the pop culture value, as blue-collar treasures are increasingly regarded as art, and the horizon is bright for this workingman's collectible.

"I see younger generations continuing to get into this hobby more and more," said Matthews. "As long as we have to put gas in our cars and food in our mouths, people will collect this stuff."

Tin sign, Stein Club All Havana Cigars, circa 1910, scarce item, 30 1/2" x 22 1/2". **$8,400**

Courtesy of Morphy Auctions, www.morphyauctions.com

Tin Sweet Orr & Co. overalls sign, circa 1890s, early frame without glass, lithography by C.W. Shonk; colors are bright and unfaded, a few small surface scratches, minor scuffs, and rubs. **$13,800**

Courtesy of Morphy Auctions, www.morphyauctions.com

Neon three-color Planters Peanuts sign, circa 1980s, acrylic, appears to be handmade, near mint condition, 30 1/4" x 27 1/4". **$1,020**

Courtesy of Morphy Auctions, www.morphyauctions.com

Cast iron Planters Mr. Peanut Hamilton scale, one-cent operation, all original paint with medium to heavy expected wear and minor rust, original wheel mounts for rolling in and out of a store, one wheel is missing and one is broken, original condition. **$19,800**

Courtesy of Morphy Auctions, www.morphyauctions.com

Red Goose Shoes figural store displays, cast iron bank embossed on both sides with Red Goose Shoes name (4 1/2" high) and three chalkware displays, 4 1/2" high, 8" high, and 11 1/2" high. Red Goose Shoes was in operation from 1869 to 1911, when it merged with another manufacturer. It wasn't until 1904, during the St. Louis World's Fair, that red was added to the image of the goose, which was trademarked in 1906. **$414**

Courtesy James D. Julia Auctioneers; www.JamesDJulia.com

Lewis Rye seldom seen reverse on glass advertising clock from Strauss Pritz & Co. of Cincinnati (1875-1918), promoting Lewis 66 rye whiskey, reverse lettering includes areas of silver foil highlights, scalloped perimeter edge has a few chips, clock mechanism not working and may not be original, 12" diameter. **$1,185**

Courtesy James D. Julia Auctioneers; www.JamesDJulia.com

De Laval Cream Separators tin sign, one of the most desirable of all De Laval advertising items, depicts farm family processing cream from fresh milk, includes mark at bottom "The H.D. Beach Co., Coshocton, O.," sign shows light mottling in lighter areas, 25 1/2" diameter. The De Laval cream separator was invented in Sweden in 1878. **$4,147**

Courtesy James D. Julia Auctioneers; www.JamesDJulia.com

Duke's Mixture porcelain door push, circa 1915, cobalt blue version with lithographic transfer process, captioned "The Roll of Fame," 4 1/4" wide x 8 1/2" high. The granulated or loose tobacco of Duke's Mixture became a popular medium- to low-priced brand of tobacco in the late 19th century. **$592**

Courtesy James D. Julia Auctioneers; www.JamesDJulia.com

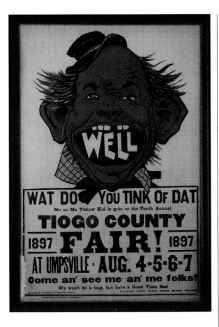

Yellow Kid county fair full-size salesman's sample poster, produced by Donaldson Litho Co. of Cincinnati, "Me an Me Yellow Kid is goin to the Tenth Annual 1897 Tioga County Fair at Umpsville. Wat do you tink of dat. Come an' see me and me' folks!," bulk pricing information for poster displayed at bottom indicates 25 posters cost $1.75 while 1,000 copies could be purchased for $20, vertical tear at bottom, 28 1/2" wide x 42 1/2" high. **$575**

Courtesy James D. Julia Auctioneers; www.JamesDJulia.com

Phoenix Pure Paint curved porcelain sign, circa 1910 to 1920, manufactured by Ingram-Richardson, rare, scarce, depicts young Native American admiring his application of face paints in hand mirror, excellent condition, 20 1/4" x 12". **$15,600**

Courtesy of Morphy Auctions, www.morphyauctions.com

Whistle Soda tin sign, 1920s, beveled edge tin over cardboard easel-back, manufactured by American Art Works, Coshocton, Ohio, scarce version, does not include orange, blue, and white Whistle Soda logo, near mint condition, 9" wide x 6 1/4" high. **$948**

Courtesy James D. Julia Auctioneers; www.JamesDJulia.com

Eveready Flashlights tin cutout flange, circa 1920s, rare, very good to excellent condition, light crazing and soiling with small marks, edge nicks, shallow crimp in bottom sign, 10" x 10 1/4". **$6,000**

Courtesy of Morphy Auctions, www.morphyauctions.com

Antique Bourbon trade figure, circa 1950s to 1960s, fiberglass construction with medium overall marks, wear, and soiling, 45" tall. **$210**

Courtesy of Morphy Auctions, www.morphyauctions.com

South Bend Watch countertop display, figural pocket watch light-up sign with a reverse-on-glass "dial" face depicting a watch frozen in a block of ice as testimony to its ability to take a licking and keep on ticking. Manufactured by the Cincinnati Sand Blast Co., includes a card from the C.C. Markham Jewelry Store, Guilford, Conn., where it originated, 12 1/2" x 17". **$4,600**

Courtesy James D. Julia Auctioneers; www.JamesDJulia.com

Tin Beeman's Pepsin Gum sign, circa 1905, handmade, tin, with old (if not original) wooden framework, stamped "Mr. Brook" at bottom, light staining, medium soiling, wear and minor marks. **$16,800**

Courtesy of Morphy Auctions, www.morphyauctions.com

Circa 1933 Goudey Gum advertising sign. A little sprite whispers in the ear of a young boy on this tin advertising sign from Goudey Gum Co. Boston - Chicago, 7 1/2" x 15 1/2". **$286**

Courtesy Heritage Auction, www.HA.com

Planters Peanuts porcelain sign, rare, used as an advertising panel in a "Highway Lighthouse." These lighthouses were found along roadways in the 1920s and '30s to alert motorists of roadway hazards ahead. Constructed with a large blinking light atop a tall rectangular base, they proved too tempting a canvas for advertising companies to pass up. The Highway Lighthouse Co. had offices located in New York and Pittsburgh in the mid-1930s, 27 1/2" x 60 1/4". **$13,800**

Courtesy James D. Julia Auctioneers; www.JamesDJulia.com

Painted tin boot and shoemaker's trade sign, American, late 19th century, double-sided painted tin panel, 20" x 14". **$237**

Courtesy of Skinner Inc., www.SkinnerInc.com

Double-sided lithographed tin die-cut flange sign advertising Pennsylvania Bicycle Tires, patent date June 7, 1907, 27 3/4" tall. **$9,200**

Courtesy Noel Barrett Antiques & Auctions Ltd., www.NoelBarrett.com

Philip Morris "Johnny" Bellhop die-cut floor display, captioned, "No Cigarette Hangover When you Smoke Philip Morris", 18" x 45", fair condition, **$172**

Courtesy James D. Julia Auctioneers, www.JamesDJulia.com

Hires Root Beer tin-on-cardboard sign, rare embossed oval illustration of soda fountain beauty set against a simulated wood grain background, 6 1/4" x 9 1/4". **$1,035**

Courtesy James D. Julia Auctioneers, www.JamesDJulia.com

Pre-1900 reverse-on-glass oval corner sign advertising Yuengling's brewery of Pottsville, Pa. **$6,600**

Courtesy of Morphy Auctions, www.MorphyAuctions.com

Sunbeam Bread die-cut standup sign, 1950s, cardboard, includes original display bread box, near mint, 40" x 27". **$373**

Courtesy of Morphy Auctions, www.MorphyAuctions.com

Linen Rub-No-More sign, late 1800s, mother elephant giving baby a bath. Fashioned similarly to "pin the tail on the donkey" game, it is uncut and retains all of its original elephant tails, 38" x 42". **$1,852**

Courtesy of Morphy Auctions, www.MorphyAuctions.com

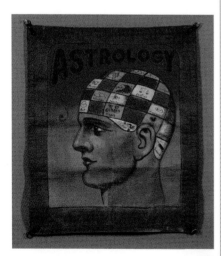

"Astrology" sideshow banner, Driver Bros. Inc. Chicago, early to mid-20th century, incorrectly titled, the banner painted with a man's head displays a phrenology diagram of the various mental faculties of the brain, 34" x 29". **$3,081**

Courtesy of Skinner Inc., www.SkinnerInc.com

Tin Paul Jones Whiskey sign, minor oxidation, 14" x 19". **$1,053**
Courtesy of Morphy Auctions, www.morphyauctions.com

Painted tin fireworks advertising sign, American, mid-20th century, 8 1/4" x 28 1/2". Has three bullet holes, some rusty surface areas. **$533**

Courtesy of Skinner Inc., www.SkinnerInc.com

Painted wood and iron "The Elm's Hotel" sign, from a house on Elm Street in Upton, Mass., early 20th century, double-sided sign with cut-out leaf-form panel, wrought-iron mount, (panel cracked), 40" x 40". **$1,067**

Courtesy of Skinner Inc., www.SkinnerInc.com

Aunt Jemima Pancake Flour cardboard premium toy, colorful die-cut advertising premium, circa 1905, from the Davis Milling Co., St. Joseph, Mo. Consists of a hinged, embossed cardboard two-piece Aunt Jemima originally tethered to a die-cut box of pancake flour with a string. By pulling on the bottom of the string, Aunt Jemima would appear to be climbing a rope to reach the box of flour at the top, 6 1/2" x 13". **$345**

Courtesy James D. Julia Auctioneers; www.JamesDJulia.com

Two embossed tin Moxie signs, circa 1930s, one bright and clean with only minor surface rubs and a few small marks, the other sign has more advanced rubs, chips, and wear, each 8 1/4" diameter. **$180**

Courtesy of Morphy Auctions, www.morphyauctions.com

Moxie cardboard floor display sign, uncommon, die-cut. Humorous illustration of "Moxie Boy" resting on a pile of Moxie crates, being teased with a feather by "Moxie Girl". Caption reads: "Wake Up! Send a Case of Moxie To Our Home – Wouldn't That Tickle You?" 22 1/2" x 37". **$1,265**

Courtesy James D. Julia Auctioneers; www.JamesDJulia.com

Hires large paper poster, circa 1940-1950, new old stock heavy paper, almost no wear or marks, 34" x 58". **$150**

Courtesy of Morphy Auctions, www.morphyauctions.com

Oertels '92 Beer advertising figure, circa 1940s, plaster, excellent condition, 16 1/2" tall. **$150**

Courtesy of Morphy Auctions, www.morphyauctions.com

Rare embossed tin Modox sign, circa 1900 to 1905, framed without glass, outstanding graphics of Indian in full headdress, light to medium overall wear with some minor chips and nicks that mostly impact background colors and border areas. **$7,200**

Courtesy of Morphy Auctions, www.morphyauctions.com

Moxie 1911 tip tray with Moxie Boy die-cut, captioned "Our Idol", shipped flat from factory and intended to be bent at a right angle for display on store counter, 6" x 11 3/4". **$632**

Courtesy James D. Julia Auctioneers; www.JamesDJulia.com

Americana

By Noah Fleisher

The collecting field of historical Americana is so broad and diverse, so infinitely parsible, that entering it with confidence can prove a daunting task to both neophyte and experienced collectors alike. For the purposes of this introduction and this section, we've chosen to keep the focus on historical Americana as it applies to key figures in American history – presidents, politicians and assorted prominent thinkers; artifacts that are, in this writer's estimation, easily identifiable and therefore easier to relate to.

For Tom Slater, director of Americana Auctions at Heritage Auctions and formerly of Slater's Americana, there is a conflict in the Americana market between an abundance of good material and a lack of erudition among "new" collectors.

"You don't see new collectors getting into Americana the same way that you see it in categories like comics or sports, which are more in-tune with current pop culture trends," he said. "New generations in these types of categories are being created by osmosis, inheriting their love of collecting – and often parts of their collections – from family members and friends, being influenced by what's clicking in the popular imagination and current public zeitgeist. When you get into more esoteric subjects, they require more commitment to develop working knowledge to be an effective collector."

Key trends in historical Americana are easy to read: signatures, ephemera, and artifacts directly related to early popular American figures – think George Washington, Thomas Jefferson and Abe Lincoln – will always command solid prices; a search through the prices realized anywhere from independent dealers, eBay and a variety of auction houses will confirm this.

A little deeper into the market, and a little further into the roster of historical figures from

Writer and author
NOAH FLEISHER has 20 years of experience in the antiques and collectibles field. He is the author of *The Beatles: Fab Finds of the Fab Four, Warman's Modern Furniture,* and *Collecting Children's Books.*

Justice & Equal Rights,

POLK

FOR VICE PRESIDENT,
GEORGE M. DALLAS,
FOR GOVERNOR
FRANCIS R. SHUNK,
CANAL COMMISSIONER
JOSHUA HARTSHORNE.

Ribbon, 1844, James Knox Polk, "Justice & Equal Rights Polk," eagle, wings spread, carries an American flag in its beak and at bottom is stately rooster, rare, 8" l. **$4,260**

Courtesy of Hakes Americana & Collectibles, www.hakes.com

They're looking for the right pieces and the right values."

While that might necessarily mean that you're going to have serious competition and have to dig a little deeper into your bank account to acquire that George Washington compass, book plate or signed letter, it also means that – if you do your homework and know what you are looking for – there is tremendous opportunity.

"Quality is key at whatever level you are collecting," said Slater. "Spend on quality, on what you love, and you'll never be disappointed with how much you enjoy something, what you pay for it or what it may bring when the time comes to sell it."

In terms of the broader market, there's a plethora of good material available, which may be a factor in the current price pause seen. The fact is that – though Americans love their history and have always actively coveted pieces of it – there is relatively little "brand new" material being found, unlike newer specialty categories like comics, sports and entertainment memorabilia. Twenty and 30 years ago, dealers and collectors alike were pulling significant pieces of historical Americana out of shows, shacks,

whom artifacts can be found and acquired, and the story begins to play out a little differently.

"At a certain point and a certain level, you can't tell what's going to sell or at what price," said Slater. "In the last five to 10 years we've seen a somewhat weaker, leaner and meaner stripe of collector emerge than we used to have. They're simply more discriminating now in how they spend and what they spend on.

attics and yard sales at incredible rates. Those glory days are done and picked over for the most part. You're not likely to find a William Stone lithograph of The Declaration of Independence in a garage sale anymore.

"When you get into areas where there aren't constantly new discoveries being made, you need to have a much deeper sense of going on," said Slater. "It seems there's a direct relationship between that and attracting new people, which is not necessarily the case in Americana right now."

Say you have done your research, read your history and have developed a fascination with the Founding Fathers. You'll have to look far and wide, and spend a pretty penny, for pieces that come directly from Washington, Adams, Jefferson, Madison or Monroe. If you know what you like, however, there is plenty to be had from those that surrounded those men, their families and their lives. Context becomes all important, as does understanding what you're looking at when it looks at you.

"Attention spans are decreasing, which means fewer collectors are willing to undergo what can be a long and steep learning curve," said Slater. "The categories that are thriving are the ones that are more easily accessible. That, however, means greater competition down the line. For collectors willing to put in the time, the reward can be significant."

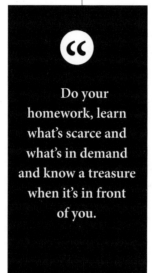

> Do your homework, learn what's scarce and what's in demand and know a treasure when it's in front of you.

What is influencing the market right now? An aging collector population, for one, and a somewhat jaded collector base at the very top of the market, for another.

Collectors who have been in the market for 40 or 50 years are aging out of active buying and are selling off their core collections. In many cases they simply have no heirs that are following them in their pursuit or they have too much in their collections for their families to efficiently and profitably disperse.

We are also living in a much more disposable culture these days. As subsequent generations come of age in an increasingly paperless society, less appreciation is created for the material culture of the past. A prime is example is the current cooling in the realm of John F. Kennedy and Camelot collecting.

"Kennedy had been a touchstone for almost three generations," said Slater. "Now those collectors, those people who were born and raised on Camelot and its attendant glamour, are aging out and the polish has faded somewhat on the perspective of those times. This has created, simultaneously, a leveling off in prices for JFK memorabilia and a golden opportunity for smart collectors willing to hold on to something for the duration. If history has taught us anything, it's that eventually everything comes around again and is eventually seen as being new."

Do your homework, learn what's scarce and what's in demand and know

Pinback, 1965, Issued by
the National Coordinating
Committee To End The
Vietnam War for national
convention, from Madison,
WI., 1-3/4" dia., **$674**

*Courtesy of Hakes Americana &
Collectibles, www.hakes.com*

Ring, 1927, brass,
commemorating Charles
Lindbergh historic Trans-
Atlantic flight, size 6, scarce,
$252

*Courtesy of Hakes Americana &
Collectibles, www.hakes.com*

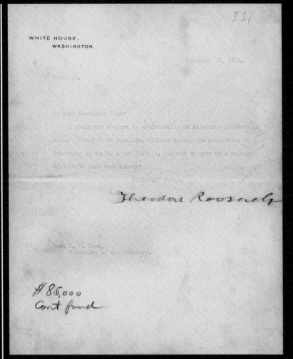

Theodore Roosevelt letter to Secretary of the Treasury Leslie
M. Shaw, Dec. 27, 1904. Roosevelt's famous letter decrying the
"atrocious hideousness" of America's coinage and suggesting
Augustus St. Gaudens redesign the nation's gold coins. Called
the "Genesis Letter" in numismatics, it led to the creation of
some of the most sought-after gold coins ever struck. **$94,000**

*Courtesy of Heritage Auctions,
www.ha.com*

a treasure when it's in front of you.
Be patient with your purchases and
diligent in your pursuit of the material
you want. Right now your purchases
– be they with a major auction house
or a reputable dealer – may have
an air more of stewardship than of
investment, but the popularity of
television shows and books on antiques
and collectibles points to an increased
awareness in the potential value of

historical material, if not its inherent
value simply as a piece of history.

"That wider recognition of value
that seems to be dawning in the
general public is the thing that is
encouraging," said Slater. "The smart,
educated collector that will endure
the vagaries of the market will, in
time, realize the full potential not only
of their investment but also of their
passion for the subject."

Sign, 1941, cardboard, color photo image of Rosemary LaPlanche, Miss America 1941. She was also Miss America in 1940, before the rule that disqualified contestants from winning the pageant more than once, 11 h. x 21" w. **$118**

Courtesy of Hakes Americana & Collectibles, www.hakes.com

Umbrella, 1900, cotton parasol or umbrella with portraits of the 1900 Republican nominees, McKinley & Roosevelt, an American flag and the imprint "Canton Republican League" on three panels, manufactured in Norwalk, Ohio, McKinley conducted the campaign from his front porch in Canton. **$300**

Courtesy of Heritage Auctions, www.ha.com

James Buchanan campaign banner, 1856, in the style of American flag, world's most valuable campaign flag sold at auction, 21-1/2" l. x 15" t. **$275,000**

Courtesy of Heritage Auctions, www.ha.com

Banner, 1860, from the John Bell campaign, hand painted silk with "Gibbs & Smith Manufacturers" below main graphic, front has allegorical image of Lady Liberty, text reads "Our Native Land, Onward To Her Rescue," reverse has Constitutional Union Party slogan "The Union, The Constitution, And The Enforcement Of The Laws," 41" w. x 50" l. **$13,700**

Courtesy of Hakes Americana & Collectibles, www.hakes.com

Kofia, early 1970s, black velvet and platinum, gold, diamonds, rubies and pearls, interior embroidered "Elijah Muhammad, Our King, Messenger of Allah," owned by Elijah Muhammad (born Elijah Poole), one of the most influential black leaders of the 20th century, 23 carats. **$32,500**

Courtesy of Heritage Auctions, www.ha.com

Pin, early 1940s, sterling silver, figural depiction of Uncle Sam seated in a chair holding the full figure of Tojo over his knees, 1-13/16" t. **$259**

Courtesy of Hakes Americana & Collectibles, www.hakes.com

Placard, 1963, "We Demand Full Employment Now", produced for the event that came to be defined by Dr. Martin Luther King's "I Have A Dream" speech, produced by Prothro Lithograph Co. Compton Calif., rare, 14" w. x 22" t. **$785**

Courtesy of Hakes Americana & Collectibles, www.hakes.com

Carving, late 19th century, cigar store Indian carving, left hand holds an actual Springfield-type musket, as made, elaborately carved, with a second bundle of cigars in the crook of his arm and an animal pelt worn regally over the right shoulder, 8' t. **$37,500**

Courtesy of Heritage Auctions, www.ha.com

Abraham Lincoln, John Wilkes Booth assassination broadside. A "Booth Reward Broadside" constitutes a Holy Grail for Lincoln collectors. Like the Charleston Mercury "The Union is Dissolved!" broadside and Ford's Theatre playbills, it is widely sought after. Measures approximately 13" x 24" and has been professionally backed with rice paper to repair a few small tears. A key relic of the Civil War and the final chapter in Lincoln's life. **$47,800**

Courtesy of Heritage Auctions, www.ha.com

◄ Bill Clinton's Fleetwood Mac-signed saxophone. Fleetwood Mac performed at President Clinton's 1993 inauguration. Excellent condition. **$8,963**

Courtesy of Heritage Auctions, www.ha.com

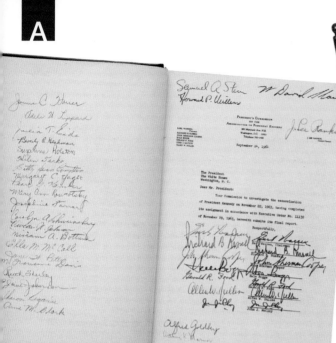

John F. Kennedy assassination-related, Warren Commission Report, signed by all seven commission members, including Chairman Earl Warren, plus the general counsel, four assistant counsel members, two staff members, and 33 aides; 47 signatures in all. **$19,120**

Courtesy of Heritage Auctions, www.ha.com

John F. Kennedy rocking chair, authenticated by the family. Kennedy used approximately 14 rocking chairs, making sure that one was available anywhere he spent a considerable amount of time. The Kennedy family affixed a brass plaque declaring it to be the late president's own chair, accompanied by a 2000 letter from Edward Kennedy, confirming that the chair was actually used by JFK, the only one ever authenticated by the family. **$65,725**

Courtesy of Heritage Auctions, www.ha.com

◄ John F. Kennedy signed photograph with a humorous inscription to Barry Goldwater. This black-and-white 8" x 10" image is an original photograph taken by Goldwater. Across the bottom JFK wrote: "For Barry Goldwater – Whom I urge to follow the career for which he has shown such talent – photography! – from his friend – John Kennedy." Near-mint condition. **$17,925**

Courtesy of Heritage Auctions, www.ha.com

Abraham Lincoln, supremely rare and important portrait campaign flag from 1860. Among categories of collectible political campaign novelties, flag-format banners are among the most highly prized. Within this subcategory, 1860 and 1864 Lincoln flags carrying the candidate's portrait are the most sought after of all. 17.5" x 10.75", custom-framed to an overall 20" x 14". **$33,460**

Courtesy of Heritage Auctions, www.ha.com

Richard M. Nixon's original White House presidential flag, latter part of Nixon's term in office. 70.5" x 57" including fringe, carefully sewn down to archival backing and custom framed. **$19,120**

Courtesy of Heritage Auctions, www.ha.com

George Washington signed U.S. patent as president for "new machinery called the Cotton Gin" issued to Hodgen Holmes, not Eli Whitney. The patent is countersigned by Timothy Pickering as secretary of state and Charles Lee as attorney general. One vellum partly printed page, 12.5" x 15", "City of Philadelphia," May 12, 1796. By signing this, Washington unwittingly signs away the freedom of future generations of African-American men and women. The invention transformed America, expanding the cotton culture in the South and spreading it westward, breathing new life into slavery, the institution that many had hoped would die a natural death. **$179,250**

Courtesy of Heritage Auctions, www.ha.com

American Art

By Noah Fleisher

American art, described here as paintings, works on paper, and sculpture from roughly 1850 to 1950 – and on occasion even earlier than 1850 – is as fascinating, accessible, and varied a wrinkle in the art market as there is. The art and the artists now considered "American" have shifted significantly in the last decade.

"Everything from Colonial portraiture and Hudson River School paintings through to Modernism, Realism, and everything in between can be considered 'American,'" said Aviva Lehmann, Director of American Art at Heritage Auctions, New York. "Of all areas of fine art, I find American art to be the most diverse. Where else can you sell a Remington, an O'Keeffe, a Cassatt, and a Rockwell in one auction? As such, my catalogs often look like a syllabus of American art, even of American history in general."

What's even better news right now for both collectors and dealers in American art, especially if your bread and butter is in the middle market –anything between $2,000 and $50,000 – and into the lower market, things are as good as they can be right now. It seems somewhat counterintuitive to hear that, perhaps, given the obscene prices being paid for high profile Modern and contemporary works at top art auction houses, but it's the truth.

There is a plethora of quality work available in all corners, and with the malleable definition of "American art," that creates opportunities by the score, especially to a determined eye.

"The state of the American art market is as healthy as it's ever been," said Lehmann. "In 2007 and early 2008 we all thought that was the peak, yet in many areas the market is at a height never achieved before."

Several areas are driving the strength we see in American art right now, like Western art, regional art of various types, and early American Modernism, with records being set at auction not just for Rockwell

Writer and author
NOAH FLEISHER has 20 years of experience in the antiques and collectibles field. He is the author of *The Beatles: Fab Finds of the Fab Four*, *Warman's Modern Furniture*, and *Collecting Children's Books*.

▲ "Flood Disaster" by
Thomas Hart Benton (1889-
1975), 1951, oil and tempera
on canvas mounted on
plywood (original), 25 1/2"
x 36-½", signed Benton and
dated 51. **$1,874,500**

Courtesy of Sotheby's, sothebys.com

◄ "Abandoned Silos" by Jon
Flaming (American, b. 1962),
oil on Masonite, 24" x 36",
monogrammed and signed
lower left: Jon Flaming. **$4,780**

Courtesy Heritage Auctions, ha.com

"Saturday Night at the
Longhorn" by John Philip
Falter (American, 1910-1982),
1976, oil on canvas, 30" x 40",
signed and dated lower left:
John Falter '76; titled, signed
and dated verso: Saturday
Night at the Longhorn / John
Falter 1976. **$16,250**

Courtesy Heritage Auctions, ha.com

"Lively Gathering
in Town Square"
by Ethel Spears
(American, 1903-
1974), oil on canvas,
29 7/8" x 40 1/4",
signed lower right.
$3,250

*Courtesy of Heritage
Auctions, ha.com*

"Wisconsin
Landscape" by
John Steuart Curry
(American 1897-
1946), oil on canvas,
18.5in. x 24.5 inches,
signed lower right.
Along with Thomas
Hart Benton and
Grant Wood, John
Steuart Curry was
one of the top artists
of the regionalist
movement. **$17,925**

*Courtesy of Heritage
Auctions, ha.com*

and O'Keeffe, but for secondary and tertiary artists in these areas, such as J.C. Leyendecker and Henry Lyman Sayan. This same pattern on down the hierarchical line of popular painters is repeating and resulting in ever better prices.

"As they say, a rising tide lifts all boats," said Lehmann.

So, knowing now that the choice of "American" arenas is so broad, the reality of price has to be considered. Most of us are not going to spend $50,000 or $100,000 on a painting. In fact, most of us will have to carefully consider spending more than $1,000-$2,000 on anything, let alone a painting. How do you decide?

"I always say to either choose a modest example by a very important artist – a Hopper drawing, for example – or a masterwork by a more obscure artist," said Lehmann. "At the end of the day, buy only what you love and cannot live without. Go from the heart."

This last bit of advice from Lehmann is perhaps the most important. It is also the most ubiquitous piece of advice a seeker in any category can get. At $100 million or so, it's probably okay to consider the investment aspect of it. At a few thousand? The market going to hold its value at most levels right now. You're not going to get filthy rich on obscure Regionalism, but you're also not going to lose.

In the end, buy from those you trust, educate yourself – read books, go to museums, galleries and auctions – and seek advice from seasoned collectors and curators.

"Never be afraid to ask too many questions," added Lehmann. "Above all, have fun."

"The Bull Fight" by Edna Reindel (American, 1894-1990), circa 1936, oil on canvas, 25" x 30 1/4", signed upper left: Reindel. **$35,000**

Courtesy Heritage Auctions, ha.com

Thomas Moran
(1837-1926)

Thomas Moran was considered the visual architect of the dramatic Western landscape, which captured the imagination of America at the turn of the century and helped inspire the creation of the National Park System. During the 1910s, Moran revisited his favorite subjects from prior decades, including Yellowstone, Yosemite, Zion and especially the Grand Canyon. A masterwork from 1914, "Mountain Lion in Grand Canyon" epitomizes Moran's technique of romanticizing landscape elements in order to evoke the sublimity of nature.

"Mountain Lion in Grand Canyon (Lair of the Mountain Lion)" by Thomas Moran, oil on canvas, 1914, 30" x 25", signed. **$612,500**

"Fertility" by Grant Wood (American 1891-1942), 1939, lithograph, 9" x 11-7/8", Ed. 250 AAA, pub., signed lower right in pencil: *Grant Wood*; **$4,780**

Courtesy of Heritage Auctions, ha.com

"Pumpkinhead – Self-Portrait, 1972" by Jamie Wyeth (b. 1946), oil on canvas, signed "James Wyeth" lower left, 30" x 30". **$1,690,000**

Courtesy of Sotheby's, sothebys.com

◀ "The Old Checkered House in Cambridge Valley" by Grandma Moses (American, 1860-1961), 1943, oil on Masonite, 21 3/4" x 29 3/4", signed lower center: MOSES. "The Old Checkered House in Cambridge Valley" derives from one of Grandma Moses's most famous series of a historic inn on the Cambridge Turnpike in Washington County near her childhood home. **$134,500**

Courtesy Heritage Auctions, ha.com

◀ "The Sentinel" by Dale Nichols (1904-1995), oil on canvas, artist signed lower left, 30" x 40". **$45,600**

Courtesy of Shannon's Auctioneers, shannons.com

▼ "Saturday Night at the Honkey Tonk" by Clementine Hunter (American, 1886-1988), oil on board, 16" x 24", initialed lower right: CH. **$5,078**

Courtesy Heritage Auctions, ha.com

"Winter in the Country, A Cold Morning" by George Henry Durrie (1820-1863), oil on canvas, circa 1863, 26" x 36". **$448,000**

Courtesy of Heritage Auctions, ha.com

"Crab Line" by David Bates (American, b. 1952), 1989, oil on board, 21 1/2" x 17 1/2", signed and dated lower right: Bates 89. **$17,500**

Courtesy Heritage Auctions, ha.com

"Sheep Pasture, Cornish, New Hampshire" by Maxfield Parrish (American, 1870-1966), 1936, oil on panel, 25" x 30", signed and dated lower right: Maxfield Parrish 1936. **$74,500**

Courtesy of Heritage Auctions, ha.com

"The assimiboins attacking a blackfoot village at fort mckenzies - 28 august 1833" by Roy Lichtenstein (American, 1923-1997), circa 1951, oil on canvas, 18" x 24", signed lower right. **$95,600**

Courtesy of Heritage Auctions, ha.com

"Golden Clouds" by Ila Mae McAfee (American, 1897-1995), oil on artists' board, 13" x 16", signed lower left: Ila McAfree, inscribed verso: "Golden Clouds." **$7,500**

Courtesy Heritage Auctions, ha.com

"Children at the Shore" by Edward Henry Potthast (American, 1857-1927), oil on canvas, 24" x 30", signed lower left: E Potthast. Beloved by audiences from the 19th century through the present for his vibrant, sunlit depictions of carefree beachgoers enjoying leisurely holidays on the coast, Edward Potthast is considered one of the most prominent of the American Impressionists. **$242,500**

Courtesy Heritage Auctions, ha.com

"The Empire State Building, Winter" by Guy Carleton Wiggins (American, 1883-1962), oil on canvas board, 12" x 9", signed lower left: Guy Wiggins; titled and signed verso: The Empire State Building / Winter / Guy Wiggins NA. **$44,813**

Courtesy Heritage Auctions, ha.com

"Jimson Weed/
White Flower No. 1"
by Georgia O'Keeffe
(1887-1986), oil on
canvas, 1932, 48" x
40". **$44,405,000**

*Courtesy of Sotheby's,
sothebys.comv*

"The Summer
Cloud" by Winslow
Homer (1836-1910),
watercolor on paper,
signed "Winslow
Homer" and dated
1881 lower left,
13 1/2" x 19 3/4".
$1,810,000

*Courtesy of Sotheby's,
sothebys.com*

Birger Sandzén
(1871-1954)

"Creek at Twilight" by Birger Sandzén (1871-1954), oil on canvas, 1927, 48" x 60", signed. The 1927 graduating class of Washington High School in Milwaukee, Wisconsin, purchased "Creek at Twilight" directly from the trunk of the artist's car, the very year in which it was painted. Sandzén had been on exhibit at the time at the Milwaukee Art Institute. Sandzén was born in Sweden, but lived for many years in Lindsborg, Kansas, where he taught art at Bethany College and worked on his own paintings. "Creek at Twilight" hung on the walls of the school for years but at some point ended up in storage. The painting was resurrected from a dusty boiler room in 2004. With its textural impasto and strong, colorful brushwork reminiscent of Vincent Van Gogh and Paul Cézanne, "Creek at Twilight" embodies the accolades showered upon Sandzén in 1920, and is as relevant and impressive today as it was when painted. Proceeds from the sale of the painting went to the school's scholarship fund. **$516,500**

Courtesy of Heritage Auctions, ha.com

Born in Canton, Mississippi, and raised in the South, **John McCrady** (1911-1968) emerged as one of the best-known 20th century southern artists. The son of an Episcopal minister, McCrady studied at the Arts and Crafts Club of New Orleans, the Art Students League of New York and the University of Pennsylvania. While in New Orleans, McCrady painted "Portrait of a Negro," a groundbreaking work that earned him a one-year scholarship in New York and launched his career. In New York he was exposed to the teaching of Thomas Hart Benton and the art of the American regionalists. Returning to Louisiana, the influence of his teachers would shape his direction and career.

In 1946 when McCrady painted this extraordinary mural "Steamboat

'Round the Bend," a nostalgic depiction of teenage boys frolicking along the banks of the Mississippi River, he was already being lauded as *the* "first-rate" painter from the South, "a star risen from the bayous." The work, an oil-on-canvas mural measuring 78" x 168", was commissioned in 1945 by Marie LaFanca, owner of Delmonico's, an upscale restaurant in New Orleans. McCrady was said to have been paid with dinners, drinks and an unknown fee for the work, which took him a year to complete. When done, the painting hung behind the restaurant bar. Illustrating the appreciation and demand for Regionalism, the painting sold at auction for **$542,500.**

Courtesy of Heritage Auctions, ha.com

Bronze Artwork

"Leda Col Cigno" by Bruno Bruni, surrealist bronze sculpture of a woman depicting a coquettish standing female with the head of a swan, signed and numbered, 18" t. $500

Courtesy of Bruneau & Co. Auctioneers, www.bruneauandco.com

When looking at bronze works of art, it's easy to be dazzled by the diversity of shapes, forms and color. Most people do not realize that bronze statues have artificial patinas applied to their surface. This is what makes bronze such an attractive art form and leads to a piece increasing in value over time.

Bronze is a metal alloy consisting primarily of copper, usually with tin as the main additive, but sometimes with other elements such as phosphorus, manganese, aluminum, or silicon. Bronze has been used by humans for thousands of years. The natural color of bronze is bright and shiny like brass. The patina seen on unearthed artifacts and antiquties take thousands of years to develop. Artists soon discovered methods to apply patinas in a way to imply age or to simply enhance the artistic look of a piece. Brown patinas were mainly used during the 15th through the 17th centuries. These works are now coveted for the manner in which artists subtly applied the brown coloration, especially on small-scale sculptures and figures.

In 19th century France and England, green patinas were in vogue. It shows details well and ages to a warm, soft glow. This patina is extremely difficult to apply and the process was left to only the most highly skilled artisans. This is one indication why green patina bronze sculptures often command higher prices at auction and generally increase in value over time.

Contemporary bronze sculptures (late 19th century to today) use "artistic patinas" to enhance sculptural forms. Ranging from russet earth tones to blacks and even white, these patinas are applied at the foundry. Surprisingly, very few foundries apply more than one patina so it is entirely up to a second artist to add elements to create subtle colorations on the bronze. It is hard to believe that in the 21st century, applying these specialty patinas is truly a lost art and one that is at risk of dying out.

"Hunter & Dog" by Marcel Debut, primitive figure of a large, proud man wearing fur garments with a spear in one hand and an axe at his belt; deep brown patina, 31" h. **$5,000**

Courtesy of Fontaine's Auction Gallery, www.fontainesauction.com

"Peace Through Chemistry" by
Roy Lichtenstein, bronze plaque,
c.1971, signed & numbered from
the edition of 38. Published by
Gemini G.E.L., Los Angeles, with
their copyright stamp lower right,
27" h. x 46" w., **$50,000-$80,000**

Courtesy of Cottone Auctions,
www.cottonauctions.com

"Maquette for a Warrior Without
Shield" by Henry Moore, 1952,
bronze statue, 8-1/2" h. x 3-1/2"
w. x 4-1/2" d., with stand. **$17,000**

Courtesy of Nye & Company Auctions,
www.neyandcompany.com

"Buddha," artist unknown, seated in the full lotus position,
he wears robes in a floral cloisonné pattern in turquoise and
edged in burgundy, 11 1/4» x 8 1/2» w. x 18» d. **$1,500**

Courtesy Converse Auctions, www.auctionsatconverse.com

"Una & The Lion," unknown artist, bronze sculpture, depicts the maiden wearing a crown and holding an overflowing cornucopia in her lap, riding on the back of a lion; stands on a rouge marble base, 19 3/4" h. x 21 1/5" w. x 8" d. **$4,000**

Courtesy of Fontaine's Auction Gallery, www.fontainesauction.com

▲"Grupo de cuatro mujeres de pie" by Francisco Zúñiga, 1972, Ed. 2 of 5, signed, dated and numbered ' Zúñiga, 1972, II/V' (on the base), bronze with green patina and wooden base, 25" h. x 22-3/4" w. x 17-3/8" d., **$68,500**

Courtesy of Christie's Auction, www.christies.com

▼ "Taking the Ducks to Market" after the model by Leonid Posen, circa 1890, bronze figural group, brown patina, inscribed 'Sculp. L. Posene', with foundry mark, on a plush covered plinth, 31 1/8" w. **$184,217**

Courtesy of Sotheby's, www.sothebys.com

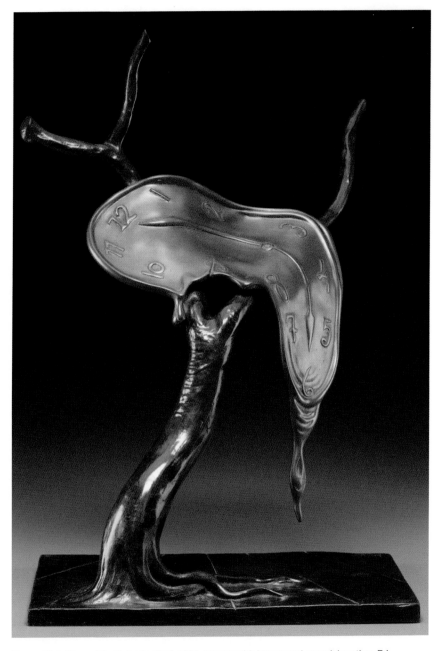

"Le profil du Temps" by Salvador Dalí, 1984, bronze with brown and greenish patina, Ed. 166/350, inscribed on base: Dali / 166/350, 20-1/2» h., **$18,750**

Courtesy of Heritage Auctions, www.ha.com

"Ocean II" by Romain "Erte" de Tirtoff, Art Nouveau figural bronze bowl, an abstracted sailing vessel with front figurehead of a nude woman, numbered 292 of 300, and impressed with the Conker foundry mark, 13 1/4" l., x 9 1/2" w. x 6 3/4" t. **$1,800**

Courtesy of Bruneau & Co. Auctioneers, www.bruneauandco.com

"Draped Reclining Figure" by Henry Moore, c. 1952, bronze sculpture maquette, original marble base. HMF reference: 2016.463, bronze edition of 10+1. **$195,500**

Courtesy of Cottone Auctions, www.cottonauctions.com

▼ Clock, monumental French Napoleon III, gilt bronze, mantel clock with cherubs, 19th century. Movement, P. Ltre., 29 1/2" h. x 34" w. x 13" d. **$35,650**

Courtesy of Cottone Auctions, www.cottonauctions.com

"Elk" by Joseph Franz Pallenberg, date unknown, bronze, signed on base, 23" h. x 20-1/2" w., **$848**

Courtesy of Copake Auction, Inc., www.copakeauction.com

▲ Chandelier, Peter Fillerup, early 21st c., Indian Drum Circle, bronze and glass, with 11Native American musician figures in high relief atop a drum form armature with amber slag glass panels, 60" h. x 37" dia., **$5,000**

Courtesy of Heritage Auctions, www.ha.com

▶ "John Wayne, Hondo Lane & Sam" by David Manuel, 1986, bronze with brown patina, Ed. 3/7, inscribed on base: John Wayne / "Hondo" Lane / & / Sam / Godensa Manuel Magroni / 1986 WF3/7, 28" h. **$11,875**

Courtesy of Heritage Auctions, www.ha.com

▲ "Anyanwu" by Benedict Chukwukadibia Enwonwu, aka Ben Enwonwu, 1956, a version of "Anyanwu" was gifted from the Nigerian state to the United Nations for its new headquarters in the 1960s, 92 15/16" h. x 27 15/16" w. x 17 11/16" d. **$461,066**

Courtesy of Bonhams, www. bonhams.com

Plaque, c. 1930s, Art Deco, silvered bronze architectural plaque depicting a fountain, 26-1/2" h. x 29-1/2" w. **$4,250**

Courtesy of Heritage Auctions, www.ha.com

"Diana" by Pierre le Faguays, bronze with green patina, inscribed on base: Le Faguays / Susse Fres Edtrs Paris, 27" h. x 9" w. x 6-1/5 d., **$3,750**

Courtesy of Heritage Auctions, www.ha.com

"Venus II" by David Bates, 2012, painted bronze, Ed. 1/6, signed on base: Bates, 36" h. **$20,000**

Courtesy of Heritage Auctions, www.ha.com

Continental School

When paintings or other fine art items are left unsigned, or they are signed indistinctly, the trained art researcher will categorize the item within a genre among artists who are from a similar place or utilize the style, technique and subject matter that place is known for, according to Chicago's Mir Appraisal Services. The Continental School genre, as the name suggests, focuses on subject matter that is recognizably "from the continent" meaning Europe, and it can be as variable as an oil on canvas depiction of the English landscape or a Parisian cityscape. The Continental School is most often associated with the late 19th century and early 20th century. Particularly in cases where Old Masters are concerned, less specific descriptions or labels such as "school of" or "follower of" or "circle of" are often used. But a label describing a piece as "19th-Century" is about as broad as possible.

The term is not limited to paintings. The Continental School genre also may also include furniture, sculpture and prints and even firearms. The common thread linking these disparate items is an expert's inability to attribute

"Royal Courier," Continental School, 19th Century, bronze, inscribed on base with 'Bronze Garanti au Titre Paris' founder's seal: Creca, 18" h. x 28" w. **$3,250**

Courtesy of Heritage Auctions, www.ha.com

the work to an artist or even a manufacturer. While it may seem like a backwater corner of the art world, Continental School works of art are sold by the thousands every year by the most reputable dealers and auction houses. As to be expected, values can be considerably lower than artworks by recognized (or even identified) artists. Continental School works of art can be had for as little as $20 or can sell well into the six figures. However, there are always diamonds in the rough that make Continental School genre artworks so intriguing.

Take the case of "Triple Portrait with Lady Fainting," a small oil on board billed as a 19th-

Triple Portrait of Lady Fainting" Or "Smell", possibly by Rembrandt, 1625, presumed by bidders to be part of the artist's series on the Five Senses, with this painting being the representation of "smell," possibly executed while Rembrandt was still a student in the studio of Dutch painter Pieter Lastman. Painting was auctioned as "Continental School, 19thC., Appears unsigned," 12 1/2" h. x 10" w. **$870,000**

Courtesy of Nye & Co.,
www.nyeandcompany.com

century Continental School painting and valued at just $500 to $800. The painting was offered in late 2015 and it quickly caught the eye of art experts. The painting sold for $870,000 on talk that the bidders who competed intensely for it believe it could be a something special. Experts believe the artwork was actually a long lost panel by a teenaged Rembrandt.

The bidding war shocked auction house owner John Nye of Nye & Company. When asked whether he or his staff had gotten wind of any presale buzz on the work, he told ArtNet News, "In a word, no. There was no inclination that it was going to do anything like what it did.

"It was really just all at once, when the lot came up and we started the bidding, it just didn't stop, it kept going and going. It was at 30 [thousand] and then 50, and I started thinking 'Wow, this is pretty cool.'"

"The Parrot Cage" after Jan Steen, Continental School, 19th century copy of the 1665 original currently in the collection in the Rijksmuseum, Amsterdam, oil on canvas, 21" h. x 16-1/2" w. **$767**

Courtesy of Eldred's Auctioneers & Appraisers, www.eldreds.com

"Riverside Fort," unsigned, Continental School, oil on canvas, 12" h. x 16" w., **$192**

Courtesy of Eldred's Auctioneers & Appraisers, www.eldreds.com

Sculpture, "Eagle," Continental School, 20th century, bronze with brown patina, 41" h., **$1,250**

Courtesy of Heritage Auctions, www.ha.com

Carpet, Oushak style, Continental, second quarter of the 20th century, the central polychrome circular medallion on the open madder field is within an ivory palmette and meandering vine border, 11' 9" l. x 8' 1" w. **$375**

Courtesy of Doyle New York, www.doyle.com

"The Fisherman,"
signed lower right:
C. Patin, Continental
School, 20th Century,
oil on canvas, 24" h x
36" w. **$375**

Courtesy of Heritage Auctions,
www.ha.com

"Portrait of Wolfgang Amadeus Mozart,"
unsigned, Continental School, oil on canvas,
32" h. x 24 1/4" w. **$5,900**

*Courtesy of Eldred's Auctioneers & Appraisers,
www.eldreds.com*

"Competing for her Affection," unsigned,
Continental School, oil on canvas, 38" h. x
26" w. **$708**

*Courtesy of Eldred's Auctioneers & Appraisers,
www.eldreds.com*

"The Abbey Ruins" Continental School, 20th
Century, oil and watercolor on paper, 9" h. x
6-3/4" w. **$137**

Courtesy of Heritage Auctions, www.ha.com

"Portrait of a woman with a hat," signed 'R,'
19th century, Continental School, framed liner
reads "George Romney", oil on canvas, period
frame, 24" h. x 20" w. **$885**

*Courtesy of Eldred's Auctioneers & Appraisers,
www.eldreds.com*

▲ "The Roman
Forum with Figures
near the Arch of
Septimius Severus
Looking toward
the Arch of Titus,"
Continental School,
19th century,
pen with brown
and gray wash
heightened with
white on paper,
4 7/8" h. x 6 3/4" w.
$593

*Courtesy of Doyle New York,
www.doyle.com*

Panels, pair, Continental
stained glass panels,
probably 16th century,
12-1/4" h. x 10" w. **$312**

*Courtesy of Doyle New York,
www.doyle.com*

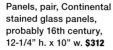

Box, Continental silver
covered dressing box, late
19th/ early 20th century,
8-1/4" l., 18 oz. **$375**

*Courtesy of Doyle New York,
www.doyle.com*

"Virgin and Child with two female saints (a triptych)." Continental School, oil and mixed media on panel, 22" h. x 28 1/2" w. **$812**

Courtesy of Heritage Auctions, www.ha.com

"Madonna and Child" unsigned, Continental School, late 19th century, hand-carved gilt frame, oil on canvas, framed 52" h. x 43" w. **$212**

Courtesy of Eldred's Auctioneers & Appraisers, www.eldreds.com

"Balloon Over the Harvest," Continental School, 20th century, oil on canvas, 22" h. x 14" w., **$36**

Courtesy of Heritage Auctions, www.ha.com

"Floral and Flight," textile, Continental School, 19th century, embroidery and beading on silk, 31" l. x 16" w. **$500**

Courtesy of Heritage Auctions, www.ha.com

Bench, Continental provincial-style walnut bench, hinged seat, 41 3/4" l. **$187**

Courtesy of Doyle New York, www.doyle.com

"Foxhounds," 1775, Continental School, 18th century, oil on canvas, signed lower right indistinctly and dated: 1775, 33 1/2" h. x 43 1/2" w. **$2,987**

Courtesy of Heritage Auctions, www.ha.com

Illustration Art

Collectors, whether looking for a distinctive decoration for a living room or seeking a rewarding long-term investment, will find something to fit their fancy – and their budget – when they turn to illustration art.

Pieces of representational art – often, art that tells some sort of story – are produced in a variety of forms, each appealing in a different way. They are created as the source material for political cartoons, magazine covers, posters, story illustrations, comic books and strips, animated cartoons, calendars, and book jackets. They may be in color or in black and white. Collectible forms include:

- Unique original art. These pieces have the widest range of all, from amateur sketches to finished paintings. The term "original art" includes color roughs produced by a painter as a preliminary test for a work to be produced, finished oil paintings, animation cels for commercials as well as feature films, and black-and-white inked pages of comic books and strips. They may be signed and identifiable or unsigned and generic.

- Mass-market printed reproductions. These can range from art prints and movie posters to engravings, clipped advertising art, and bookplates. While this may be the least-expensive art to hang on your wall, a few rare items can bring record prices.

- Limited-run reproductions. These range from signed, numbered lithographs to numbered prints.

- Tangential items. These are hard-to-define, oddball pieces. One example is printing plates (some in actual lead; some in plastic fused to lightweight metal) used by newspapers and comic-book printers to reproduce the art.

Illustration art is often differentiated from fine art, but its pop culture nature may increase the pool of would-be purchasers and even value. Alberto Vargas (1896-1982) and Gil Elvgren (1914-1980) demand high prices for pin-up art; Norman Rockwell (1894-1978), James Montgomery Flagg (1877-1960), and J. C. Leyendecker (1874-1951) were masters of mainstream illustration and the value for their work reflects that; and Margaret Brundage (1900-1976) and Virgil Finlay (1914-1971) are highly regarded pulp artists, a genre that continues to grow in popularity.

Ringling Brothers Barnum and Bailey Circus program cover, 1950, James Montgomery Flagg, oil on canvas, 33" x 25", signed. **$8,365**

Courtesy of Heritage Auctions, ha.com

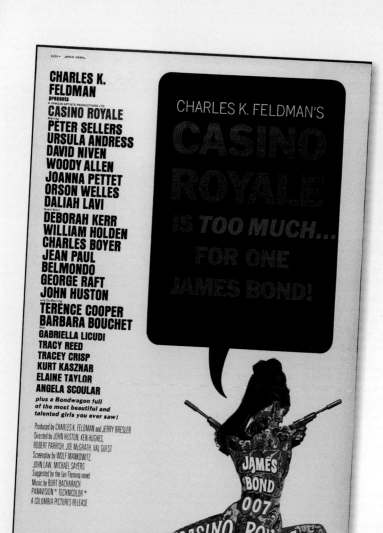

"Casino Royale" by
Robert McGinnis
(American, b. 1926),
original DVD illustration,
2002, gouache and
pencil on board, signed,
23 1/2" x 30 1/2". $47,500
*Courtesy of Heritage Auctions,
ha.com*

"Noisy Neighbor" by Charles Addams full-page cartoon for *The New Yorker,* with their stamps and a pencil sketch by Addams on verso, published April 28, 1951, watercolor, ink and wash on board, 19 1/4" x13 3/4", signed "Chas Addams". **$15,000**

Courtesy of Swann Galleries, swanngalleries.com

"E.T. the Extra-Terrestrial" by John Alvin (1948-2008), original promotional movie illustration,1982, acrylic on board, 41" x 27", signed. Alvin is among the greatest cinematic artists in history and created iconic images for more than 135 films, including *Blade Runner*, *The Goonies*, *Aladdin*, *The Princess Bride*, *Batman Returns*, *Jurassic Park*, and *The Lion King*. Utilizing his daughter's hand as a model and taking inspiration from Michelangelo's "The Creation of Adam," Alvin created this world-renowned image for E.T. **$394,000**

Courtesy of Heritage Auctions, ha.com

▲ TOP OF PAGE "Peanuts" by Charles M. Schulz, original 4-panel, "Here comes the big Polar Bear stalking across the snow!" published February 9, 1957, with United Feature Syndicate, Inc., pen and ink on thick paper. 7" x 28 3/4" inches, signed and dated. **$12,500**

Courtesy of Swann Galleries, swanngalleries.com

▲ "Weekend Chores" by Lucille Corcos, highly detailed image of a suburban neighborhood bustling with activity, egg tempera on masonite, 21 1/4" x 26 1/4", signed. **$10,000**

Courtesy of Swann Galleries, swanngalleries.com

◄ Mr. Earbrass by Edward Corey, unknown publication, but similar to Mr. Earbrass-style characters used for Christmas cards in the 1970s. Watercolor, pen, and ink on paper. 3 1/2" x 2" inches. **$11,875**

Courtesy of Swann Galleries, swanngalleries.com

"In Pharaoh's Tomb" by Frank Frazetta, 1978, published in TV Guide and appeared as an advertisement for the TV show "Battlestar Galactica," 17 1/2" x 23 1/2", signed and dated 1978 at lower left. **$191,200**

Courtesy of Heritage Auctions, ha.com

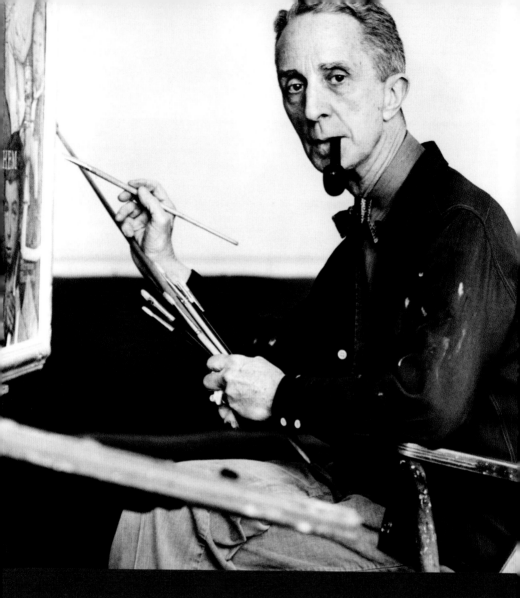

Norman Rockwell
(1894-1978)

Arguably America's favorite and most famous artist, Norman Rockwell produced more than 4,000 original works, earning widespread fame for his cover illustrations of everyday life for *The Saturday Evening Post*. Rockwell considered the illustration found on the opposite page his best work. One of the most memorable self-portaits in art history, the illustration captures Rockwell working in his studio in Stockbridge, Massachusetts, circa 1960.

Photo by Underwood Archives/Getty Images

Study for "Triple Self Portrait" by Norman Rockwell (1894-1978), 1960.
Rockwell's oil study of his self-described "masterpiece" was created
for a 1960 cover of *The Saturday Evening Post*; oil on photographic
paper laid on panel, 11 1/2" x 9 1/4", signed and inscribed lower right.
$1,332,500

Courtesy of Heritage Auctions, ha.com

James Montgomery Flagg
(1877-1960)

American painter and illustrator James Montgomery Flagg was best known for the World War I Uncle Sam recruiting poster with the words "I Want You." More than four million copies of the poster were printed during the war. The poster was revived for World War II.

"Jimmie Loves Mary" by Revere F. Wistehuff, image of young unrequited love, circa 1930s, oil on canvas. 29" x 22 3/4", signed. **$8,750**

Courtesy of Swann Galleries, swanngalleries.com

"Dancing Cheek to Cheek" by James Montgomery Flagg, watercolor on board, 27" x 18 1/2", signed. **$3,585**

Courtesy of Heritage Auctions, ha.com

"It's Time to Build a Stronger America" by James
Montgomery Flagg (1877-1960), Uncle Sam American Industry
advertisement, 1932, oil on canvas, 36 1/4" x 30", signed and
dated lower right: James Montgomery Flagg / 1932. **$30,000**

Courtesy of Heritage Auctions, ha.com

Joseph Christian Leyendecker
(1874-1951)

Before Norman Rockwell's arrival, Joseph Christian "J.C." Leyendecker was the most prominent artist associated with *The Saturday Evening Post*. Leyendecker produced 322 covers for the magazine. As a commercial artist, Leyendecker created The Arrow Collar Man, work that came to define the fashionable American man during the early decades of the 20th century.

"Thanksgiving, 1628-1928: 300 Years (Pilgrim and Football Player)" by Joseph Christian Leyendecker (American, 1874-1951), *The Saturday Evening Post* cover, November 24, 1928, oil on canvas, 28 1/4" x 21". **$365,000**

Courtesy of Heritage Auctions, ha.com

OPPOSITE PAGE

"To the Vanguished" by Joseph Christian Leyendecker, *The Saturday Evening Post* cover, March 10, 1934, oil on canvas, 32" x 24", signed. **$200,000**

Courtesy of Heritage Auctions, ha.com

Untitled cover for American Weekly by Joseph Christian Leyendecker, magazine published December 19, 1948, oil on canvas, signed. **$131,450**

Courtesy of Heritage Auctions, ha.com

"Honeymoon" by Joseph Christian Leyendecker, *The Saturday Evening Post* cover, July 17, 1926, oil on canvas, 28 1/4" x 21 1/4". Leyendecker was firmly established as a master illustrator by the early 1930s. He completed advertising illustrations for Boy Scouts of America, Cream of Wheat and Ivory Soap. **$194,500**

Courtesy of Heritage Auctions, ha.com

Untitled (Woman with Horse) by Patrick Nagel, acrylic on canvas, 30" x 22", signed and dated. **$161,000**

Courtesy of Heritage Auctions, ha.com

"Susan" by Patrick Nagel (American, 1945-1984), 1982, acrylic on board, 19 1/2" x 13 1/4", signed. **$47,500**

Courtesy of Heritage Auctions, ha.com

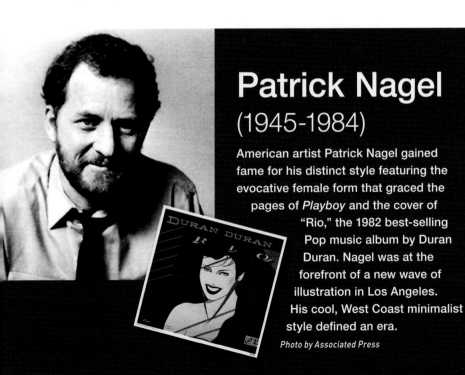

Patrick Nagel
(1945-1984)

American artist Patrick Nagel gained fame for his distinct style featuring the evocative female form that graced the pages of *Playboy* and the cover of "Rio," the 1982 best-selling Pop music album by Duran Duran. Nagel was at the forefront of a new wave of illustration in Los Angeles. His cool, West Coast minimalist style defined an era.

Photo by Associated Press

"Geometric Plaid" by Patrick Nagel, acrylic on board, 35" x 22 3/4". **$93,750**

Courtesy of Heritage Auctions, ha.com

LeRoy Neiman (1921-2012)

Immediately recognized by his handlebar mustache and ever-present cigar,
LeRoy Neiman gained fame with his distinctive impressionistic style. He
captured athletes, singers and other celebrities in brilliant Technicolor bursts of
electricity and pure energy. Neiman said his favorite subject was Muhammad
Ali because he was drawn to larger-than-life figures.

Photo by Nancy R. Schiff/Getty Images

"Roulette Las Vegas" by LeRoy Neiman, 1958, oil on canvas, signed and dated lower left: *LeRoy Neiman 58*, 44 1/4" x 36". **$125,000**

Courtesy of Heritage Auctions, ha.com

"Blonde Pin-Up in White Bikini" by LeRoy Neiman (American, 1921-2012), Playboy magazine, 1964, oil on Masonite, signed and dated lower right: Leroy Neiman / '64 30" x 22 1/2". **$112,500**

Courtesy of Heritage Auctions, ha.com

"Regatta of the Gondoliers" by LeRoy Neiman, oil on canvas 30" x 401/2", exhibited at the Minnesota Museum of Art, St. Paul, Minnesota, "Leroy Neiman: Retrospective 1949-1975," 1975. **$50,000**

Courtesy of Heritage Auctions, ha.com

Modern & Contemporary Art

By Noah Fleisher

The proliferation of eight- and nine-figure artworks in the last decade has been hard to miss, and no sector has seen a bigger uptick than contemporary art.

According to Brandon Kennedy, a Contemporary and Modern Art Specialist at Heritage Auctions, "Things are definitely on the upswing. There's always a little bit of the 'good, bad, and the ugly' in the market and it largely depends on where you're standing."

The best place to stand would be on your own two feet on a firm foundation. That foundation has to be built on a solid understanding of exactly what you are looking at. Just what is the definition of contemporary art, and how is it separated from modern art?

According to Kennedy, the term "modern art" is used to define a period starting in the late 19th century and extending to sometime in the 1960s-1970s, depending on who you ask, largely defined by styles and movements within a certain historical moment. "Contemporary art" is generally thought of taking shape post-1965 or so, when the lines between strict divisions and traditional mediums begin to dissolve and even wander outside the gallery or institutional framework.

Kennedy is quick to point out that, with the rapid evolution of mediums (including digital artwork, 3-D printers, and new mediums for sculpture), even those definitions are becoming hazy. There is a definite post-modern movement, but is such a thing as post-contemporary even possible?

What can we make of recent sales at big auction houses and galleries of work by young artists done in those non-traditional mediums, specifically computer prints that sell for seven and eight figures? How philosophically and financially sound or unsound is this?

"Artwork created by digital or other technological means is now always present and will continue to

Writer and author **NOAH FLEISHER** has 20 years of experience in the antiques and collectibles field. He is the author of *The Beatles: Fab Finds of the Fab Four*, *Warman's Modern Furniture*, and *Collecting Children's Books*.

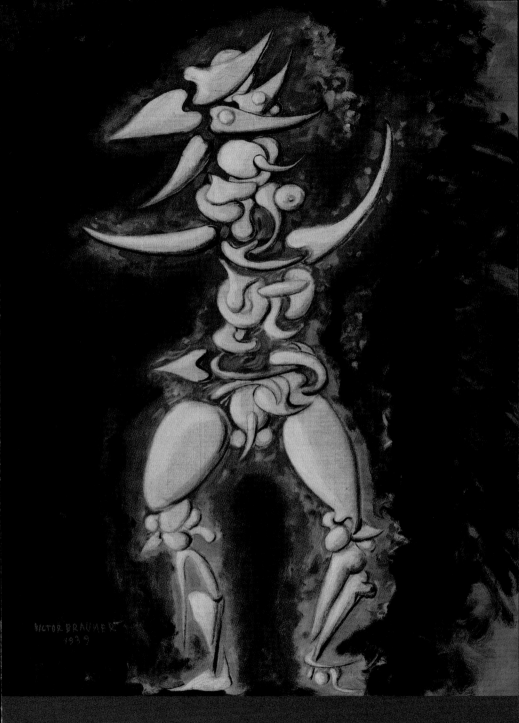

"Denombrement III" by Victor Brauner, 1938-39, oil on canvas, signed and dated lower left: Victor Brauner / 1939, inscribed on the stretcher: 1938 Victor Brauner "Denombrement 3", 25-1/2" h. x 21" w. **$150,000**

Courtesy of Heritage Auctions

"Abstract Composition" by Toshimitsu Imai, heavy impasto abstract composition in green and blue acrylic paint on wove C.M. Fabriano paper. Signed and dated at bottom right: "Imai 80 / New York," in black felt tip, 22" h. x 30" w. **$3,000**

Courtesy of Roland New York

evolve with the available technology at hand," said Kennedy. "Whether sound or unsound, it largely boils down to the market and personal taste and where the two overlap."

Doesn't the very artificiality of such a medium change value for the lower in the long run?

"There are plenty of high rollers and lower-level speculators treating contemporary art like a futures market," Kennedy said, "and many others simply follow along and get burnt on the back-side of a transaction when they try to resell the work. A lot of the time, the contemporary art market can sound like it's somewhere in-between a horse race and interior decorating, and, unfortunately, it is sometimes as simple as that."

Can't an artist just print out another print, if it's a digital piece? Absolutely, and sometimes they do. In the topsy-turvy modern world, that can even enhance the value of a piece, at least in the short-term, even when an artist "creates" more digital work in a sort of protest against what could become a quickly bloated market.

If you're serious about getting in, where do you even begin? What area of contemporary art is the hottest right now and who are the hottest artists who might not necessarily be household names?

"Names like Warhol, Bacon, and Gerhard Richter are still fetching premium prices, at all levels of work, and that's no surprise," Kennedy said. "Bruce Nauman and Ed Ruscha are

"Woman from Velarde, New Mexico" by Miguel Martinez, pastel and oil on paper, 30" h. x 40" w.
$6,500

Courtesy of Bruneau & Co. Auctioneers

still producing great work and fetching premium prices, as is the work of artists like David Hammons, John Baldessari, Jasper Johns, and Richard Serra. There are also a slew of hot, young artists who graduate from the gallery scene to the auction block in the blink of an eye and, by the time you realize that you could've capitalized on their ascendancy, they're already on the decline. I won't name names specifically because of the aforementioned problem."

Is contemporary art, then, a market that's even open to first-time buyers and those without massive bank accounts?

"Absolutely," said Kennedy. "Start small and look at editions and prints of an established artist that you have heard of before. Pop and abstract expressionism are good movements to consider when pondering this question. Otherwise, get out and visit local art galleries and the artists who show there. Spend a season or two surveying what's available and educating yourself, and eventually your heart and taste will lead you down the right road."

Kennedy is 100% right in this approach, which will work no matter what the category. Ask experts for their opinion. Get to know the people behind the industry, go to auctions and gallery openings and museum exhibitions. Continue to educate yourself in every aspect of art culture and the market.

"Educate yourself and continue to do so over the course of your life," he said, "but only buy what you love and can't stop thinking about."

"Nemesis" by Robert Motherwell, 1981-82, acrylic on canvas,
signed and dated on the reverse: R. Motherwell / 1982,
60" h. x 44" w. **$380,000**

Courtesy of Heritage Auctions

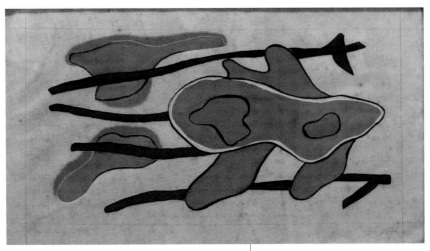

▲ "Untitled" by Fernand Leger, gouache, ink and pencil on paper depicting an aircraft in the sky, pencil signed lower right, 19 1/4" h. x 10 1/2" w. **$13,500**

Courtesy of Antiques & Modern Auction Gallery

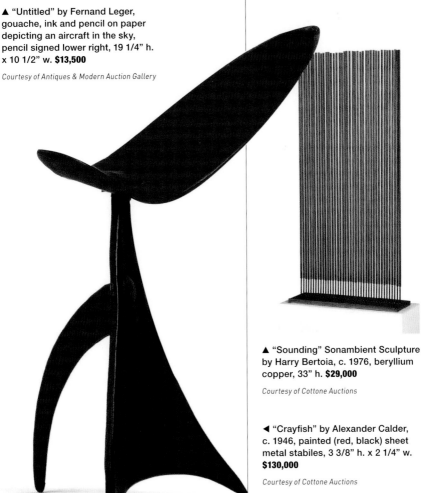

▲ "Sounding" Sonambient Sculpture by Harry Bertoia, c. 1976, beryllium copper, 33" h. **$29,000**

Courtesy of Cottone Auctions

◄ "Crayfish" by Alexander Calder, c. 1946, painted (red, black) sheet metal stabiles, 3 3/8" h. x 2 1/4" w. **$130,000**

Courtesy of Cottone Auctions

Hans Hofmann
(1880-1966)

Hans Hofmann is one of the most important figures of postwar American art. Celebrated for his exuberant, color-filled canvases, and renowned as an influential teacher for generations of artists—first in his native Germany, then in New York and Provincetown—Hofmann played a pivotal role in the development of Abstract Expressionism.

From his early landscapes of the 1930s, to his "slab" paintings of the late 1950s, and his abstract works at the end of his career, Hofmann continued to create boldly experimental color combinations and formal contrasts that transcended genre and style.

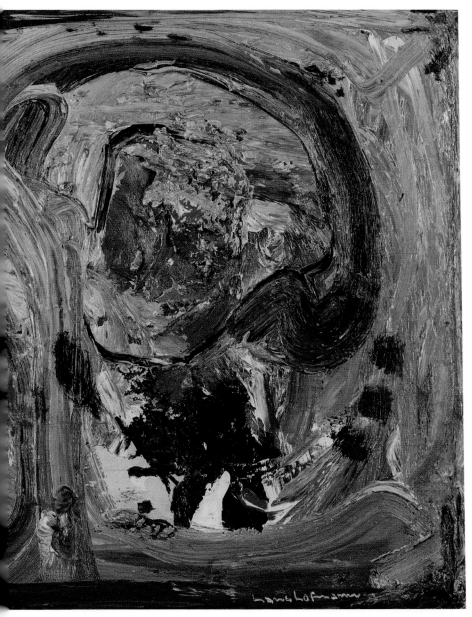

"Pink Phantasie" by Hans
Hofmann, 1950, oil on panel,
signed lower right: hans hofmann,
inscribed verso: Cat. 1091 / 1090,
14-1/4" h. x 20-1/4" w. **$55,000**

Courtesy of Heritage Auctions

"Allegro" by Alice Mattern, oil on canvas
42 1/4" h. x 39" w. **$55,200**

Courtesy of Shannon's Fine Art Auctioneers

"Cavaliers sous les branches a Fère en
Tardenois" by Andre Brasilier, oil on canvas,
38 1/2" h. x 51" w. **$78,000**

Courtesy of Shannon's Fine Art Auctioneers

"Yankee Stadium at Night" by Craig McPherson, mezzotint on BFK Rives print paper, pencil
signed, titled and numbered 3 of 75, 23 1/4" h. x 35" w. **$1,600**

Courtesy of Bruneau & Co. Auctioneers

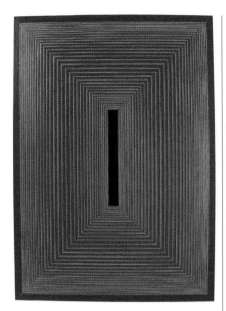

"Inner Red II" by Richard Anuszkiewicz, 1984, rectangular geometric composition. Inscribed, signed, dated, and titled on verso "762 / (c) Richard Anuszkiewicz / 1984 / 'Inner Red'," 17" h. x 12" w. **$18,000**

Courtesy of Roland New York

"NEGRITUDE" by Ben Enwonwu, 1978, gouache on paper, signed and dated, 29 1/2" h. x 21-1/2" w. **$93,685**

Courtesy of Sotheby's

"Province By The Sea" by Will Barnet, 1957, signed bottom right, inscribed with artist's name and title verso, oil on canvas, 54" h. x 46" w. **$11,250**

Courtesy of Freeman's

"Maquette Jubilee II" by Lynn Chadwick, 1983, both stamped 'C3S,' dated 1983 and numbered 1/9, one with the Morris Singer Founders London stamp, bronze with black and polished patina, in two parts, 35 1/2" h. x 56 3/4" w. x 45 3/4" d. **$466,000**

Courtesy of Freeman's

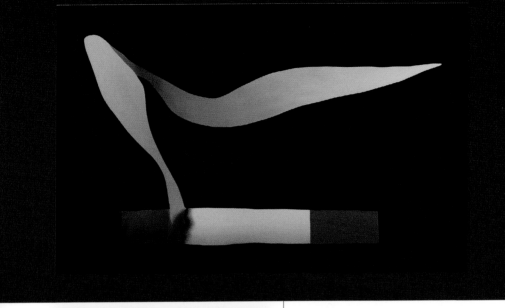

▲ Smoking Cigarette II" by Tom Wesselmann, 1980, acrylic on shaped Masonite, signed and dated Wesselmann 80 on the reverse, mounted on board and framed. **$449,000**

Courtesy of Dorotheum

◄ "Portrait De Barabowski" by Amedeo Modigliani, 1918, oil on canvas, 44 1/4" h. x 22" w. **$19.8 million**

Courtesy of Sotheby's

▼ "Self Portrait" by Alex Israel, 2014, acrylic and bondo on fiberglass, signed and dated by the artist, with the Warner Bros. Studios stamp on the reverse, 69" h. x 60" w. x 3 "d. **$275,000**

Courtesy of Heritage Auctions

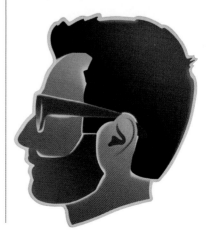

"Homage to Piranesi" by Herbert Ferber, 1965,
corten steel, incised with signature and date
on the base, 19 1/2" h. x 12" w. x 11" d. **$17,500**

Courtesy of Heritage Auctions

Prints & Multiples

The increasing popularity in Prints & Multiples is based on fine art collectors looking for impressive representations from top name Modern and Contemporary artists without the high six-figure price tags. Values generally range from $500 but can surpass $100,000 for pop artist such as Andy Warhol and Jasper Johns and recognizable printmakers including Chuck Close, Keith Haring, M.C. Escher and Pablo Picasso. In many cases, these prints and multiples are personally signed by the artist.

"Prints & Multiples is an exciting and growing category," said Taylor Curry, Consignment Director of Modern & Contemporary Art at Heritage Auctions. "We have seen interest from collectors all over the world. We've found hosting both live and online auctions with affordable pieces for beginning collectors makes collecting accessible to a wider audience. It is a testament to the variety and quality of the items."

The diversity of the Prints & Multiples collecting category often includes mid-century artworks but predominately includes works created in the last 20 to 25 years. It is also not limited to works on paper. The artist known as KAWS works with painted cast vinyl. His 2016 open edition 11-inch sculptures command $3,000 to $5,000 at auciton. Likewise, editions from Jeff Koons' oeuvre from his 2015 "Balloon Dog" editions regularly sell for as much as $7,500.

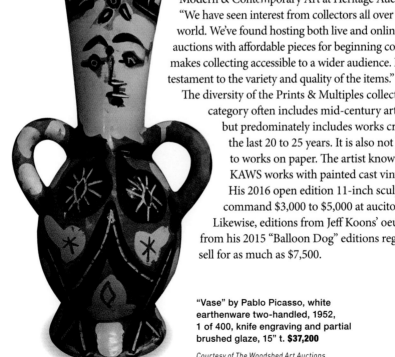

"Vase" by Pablo Picasso, white earthenware two-handled, 1952, 1 of 400, knife engraving and partial brushed glaze, 15" t. **$37,200**

Courtesy of The Woodshed Art Auctions

"Take Me to Your Leader" by George Rodrigue, 1997, silkscreen, 46/120, silver pen signed and numbered lower left, framed, 15 5/8" h. x 11" w. **$1,500**

Courtesy of Crescent City Auction Gallery, crescentcityauctiongallery.com

"The Star" by Andy Warhol, screenprint in color, 4/200, from his "Myths" portfolio, depicts actress Greta Garbo (1905-1990) as Dutch exotic dancer Mata Hari, pencil signed, 37 7/8" x 37 7/8". **$52,000**

Courtesy Bruneau & Co. Auctioneers, www.bruneauandcom.com

"Balloon Dog (Yellow)" by Jeff Koons, 2015, porcelain sculpture painted in chrome, Ed. 425/2300, printed signature and number on the underside, produced by Bernardaud, Limoges, France, 10-1/2" dia., **$7,500**

Courtesy of Heritage Auctions, www.ha.com

"Companion (set of six)" by KAWS, 2016, painted cast vinyl, open edition, each stamped to the bottom of the feet, produced by Medicom Toy, 11" h. **$4,250.**

Courtesy of Heritage Auctions, www.ha.com

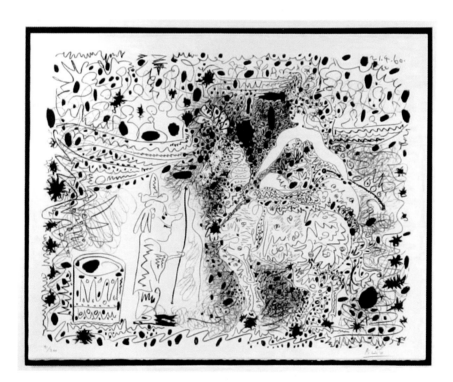

"L'Ecuyère" by Pablo Picasso, limited edition, pencil signed and numbered 91of 200 in the margin and dated, 21 1/2" x 27 1/8". **$4,065**

Courtesy of Bruneau & Co. Auctioneers, www.bruneauandcom.com

"View of Baltimore Canvas Back Ducks, 2 Male, 1 female" by Julius Bien, 1860, Plate 395, chromolithograph on wove paper, 27" h. x 39" w. **$5,000**

Courtesy of John McInnis Auctioneers

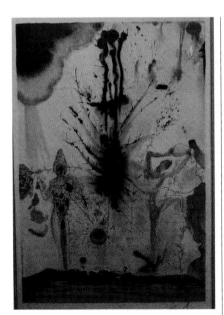

"Land Come to Life" by Salvador Dali, from The Aliyah, signed and numbered 116/250, lithograph, 22" h. x 15" w. **$750**

Courtesy of The Woodshed Art Auctions

"Female Figure" by Man Ray, 1951, signed and dated. **$7,500**

Courtesy The Woodshed Art Auctions

"Train Tracks" by Bob Dylan, 2014, giclee print, from
the Drawn Blank Series, pencil signed and numbered
75/295, 42" h. x 33" w. **$4,250**

Courtesy The Woodshed Art Auctions

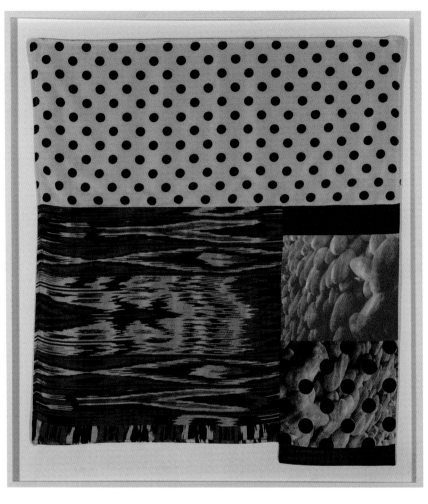

▲ "Samarkand Stitches #VII" by Robert Rauschenberg, 1988, screenprint with mixed media, from an edition of 72, inscribed #11 on the reverse in black ink, 48" h. x 43" w. **$8,750**

Courtesy of Heritage Auctions, www.ha.com

◄ "Cycle 3" by Jay Rosenblum, 1979, screenprint in colors, AP 3/25, signed, titled, dated and numbered in the lower margin in pencil, 21" h. x 25 3/4" w. **$625**

Courtesy of Heritage Auctions, www.ha.com

"American Flag III" by Paul von Ringelheim, 1979, screenprint in colors, ed. 56/300, signed and numbered in the lower margin in pencil, 31" h. x 23" w. **$525**

Courtesy of Heritage Auctions, www.ha.com

"Backstage Dressing Room" by Bob Dylan, 2013, giclee print, from the Drawn Blank Series, pencil signed and numbered 189/295, 33 1/2" h x 26 3/4" w. **$1,200**

Courtesy The Woodshed Art Auctions

"Portrait of Martin Luther King" by Mr. Brainwash, 2017, screenprint, from an edition of 88, signed in the lower right margin recto, dated with the artist's thumbprint verso, published by artist, 44" h. x 31-3/4" w. **$625**

Courtesy of Heritage Auctions, www.ha.com

"Souper Dress" inspired by Andy Warhol, circa 1968, color screenprint on cellulose and cotton, dress inspired by Warhol's 1962 "Campbell's Soup Cans." Dress was made and sold by Campbell's Soup in the late 1960s at a time when disposable paper dresses were a popular trend, 37 1/2" h. x 21 1/2". **$1,750**

Courtesy of Heritage Auctions, www.ha.com

◀ "Pumpkin (Yellow)" by Yayoi Kusama, 2013, painted cast resin, stamped with the artist's copyright on the underside, published by Benesse Holdings, Inc., Naoshima, Japan, 4" h. x 3 1/4 w. x 3 1/4 d. **$750**

Courtesy of Heritage Auctions, www.ha.com

▼ "Six Pills" by Damien Hirst, 2005, digital pigment print, ed. 10/75, signed and numbered in the lower margin in pencil, 19 5/8" h. x 26 5/8" w. **$3,750**

Courtesy of Heritage Auctions, www.ha.com

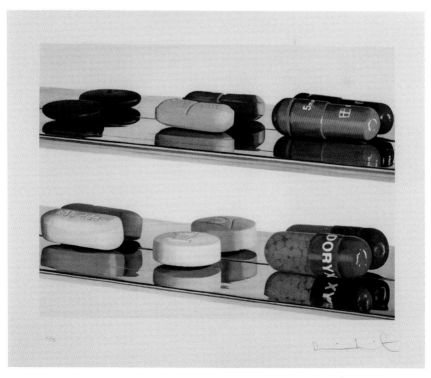

Urban Art

The emerging American art movement called Urban Art (sometimes referred to as Street Art) combines traditional art and graffiti and is often used to summarize all visual art forms arising in urban areas, being inspired by urban architecture or urban lifestyle. The notion of Urban Art developed from street art, which is primarily concerned with graffiti culture. Urban Art is seen as the next American art movement to follow Modern & Contemporary Art.

Street artists often use traditional media but with subject matter that deals with urban and political issues; but because urban art is characterized by existing in the public space, it is often viewed as vandalism and destruction of private property. Though starting as an underground movement, urban artists like Banksy and Adam Neate have now gained mainstream status and their work commands six figures at art auctions.

Urban Art auctions have been successful events and a respected art form in Europe for some time. In fact, the Le Mur museum was founded as a public urban art spot in Paris in 2007.

The first Urban Art auction held in the United States was in 2000 by Guernsey's of New York, which came up short on sales. Doyle New York broached the category in 2013 with success as it set several artist auction records. Angelo Madrigale, Doyle New York's Specialist in Street Art, said sales like his "can be a platform to debut important emerging artists, like Dabs Myla or Grotesk,

"Air Mag (Back to the Future)" by Nike, 2016, multi-color/multi-color, size 11, original box with signed numbered plate, display and charging accessories, plate signed by Tinker Hatfield. **$52,500.**

Courtesy of Heritage Auctions, www.ha.com

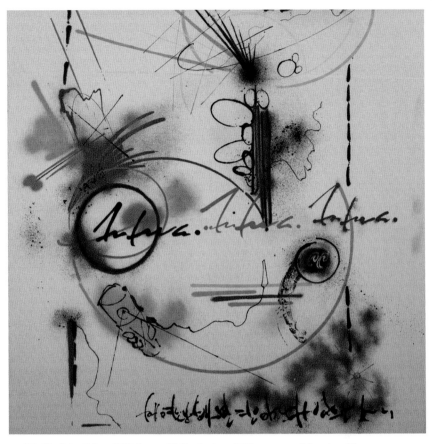

"Untitled" by Futura 2000 (Lenny McGurr), circa 1980s, spray paint and acrylic on canvas, 72" x 72". **$35,000**

Courtesy of Heritage Auctions, www.ha.com

to the auction world, as well as to showcase the masters we all know, whether itís a classic NYC Graffiti legend like Crash, or a UK Street Art legend like Banksy. We've all lived with graffiti most, if not all, of our lives. However, it's only recently, for a lot of people, that it is finally being seen as art - I think Graffiti and Street Art are the last true American movements."

Heritage Auctions launched a foray in the category in 2017, realizing $317,000 on 106 lots. The auction, titled The Future is Now, expanded the category and brought together rare pop culture and urban art objects, sneakers with street art. The auction set a world record for a collectible sneaker at public auction when a pair of Nike Air Mag self-lacing sneakers sold for $52,500 (see image opposite page).

"It's an exciting moment to bridge the gap and draw similarities between industries that have been heavily influenced by street culture and contemporary art," said Leon Benrimon, Director of Modern & Contemporary Art at Heritage Auctions. "Collectors were excited to see their passions displayed on a public stage, giving them a platform and a voice."

◀ "Flower Girl" by Banksy, 2008, black and silver aerosol and exterior semi-gloss on brick facade, mural of a young girl in a dress holding a flower basket and staring quizzically up at a leafy vine upon which a surveillance camera with a rat tail, executed with stencils on a Hollywood gas station wall in the dead of night by the notorious graffiti artist Banksy, the global industrial complex and the government's prying eye are common themes in Banksy's work, 9' x 8'. **$212,500**

Courtesy of Julien's Auctions, www.juliensauctions.com

"Monopoly Man" by Alec Monopoly, 2014, aerosol on canvas, signed in black aerosol lower right, signed and dated in black aerosol on verso, 48" h. x 36" w. **$6,875**

Courtesy of Julien's Auctions, www.juliensauctions.com

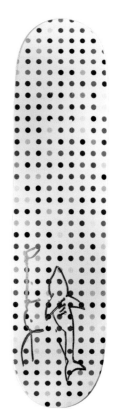

"Dots 5- Little Shark" by Damien Hirst, skatedeck, hand signed and hand drawn, signed in marker verso, 31" l. x 8" w. **$12,500**

Courtesy of Heritage Auctions, www.ha.com

"New World Odor" by Shepard Fairey, 2005, spray paint stencil
and collage on paper, 44 3/4" h. x 30" w. **$33,750**

Courtesy of Julien's Auctions, www.juliensauctions.com

Jean-Michel Basquiat (1960-1988)

The Brooklyn-born Jean-Michel Basquiat went from graffiti artist to an art-collector darling in the span of a mere seven years. He gained early fame as part of SAMO, an informal graffiti duo with friend Al Diaz that began spray-painting sides of buildings in lower Manhattan. By the time he died at age 27 of a drug overdose in 1988, Basquaint had emerged as a powerful voice in the Urban Art Movement. His piece, "Untitled" (1982), an acrylic, spray paint and oil stick on canvas (see opposite page), sold at auction for an impressive $110.5 million at Sotheby's.

The Japanese billionaire Yusaku Maezawa revealed himself to be the buyer through a post on his Instagram account. "When I first encountered this painting, I was struck with so much excitement and gratitude for my love of art," he said in his post. "I want to share that experience with as many people as possible."

It was Mr. Maezawa, the 41-year-old founder of Contemporary Art Foundation, who set the previous auction high for Basquiat, paying $57.3 million for the artist's large 1982 painting of a horned devil during an auction Christie's. Maezawa is the founder of Japan's large online fashion mall, Zozotown. "I hope it brings as much joy to others as it does to me, and that this masterpiece by the 21-year-old Basquiat inspires our future generations."

**"Untitled" by Jean-Michel Basquiat, 1982,
72 1/8" h. x 68 1/8" w.**

Courtesy of Sotheby's, www.southebys.com

"Morons (White & Gold)" by Banksy, 2006, silkscreen on paper, 39/150, signed and dated by Banksy to the lower right, contrary to the marked limitation it is believed that only 50 of these original gold-frame prints were ever actually produced and that they were available only to friends and associates of the artist, 293/4 h. x 223/8" w. **$33,750**

Courtesy of Julien's Auctions, www.juliensauctions.com

▶ "All You Need Is Love (Icon Series)" by Mr. Brainwash, 2010, Ed. 21/250, signed vertically to the center right, 36" h. x 28-1/2" w. **$4,375**

Courtesy of Julien's Auctions, www.juliensauctions.com

▼ "Tigre" by Richard Orlinski, sculpture, resin and bomb aerosol and graffiti, signed, 51" l. **$28,750**

Courtesy of Le Chesnay Enchères, Copyright Alex Guinot

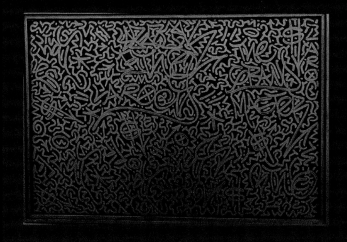

"Grand Master" by LA Ii (Angel Ortiz), New York City urban graffiti painting, year of creation: Lower East Side New York City early 1990s, burgundy acrylic base with metallic gold paint marker, LA Ii collaborated with Keith Haring on a substantial collection of works from paintings, murals, sculptures and found objects, 43" h. x 29" w. **$1,100**

Courtesy Kensington Estate Auction

"America's Nightmare" by Pure Evil, 2017, spray paint on canvas, signed, titled, and dated on the reverse: 2017 / Pure Evil / America's Nightmare / 3/10, 29 3/4" h. x 29 3/4" w. **$1,250**

Courtesy of Heritage Auctions, www.ha.com

"Showpaper Box" by Cost, 2010, mixed media on newspaper box; Cost is considered one of the lynchpins in the progression of graffiti and transition to Street Art, signed repeatedly with artist's device, 48" h. x 16 1/4" w. x 19 1/4 d. **$11,850**

Courtesy of Doyle New York

"Untitled (Figure in a box)" by Keith Haring, 1985, marker on paper, signed and dated in marker, 12" h. x 8 7/8" w. **$8,125**

Courtesy of Heritage Auctions, www.ha.com

"Weber Feather model" by Dewey Weber, late 1960s, vintage surfboard, fiberglass and resin with silk-screened printed laminate, 8' x 10 1/2" w. **$2,125**

Courtesy of Heritage Auctions, www.ha.com

"Be@rbrick Jackson Pollock Toy 1000%" by Medicom Toy and Jackson Pollock Studio, 2015, vinyl, original box, produced in collaboration with the Pollock/Krasner House/Sony Brook Foundation, 11" h. x 5" w. x 4" d. **$525**

Courtesy of Heritage Auctions, www.ha.com

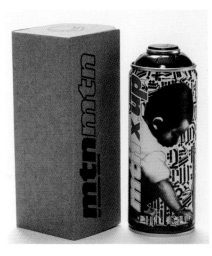

"MTN x up, El Mac/Retna Hardcore (Black R-9011) - Spray paint can" by RETNA with El Mac, from a limited edition of 500, this series is a collaboration between Upper Playground and Montana Colors to create artist series Hardcore cans by four artists, this can is the collaborative work of El Mac and Retna, 7 1/2" h. x 2-1/2" w. x 2 1/2 d. **$250**

Courtesy of Heritage Auctions, www.ha.com

"McSupersized" by Ron English, plastic, 6 1/4" h. x 4 1/2" w. **$137**

Courtesy of Heritage Auctions, www.ha.com

"Di-Faced Tenner, 10 GBP Note" by Banksy, 2005, offset lithograph in colors, 3" h. x 5 5/8" w. **$5,750**

Courtesy of Heritage Auctions, www.ha.com

Asian

Art and antiques from Asia have fascinated collectors for centuries because they are linked with the rich culture and fascinating history of the Far East. Their beauty, artistry and fine craftsmanship have lured collectors through the ages.

The category is vast and includes objects ranging from jade carvings to cloisonné to porcelain, the best known of these being porcelain.

Large quantities of porcelain have been made in China for export to America from the 1780s. A major source of this porcelain was Ching-te-Chen in the Kiangsi province, but the wares were also made elsewhere. The largest quantities were blue and white.

Prices for Asian antiques and art fluctuate considerably depending on age, condition, decoration, etc.

Vase, late Meiji Period, Japan, bronze, 36" t. **$718**

Courtesy of Heritage Auctions, www.ha.com

Statue, gold gilt bronze and cloisonnè Buddha, shown seated in a full lotus position, wearing floral pattered robes, 11" t. $1,000-$1,500

Courtesy of Converse Auctions, www.auctionsatconverse.com

Vase, Chinese Qianlong-style cloisonnè enamel vase; of elaborate tiered form; showing scrolling floral motifs reserved on a teal-blue ground; with various registers of intricate metalwork; featuring several enamel on copper figural panels showing ‹foreigners›; four character mark to base, 16" h. **$340,000**

Courtesy of I.M. Chait Gallery/Auctioneers, www.chait.com

Jar, Guan Ming Dynasty, 15th century, Chinese blue and white porcelain Windswept jar, 13-7/8" h. **$118,750**

Courtesy of Heritage Auctions, www.ha.com

Vessel, Archaic-style Chinese bronze covered vessel; of ding form with two flaring handles; exhibiting elaborately cast scrolling motifs in relief; the cover featuring four loop handles, 11-1/2" h. **$600**

Courtesy of I.M. Chait Gallery/Auctioneers, www.chait.com

Vase, Chinese porcelain Hundred Deer Hu-Form vase, Qianlong seal in underglaze blue but of a later period, 12-7/8" h. **$18,750**

Courtesy of Heritage Auctions, www.ha.com

▲ Cabinets, pair of large Chinese hardwood sectional cabinets; the rectangular stacked forms each with inset design of scholarly objects and flowering precious vessels to the doors, 88-3/4" h. **$1,500**

Courtesy of I.M. Chait Gallery/ Auctioneers, www.chait.com

◄ Bowl, Chinese gilt porcelain bowl; of wide circular form with raised base; exhibiting gilt flora, dragon and butterfly motifs atop a cobalt blue ground; with double concentric mark to base, 8" d. **$550**

Courtesy of I.M. Chait Gallery/ Auctioneers, www.chait.com

**Painting, Tibetan thangka,
(Tibetan Buddhist paintings on
cotton, or silk applique).
$300-$1,200**

*Courtesy of Converse Auctions,
www.auctionsatconverse.com*

Seal, Jade, double dragon seal in a gilt bronze case, elaborately
carved on all sides with a central dragon over waves surrounded
by ruyi clouds and a flaming pearl, 5-3/4" w. x 5-3/4" t. x 6-3/4" d.
$3,000-$5,000

Courtesy of Converse Auctions, www.auctionsatconverse.com

Chairs, pair of Huanghuali dragon arm folding chairs with heavily
carved legs, arm rests and back all in a dragon and cloud motif,
31" t. **$3,000-$5,000**

Courtesy of Converse Auctions, www.auctionsatconverse.com

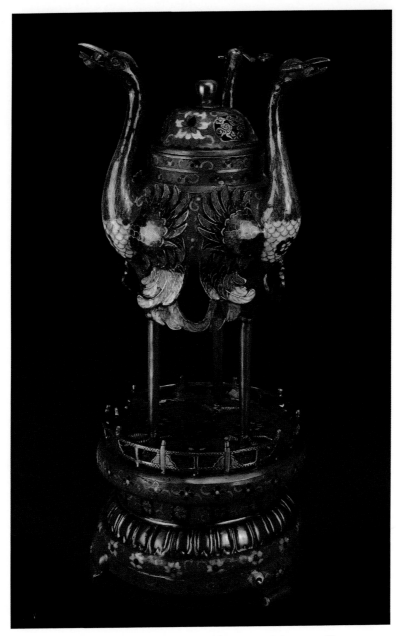

Censer, cloisonnè tripod censer of three enameled cranes with each crane shown holding a ruyi in its beak, 9" t. **$3,000-$5,000**

Courtesy of Converse Auctions, www.auctionsatconverse.com

▲ Panel, late Qing Dynasty, framed Chinese silk embroidered, with floral silk border framing interior narrative court scene of nine male figures outdoors, 29-1/2" h. x 60" w. **$1,500**

Courtesy of Heritage Auctions, www.ha.com

◀ Panel, Chinese carved, parcel-gilt and lacquered wood panel; depicting an official on horseback, riding past forested pavilions as women gaze down from the windows, 15" w. x 11" t. **$900**

Courtesy of I.M. Chait Gallery/ Auctioneers, www.chait.com

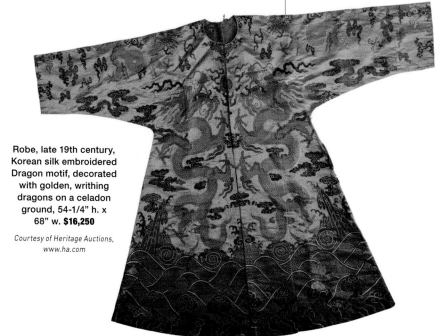

Robe, late 19th century, Korean silk embroidered Dragon motif, decorated with golden, writhing dragons on a celadon ground, 54-1/4" h. x 68" w. **$16,250**

Courtesy of Heritage Auctions, www.ha.com

Banks

By Eric Bradley and Karen Knapstein

ERIC BRADLEY is the author of *Harry Potter – The Unofficial Guide to the Collectibles of Our Favorite Wizard*, as well as *Mantiques: A Manly Guide to Cool Stuff*. He is the public relations director at Heritage Auctions, Dallas.

KAREN KNAPSTEIN is the print editor of *Antique Trader* magazine. A lifelong collector and student of antiques, she has written dozens of articles on antiques and collectibles.

Banks that display some form of action while accepting a coin are considered mechanical banks. Mechanical banks date back to ancient Greece and Rome, but the majority of collectors are interested in those made between 1867 and 1928 in Germany, England, and the United States. More than 80 percent of all cast-iron mechanical banks produced between 1869 and 1928 were made by J. & E. Stevens Co. of Cromwell, Connecticut. Tin banks are usually of German origin.

The mechanical bank hobby continues to catch headlines as some of the best examples of rare banks head to the auction block. Morphy Auctions is a world leader in selling mechanical and still banks most desired by collectors.

According to Dan Morphy, owner and founder of Morphy Auctions, condition – like all other categories of collecting – is king. "Banks in top condition seem to be the trend these days," he said.

Bertoia Auctions, founded by the late Bill Bertoia and Jeanne Bertoia in 1986, has sold some of the rarest and most desirable mechanical and still (with no mechanical action) banks to come to market. The firm is known for achieving record-setting results. In November 2014, Preacher at Pulpit, circa 1876 by J. & E. Stevens Co., realized an astounding $252,000. The preacher bank, in pristine condition, was from the Max Berry collection and one of three known examples.

It's not uncommon for desirable banks to earn four and five figure results. But you don't need to be able to fill a bank to start collecting toy and mechanical banks. Auctions abound with more affordable character banks and premium banks from the mid-20th century. Designs are as varied as your imagination and cover a number of historical events, political figures, and landmarks. Unlike other collecting areas, many rare forms of mechanical and still banks are highly valued,

Trick Dog, cast iron, Shepard Hardware Co. Six-part base variation. All original. **$920**

Courtesy of Morphy Auctions, www.morphyauctions.com

even if they are not in perfect condition. However, one should always buy the best condition afforded; when investing in a collection, quality should always outweigh quantity.

Those interested in mechanical banks are encouraged to learn more about the Mechanical Bank Collectors of America (www.mechanicalbanks.org), a non-profit organization consisting of around 400 members from the United States

> ❝
>
> It's not uncommon for desirable banks to earn four and five figure results at auction.

and several foreign countries. Organized in 1958, it is dedicated to expanding the knowledge and availability of antique mechanical banks.

Another valuable resource is the Still Bank Collectors Club of America (www.stillbankclub.com), a non-profit organization founded in 1966 with collectors from the United States, Canada, Germany, Denmark, Australia and England.

Bill E Grin mechanical bank, J. & E. Stevens Co., painted cast iron, working, missing trap. **$1,050**

Courtesy of Lloyd Ralston Gallery, www.lloydralstontoys.com

Lion Hunter mechanical bank, J. & E. Stevens Co., circa 1911, cock device on gun barrel and place coin in front, press lever and hunter takes aim and fires, causing coin to strike lion and fall into receptacle below, 7" high. **$2,000**

Courtesy of Heritage Auctions, www.ha.com

Penny Pineapple cast iron mechanical bank, excellent condition, 9" high. **$330**

Courtesy of Morphy Auctions, www.morphyauctions.com

Tammany Hall, J. & E. Stevens and Co. Brown-jacket variation. All original, including trap, 5 3/4". **$1,150**

Courtesy of Morphy Auctions, www.morphyauctions.com

Painted cast-iron lighthouse mechanical bank, 10 1/2", working and all original. **$11,000**

Courtesy of Morphy Auctions; www.MorphyAuctions.com

'Spise a Mule, cast iron, J. & E. Stevens and Co. bench variation. **$517**

Photo courtesy Morphy Auctions, Denver, Pa; www.MorphyAuctions.com

Tiger, tin mechanical, Saalheimer and Strauss, with advertisement for Lyons Toffee on back, 5 1/8". **$12,075**

Courtesy of Morphy Auctions, www.morphyauctions.com

Jonah & the Whale, J. & E. Stevens and Co. Cast iron, pedestal variation, extremely rare. One small break at tab by the back tail, which is common for this bank. Old repaint with some remnants of original paint. **$17,250**

Courtesy of Morphy Auctions, www.morphyauctions.com

Uncle Remus cast iron mechanical bank, Kyser & Rex, fence at house repainted and club in cop's hand pinned, 6" long. **$33,000**

Courtesy of Morphy Auctions, www.morphyauctions.com

Cast iron Mikado mechanical bank by Kyser & Rex, blue variation, 6 3/4" tall. **$198,000**

Courtesy of Morphy Auctions; www.MorphyAuctions.com

Cast iron rooster mechanical bank by Kyser & Rex, highlights to base, 6" tall. **$2,700**

Courtesy of Morphy Auctions; www.MorphyAuctions.com

J. & E. Stevens, around 1907, the Clown, Harlequin and Columbine bank features an intricate action involving all three figures. As the columbine (harlequin's mistress in the Italian commedia dell'arte) dancer spins, the coin is deposited, ex-Stephen and Marilyn Steckbeck collection. **$103,500**

Courtesy of Morphy Auctions, www.morphyauctions.com

> ❝ Bank designs from the mid-20th century are as varied as your imagination, covering historical events, political figures and landmarks.

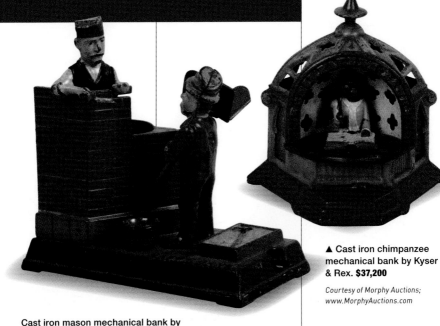

▲ Cast iron chimpanzee mechanical bank by Kyser & Rex. **$37,200**

Courtesy of Morphy Auctions; www.MorphyAuctions.com

Cast iron mason mechanical bank by Shepard Hardware Company, 7" tall. **$5,100**

Courtesy of Morphy Auctions; www.MorphyAuctions.com

Butting Ram/Man Thumbs Nose cast-iron mechanical bank, circa 1895, made by Wagner & Zwiebel Machine Shop, Burlington, Wis. **$27,945**

Courtesy of RSL Auction Co.; www.rslauctions.com

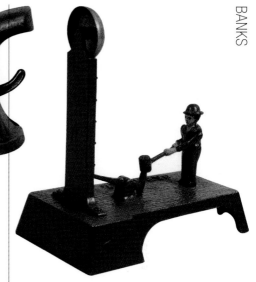

Cast iron carnival mechanical bank, original working condition, 8 1/4" tall. **$12,000**

Courtesy of Morphy Auctions; www.MorphyAuctions.com

Painted-lead still bank depicting Mickey Mouse on a round of cheddar cheese, 5". **$4,600**

Courtesy of Morphy Auctions; www.MorphyAuctions.com

Organ monkey bank, made by Kyser & Rex Company, Frankford, Pennsylvania. Place coin in tray, turn handle and monkey lowers coin into organ while he tips his hat and cat and dog revolve, 4" x 5 1/4" x 7 1/4" tall overall. **$420**

Courtesy of Hakes Americana & Collectibles

Only known example of
J. & E. Stevens' cast-iron
mechanical "Novelty" bank in
a sea-foam green, cream, tan
and red color motif. **$29,160**

*Courtesy of RSL Auction Co.;
www.rslauctions.com*

Initiating First Degree cast-iron mechanical bank, circa
1880, manufactured by Mechanical Novelty Works of New
Britain, Conn. **$60,850**

Courtesy of RSL Auction Co.; www.rslauctions.com

J. & E. Stevens "Calamity"
football cast-iron mechanical
bank, circa 1905, with original
wooden box. **$78,975**

*Courtesy of RSL Auction Co.; www.
rslauctions.com*

J. & E. Stevens Owl Turns
Head cast-iron mechanical
bank, circa 1880. **$23,085**

*Courtesy of RSL Auction Co.;
www.rslauctions.com*

J. & E. Stevens Chief Big Moon cast-iron mechanical bank,
circa 1899. **$42,310**

Courtesy of RSL Auction Co.; www.rslauctions.com

'Spise a Mule, cast iron, J. & E. Stevens and Co., jockey-over variation with brown base. **$517**

Courtesy of Morphy Auctions, www.morphyauctions.com

Cast iron Santa at chimney mechanical bank, gray coat variation, 6" tall. **$1,320**

Courtesy of Morphy Auctions; www.MorphyAuctions.com

Roller Skating cast iron mechanical bank, Kyser & Rex, near mint condition, 9" long. **$88,800**

Courtesy of Morphy Auctions, www.morphyauctions.com

Mule Entering Barn cast iron mechanical bank, J. & E. Stevens Co., trap present, overall good condition. $425

Courtesy of Pook & Pook, Inc., www.pookandpook.com

The Beatles

The first wave of Beatlemania broke over the U.S. in 1964 when The Beatles appeared on *The Ed Sullivan Show*. More than 50 years after that historic evening, that storm has swelled into a tsunami as a new era of Beatlemania has hit the collecting world hard.

"The Beatles rule the world of music and entertainment memorabilia like few others," says Noah Fleisher, author of *The Beatles: Fab Finds of the Fab Four*. "I might even venture to say, having watched the market for the best Beatles material explode in the last five years, that they may well be the only sure-fire bet in music memorabilia that a collector could have right now."

Recent auction results support Fleisher's contention. At auction, John Lennon's lost Gibson J-160E guitar sold for $2.4 million; the drum head on Ringo Starr's drum kit from that *Ed Sullivan Show* sold for more than $2 million; and a Beatles-signed "Sgt. Pepper's Lonely Hearts Club Band" album gatefold sold for nearly $300,000.

Everything from autographs to photos, albums, clothing, licensed plastic Beatles guitars and especially the real things are hotly pursued.

"The music was the doorway and the merchandising was the fix," Fleisher says. "We're all so fascinated by how they did what they did that we got personally involved with their stories and their images. How do you feel close to your idols? To people that you love with all your heart and soul but to whom you have almost no chance of ever meeting? You buy the stuff."

When it comes to selling Beatles memorabilia there are few, if any, who can match Darren Julien, the CEO and president of Julien's Auctions in Los Angeles.

"The Beatles are so popular because their music is still relevant and their fan base is not only global but it transcends all age groups," Julien said. "Their fan base only continues to increase and, for many, buying an item from their life or career is like buying a memory from their past."

**THE BEATLES –
FAB FINDS OF THE
FAB FOUR**

LIKE A modern-day archeological dig, The Beatles — Fab Finds of The Fab Four (Krause Publications, $26.99) unearths a treasure trove of rock relics in a stunning pictorial guide to a new era of Beatlemania. Showcasing more than 600 color and black-and-white photos, the book by author Noah Fleisher shines a fresh spotlight on rock's never-ending magical mystery tour.

"Beatles memorabilia is the blue chip of the collectibles market. Items from their career tend to go up gradually and consistently, unlike some celebrities who spike high and sometimes end low."

As a matter of debate, there may be no better investment in the memorabilia market today than a Beatles item.

"The items that bring the most and are the most sought-after are items that were used/worn on stage," Julien says. "The market for these items has dramatically increased. For instance, guitars that Christie's sold for around $100,000 in recent years, we now sell for more than $500,000. Beatles garments have also dramatically increased in recent years as museums and investors now look for iconic items that can be on display or that will increase in value."

"The Beatles are not going anywhere. I think their legendary status and collectability will only continue to increase. Items that we see selling for $500,000 now, I believe, will someday soon be worth $2 million to $3 million."

The value of the memorabilia mirrors the band's career to a tee, Fleisher says.

"The early part of their fame can be documented by massive amounts of material that was released with their names and images on it, much of which they didn't control" Fleisher notes. "The middle period, when they stopped touring, and the end, saw a good bit less of the trinket type pop culture material. Their image was more mature and the market in memorabilia matured the same way, focusing on autographs, records and more personal material. The end of the band saw very little material, and you can see in the book it's much more scarce from the final period of the band's time together and more valuable for that scarcity."

Items closely tied to The Beatles demand top dollar. Band-used gear – guitars, drums, even cases that carried equipment – are the ultimate prize for the biggest players in the Beatles memorabilia field.

"With this band it all comes back to the music," Fleisher says. "They are working now on their fifth successive generation and the music sounds as fresh, innovative and inspiring as it ever has. As long as the tunes these men wrote and recorded together continue to sound so damn good, I cannot imagine that the attendant memorabilia won't continue to bring a premium. The $2.4 million paid for John's Gibson J-160E is going to look like a bargain in 20 years."

Early pre-Beatles photograph, (from left) George Harrison, John Lennon and Paul McCartney, 1958. Photo taken by Mike McCartney, Paul's brother, at a wedding reception. Harrison was a mere 15 in the photo. **$1,000**

Courtesy of Julien's Auctions, www.juliensauctions.com

Sgt. Pepper's Lonely Hearts Club Band Gold Record from the Record
Industry Association of America, commemorating more than $1 million worth
of sales for The Beatles' 1967 release, Sgt. Pepper's Lonely Hearts Club
Band, an album that spent 175 weeks on the American charts. **$8,125**

Courtesy of Julien's Auctions, www.juliensauctions.com

▲ Beatles publicity photograph, 1962, by Peter Kaye, Liverpool. The leather jackets are gone, replaced by the suits that would come to define their early rise to fame. **$2,240**

Courtesy of Julien's Auctions, www.juliensauctions.com

▲ The Beatles Flip Your Wig Game, 1964, Milton Bradley, includes game board, cardboard cutouts for each member of The Beatles, numbered die and two decks of cards. **$140**

Courtesy of Heritage Auctions, HA.com

▶ Cavern Club stage-used microphone, late 1950s/early 1960s, from the famous Liverpool, England, club where The Beatles performed nearly 300 times early in their career. **$10,625**

Courtesy of Heritage Auctions, HA.com

Beatles signed tour program, 1965, depicting the band as Saturday morning cartoon. **$19,200**

Courtesy of Heritage Auctions, HA.com

Beatles blue Lunchbox with original matching Thermos, Aladdin, 1965. The first Aladdin lunchbox dedicated to a rock group. **$750**

Courtesy of Heritage Auctions, HA.com

Beatles Bobb'n Head Figures, Car Mascots, Inc., 1964, with original box and cardboard insert that keeps the heads from "bobb'n." **$1,075**

Courtesy of Heritage Auctions, HA.com

Beatles Wrist Watch, Bradley Time, 1963, dial bears the group's individual portraits placed at the 12:00, 3:00, 6:00, and 9:00 positions with the text: "The Beatles", "Shockproof" and "Made in Gt Britain".

Courtesy of Heritage Auctions, HA.com

Beatles School Bag, Burnel Ltd. of Canada, 1964, 12" x 9", gusseted tan vinyl school bag with handle and shoulder strap with Beatle images in brown below the flap and on either side of the latch with facsimile signatures between the images. **$1,750**

Courtesy of Heritage Auctions, HA.com

Beatles "Official Beatles Fan" Vintage Pinback Button, Green Duck/NEMS, 1964, original 4" litho pinback button featuring photo images of Paul McCartney, Ringo "Rings" Starr, George Harrison, and John Lennon. **$55**

Courtesy of Heritage Auctions, HA.com

Beatles Record Player, NEMS, 1964, four-speed portable record player with carrying case. With only about 5,000 produced, the record player is considered by most collectors to be one of the ultimate pieces to own of all commercial Beatles memorabilia. **$2,750**

Courtesy of Heritage Auctions, HA.com

The Beatles line-up photograph signed on back by George Harrison, Paul McCartney and Pete Best. Albert Marion, a local wedding photographer, took the photograph on Dec. 17, 1961, during The Beatles' first professional photography session. **$4,800**

Courtesy of Julien's Auctions, www.juliensauctions.com

The Beatles at the Cavern Club photo, 1961, 8" x 10" photo of The Beatles, with Pete Best on drums, taken at Liverpool club that first brought them attention. Photo taken by Gloria Stavers. **$750**

Courtesy of Julien's Auctions, www.juliensauctions.com

John Lennon's Gibson J-160E guitar, which was used to compose the songs "I Want to Hold Your Hand," "Please, Please Me," "All My Loving" and others, sold for **$2,410,000** at auction.

Courtesy of Julien's Auctions, www.juliensauctions.com

Abbey Road Gold Record from the Record Industry Association of America, commemorating more than $1 million worth of sales for The Beatles' 1969 release, Abbey Road, an album that spent 129 weeks on the American charts. **$5,937**

Courtesy of Julien's Auctions, www.juliensauctions.com

Books

By Noah Fleisher

Joe Fay, manager of the Rare Books Department at Heritage Auctions, has an encyclopedic knowledge of the printed word. He can wax poetic about the mysteries of incunabula, then turn around and extol the virtues of Stephen King or Sherlock Holmes, his personal favorite, finding the common thread between them. He's got an eye for early copies of *The Federalist Papers* and can spot a rare first edition of J.K. Rowling's *Harry Potter and the Philosopher's Stone,* reciting from memory exactly what makes it a true first edition.

Warman's: Give me an overview of rare books.
Joe Fay: As always, the top of the market is very stable. The market seems to be holding steady against a fairly violent public assault on the printed word.

I hear the question all the time: "Will the Kindle kill the printed book?" Of course not. Folks bemoan the death of the printed word, but it's not going to happen anytime soon. It seems like every new technology that transmits information has called for the death of the book, but it hasn't happened yet and I don't think it will.

I think rare books will become increasingly more precious because of their physicality. People will come to interact with books in a different, more intimate way because of their relative scarcity.

Warman's: Is the market improving? Where are the best buying opportunities?
Joe Fay: The market is improving. There is strength in special or unique books: examples with wonderful inscriptions, association copies, fine bindings, etc. Also, with the prevailing cultural obsession with superheroes and comic book-related material, there has never been a stronger market for science fiction and genre fiction.

You can also never go wrong with incunabula, books printed before 1500, or great copies of great works in

Writer and author
NOAH FLEISHER has 20 years of experience in the antiques and collectibles field. He is the author of *The Beatles: Fab Finds of the Fab Four, Warman's Modern Furniture,* and *Collecting Children's Books.*

the major collecting categories.

Early printed books are always strong, the incunabula I just mentioned. Important first editions in the major categories, such as history, science and medicine, natural history, travel, religion, maps and atlases, literature, economics, early American imprints, children's books, and illustrated books.

Fine press printing and artists' books seem to be on the upward trend, too, as books become more of a specialty in the face of competing technologies.

Warman's: Is there room for new and younger collectors in rare books right now?
Joe Fay: I think it's a good market to get into at any time and any age. The rule I live by when talking about book collecting, as any expert in any category will tell you: Collect what you like. Find some focus within a subject area, author, printer or publisher, and collect everything you can.

Don't limit yourself to just the books, either. For a given author, seek out autograph material, posters, artifacts, original art if applicable, and so on. It can be rewarding to walk into a person's personal library and not only see an incredible run of first editions by Ray Bradbury, but also find a *Fahrenheit 451* poster on the wall, next to a framed letter from the author. I guess this is a disguised version of diversification, in a way.

Warman's: It's a huge field. How do you go about starting or bolstering a collection if you've been out for a while?
Joe Fay: Vigilance. It's a great time to be a buyer of rare books because they are so readily available to be bought.

Build a relationship with a reputable dealer, save keyword searches at online sites like eBay and Heritage, places

where you get email reminders when material matching your interests becomes available.

Warman's: What is it that draws people to rare books?
Joe Fay: That's a really big question. I think the desire to collect rare books started with a thirst to converse with the great minds of the past, which encompasses really anything. There are practically limitless possibilities for a subject area to collect in rare books.

For me, personally, the allure of rare books comes down to both what they are, physically, and what they represent. Books are wonderful to handle. If a book is well put together, it fits nicely in the hand or lies well when opened on a table, it stimulates both the eye to flip through and the mind to read, and is a pleasure to look at on the shelf. Even the smell of a book is a unique phenomenon that evokes myriad emotions and memories.

A first printing of a given important novel is rare in itself, but it also represents a viewpoint and a cultural zeitgeist that is usually universal, that mattered both when the book was published and today. They are a window into the minds of people long gone, markers of our evolution as humans. This is not something you get with many other collecting categories.

Warman's: Looking back 10 years and looking ahead 10 years, how does/will the market look in comparison?
Joe Fay: A couple of generations ago everyone had books in their house. For 550 years books have been the primary method by which people learned. Now there are so many competing delivery systems for information that print culture has obviously taken a hit.

I think the number of collectors 10 years from now will be smaller in number but more intense in terms of who is collecting. Rare books have become a bit of a niche market, but you can see the contraction markedly at regional book fairs. More people used to come to fairs than they do now. High-end fairs like the New York Antiquarian Book Fair are still going strong and will likely continue to do so because the top end of the market is not going anywhere. Truly valuable rarities always bring premium prices.

Warman's: You hear how technology has hurt books. Tell me how it has helped.
Joe Fay: The Internet and the eReader have certainly had an effect on the trade, no doubt – we have fewer bookstores these days – but the web has also opened up thousands upon millions of avenues for finding books, especially those that people once thought were rare or even unique. The Internet has also had a positive effect on some titles by reinforcing their rarity.

The Internet helped to stratify the rare book world. With so much information, no one can pay – and no one will ask – unreasonable prices for common books. I talk to book dealers all the time who say something to the effect of, "I used to be able to get $500 for that book, now I can't give it away." Then they turn around and say, "You know that book I sold in your Internet weekly auction for $1,000? I've had that book on my table at book fairs for 10 years for $150 and barely anyone looked at it."

Obviously, the web can now help actually identify rarity instead of proving commonness.

Warman's: How much homework should a collector do before entering the category, or is it best to consult experts and let them fill in the gaps?
Joe Fay: Do a lot of homework. Many people have been burned by casually starting to collect books or by trusting the wrong dealer.

Book, 1895, "It's All in the Draw," humorous look at the game of poker, with pictures of cards facing witty passages about the game, 10 leaves including wrappers, on thin card stock. Color lithographed throughout, 5" t. x 9" w. **$650**

Courtesy PBA Galleries, www.PBAgalleries.com

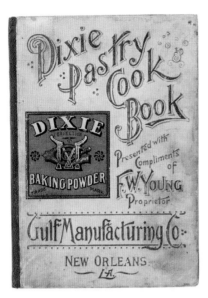

Cookbook, 1893, Gulf Manufacturing Co., "Dixie Pastry Cook Book. Presented with compliments of F.W. Young, proprietor", 22 pages, five inserted chromolithographed plates with illustrations on both sides. **$650**

Courtesy PBA Galleries, www.PBAgalleries.com

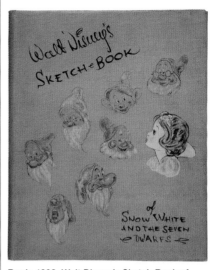

Book, 1938, Walt Disney's Sketch Book of Snow White and the Seven Dwarfs, first edition, Collins Sons & Co., 12 color plates. **$687**

Courtesy of Heritage Auctions, www.ha.com

Codicem, 1517, Cini de Pistorio in Codicem, Vol. II, handwritten and illuminated manuscript, second of nine books dedicated to Justinian Law, in Latin, 16" t. x 11-1/2" w x 2-1/2" d. **$1,400**

Courtesy Michaan's Auctions

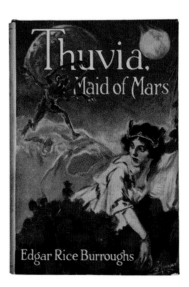

Edgar Rice Burroughs, Thuvia, Maid of Mars. Chicago: A.C. McClurg & Co., 1920, first edition, inscribed and signed by Burroughs on front free endpaper, 256 pages plus 12-page publisher's catalog. **$9,560**

Courtesy of Heritage Auctions, www.ha.com

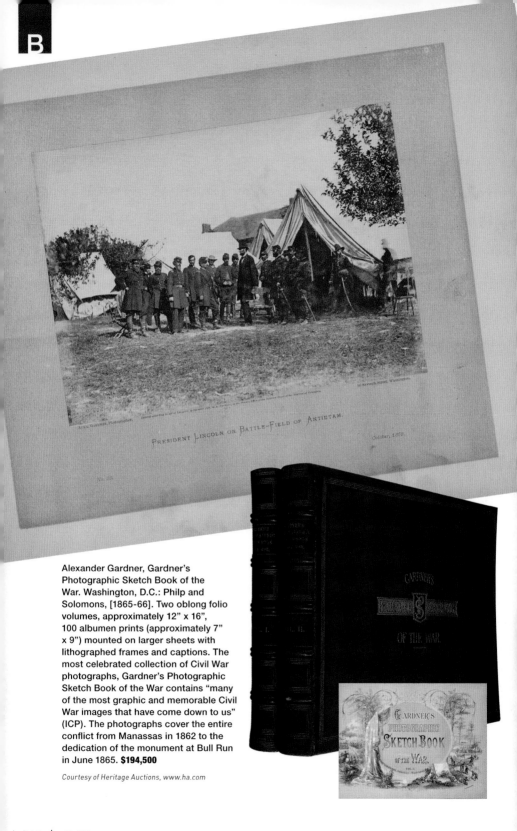

B

President Lincoln on Battle-Field of Antietam. *October, 1862.*

Alexander Gardner, Gardner's Photographic Sketch Book of the War. Washington, D.C.: Philp and Solomons, [1865-66]. Two oblong folio volumes, approximately 12" x 16", 100 albumen prints (approximately 7" x 9") mounted on larger sheets with lithographed frames and captions. The most celebrated collection of Civil War photographs, Gardner's Photographic Sketch Book of the War contains "many of the most graphic and memorable Civil War images that have come down to us" (ICP). The photographs cover the entire conflict from Manassas in 1862 to the dedication of the monument at Bull Run in June 1865. **$194,500**

Courtesy of Heritage Auctions, www.ha.com

Stephen King, Christine. West Kingston: Donald M. Grant, 1983, first edition, limited to 1,000 numbered copies of which this is number 121, signed by King, 544 pages. **$598**

Courtesy of Heritage Auctions, www.ha.com

Robert A. Heinlein, Stranger in a Strange Land. New York: G.P. Putnam's Sons, 1961, first edition, first printing. **$7,768**

Courtesy of Heritage Auctions, www.ha.com

E.B. White, Charlotte's Web. New York: Harper and Brothers, 1952, first edition, pictures by Garth Williams, 1953 Newberry Award winning book. **$1,554**

Courtesy of Heritage Auctions, www.ha.com

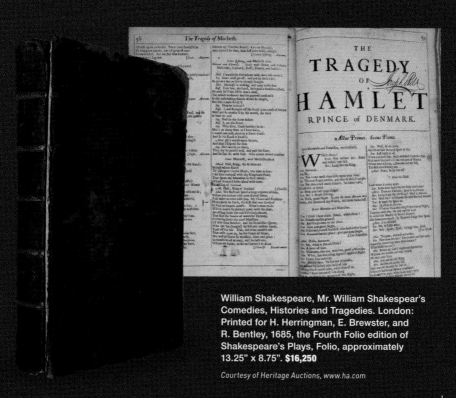

William Shakespeare, Mr. William Shakespear's Comedies, Histories and Tragedies. London: Printed for H. Herringman, E. Brewster, and R. Bentley, 1685, the Fourth Folio edition of Shakespeare's Plays, Folio, approximately 13.25" x 8.75". **$16,250**

Courtesy of Heritage Auctions, www.ha.com

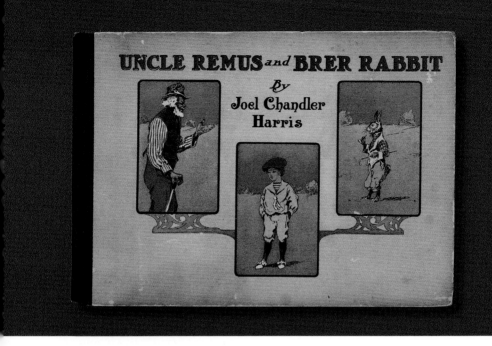

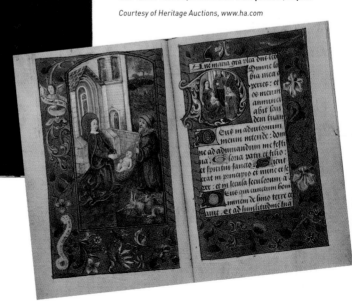

▲ Joel Chandler Harris, Uncle Remus and
Brer Rabbit, New York, 1907, first edition,
Oblong quarto. [64] leaves. Rectos only.
Illustrated in color. **$438**

Courtesy of Heritage Auctions, www.ha.com

◀ Book of Hours, Artois [St.-Omer]
France, circa 16th century, small quarto,
approximately 8.5" x 5.75", 76, lacking one
leaf after fol. 31, otherwise complete. **$68,500**

Courtesy of Heritage Auctions, www.ha.com

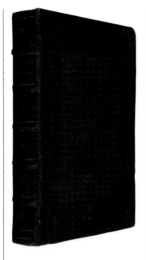

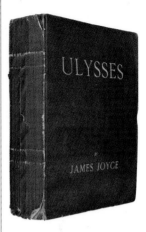

Charles Darwin, On the Origin of Species by Means of Natural Selection, or The Preservation of Favored Races in the Struggle for Life. London: John Murray, 1859, first edition, two quotations on p. [ii]. Octavo in twelves (7 13/16" x 4 15/16"). ix, [1], 502 pages, plus 32-page publisher's catalog dated June, 1859. One of the most influential scientific works of the 19th century. From the James and Deborah Boyd Collection. **$83,500**

Courtesy of Heritage Auctions, www.ha.com

Sir Isaac Newton, Opticks, or, A Treatise of the Reflexions, Refractions, Inflexions and Colours of Light. Also Two Treatises of the Species and Magnitude of Curvilinear Figures. London: Printed for Sam. Smith, and Benj. Walford, 1704, first edition, two parts in one quarto volume. Opticks provided the scientific framework for the study of optics, collecting together all of Newton's researches for the first time. **$43,750**

Courtesy of Heritage Auctions, www.ha.com

James Joyce, Ulysses. Paris: Shakespeare and Co., 1922, first edition, number 513 of 750 numbered copies printed on handmade paper (total edition 1,000 copies). **$35,000**

Courtesy of Heritage Auctions, www.ha.com

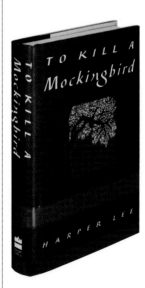

George Orwell, Nineteen Eighty-Four [1984]. London: Secker & Warburg, 1949, first edition, "First Published 1949" stated on copyright page, 312 pages. **$4,48**

Courtesy of Heritage Auctions, www.ha.com

Margaret Mitchell, Gone With the Wind, Macmillan and Co., 1936, first edition. **$11,250**

Courtesy of Heritage Auctions, www.ha.com

Harper Lee, To Kill a Mockingbird, 1995, 35th anniversary edition, later printing, signed by author. **$300**

Courtesy of Heritage Auctions, www.ha.com

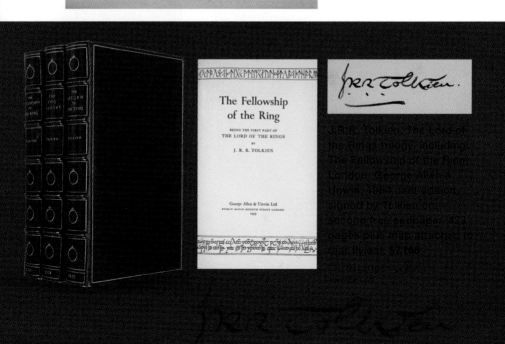

Isaac Asimov, The Foundation Trilogy, including: Foundation, Foundation and Empire, and Second Foundation. Garden City: Gnome Press, [1951-1953], all volumes first editions, each a presentation copy, inscribed by Asimov on front free endpaper. **$21,250**

Courtesy of Heritage Auctions, www.ha.com

The Fellowship of the Ring

BEING THE FIRST PART OF
THE LORD OF THE RINGS

BY

J. R. R. TOLKIEN

George Allen & Unwin Ltd
RUSKIN HOUSE MUSEUM STREET LONDON
1954

J.R.R. Tolkien, The Lord of the Rings trilogy, including: The Fellowship of the Ring. London: George Allen & Unwin, 1954, first edition, signed by Tolkien on second free endpaper, 423 pages, plus map attached to rear flyleaf. $7,768

Galileo Galilei, Dialogo...Doue ne I congressi di Quattro giornate si discorre sopra I due Massimi Sistemi del Mondo Tolemaico, e Copernicano... Florence: Giovanni Batista Landini, 1632, first edition, quarto. **$65,725**

Courtesy of Heritage Auctions, www.ha.com

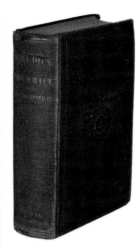

Herman Melville, Moby-Dick; or The Whale, first U.S. edition, Harper & Brothers, 1851. **$21,250**

Courtesy of Heritage Auctions, www.ha.com

H.P. Lovecraft, The Outsider and Others. Collected by August Derleth and Donald Wandrei. Sauk City, Wisconsin: Arkham House, 1939, first edition of first collection of Lovecraft's writings, rare and important first book and first publication printed by Arkham House, one of only 1,268 copies printed, 553 pages. **$5,079**

Courtesy of Heritage Auctions, www.ha.com

J.K. Rowling, first five Harry Potter Delux editions, various dates, all inscribed, housed in the common purple publisher's slipcase. **$6,000**

Courtesy of Heritage Auctions, www.ha.com

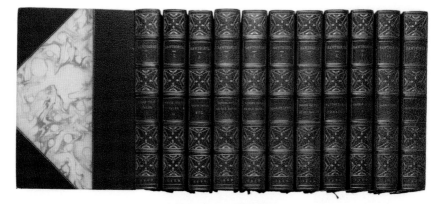

Nathaniel Hawthorne, "Complete Writings of Nathaniel Hawthorne," Houghton, Mifflin & Co., Boston, 1900, limited to 500 numbered sets, signed by Hawthorne, from the private library of actor Sylvester Stallone. **$1,375**

Courtesy of Heritage Auctions, www.ha.com

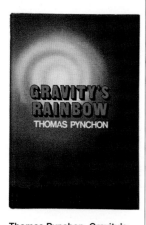

Thomas Pynchon, Gravity's Rainbow. New York: Viking, 1973, first edition, first printing, inscribed and signed by Pynchon on half-title page, "10/86 / To Michael Urban, / Best Wishes, / Thomas Pynchon," 760 pages. **$16,250**

Courtesy of Heritage Auctions, www.ha.com

Ernest Hemingway, Three Stories & Ten Poems. Paris: Contact Publishing Co., 1923, first and only edition of Hemingway's first book, one of only 300 copies printed, with inscription from author to editors of The Little Review, the "little magazine" in Paris that published his first mature prose work the same year: "For j.h. and Margaret Anderson with love from Hemingway" ("j.h." being Jane Heap). Twelvemo, 58 pages plus printer's imprint. **$68,500**

Courtesy of Heritage Auctions, www.ha.com

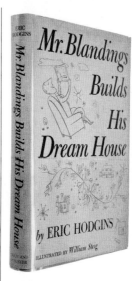

Eric Hodgins, Mr. Blandings Builds His Dream House. New York: Simon and Schuster, 1946, first edition, signed and inscribed by author on front endpaper. **$538**

Courtesy of Heritage Auctions, www.ha.com

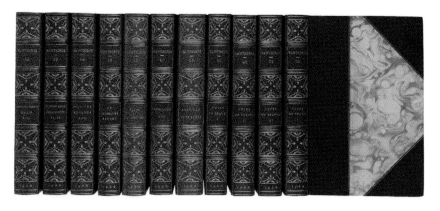

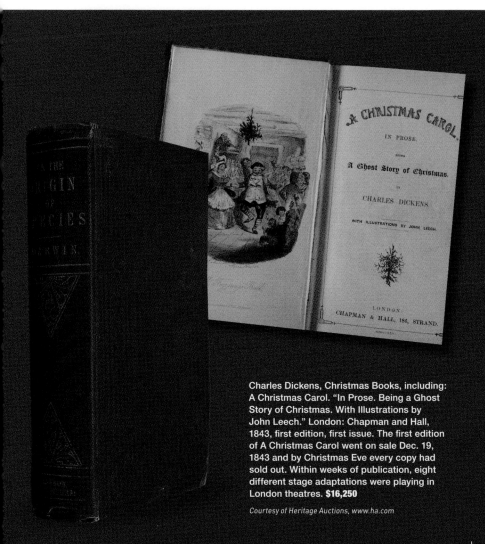

Charles Dickens, Christmas Books, including: A Christmas Carol. "In Prose. Being a Ghost Story of Christmas. With Illustrations by John Leech." London: Chapman and Hall, 1843, first edition, first issue. The first edition of A Christmas Carol went on sale Dec. 19, 1843 and by Christmas Eve every copy had sold out. Within weeks of publication, eight different stage adaptations were playing in London theatres. **$16,250**

Courtesy of Heritage Auctions, www.ha.com

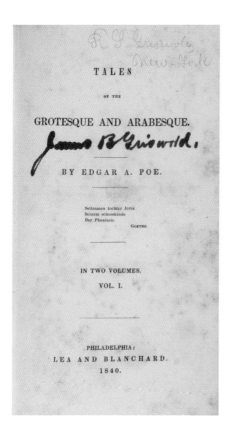

Edgar Allan Poe, Tales of the Grotesque and Arabesque. Philadelphia: Lea and Blanchard, 1840, first edition, one of 750 printed, very good complete copy, rare in original cloth with original critical notices and flyleaves present. **$21,850**

Courtesy of Heritage Auctions, www.ha.com

Children's book, 1802, The Cries of Large Cities Alphabetically Arranged, Published by J. Johnson, American miniature, [22] leaves. Illustrated with woodcuts, rare, **$2,750**

Courtesy PBA Galleries

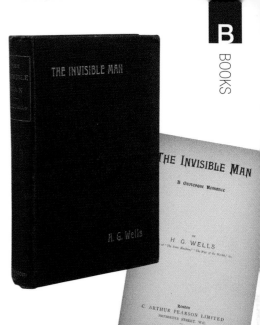

Thomas L. M'Kenney and James Hall,
History of the Indian Tribes of North America.
Philadelphia: Daniel Rice & James G. Clark,
1842-1842-1844, first edition. **$43,750**

Courtesy of Heritage Auctions, www.ha.com

H.G. Wells, The Invisible Man, A Grotesque
Romance. London: C. Arthur Pearson Limited,
1897, first edition, 245 pages plus two pages
of advertisements. **$538**

Courtesy of Heritage Auctions, www.ha.com

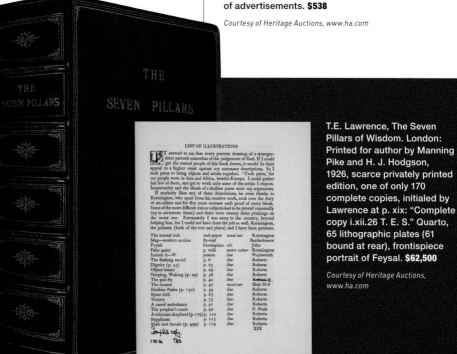

T.E. Lawrence, The Seven
Pillars of Wisdom. London:
Printed for author by Manning
Pike and H. J. Hodgson,
1926, scarce privately printed
edition, one of only 170
complete copies, initialed by
Lawrence at p. xix: "Complete
copy i.xii.26 T. E. S." Quarto,
65 lithographic plates (61
bound at rear), frontispiece
portrait of Feysal. **$62,500**

*Courtesy of Heritage Auctions,
www.ha.com*

Peter Pan
In Kensington Gardens

By

J. M. Barrie

(From 'The Little White Bird')

With Drawings by
Arthur Rackham, A.R.W.S.

Hodder & Stoughton
London
1906

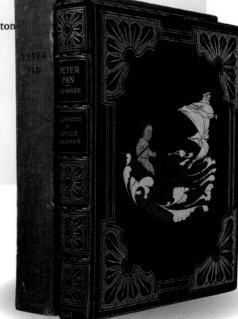

J. M. Barrie, Peter Pan in Kensington Gardens (from "The Little White Bird") with drawings by Arthur Rackham. London: Hodder & Stoughton, 1906, limited to 500 copies, this is number 49, numbered and signed by Arthur Rackham, 125 pages, 50 color plates mounted on brown paper with descriptive tissue guards. **$10,158**

Courtesy of Heritage Auctions, www.ha.com

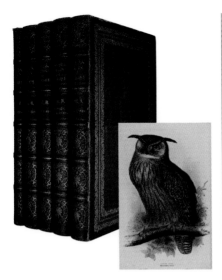

John Gould, The Birds of Europe. London: Richard and John E. Taylor, [1832-] 1837. Five imperial folio volumes, 21.5" x 14.25" each, 449 hand-colored illustrations on 448 lithographed plates printed by Charles Hullmandel, majority of plates by Elizabeth Gould from sketches by Gould, with remainder by Edward Lear. **$80,500**

Courtesy of Heritage Auctions, www.ha.com

Johannes Kepler, Strena Seu De Nive Sexangula. Frankfurt: Gottfried. Tampach, 1611, first edition, quarto, woodcut printer's device, three woodcut illustrations in text. **$20,000**

Courtesy of Heritage Auctions, www.ha.com

H. A. Rey, Curious George. Boston: Houghton Mifflin, 1941, first edition, quarto, unpaginated, illustrations by author, publisher's brick red cloth with Curious George vignette in black on front board and lettering in black on spine, illustrated endpapers, original dust jacket with $1.75 price. **$26,290**

Courtesy of Heritage Auctions, www.ha.com

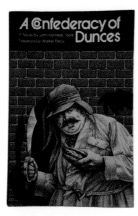

John Kennedy Toole, A Confederacy of Dunces. Foreword by Walker Percy. Baton Rouge: Louisiana State University Press, 1980, first edition signed by Walker Percy, 338 pages. **$4,482**

Courtesy of Heritage Auctions, www.ha.com

Raymond Chandler, Farewell, My Lovely. New York: Alfred A. Knopf, 1940, first edition, first printing of Chandler's second Philip Marlowe novel. **$8,066**

Courtesy of Heritage Auctions, www.ha.com

Ken Kesey, One Flew Over the Cuckoo's Nest. New York: The Viking Press, 1962, first edition, first printing, inscribed by Kesey: "For / Darrel / Kesey / 1993," 311 pages. **$8,365**

Courtesy of Heritage Auctions, www.ha.com

Jules Verne, The Green Ray, translated from French by Mary de Hauteville. London: Sampson Low, Marston, Searle, & Rivington, 1883, first English edition. **$8,125**

Courtesy of Heritage Auctions, www.ha.com

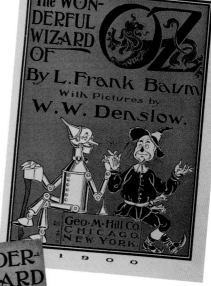

Joseph Smith, Junior, The Book of Mormon: An Account Written by the Hand of Mormon, Upon Plates Taken From the Plates of Nephi. By Joseph Smith, Junior, Author and Proprietor. Palmyra, [New York]: Printed by E. B. Grandin for author, 1830, first edition, John Wesley Brackenbury's copy, with his name on front pastedown: "J. W. Brackenbury / His Book / White Cloud / Kansas" written in pencil by Brackenbury. The Book of Mormon, rare in the first edition, is one of the most collectible books on religion issued in the United States. **$47,800**

Courtesy of Heritage Auctions, www.ha.com

L. Frank Baum, The Wonderful Wizard of Oz. Chicago and New York: George M. Hill Co., 1900, first edition, first state of the text. **$9,375**

Courtesy of Heritage Auctions, www.ha.com

Bottles

By Michael Polak

MICHAEL POLAK has collected more than 3,000 bottles since entering the hobby in 1976. He is a regular contributor to a variety of antiques publications and is the author of *Antique Trader Bottles Identification & Price Guide,* 7th edition, and *Picker's Pocket Guide: Bottles.*

Glass bottles are not as new as some people believe. In fact, the glass bottle has been around for about 3,000 years. In the late first century B.C., the Romans, with the assistance of glassworker craftsmen from Syria and Egypt, began making glass vials that local doctors and pharmacists used to dispense pills, healing powders, and miscellaneous potions.

The first attempt to manufacture glass in America is thought to have taken place at the Jamestown settlement in Virginia around 1608 by the London Co. The first successful American glass house was opened in 1739 in New Jersey by Caspar Wistar, who immigrated from Germany to Philadelphia in 1717.

Throughout the 19th century, glasshouses opened and closed because of changes in demand and technological improvements. Between 1840 and 1890, an enormous demand for glass containers developed to satisfy the demands of the whiskey, beer, medical and food-packing industries. Largely due to this steady demand, glass manufacturing in the United States evolved into a stable industry.

Unlike other businesses of the time that saw major changes in manufacturing processes, production of glass bottles remained unchanged. The process gave each bottle character, producing unique shapes, imperfections, irregularities, and various colors. That all changed at the turn of the 20th century when Michael J. Owens invented the first fully automated bottle-making machine. Although many fine bottles were manufactured between 1900-1930, Owens' invention ended an era of unique bottle design that no machine process could ever duplicate. The modern antique bottle-collecting craze started

Target ball (motif of man shooting on two sides), medium amethyst, English 1877-1895, 2 5/8" diameter. **$200-$250**

Four A.G. Smalley & Co. milk bottles – half-pint, pint, quart, and half-gallon, patent April 5, 1898, Boston, Massachusetts, American 1900-1910. $400-$425

in the 1960s with dump digging. Since then, interest in bottle collecting continues to grow, and more collectors are spending their free time digging through old dumps and foraging through ghost towns, digging out old outhouses, exploring abandoned mine shafts, and searching favorite bottles or antiques shows, swap meets, flea markets, and garage sales. In addition, the Internet offers collectors numerous opportunities and resources to buy and sell bottles with many new auction websites. Many bottle clubs have websites providing even

> **"**
>
> Collectors dig through old dumps, forage through ghost towns, dig out old outhouses and explore abandoned mine shafts searching for treasured bottles.

more information for the collector. These technologies and resources have helped bottle collecting to continue to grow and gain interest.

Most collectors, however, still look beyond the type and value of a bottle to its origin and history. Researching the history of a bottle is almost as interesting as finding the bottle itself. Both pursuits have close ties to the rich history of the settling of the United States and the early methods of merchandising.

Bitters bottle, "Suffolk Bitters – Philbrook & Tucker – Boston," light golden yellow amber, figural pig, smooth base, applied tapered collar top, 1865-1875, 10 1/8". **$800-$900**

Barber bottle, medium pink over white with fancy enameled decoration, pontiled base, tooled lip, American 1885-1920, 7-1/2". **$100-$125**

Bitters bottle, Celebrated Nectar / Stomach Bitters / And Nerve Tonic – The / Nectar Bitter Co. / Toledo, O, bright yellow green, American 1890-1900, 9 3/8". **$275-$475**

Bitters bottle, St / Drakes / 1860 / Plantation / X / Bitters – Patented / 1862, yellow green (citron), American 1862-1875, 9 3/4". **$1,500-$2,500**

Beer bottle, E.A. Olendorf / Sarsaparilla Lager (in slug plate) This Bottle / Is Never Sold, medium orange amber, American 1885-1895, 9 1/4". **$250-$300**

Pitkin flask, Midwestern, circa 1815-1825, bluish aqua, 32-broken rib pattern swirled to right, open pontil, sheared and tooled lip, blown in German half-post method, 7" high. **$600**

Courtesy of Glass Works Auctions, www.glswrk-auction.com

Rare history flask, cobalt blue "Washington Bust / Tree in Leaf" portrait flask (GI-35), 1845-1860. **$24,000**

Courtesy of Norm Heckler Auctions

Gin bottle, Royal Imperial Gin, London, sapphire blue, American 1860-1870, 9 7/8". **$1,000-$1,200**

Unger Brothers Love's Dream pattern silver and glass flask, Newark, New Jersey, circa 1900, cut glass bottle with silver hinged lid, silver base with putto kissing woman in cloud of waves, marks: UB (interlaced), STERLING, 925, FINE, 6 1/2" high. **$406**

Courtesy of Heritage Auctions, ha.com

Hawaiian bottle, Hawaiian Soda Works – Honolulu, H.I., 1899. **$1,700-$4,600**

Hawaiian bottle, "Siphon Co. LTD. – Honolulu, T. H. – Contents 35 Fl. Oz.," 1935. **$1,800-$2,500**

Fire grenade, (motif of fireman's helmet) / "HEATHMANS / SWIFT / FIRE / GRENADE," English, circa 1880-1900, light pink, smooth base, rough sheared lip, original mouth plug with embossed on red wax sealant, "Parsons / Green / Heathman / Fulham," 6 1/2" high. **$1,500**

Courtesy of Glass Works Auctions, www.glswrk-auction.com

Umbrella ink bottle, Baltimore Star, light sapphire blue, 2 1/2", eight concave panels, open pontil, rolled lip, American 1840-1860. **$1,100-$1,200**

▲ Soda fountain syrup dispenser, Grape Crush, amethyst glass, American 1900-1930, 15". **$1,150**

◄ Poison bottle, cobalt blue, American 1885-1900, 4 1/4" long. **$1,500-$2,000**

Warner bottle, "Warner's Safe Cure – Trade Mark – London," English 1890-1900, 7 3/8" and 9 3/8". **$150-$250**

Handled whiskey bottle, Wharton's – Whiskey – 1850 – Chestnut Grove – Whitney Glass Works – Glassboro NJ, medium amber, 10 1/8", American 1860-1870. **$900-$1,000**

Medicine bottle, "DR. TOWNSEND'S – SARSAPARILLA – ALBANY / N.Y.," New York, circa 1840-1860, teal blue with green tone, iron pontil, applied tapered collar mouth, 9 3/8" high. **$2,750**

Courtesy of Glass Works Auctions, www.glswrk-auction.com

French Wine Coca bottle with original paper labels, embossed at base of neck "Pemberton's Wine Coca," typical of medicinal bottles made during 1880s, with applied lip and some residue or "sickness" to inside, 11" high. **$13,750**

Courtesy of Heritage Auctions, ha.com

Whiskey bottle, Turner Brothers / New York, yellow amber, American 1855-1860, 10". **$400-$600**

Cameras

It's ironic that the same year auction companies saw more vintage cameras sell well also marked the lowest sales ever on modern cameras and equipment.

Values for vintage cameras are holding strong, with several private collections coming to market. Auction houses in both America and Europe recorded strong sales during the last two years for even mass-produced models by Kodak, Canon and Leica. The main driver for most sales has nothing to do with bringing these machines back into service. Most all are sold for decorative and collector use as it is getting increasingly more difficult to source original film.

Lenses prove to be highly popular with collectors. Prototypes from Leica jumped from a starting price of $20,000 to a sensational $90,000 at a 2017 auction. A prototype lens of an Elmarit 21mm also exceeded expectations and reached $48,000.

Since few collectors expect these vintage machines in working condition, the top of the market in cameras is defined by raritiy. An extremely rare ladies bellows handbag camera, often referred to as a "Gem Camera," sold at auction for $28,800. It was one of just six known to exist.

As always, cameras with historical significance or previously owned by a famous person remain in demand.

Camera, circa 1919, probably English, 35mm movie camera, hand-cranked, wooden body, with Bausch & Lomb-Zeiss Tessar Series Ic 50mm f/3.5 lens, **$5,000**

Courtesy of Heritage Auctions, www.ha.com

Camera, circa 1938, Kodak Bantam Special, folding rangefinder camera in art deco finish, Anastigmat Ektar 2/45mm no.1883 in Compur-Rapid shutter. **$400**

Courtesy of WestLicht Photographica Auction

Camera, Brand Camera Co., large format, 4x5 graphic camera, serial #2053, a Kodak Anastigmat No.32 lens and an accordion folding body, 9" h. x 9" w., **$60**

Courtesy of Leonard Auction, Inc.

Camera, Sweden, Hasselblad 500C, with Zeiss Planar, 80 mm f/2.8 lens No. 2575552, in the original Hasselblad case and user guides, **$475**

Courtesy of Susanin's Auctions

Camera, Conley View with original tripod, Wollensak optical lens, **$225**

Courtesy of Susanin's Auctions

Camera, Le' Marsouin Brevete, leather carrying case, with tripod in leather case, along with equipment, 5-3/4" x 4: x 4" **$550**

Courtesy John Nicholson Auctioneers

◀ Abraham Lincoln visited Mathew Brady's photo studio in Washington, D.C., at least three times in 1864. This is one of the surviving portraits.

Courtesy of Library of Congress

Mathew Brady

Historic camera used by Mathew Brady, one of the earliest photographers in American history, best known for his pictures of the Civil War. Brady photographed 18 American presidents, including Abraham Lincoln. The images of Lincoln were later used for the $5 bill and Lincoln penny. Yet it was his work documenting the Civil War that lead to Brady being recognized as the father of photojournalism. He took thousands of photos of Civil War scenes, which formed the basis of our understanding of the war.

This camera, from Brady's studio, is made of dark wood and is fitted with a Petzval-type brass barrel lens bearing the serial number 1195. It features a black fabric bellows, rack and pinion focusing, with wooden knob on rear of back section, and wide casement to accommodate side-loading plates. The camera is mounted on an 11" x 15" base rail. It is accompanied by a ground glass plate (glass replaced) for focusing, which allowed 10 3/8" x 10 3/8" exposures, as well as a dark slide. **$66,725**

Courtesy of Heritage Auctions, www.ha.com

Camera, Century Master Studio, consisting of a Century Master Studio original stand and a Graflex cameral with a Wollensak Alphax Sychromatic, 11 7/8 302mm lens, **$325**

Courtesy of Susanin's Auctions

Camera, circa 1929, Kodak, for exposures 4.5 x 6cm on 127 roll film, in green finish with matching case, **$89**

Courtesy of Heritage Auctions, www.ha.com

Camera, circa 1845, daguerreotype sliding box, with a Darlot Paris brass encased lens, complete, less ground glass plate, daguerreotype half plate 15cm focal length, 20 cm extended, lens extends 8 cm., **$4,800**

Courtesy of Affiliated Auctions

Camera, circa 1930, 'Night-Camera' for 3x4", with focal plane shutter to 1/1000 sec., fast and rare (Taylor-Hobson) 2.9/8", no maker's markings on the camera or lens, with one double film holder, rare. **$300**

Courtesy of WestLicht Photographica Auction

Orson Welles

An Orson Welles-owned Bell & Howell 240 16mm movie camera, circa 1957, handheld, used by Welles in 1962 to film his documentary "The Land of Don Quixote." The film wasn't released until 2000 in Spain. The famed actor, director, writer and producer, whose work included "Citizen Kane," also used the camera to shoot home and travel movies while living in Spain and Italy. **$37,500**

Courtesy of Heritage Auctions, www.ha.com

▲ Orson Welles' debut film, *Citizen Kane* (1941), was a revolutionary work of art nominated for nine Academy Awards. Welles co-wrote, produced, directed and starred in the movie that is considered one of the greatest achievements in film history.

Camera, 1925, Leica I Mod. A Elmax, No. 451, early first type 'Elmax', early features of the first Leica cameras, **$15,000**

Courtesy of WestLicht Photographica Auction

Leica M7 Black Chrome Rangefinder Camera German, 2001, No. 2781977, for exposures 24 x 36mm on 35mm film, with Leitz Summicron 50mm f/2 lens No. 2407980, with 0.72 viewfinder. In leather ever-ready case. **$2,750**

Courtesy of Heritage Auctions, www.ha.com

◄ Camera, circa 1930, Zeiss Ikon Baby Box Stereo, custom made stereo camera based on two Baby Box bodies, with dial Ludwig Victar 4.5/5cm no.386900 and 386897, **$1,100**

Courtesy of WestLicht Photographica Auction

Watch camera, circa 1890, Lancaster, extremely rare detective camera designed like a pocket watch with self-erecting spring loaded telescoping tubes, men's model for 1 1/2x2" plates, in original condition. **$22,000**

Courtesy of WestLicht Photographica Auction

◄ Camera, 1946, Kodak Ektra Rangefinder, American, American, No. 2356, for exposures 24 x 36mm on 35mm film in interchangeable backs, with Kodak Ektar 50mm f/1.9 lens No. EY 1000, and Kodak Ektar 90mm f/3.5 telephoto lens No. EO 470, in Kodak leather case. **$1,062.**

Courtesy of Heritage Auctions, www.ha.com

Camera, 1961, Rolleiflex 3.5F TLR Camera, German, No. 2288594, for exposures 6 x 6cm on 120 roll film, with Zeiss Xenotar 75mm f/3.5 lens in Synchro-Compur shutter, and coupled light meter. **$812**

Courtesy of Heritage Auctions, www.ha.com

▶ Camera, 1980s, U.S.S.R., based on a Kiev subminiature camera for exposures 13 x 17mm on 16mm film, metal body painted to look like a pack of John Player cigarettes. **$550**

Courtesy of Heritage Auctions, www.ha.com

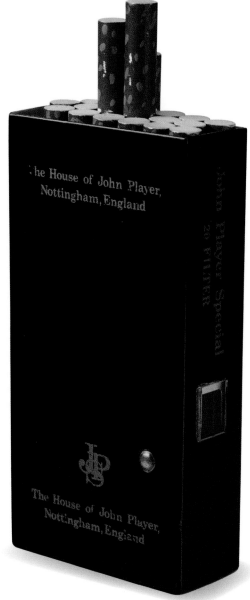

The Evolution of the American Art Pottery Market

By David Rago

DAVID RAGO began dealing in American decorative ceramics when he was 16, at a flea market in his home state of New Jersey. Today, with partners Suzanne Perrault and Miriam Tucker, he oversees the auction house that bears his name, sells privately in the field of 20th/21st Century Design, lectures nationally and appears as an expert appraiser for the PBS series, *Antiques Roadshow*, where he specializes in decorative ceramics and porcelain.

While the market for American decorative ceramics is relatively young, especially when compared to those of traditional antiques, it's been 40 years since the landmark exhibition *The Arts and Crafts Movement in America* first put the material on the map. During that span markets for some American companies came and went, while select others have seen almost a continuous upward spiral. This brief article will describe some of those disparities and explain why they exist.

Early on, before 1980, collectors and dealers both were mostly left to their own devices in determining what was good, rare, or even available. Who knew? There were very few books in print and most of them were incomplete if not outright misleading. Pricing was like throwing a dart at numbers. Imagine if you can, the total absence of auction records, online pricing information, or eBay. If you had a push button phone you were on the cutting edge of existing technology.

So we stumbled, gathering at the few shows where art pottery might be for sale, laboring through books like Lucille Henzke's *American Art Pottery* or the Purviance spiral bounds, both of which mixed serious work with flower shop ware, reflecting more the confusion than dispelling it. It is for the reasons above that early collectors bought things like Japanese influenced Rookwood, Limoges-style faience, and other such art ware that had a foundation in cultures other than American. Never mind that it was derivative, inferior and little more than a rest stop on the way to discovering the best of what was made here.

To illustrate, in 1970 when James Carpenter brought the 10,000-piece cache of George Ohr pottery to New Jersey from Biloxi, Mississippi, it proved almost impossible to sell. There was no market to speak of for even better known names such as Rookwood or Roseville, much less the weird creations by the

Mad Pottery of Biloxi. Red, twisted, scrunched, crimped 8-inch, two handled vases with black drips and the occasional applied snake didn't sell well in Biloxi 70 years earlier, and they found little more acceptance in sylvan New Jersey in 1970. What did initially sell of Ohr's work were his early, more traditional, folk pottery pieces bought by prominent folk art dealers and collectors in and around the New York area. They were something this nascent market could get their heads around. But like the Japanese and French influenced ware described above, it really had little to do with the heart of the matter. (Let's use that piece of Ohr above to show price progression. That 8-inch scrunched vase in 1975 would sell for $500)

The Jordan Volpe gallery opened in 1975 and, while the famous institution showcased a balance of great art and terrible ethics (one owner, Todd Volpe, spent 27 months in jail for fraud), it succeeded in defining the future of the art pottery market. They championed George Ohr as well as Robineau, Grueby, Newcomb College, and a host of other potteries heretofore known only to a few stalwart collectors and academics. By the mid 1980s American art pottery was no longer a secret. (Our red-scrunched Ohr vase is now a $10,000 piece)

The next big thing was the Boston Museum of Fine Art's sensational Arts and Crafts exhibition, "The Art That is Life". Princeton came first, but Boston took things to a whole other level. Though the show included all aspects of Period material such as furniture, lighting and textiles, it also displayed the beauty, diversity and accessibility of decorative ceramics. Furniture was mostly angular and deep brown. Textiles were lovely but flat and, by nature, dull. Pottery stood out, the Cartier diamond pin on the basic black dress of the staid Arts and Crafts interior. And it was small, easy to transport and trade, and most of all fun.

It was during this time that the markets for important potteries such as Newcomb College, Marblehead, Ohr, Grueby and works by Frederick Rhead separated themselves from the pack. Certainly the average artist decorated piece of Rookwood or nicely glazed Fulper continued to find new homes, but the gap between the early collectors and the new wave of serious buyers was widening. Hollywood, and Hollywood money, entered the mix.

Grueby, three-color squat adecorated with tooled and applied water lilies and lily pads in yellow and green against a leathery dark green ground, 1914. $54,825

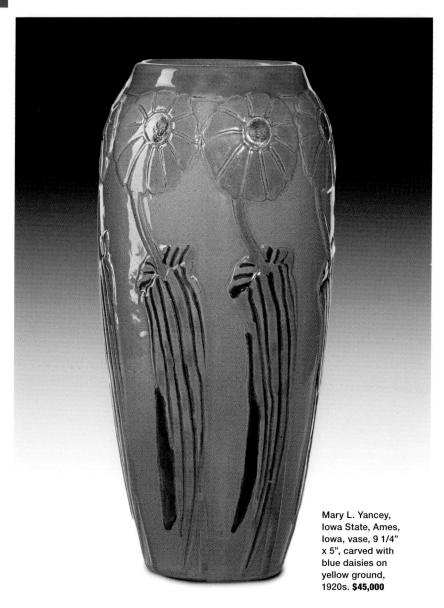

Mary L. Yancey,
Iowa State, Ames,
Iowa, vase, 9 1/4"
x 5", carved with
blue daisies on
yellow ground,
1920s. **$45,000**

Barbra Streisand featured a piece of Teco on the cover of one of her albums. Brad Pitt and Joel Silver were consistent players at auction. Suddenly many of the schoolteachers and academics that bulwarked the early collectors could no longer afford the insurance premiums

for, much less the prices, art pottery was now costing. Many of them cashed in pieces they'd taken off the market 20 years earlier. The second generation of collecting art pottery began.

At this time the darlings of the market were mostly the high-end companies mentioned above, but new scholarship was finding print at a startling rate. When the Paul Evans, book on art was published in 1975 you might see only a two-page chapter on an important but obscure pottery such as Arequipa or North Dakota School of Mines. But by the mid 1990s you could find monographs on individual artists or these companies alone. This in turn encouraged even more collecting and prices rose (with the exception of the 1993 recession) inexorably. (Our red Ohr vase? $50,000)

Enter the millennium. Swept up along with the excesses of the dot-com boom, Arts and Crafts material was at an all-time high. Furniture, wrought copper and art pottery objects were finding new buyers including public and private museums as well as determined collectors. Even after the dot-com crash prices held steady for most Period material, though there was some softening by 2005 for commercial ware such as production Roseville and non-artist decorated Rookwood. (The Ohr? $100,000)

September 2008 was a different matter; with the cratering of Lehman Brothers and the credit default swap fiasco. In fairness, ALL markets, antiques and otherwise, suffered through much of 2009. But it remains clear that the forty-year run the Arts and Crafts market had enjoyed was at least slowing down and, in some places, coming to a standstill. Collecting is generational and perhaps younger collectors aren't interested in buying what their parents coveted. The demographic is aging and the under-40 crowd is buying Modern.

This is most apparent in prices for Mission furniture, where all but the very best, in pristine condition, is selling for a fraction of what they'd have brought a decade ago. This is less true for art pottery, however. You probably don't need another bookcase, and changing

one out for an upgrade is a lot of work, between emptying, moving the old one out, moving the new one in, and refilling. Not so for your ceramics collection, where you can more easily add or subtract pieces. You can't mail a bookcase using UPS.

While work by some famous companies sell for below historic record prices, we're seeing staggering levels for the Period's best. Average pieces of Newcomb College have settled at about 80% of their high, but that elusive 1% of their production will easily sell for over $100,000. Grueby pottery also has faltered as of late, but the past few years have seen their best examples match or exceed past results. On the other end of the scale, production Roseville pieces are a full 35% lower than a decade ago, which suggests this is the best time in years to pursue such work.

We realized a record price for a piece of American art pottery six years ago when we sold a vase by Frederick Rhead, from his Santa Barbara Pottery (circa 1915), for $519,000. More recently, we sold another piece by Rhead, from his tenure at University City (circa 1911), for $637,000. And finally, that Ohr vase? It is valued at $150,000 on today's market.

All markets are always in a state of flux. What remains constant is the desire of American collectors, surfing the ebb and flow of value but continuing to collect, preserve and educate. While the current climate in some collecting areas has definitely cooled, the market for most art pottery is doing just fine.

The following images and those in the previous pages are from a collection of favorites and best-selling pieces as selected by Rago Arts and Auction Center.

Rhead Pottery, Santa Barbara, Calif., iconic Arts and Crafts piece, tall vase etched with a stylized landscape, 11 1/4" x 6". **$518,000**

Frederick Hurten Rhead signed four-part tile panel with peacock, 20 3/4" square, University City, Mo., 1910. **$637,500**

George Kendrick Grueby, rare seven-handled vase, Boston, Mass., ca. 1900, 10 3/4" x 8 1/2". **$37,500**

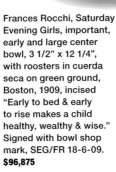

Frances Rocchi, Saturday Evening Girls, important, early and large center bowl, 3 1/2" x 12 1/4", with roosters in cuerda seca on green ground, Boston, 1909, incised "Early to bed & early to rise makes a child healthy, wealthy & wise." Signed with bowl shop mark, SEG/FR 18-6-09. **$96,875**

Newcomb College, rare tall vase, 11 1/2" x 5 1/2", carved by Sadie Irvine, fenced-in cabin under moss-laden live oaks and a full moon, 1922. **$22,325**

Newcomb College, exceptional early vessel, 7 1/2" x 9 1/2", carved by Marie de Hoa LeBlanc, features five stylized blue and white rabbits, 1902. **$84,000**

Newcomb College, tall vase, 15 1/4" x 7 1/2", carved by Sadie Irvine, pine trees with green needles on bright blue trunks against a blue-green and ivory ground, 1909. **$96,000**

Fulper, rare mushroom-shaped lamp, 17" x 17", covered in Leopard-Skin Crystalline glaze, shade inset with leaded glass, on a flaring, two-socket base. **$36,000**

Fulper, rare corseted vase, 11 1/4" x 8 1/4", Copperdust Crystalline glaze, raised racetrack mark. **$11,160**

Grueby, gourd-shaped vase with tooled and applied full-height ribbed leaves, 9 1/4" x 8 1/2" covered in feathered matte green glaze, extremely rare. **$84,000**

George Ohr, vase with two ribbon handles, 8 1/2" x 5 3/4", covered in a spectacular red and green mottled glaze. Stamped G.E. OHR, Biloxi, Miss. **$84,000**

George Ohr, bisque vase, 9" x 5", with folded rim, deep in-body twist, dimpled middle, and notched pattern on base and neck. Incised on body, "Made in the presence of owner John Power/By his friend/G E Ohr/Biloxi 1-24-1903," and on bottom, "Mary had a little Lamb & Ohr has a little Pottery." **$23,000**

Louis Comfort Tiffany, exceptional cabbage-shaped vase, 8 1/2" x 8", in mottled polychrome matte glaze. **$50,020**

George Ohr, rare corseted teapot, 6 3/4" x 8", with two different glazes, Biloxi, Miss., 1890s. **$46,875**

George Ohr, oversized pitcher, 5 1/2" x 8", with mottled raspberry, blue and green glaze, Biloxi, MS, ca. 1900. Stamped G.E. OHR, Biloxi, Miss. **$50,000**

Rookwood, "Chief Hollow Horn Bear, Sioux," 16" x 15", 1900, standard glaze pillow vase by Matthew A. Daly, shows striking detail of a Native American Chief in full headdress and breast plate. **$76,375**

Roseville, Tourist 10" wall pocket. Stamped 1209. **$5,185**

Rookwood, vase, 13 1/4" x 10 1/2" decorated by William Hentschell, 1929, perfectly fired. Flame mark/XXIX/WEH/6080. **$14,400**

Roseville, Della Robbia vase, 15 ½" x 6", with wild roses and cut-out rim, Zanesville, Ohio, ca. 1910. **$43,750**

Roseville, rare Futura "Tank" vase, 10" x 9", in blue to ivory shaded glaze. Unmarked. **$22,800**

Teco, Fritz Albert designed massive vase, 22 1/2" x 8", with iris blossoms, Terra Cotta, Ill., ca. 1905, Stamped Teco twice. **$212,500**

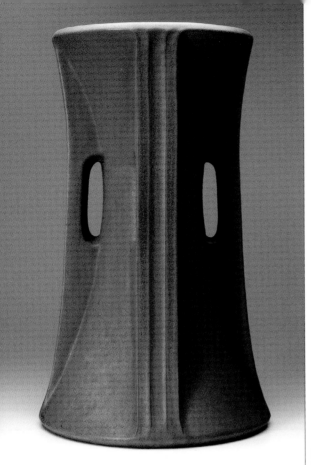

Arequipa, exceptional and large vase, 10" x 5", 1912, decorated with irises and leaves on a purple ground. Marked 670 Arequipa/California. **$74,750**

Teco, massive architectonic corseted vase, 18" x 10 1/2" with four buttressed handles, covered in a smooth matte green glaze with charcoaling. Stamped Teco 416. **$60,000**

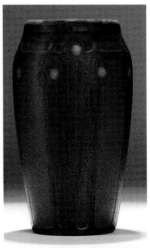

Marblehead, Arthur Hennessey exceptional carved vase, 7" x 4", with stylized blossoms. One of only four known. **$134,200**

Marblehead, tile incised with a landscape of poplar trees reflected in a pond. Tile mounted in new Arts and Crafts frame. 6-inch square. **$114,000**

Fiesta

The Homer Laughlin China Co. originated with a two-kiln pottery on the banks of the Ohio River in East Liverpool, Ohio. Built in 1873-'74 by Homer Laughlin and his brother, Shakespeare, the firm was first known as the Ohio Valley Pottery, and later Laughlin Bros. Pottery. It was one of the first white-ware plants in the country.

After a tentative beginning, the company was awarded a prize for having the best white-ware at the 1876 Centennial Exposition in Philadelphia.

Three years later, Shakespeare sold his interest in the business to Homer, who continued on until 1897. At that time, Homer Laughlin sold his interest in the newly incorporated firm to a group of investors, including Charles, Louis, and Marcus Aaron and the company bookkeeper, William E. Wells.

Under new ownership in 1907, the headquarters and a new 30-kiln plant were built across the Ohio River in Newell, West Virginia, the present manufacturing and headquarters location.

In the 1920s, two additions to the Homer Laughlin staff set the stage for the company's greatest success: the Fiesta line.

Dr. Albert V. Bleininger was hired in 1920. A scientist, author, and educator, he oversaw the conversion from bottle kilns to the more efficient tunnel kilns.

In 1927, the company hired designer Frederick Hurten Rhead, a member of a distinguished family of English

Special-order promotional disk juice pitcher in red. **$650**

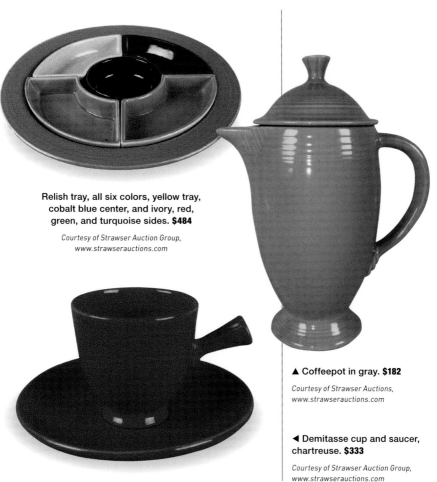

Relish tray, all six colors, yellow tray, cobalt blue center, and ivory, red, green, and turquoise sides. **$484**

Courtesy of Strawser Auction Group, www.strawserauctions.com

▲ Coffeepot in gray. **$182**

Courtesy of Strawser Auctions, www.strawserauctions.com

◄ Demitasse cup and saucer, chartreuse. **$333**

Courtesy of Strawser Auction Group, www.strawserauctions.com

ceramists. Having previously worked at Weller Pottery and Roseville Pottery, Rhead began to develop the artistic quality of the company's wares, and to experiment with shapes and glazes. In 1935, this work culminated in his designs for the Fiesta line.

Fiesta was produced until 1973, when waning popularity and declining sales forced the company to discontinue the line. But renewed appreciation of Art Deco design, coupled with collectors scrambling to buy the discontinued items on the secondary market, prompted the company to reintroduce the line on Fiesta's 50th anniversary in 1986. Spawning a whole new generation of collectors, Post-'86 Fiesta is still produced today.

For more information on Fiesta, see *Warman's Fiesta Identification and Price Guide* by Glen Victorey.

◄ Set of seven nesting bowls, all marked, overall light to moderate wear commensurate with age, some abrasions and bruising, tallest 7 1/2" high, 11" diameter. **$640**

Courtesy of Rago Arts and Auctions, www.ragoarts.com

Fiesta Colors

From 1936 to 1972, Fiesta was produced in 14 colors (other than special promotions). These colors are usually divided into the "original colors" of cobalt blue, light green, ivory, red, turquoise, and yellow (cobalt blue, light green, red, and yellow only on the Kitchen Kraft line, introduced in 1939); the "1950s colors" of chartreuse, forest green, gray, and rose (introduced in 1951); medium green (introduced in 1959); plus the later additions of Casuals, Amberstone, Fiesta Ironstone, and Casualstone ("Coventry") in antique gold, mango red, and turf green; and the striped, decal, and Lustre pieces. No Fiesta was produced from 1973 to 1985. The colors that make up the "original" and "1950s" groups are sometimes referred to as "the standard 11."

In many pieces, medium green is the hardest to find and the most expensive Fiesta color.

Fiesta Colors and Years of Production to 1972

Antique Gold – dark butterscotch............................... 1969-1972
Chartreuse – yellowish green....................................... 1951-1959
Cobalt Blue – dark or royal blue................................. 1936-1951
Forest Green – dark hunter green 1951-1959
Gray – light or ash gray.. 1951-1959
Green – often called light green when comparing it to other
      green glazes; also called "Original" green 1936-1951
Ivory – creamy, slightly yellowed................................. 1936-1951
Mango Red – same as original red.............................. 1970-1972
Medium Green – bright rich green............................... 1959-1969
Red – reddish orange .... 1936-1944 and 1959-1972
Rose – dusty, dark rose 1951-1959
Turf Green – olive.. 1969-1972
Turquoise – sky blue, like the stone 1937-1969
Yellow – golden yellow... 1936-1969

Reintroduced in 1986, Fiesta offered five colors:

Rose – pink... 1986-2005
Black... 1986-2015
Cobalt – dark blue .... 1986-still produced
White.. 1986-still produced
Apricot – pale peach 1986-1998

Platter, medium green. **$67**

Courtesy of Strawser Auction Group, www.strawserauctions.com

Carafe in red with original cork, circa 1936-1944, marked "Fiesta / HLC, U.S.A." under base, undamaged, 9 3/4" high overall. **$192**

Courtesy of Jeffrey S. Evans & Associates,
www.jeffreysevans.com

Jubilee juice set, celadon disk juice pitcher and pink, beige, rose, and gray tumblers. **$484**

Courtesy of Strawser Auction Group, www.strawserauctions.com

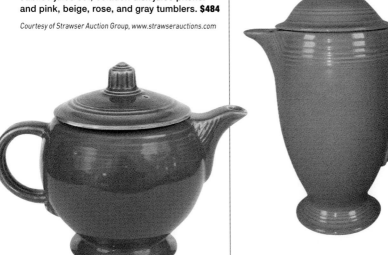

Medium teapot in turquoise. **$295**

Courtesy of Strawser Auctions, www.strawserauctions.com

Rare original design Post-'86 coffeepot in apricot; production problems led to current coffeepot style. **$454**

Courtesy of Strawser Auctions, www.strawserauctions.com

Vase in yellow, 12" high. **$484**

Courtesy of Strawser Auctions, www.strawserauctions.com

Vase, turquoise, 12". **$908**

Courtesy of Strawser Auction Group, www.strawserauctions.com

Vase in red, circa 1936-1944, marked "Fiesta / HLC U.S.A." under base, undamaged, 8" high. **$300**

Courtesy of Jeffrey S. Evans & Associates, www.jeffreysevans.com

Rare Post-'86 teapot in sapphire. **$1,392**

Courtesy of Strawser Auctions, www.strawserauctions.com

▲ Ice lip pitcher in red, circa 1936-1944, marked "Fiesta / HLC, U.S.A." under base, undamaged, 6 1/8" high. **$108**

Courtesy of Jeffrey S. Evans & Associates, www.jeffreysevans.com

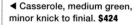

◄ Casserole, medium green, minor knick to finial. **$424**

Courtesy of Strawser Auction Group, www.strawserauctions.com

◀ Rare red stripe ivory demitasse pot. **$847**

Courtesy of Strawser Auction Group, www.strawserauctions.com

Vase in ivory, 12" high. **$545**

Courtesy of Strawser Auctions, www.strawserauctions.com

Fiesta creamer and sugar, medium green. **$182**

Courtesy of Strawser Auction Group, www.strawserauctions.com

Rare onion soup bowl with lid in ivory with red stripe, outstanding color. **$12,705**

Courtesy of Strawser Auctions, www.strawserauctions.com

▲ Rare Post-'86 sapphire pyramid candleholders, slight glaze rub to one pyramid, only pair known to exist. **$1,815**

Courtesy of Strawser Auction Group, www.strawserauctions.com

▲ Syrup pitcher in red with original orange/red lid, circa 1936-1944, marked "Fiesta / Made in U.S.A. / 29" under base, undamaged, 5 5/8" high overall. **$390**

Courtesy of Jeffrey S. Evans & Associates, www.jeffreysevans.com

Onion soup bowl with cover, red. **$787**

Courtesy of Strawser Auction Group, www.strawserauctions.com

Grueby

William Grueby was active in the ceramic industry for several years before he developed his own method of producing matte-glazed pottery and founded the Grueby Faience Co. of Boston in 1897.

The art pottery was hand-thrown in natural shapes, hand-molded, and hand-tooled. A variety of colored glazes, singly or in combinations, was produced, but green was the most popular. In 1908, the firm was divided into the Grueby Pottery Co. and the Grueby Faience and Tile Co. The Grueby Faience and Tile Co. made art tile until 1917, although its pottery production was phased out about 1910.

▲ Squat vessel with yellow buds, circa 1905, glazed-over circular stamp, overall excellent condition, 6" x 8". **$5,313**

Courtesy of Rago Arts and Auctions, www.ragoarts.com

▶ Tile decorated with white and brown swan against green grass and blue sky by Ruth Erickson, marked with artist's initials "RE" on back, 4" x 4". **$2,600**

Courtesy of Humler & Nolan, humlernolan.com

▲ Art pottery tile decorated by Kiichi Yamada, Cuenca decoration of turtle under garland of leaves in yellow, brown and green glazes, white clay body, decorator's initials on back, 1" x 6" square. **$1,476**

Courtesy of Skinner, Inc., www.skinnerinc.com

◄ Compact vase carved with broad foliage, organic green matte glaze on bottom obscuring factory marks, 2 3/4" high x 4 1/4" wide. **$1,100**

Courtesy of Humler & Nolan, humlernolan.com

Vase with leaves and buds, rare matte mauve glaze, circa 1900, circular Faience stamp, CP, 7 1/4" x 5". **$1,875**

Courtesy of Rago Arts and Auctions, www.ragoarts.com

Vase with leaves and leathery glaze, Ruth Erickson, circa 1905, incised "RE" with circular Grueby Pottery stamp, overall excellent condition, 6 3/4" x 9 1/2". **$6,250**

Courtesy of Rago Arts and Auctions, www.ragoarts.com

Squat, bulbous, ribbed art pottery vessel, circa 1900, matte yellow glaze, marked GRUEBY, BOSTON MASS (impressed), 3" high x 6" wide. **$500**

Courtesy of Heritage Auctions, ha.com

Massive, rare vase with leaves and buds, circa 1900, circular Faience stamp, 23" x 9". **$21,250**

Courtesy of Rago Arts and Auctions, www.ragoarts.com

Flower form bowl in mat green glaze, marked on bottom with circular Grueby Pottery Boston USA mark and incised with initials of artist Ruth Erickson, fine crazing inside vessel and professional repair to rim, 2" high x 6" wide. **$700**

Courtesy of Humler & Nolan, humlernolan.com

Early Kendrick vase, matte green glaze, circa 1900, circular Faience stamp, paper label, 12" x 8 1/2". **$31,250**

Courtesy of Rago Arts and Auctions, www.ragoarts.com

Rare and early vase carved with leaves, circa 1900, horizontal stamp GRUEBY BOSTON, MASS., 12" x 7 1/2". **$5,313**

Courtesy of Rago Arts and Auctions, www.ragoarts.com

Early bulbous vase carved with leaves, circa 1900, circular Faience stamp/152, paper label 1114, artist's cipher, 12" x 9". **$5,000**

Courtesy of Rago Arts and Auctions, www.ragoarts.com

Rare large vase with lilies, circa 1905, circular Grueby Pottery stamp, professional restoration to two chips and bruise at rim, 14" x 7 1/4". **$12,500**

Courtesy of Rago Arts and Auctions, www.ragoarts.com

Two-color vase with leaves and buds, circa 1905, circular Grueby Pottery stamp, professional restoration to area of rim, tight hairline from rim, 9" x 4". **$2,875**

Courtesy of Rago Arts and Auctions, www.ragoarts.com

Matte glaze vase with five hand-tooled leaves and bud,s impressed Grueby Faience Co. Boston on bottom, 7 3/8" high. **$1,200**

Courtesy of Humler & Nolan, humlernolan.com

Rare floor vase carved
with leaves and buds,
curdled green glaze,
circa 1900, unmarked,
26" x 11 1/2". **$6,875**

*Courtesy of Rago Arts and
Auctions, www.ragoarts.com*

◄ Rare wall pocket, unusual shape with carved and applied leaves, suspended green matte glaze, 3 1/2" wide x 8 1/2" long. **$1,952**

Courtesy of Treadway/Toomey Auctions

Spherical vase carved with leaves, circa 1905, circular pottery stamp, chip to rim, 3 3/4" x 4". **$3,000**

Courtesy of Rago Arts and Auctions, www.ragoarts.com

Tile with yellow tulip, circa 1905, decorator's initials, 1" x 6" sq. **$2,125**

Courtesy of Rago Arts and Auctions, www.ragoarts.com

Tile with tulip, circa 1905, unmarked, chip to bottom right corner, restoration to areas around edges, glaze shaved off one side, 1" x 6" square. **$550**

Courtesy of Rago Arts and Auctions, www.ragoarts.com

Vase with lobed rim and full-height leaves and buds, curdled green glaze, circa 1905, obscured stamp, glaze pop to body, some minor efflorescence, light wear around rim, 7 1/2" x 4 1/2". **$1,600**

Courtesy of Rago Arts and Auctions, www.ragoarts.com

Limoges

"Limoges" has become the generic identifier for porcelain produced in Limoges, France, and the surrounding vicinity. Over 40 manufacturers in the area have, at some point, used the term as a descriptor of their work, and there are at least 400 different Limoges identification marks. The common denominator is the product itself – fine hard paste porcelain created from the necessary components found in abundance in the Limoges region: kaolin and feldspar.

Until the 1700s, porcelain was exclusively a product of China, introduced to the Western world by Marco Polo and imported at great expense. In 1765, the discovery of kaolin in St. Yrieixin, a small town near Limoges, made French production of porcelain possible. (The chemist's wife credited with the kaolin discovery thought at first that it would prove useful in making soap.)

Limoges entrepreneurs quickly capitalized on the find. Adding to the area's allure were expansive forests providing fuel for wood-burning kilns; the nearby Vienne River, with water for working clay; and a workforce eager to trade farming for a (they hoped) more lucrative pursuit. Additionally, as the companies would operate outside metropolitan Paris, labor and production costs would be significantly less.

By the early 1770s, numerous porcelain

◀ Vase with large central oval medallion with portrait of young woman in purple gown and cherub against shaded blue, white, and red sky, central medallion framed by gilt border of scrolls and flowers with turquoise enameled beaded cross at top and bottom, remainder of vase in yellow glaze, flaring lip in gilt, signed "W.G. & Co. Limoges, France" on underside, very good to excellent condition, 14" high. **$711**

Courtesy of James D. Julia Auctioneers, Fairfield, Maine, jamesdjulia.com

Six hand-painted chargers
(three shown), late 19th/
early 20th century, Orientalist
scene by Morley, four avian
scenes by Boumy, Puisoye,
Valantin, and Dubois, and
unsigned pastoral scene,
largest 13 1/2" diameter. **$531**

*Courtesy of Rago Arts and Auction
Center, ragoarts.com*

manufacturers were at work in Limoges and its environs. Demand for the porcelain was high because it was both useful and decorative. To meet that demand, firms employed trained, as well as untrained, artisans for the detailed hand painting required. (Although nearly every type of Limoges has its fans, the most sought-after—and valuable—are those pieces decorated by a company's professional artists.) At its industrial peak in 1900, Limoges factories employed over 8,000 workers in some aspect of porcelain production.

A myriad of products classified as Limoges flooded the marketplace from the late 1700s onward. Among them were tableware pieces, such as tea and punch sets, trays, pitchers, compotes, bowls and plates. Also popular were vases and flower baskets, dresser sets, trinket boxes, ash receivers, figural busts, and decorative plaques.

Although produced in France, Limoges porcelain was soon destined for export overseas; eventually over 80 percent of Limoges porcelain was exported. The United States proved a particularly reliable customer.

Six rare barrel-shaped mugs with hand-painted rabbit décor, 3 1/2" high. **$207**

Courtesy of Woody Auction, woodyauction.com

Notable among the importers was the Haviland China Co.; until the 1940s, its superior, exquisitely decorated china was produced in Limoges and then distributed in the United States.

By the early 20th century, many exporters in the United States were purchasing porcelain blanks from the Limoges factories for decoration stateside. The base product was authentically made in France, but production costs were significantly lower: Thousands of untrained porcelain painters put their skills to work for a minimal wage. Domestic decoration of the blanks also meant that importers could select designs suited to the specific tastes of target audiences.

Because Limoges was a regional designation rather than the identifier of a specific manufacturer, imported pieces were often marked with the name of the exporting firm, followed by the word "Limoges." Beginning in 1891, "France" was added. Some confusion has arisen from products marked "Limoges China Co." (aka "American Limoges"). This Ohio-based firm, in business from 1902-1955, has no connection to the porcelain produced in France.

The heyday of quality French Limoges lasted roughly into the 1930s. Production continues today, but after World War II, designs and painting techniques became much more standardized.

Vintage Limoges is highly sought-after by today's collectors. They're drawn to the delicacy of the porcelain as well as the colors and skill of decoration. Viewing a well-conceived Limoges piece is like seeing a painting in a new form. Valuation is based on age, decorative execution, and, as with any collectible, individual visual appeal.

Enamel on copper plaque depicting procession of the Magi, France, 19th century, after Benozzo Gozzoli (circa 1421-1497), in polychrome and gilt with raised "jewel" accents, back incised "France," metal frame, plaque 11" x 7". **$2,760**

Courtesy of Skinner, Inc., skinnerinc.com

▲ French bronze gilt enameled box, 2 1/4" high x 7" wide x 4 1/4" deep. **$850**

Courtesy of Kaminski Auctions, kaminskiauctions.com

▶ Thirteen-piece fish set, oval tray with fish and underwater décor, green border, heavy gold trim, 12 matching plates, good condition, tray 23 1/2" long. **$1,180**

Courtesy of Woody Auction, woodyauction.com

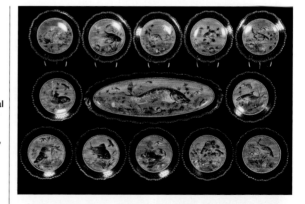

Art Nouveau Haviland punch bowl set, early 20th century, punch bowl and 10 cups, red ground with poppy motif and gilt banding, signed "GASPER" in gilt, hand-painted by Wilder Pickard Studios, marked, 8" high, 14" diameter. **$2,100**

Courtesy of Neal Auction, nealauction.com

Twelve black and white Hèrmes Estampe de Toucans place settings printed with toucans (part shown), 11 teacups, 12 saucers, 12 bread plates, 12 salad plates, 12 dinner plates, and 12 large bowls, excellent condition, one teacup missing, each bowl with dustbag, teacups 2 1/2" wide x 2 1/2" high, saucers 5 1/2" diameter, bread plates 6" diameter, salad plates 8 1/2" diameter, dinner plates 11" diameter, bowls 12" diameter. **$5,750**

Courtesy of Heritage Auctions, ha.com

Hand-painted porcelain plaque with two women, one lying and one seated on garden bench, with scenic background, gilded edge, artist signed "Dubois," signed on back "Coronet, Limoges, France," excellent condition with no scratches, chips, or repairs, 15 1/2". **$726**

Courtesy of Fontaine's Auction Gallery, fontainesauction.com

Enamel portrait plaque, early 20th century, rectangular, with polychrome enameled depiction of Titian, artist signed "C. Faure," in wood frame, 8 1/2" x 12". **$308**

Courtesy of Skinner, Inc., skinnerinc.com

French Barbotine De Marcel Chaufriasse pate-sur-pate vase, circa 1900, marks: BARBOTINE DE MARCEL CHAUFRIASSE, LIMOGES, rubbing to gilt, surface wear commensurate with age, 6" high. **$375**

Courtesy of Heritage Auctions, ha.com

Eight porcelain Mary Bacon Jones-designed plates, circa 1905, each polychrome enamel-decorated design based on Rudyard Kipling's The Jungle Book, printed Wm. Guerin & Co. Limoges mark, 10 7/8" diameter. **$2,400**

Courtesy of Skinner, Inc., skinnerinc.com

Eleven hand-painted porcelain plates depicting orchids, early 20th century, retailed by Ovington Bros., New York, each with gilded border decorated with floral garlands, polychrome enameled orchids in center, signed "L. Meage," Latin names for specimens on reverse, 9 3/8" diameter. **$1,140**

Courtesy of Skinner, Inc., skinnerinc.com

Porcelain potpourri vase and cover, 19th century, oval shape heavily pierced with gilded borders to pink ground and polychrome floral cartouches to either side, paneled cover with colored flowers and gilded flower finial, 10 3/4" high. **$500-$700**

Courtesy of Skinner, Inc., skinnerinc.com

Bawo & Dotter hand-painted covered handled tureen with matching floral serving platter, each with floral designs with crimson ground and gild accenting, bottoms have green Limoges mark with gold Bawo & Dotter mark, serving platter signed Ribes, 19th/20th century; tureen 10 1/2" high x 15" long, platter 19" long x 12 3/4" wide. **$610**

Courtesy of Elite Decorative Arts, eliteauction.com

Two-handled footed porcelain bowl and matching 11" tray, green tones with berry and vine décor, artist marked "LHS," no chips, cracks, or repairs, 4 3/4" x 12 1/2". **$266**

Courtesy of Woody Auction, woodyauction.com

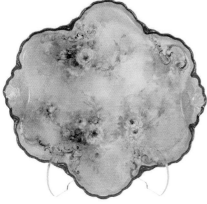

Unusual Haviland & Co. barbotine vase painted by Emile-Justin Merlot, circa 1875, scenic decoration of houses on bank of river with chickens in foreground, signed by Merlot on front of form and impressed "Haviland & Co. Limoges" on bottom, fine overall crazing and professional restoration to small chip on back of foot, 8 7/8" high x 13 1/4" wide. **$1,694**

Courtesy of Mark Mussio, Humler & Nolan, humlernolan.com

Tray in green, blue, yellow, and pink with pink and yellow roses and gold border, 18" x 17". **$590**

Courtesy of Woody Auction, woodyauction.com

Arts & Crafts silver and Limoges enamel box, Frank Gardner Hale, enamel panel depicting butterfly and mounted into silver box, box marked F.G. HALE, enamel approximately 3 3/4" x 3 1/4", box 6 1/4" x 4 1/4" x 1 7/8". **$6,765**

Courtesy of Skinner, Inc.; skinnerinc.com

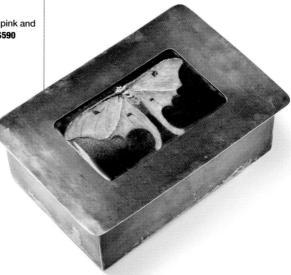

Ormolu mirror with Limoges enameled scene of maiden in distress being attacked by two
bandits, maiden holding hand mirror high above her head and looking into distance as if
signaling someone; enameled panel is artist signed, reverse side houses what appears to be
original beveled glass mirror, mirror and enameled panel housed in ormolu frame that swivels in
matching stand decorated with lion's paw feet and gargoyles; very good to excellent condition
with some minor pitting to silvering on mirror; mirror
10 1/4" high overall; Limoges panel approximately 4" x 5 3/4". **$5,036**

Courtesy of James D. Julia, Inc., jamesdjulia.com

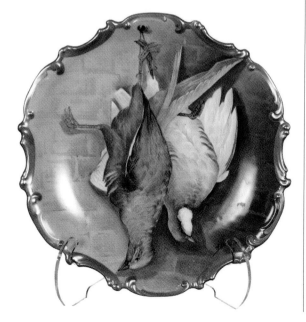

▲ Hand-painted punch bowl, 6 3/4" x 16" diameter. **$250**

Courtesy of Kaminski Auctions, kaminskiauctions.com

◀ Fish service with scalloped gilt border centering trout in river, 12 luncheon plates, 9 1/2" diameter; large serving tray, 24" wide; and sauce boat with undertray, signed de Solis. **$671**

Courtesy of Clars Auction Gallery, clars.com

◀ Charger with scene of two game birds hanging from hook, gold trim, marked, signed "A. Brounssillon" by artist, 16 1/2" diameter. **$325**

Courtesy of Woody Auction, woodyauction.com

Majolica

In 1851, an English potter was hoping that his new interpretation of a centuries-old style of ceramics would be well received at the Great Exhibition of the Industries of All Nations set to open May 1 in London's Hyde Park.

Potter Herbert Minton had high hopes for his display. His father, Thomas Minton, founded a pottery works in the mid-1790s in Stoke-on-Trent, Staffordshire. Herbert Minton had designed a "new" line of pottery, and his chemist, Leon Arnoux, had developed a process that resulted in vibrant, colorful glazes that came to be called "majolica."

Trained as an engineer, Arnoux also studied the making of encaustic tiles, and had been appointed art director at Minton's works in 1848. His job was to introduce and promote new products. Victorian fascination with the natural world prompted Arnoux to reintroduce the work of Bernard Palissy, whose naturalistic, bright-colored "maiolica" wares had been created in the 16th century. But Arnoux used a thicker body to make pieces sturdier. This body was given a coating of opaque white glaze, which provided a surface for decoration.

Rare Wardle three-piece tea set with matching tray, minor spout nick to teapot and creamer, staining to sugar bowl, tray 10 3/4" diameter. **$726**

Courtesy of Strawser Auction Group, www.strawserauctions.com

Pieces were modeled in high relief, featuring butterflies and other insects, flowers and leaves, fruit, shells, animals, and fish. Queen Victoria's endorsement of the new pottery prompted its acceptance by the general public.

When Minton introduced his wares at Philadelphia's 1876 Centennial Exhibition, American potters also began to produce majolica.

For more information on majolica, see *Warman's Majolica Identification and Price Guide* by Mark F. Moran.

Other Majolica Makers

John Adams & Co., Hanley, Stoke-on-Trent, Staffordshire, England, operated the Victoria Works, producing earthenware, jasperware, Parian, majolica, 1864-1873.

Another Staffordshire pottery,

Samuel Alcock & Co., Cobridge, 1828-1853; Burslem, 1830-1859, produced earthenware, china and Parian.

The **W. & J.A. Bailey Alloa Pottery** was founded in Alloa, the principal town in Clackmannanshire, located near Edinburgh, Scotland.

The **Bevington** family of potters worked in Hanley, Staffordshire, England in the late 19th century.

W. Brownfield & Son operated in Burslem and Cobridge, Staffordshire, England from 1850-1891.

T.C. Brown-Westhead, Moore & Co. produced earthenware and porcelain at Hanley, Stoke-on-Trent, Staffordshire, from about 1862 to 1904.

The Choisy-le-Roi faience factory of Choisy-le-Roi, France, produced majolica from 1860 until 1910. The firm's wares are not always marked. The common mark is usually a black ink stamp "Choisy-le-Roi" pictured to the right with a large "HBm" that stands for Hippolyte Boulenger, a director at the pottery.

William T. Copeland & Sons pottery of Stoke-on-Trent, Staffordshire, England, began producing porcelain and earthenware in 1847. (Josiah Spode established a pottery at Stoke-on-Trent in 1770. In 1833, the firm was purchased by William Copeland and Thomas Garrett. In 1847, Copeland became the sole owner. W.T.

Copeland & Sons continued until a 1976 merger when it became Royal Worcester Spode. Copeland majolica pieces are sometimes marked with an impressed "COPELAND," but many are unmarked.)

Jose A. Cunha, Caldas da Rainha, southern Portugal, also worked in the style of Bernard Palissy, the great French Renaissance potter.

Julius Dressler, Bela, Czech Republic, was founded 1888, producing faience, majolica and porcelain. In 1920, the name was changed to EPIAG. The firm closed about 1945.

Eureka Pottery was located in Trenton, New Jersey, circa 1883-1887.

Railway Pottery was established by S. Fielding & Co., Stoke-on-Trent, Staffordshire, England, 1879.

There were two **Thomas Forester** potteries active in the late 19th century in Staffordshire, England. Some sources list the more famous of the two as Thomas Forester & Sons, Ltd. at the Phoenix Works, Longton.

Established in the early 19th century, the **Gien** pottery works is located on the banks of France's Loire River near Orleans.

Joseph Holdcroft majolica ware was produced at Daisy Bank in Longton, Staffordshire, England, from 1870 to 1885. Items can be found

◄ Delphin Massier rooster alongside cornhusk, Vallauris, France, early 20th century, polychrome decoration, 12 3/4" high. **$861**

Courtesy of Skinner, Inc., www.skinnerinc.com

George Jones strawberry serving platter, 14 1/2" long. **$514**
Courtesy of Strawser Auction Group, www.strawserauctions.com

marked with "J HOLDCROFT," but many pieces can only be attributed by the patterns and colors that are documented to have come from the Holdcroft potteries.

George Jones & Sons, Ltd., Stoke, Staffordshire, started operation in about 1864 as George Jones and in 1873 became George Jones & Sons, Ltd. The firm operated the Trent Potteries in Stoke-on-Trent (renamed "Crescent Potteries" in about 1907).

In about 1877, **Samuel Lear** erected a small china works in Hanley, Staffordshire. Lear produced domestic china and, in addition, decorated all kinds of earthenware made by other manufacturers, including "spirit kegs." In 1882, the firm expanded to include production of majolica, ivory-body earthenware, and Wedgwood-type jasperware. The business closed in 1886.

Robert Charbonnier founded the **Longchamp** tile works in 1847 to make red clay tiles, but the factory soon started to produce majolica. Longchamp is known for its "barbotine" pieces (a paste of clay used in decorating coarse pottery in relief) made with vivid colors, especially oyster plates.

Hugo Lonitz operated in Haldensleben, Germany, from 1868-1886, and later Hugo Lonitz & Co., 1886-1904, producing household and decorative porcelain, earthenware, and metalwares. Look for a mark of two entwined fish.

The **Lunéville** pottery was founded about 1728 by Jacques Chambrette in the city that bears its name, in the Alsace-Lorraine region of northeastern France. The firm became famous for its blue monochromatic and floral patterns. Around 1750, ceramist Paul-Louis Cyfflé introduced a pattern with animals and historical figures. Lunéville products range from hand-painted faience and majolica to pieces influenced by the Art Deco movement.

The **Massier** family began producing ceramics in Vallauris, France, in the mid-18th century.

François Maurice, School of Paris, was active from 1875-1885 and also worked in the style of Bernard Palissy.

George Morley & Co. was located in East Liverpool, Ohio, 1884-1891.

Morley & Co. Pottery was founded in 1879, Wellsville, Ohio, making graniteware and majolica.

Orchies, a majolica manufacturer in northern France near Lille, is also known under the mark "Moulin des Loups & Hamage," 1920s.

Faïencerie de Pornic is located near Quimper, France.

Quimper pottery has a long history. Tin-glazed, hand-painted pottery has been made in Quimper, France, since the late 17th century. The earliest firm, founded in 1685 by Jean Baptiste Bousquet, was known as HB Quimper. Another firm, founded in 1772 by Francois Eloury, was known as Porquier. A third firm, founded by Guillaume Dumaine in 1778, was known as HR or Henriot Quimper. All three companies made similar pottery decorated with designs of Breton peasants, and sea and flower motifs.

The **Rörstrand** factory made the first faience (tin-glazed earthenware) produced in Sweden. It was established in 1725 by Johann Wolff, near Stockholm.

The earthenware factory of **Salins** was established in 1857 in Salins-les-Bains, near the French border with Switzerland. Salins was awarded the gold medal at the International Exhibition of Decorative Arts in Paris in 1912.

Sarreguemines wares are named for the city in the Lorraine region of northeastern France. The pottery was founded in 1790 by Nicholas-

Figural center bowl, Minton, Stoke-on-Trent, Staffordshire, England, circa 1870, in basket weave, supported by three fantailed pigeons on oak leaf branches ,11" wide. **$1,000**

Courtesy of Heritage Auctions, www.ha.com

Tureen and cover, St. Honoré, France, circa 1870, modeled and colored as a duck on oval weave base, 7 1/2" x 11 1/2" x 8". **$1,314**

Courtesy of Heritage Auctions, www.ha.com

Henri Jacobi. For more than 100 years, it flourished under the direction of the Utzschneider family.

Wilhelm Schiller and Sons, Bodenbach, Bohemia, was established 1885.

Thomas-Victor Sergent was one of the School of Paris ceramists of the late 19th century who was influenced by the works of Bernard Palissy.

St. Clement was founded by Jacques Chambrette in Saint-Clément, France, in 1758. Chambrette also established works in Lunéville.

The **St. Jean de Bretagne** pottery works are located near Quimper, France.

Vallauris is a pottery center in southeastern France, near Cannes. Companies in production there include Massier and Foucard-Jourdan.

Victoria Pottery Co. was located in Hanley, Staffordshire, England from 1895-1927.

Wardle & Co. was established 1871 at Hanley, Staffordshire, England.

Josiah Wedgwood was born in Burslem, Staffordshire, England, on July 12, 1730, into a family with a long pottery tradition. At the age of nine, after the death of his father, he joined the family business. In 1759, he set up his own pottery works in Burslem. There he produced cream-colored earthenware that found favor with Queen Charlotte. In 1762, she appointed him royal supplier of dinnerware. From the public sale of "Queen's Ware," as it came to be known, Wedgwood was able to build a production community in 1768, which he named Etruria, near Stoke-on-Trent, and a second factory equipped with tools and ovens of his own design. (Etruria is the ancient land of the Etruscans, in what is now northern Italy.)

Fielding wheat and daisy pewter top syrup pitcher, 5" high. **$272**

Courtesy of Strawser Auction Group, www.strawserauctions.com

Minton stag head sweetmeat dish, England, 1864, polychrome enamel decorated and modeled with circular dish set atop cornucopia-shaped stem terminating at stag head, all set on raised oval base, impressed marks, areas of antlers professionally restored, 4 1/4" high. **$570**

Courtesy of Skinner, Inc., www.skinnerinc.com

Minton beehive cheese dome and stand, England, circa 1865, polychrome enamel decorated and modeled with twig handle on coiled straw body with vines, octagonal twig-form stand with scattered leaves, impressed mark, dome and stand each with professional restorations, 13 1/4" high overall. **$3,444**

Courtesy of Skinner, Inc., www.skinnerinc.com

George Jones punch bowl, England, circa 1870, enameled earthenware with reclining figure of Punch holding textured orange ground bowl with holly and berries, painted design number 3468 and impressed registry mark, 13 1/4" diameter, 9 3/4" high. **$3,075**

Courtesy of Skinner, Inc., www.skinnerinc.com

Victorian centerpiece, Stoke-on-Trent, Staffordshire, England, 1870, nautilus shell-form with cobalt blue ground and turquoise glazed interior, decorated with relief figures of water nymphs and tritons, supported on the backs of two tritons on oval base. 20 7/8" x 17 1/2" x 7 7/8". **$4,300**

Courtesy of Heritage Auctions, www.ha.com

Monkey Handle Teapot, George Jones & Sons, Staffordshire, England, circa 1880, cobalt blue with molded dogwood decoration to body and blossom finial to lid, monkey handle to back, naturalistic branch spout, 6" tall. **$1,500**

Courtesy of Heritage Auctions, www.ha.com

Fielding turquoise shells and fishnet pitcher with coral handle, base chip to underside, 6 1/2" high. **$303**

Courtesy of Strawser Auction Group, www.strawserauctions.com

Victorian jug, Minton, Stroke-on-Trent, Staffordshire, England, circa 1867, pineapple motive, 9" x 6 1/2" diameter, **$1,195.**

Courtesy of Heritage Auctions, www.ha.com

Continental garden seat, circa 1880, round base with three figural sea monsters to stem, round seat with Greek key border to geometric floral motif to center, 18 1/8" high x 12 3/4" diameter. **$937**

Courtesy of Heritage Auctions, www.ha.com

Fielding shells and fishnet pitcher with coral handle, hairline crack on spout, minor surface wear, 7" high. **$272**

Courtesy of Strawser Auction Group, www.strawserauctions.com

Shells and coral on waves pitcher, 8" high. **$575**

Courtesy of Strawser Auction Group, www.strawserauctions.com

Minton bowl, England, date cipher for 1867, circular shape with pale pink exterior and orange interior, three frogs on faux cobblestone base, impressed factory mark and cipher marks, 4 1/8" high. **$984**

Courtesy of Skinner, Inc., www.skinnerinc.com

▲ Delphin Massier jardinière and pedestal, France, early 20th century, enameled earthenware with five scrolled foliate handles on allover foliate molded body, pedestal with standing flamingo, professionally restored rim chips and body on jardinière, jardinière 14 1/2" high, 46 1/4" high overall. **$3,567**

Courtesy of Skinner, Inc., www.skinnerinc.com

▶ Sarreguemines Coupe Sandier, France, late 19th century, designed by Alexandre Sandier, large bowl molded with classical children among chain festoons terminating at ribbon ties, pedestal with central urn framed within three caryatid supports on radiating circular base, 29" diameter, 47 1/2" high overall. **$2,706**

Courtesy of Skinner, Inc., www.skinnerinc.com

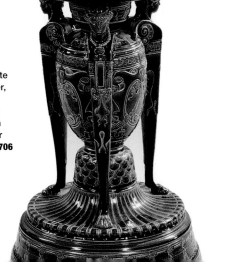

Rookwood

Maria Longworth Nichols founded Rookwood Pottery in 1880. The name, she later reported, paid homage to the many crows (rooks) on her father's estate and was also designed to remind customers of Wedgwood. Production began on Thanksgiving Day 1880 when the first kiln was drawn.

Rookwood's earliest productions demonstrated a continued reliance on European precedents and the Japanese aesthetic. Although the firm offered a variety of wares (Dull Glaze, Cameo, and Limoges for example), it lacked a clearly defined artistic identity. With the introduction of what became known as its "standard glaze" in 1884, Rookwood inaugurated a period in which the company won consistent recognition for its artistic merit and technical innovation.

Rookwood's first decade ended on a high note when the company was awarded two gold medals: one at the Exhibition of American Art Industry in Philadelphia and another later in the year at the Exposition Universelle in Paris. Significant, too, was Maria Longworth Nichols' decision to transfer her interest in the company to William W. Taylor, who had been the firm's manager since 1883. In May 1890, the board of a newly reorganized Rookwood Pottery Co. purchased "the real estate, personal property, goodwill, patents, trade-marks… now the sole property of William W. Taylor" for $40,000.

Under Taylor's leadership, Rookwood was transformed from a fledgling startup to successful

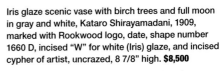

Iris glaze scenic vase with birch trees and full moon in gray and white, Kataro Shirayamadani, 1909, marked with Rookwood logo, date, shape number 1660 D, incised "W" for white (Iris) glaze, and incised cypher of artist, uncrazed, 8 7/8" high. **$8,500**

Courtesy of Mark Mussio, Humler & Nolan, humlernolan.com

Rare Iris glaze plaque with four-masted ship near Kennebuck, Maine, by Sturgis Laurence in 1903, signed SL in lower left-hand corner and marked on back with large Rookwood logo, date, notation X1168X, and incised notation "Mouth of the Kennebuck Sturgis Laurence," uncrazed, 10 1/8" x 14 3/8". **$12,100**

Courtesy of Mark Mussio, Humler & Nolan, humlernolan.com

business that expanded throughout the following decades to meet rising demand.

Throughout the 1890s, Rookwood continued to attract critical notice as it kept the tradition of innovation alive. Taylor rolled out three new glaze lines—Iris, Sea Green and Aerial Blue—from late 1894 into early 1895.

At the Paris Exposition in 1900, Rookwood cemented its reputation by winning the Grand Prix, a feat largely due to the favorable reception of the new Iris glaze and its variants.

Over the next several years, Rookwood's record of achievement at domestic and international exhibitions remained unmatched.

Throughout the 1910s, Rookwood continued in a similar vein and began to more thoroughly embrace the simplified aesthetic promoted by many Arts and Crafts figures. Production of the Iris line, which had been instrumental in the firm's success at the Paris Exposition in 1900, ceased around 1912. Not only did the company abandon its older, fussier underglaze wares, but the newer lines the pottery introduced also trended toward simplicity.

Unfortunately, the collapse of the stock market in October 1929 and ensuing economic depression dealt Rookwood a blow from which it did not recover. The Great Depression took a toll on the company and eventually led to bankruptcy in April 1941.

Rookwood's history might have ended there were it not for the purchase of the firm by a group of investors led by automobile dealer Walter E. Schott and his wife, Margaret. Production started once again. In the years that followed, Rookwood changed hands a number of times before being moved to Starkville, Mississippi, in 1960. It finally closed its doors there in 1967.

For more information on Rookwood, see *Warman's Rookwood Pottery Identification and Price Guide* by Denise Rago and Jonathan Clancy.

Porcelain lidded coffee pot with spout stopper, decorated by Arthur Conant in 1933 with scene of wild hog peering through reeds, impressed Rookwood symbol, date and shape 6330, pot, lid and stopper in excellent original condition, 11 1/2" high. **$4,200**

Courtesy of Mark Mussio, Humler & Nolan, humlernolan.com

Rare Double Bunny paperweight in violet gray glaze, Kataro Shirayamadani design, 1953, marked with company logo, date, and shape number 6643, uncrazed excellent condition, 3" high. **$2,420**

Courtesy of Mark Mussio, Humler & Nolan, humlernolan.com

Early vase decorated by Laura Fry, 1882, incised geometric pattern along rim, incised blue and green fronds with gilt outlines, 1882 Rookwood logo, artist's initials, reads 1882 Cincinnati Pottery Club, even crazing with slight loss to gilt, 6 3/4" high. **$2,829**

Courtesy of Cowan's Auctions, Inc., cowanauction.com

"Hazy Day" landscape Vellum plaque of country road and trees beneath variegated sky, Fred Rothenbusch, 1925, signed with artist monogram in lower right-hand corner, impressed with Rookwood symbol and date on back, label attached to original frame with title and identification of artist, excellent original condition, 11 3/4" x 8 3/4". **$4,100**

Courtesy of Mark Mussio, Humler & Nolan, humlernolan.com

Rare oil lamp with matching ceramic oil font and matching glass shade with carved and hand-colored green and mauve thistles and rare shade in two colors, Rose Fechheimer, 1903, marked with company logo, shape number 652 Z (later becoming shape number 1041 in regular line), and Fechheimer's full name in black slip, excellent original condition, converted to electricity, 24 3/4" high, ceramic portion 14 3/4" high. **$6,250**

Courtesy of Mark Mussio, Humler & Nolan, humlernolan.com

Rookwood advertising sign with dark blue rook perched on branch with green leaves and name of pottery, made in 1915, impressed on back with Rookwood insignia, date and shape 1622, minor edge and corner chips, 4 1/4" x 8 1/2". **$5,250**

Courtesy of Mark Mussio, Humler & Nolan, humlernolan.com

Pair of Union Terminal bookends, designed by Arthur Conant, cast in 1933 and covered with Ivory Mat Glaze, impressed Rookwood symbol, date and shape 6378, uncrazed with fine detail, excellent original condition, 4 1/2" x 7". **$6,250**

Courtesy of Mark Mussio, Humler & Nolan, humlernolan.com

Hand-carved Vellum glazed advertising tile from 1908, Rookwood Pottery banner near top with three rooks sitting on carved perch below, marks: Rookwood logo, date, impressed V and incised V for Vellum, overall crazing with small glaze skips in white Vellum field, 5 1/2" x 7 3/8". **$2,700**

Courtesy of Mark Mussio, Humler & Nolan, humlernolan.com

Porcelain covered box decorated by Sara Sax in 1930, stylized flowers and geometric details in Art Deco tradition, impressed on base with Rookwood symbol, date, shape 6205 and fan-shaped esoteric mark, artist's monogram in black slip, 5" high x 7" x 4 1/2". **$2,300**

Courtesy of Mark Mussio, Humler & Nolan, humlernolan.com

Round lidded box in blue Vellum glaze decorated with cherries and leaves by Sarah "Sallie" E. Coyne, impressed Rookwood logo, dated 1926, shape 2927, and artist's initials on underside of base and lid, 8 1/4" diameter. **$1,680**

Courtesy of Cowan's Auctions, Inc., cowanauctions.com

Three-piece inkwell modeled by Anna Valentien in 1902 with nude draped around opening, mat green glaze, impressed with Rookwood insignia, date and shape 156 Z, incised with artist monogram, ink cup has chip to one edge, tiny nick to interior edge that supports ink cup, both unseen when lid is in place, 4 1/4" high. **$1,200**

Courtesy of Mark Mussio, Humler & Nolan, humlernolan.com

Cameo potpourri jar by A. R. Valentien with a bird on a branch, 1886, stamped ROOKWOOD 1886/Y/27 A.R.V., 7 1/2" x 6". **$1,000-$1,500**

Standard Glaze mug of lion in midst of roar by E.T. Hurley in 1898, impressed Rookwood insignia indicating date and shape number 587 C, lightly incised with Hurley's cipher, excellent original condition with faint crazing, 4 5/8" high. **$726**

Courtesy of Mark Mussio, Humler & Nolan, humlernolan.com

Standard glaze mug with kitten skipping rope with piece of yarn, decorated by Bruce Horsfall in 1893, marks: Rookwood logo, date, shape 587, impressed W for white clay and artist's cipher, excellent original condition with no crazing, 4 5/8" high. **$1,400**

Courtesy of Mark Mussio, Humler & Nolan, humlernolan.com

Dull Glaze pitcher with butterflies, A. R. Valentien, 1886, impressed Rookwood symbol with date, shape 308 X, and Y for yellow clay, incised with artist's monogram, professional restoration to rim and upper portion of handle where it attaches to body, 19 3/4" high. **$1,500**

Courtesy of Mark Mussio, Humler & Nolan, humlernolan.com

Vase by Kitaro Shirayamadani, 1899, painted with a heron spreading its wings amidst tall grasses, the bottom wrapped in a bronze overlay of flowers and large leaves, 12 1/2" x 5". **$35,000-$45,000**

Silver-overlaid Standard Glaze two-handled vase by Kitaro Shirayamadani, 1898, painted with orange and golden yellow chrysanthemums and green leaves, and covered in Gorham silver with whiplash strands, 12" x 6 1/2". **$10,000-$15,000**

Sea Green pillow vase with crescent rim, decorated by Edward Diers, 1899, with tall stems and leaves in green against a blue and celadon ground, wrapped in a bronze overlay of iris blossoms, 4 1/2" x 4". **$17,500-$25,000**

Carved and incised mat glaze vase with dandelion decoration by Kataro Shirayamadani in 1902, Arts & Crafts style, repeating dandelion leaves, stems, and flowers in green and yellow on rose-colored ground, concentric lines encircle shoulder with small dots of green between lines, marked with Rookwood logo, date, shape number 927 E, and incised cypher of artist, excellent condition, 6 5/8" high. **$6,655**

Courtesy of Mark Mussio, Humler & Nolan, humlernolan.com

Iris glaze vase with five fish against background of green, cream, and white, E. T. Hurley, 1904, marked with Rookwood logo, date, shape number 942 C, incised "W" for white (Iris) glaze, and incised initials of Hurley, uncrazed, 6 1/4" high. **$6,000**

Courtesy of Mark Mussio, Humler & Nolan, humlernolan.com

Large, rare Vellum glaze vase decorated by A.R. Valentien, with two carved rooks on branch, ombred green background, signed, dated 1901, and marked 198 AZ, fine condition, small scuffs inside mouth, 13" high x 7" diameter. Albert Robert Valentien or Valentine was head of the decorating department at Rookwood in Cincinnati. Namesake rooks seldom appeared on pieces, but were done by special request. **$25,875**

Courtesy of Thomaston Place Auction Galleries, thomastonauction.com

Modeled Mat vase by William Hentschel with deeply mottled poppies and curvilinear stems in flowing light green on a maroon ground, 1912, flame mark/XII/907B/artist's cipher, 17 1/2" x 7". **$4,500-$6,500**

Rare, important and monumental Iris glaze vase with life-size white cattleya orchids, Carl Schmidt, 1903, marked with special shape number of S 1611 A (denoting largest size, A), company logo, date, shape number, incised "W" for white (Iris) glaze, and impressed monogram of Schmidt, uncrazed, two scratches, 19 1/8". **$15,000**

Courtesy of Mark Mussio, Humler & Nolan, humlernolan.com

Large Later Mat/Mat Moderne urn, 1930, flame mark / XXX / 6010C / artist cipher, 11 1/2" x 10 1/2". **$1,000**

Courtesy of Rago Arts and Auctions, ragoarts.com

Roseville Pottery

Roseville is one of the most widely recognizable of potteries in the United States. Having been sold in flower shops and drugstores across the country, Roseville art and production wares became a staple in American homes until the company closed its doors in the 1950s.

The Roseville Pottery Co., located in Roseville, Ohio, was incorporated on Jan. 4, 1892, with George F. Young as general manager. The company had been producing stoneware since 1890, when it purchased the J. B. Owens Pottery, also of Roseville.

The popularity of Roseville Pottery's original lines of stoneware grew. The company acquired new plants in 1892 and 1898, and production started to shift to Zanesville, just a few miles away. By about 1910, all of the work was centered in Zanesville, but the company name was unchanged.

Young hired Ross C. Purdy as artistic designer in 1900, and Purdy created Rozane – a contraction of the words "Roseville" and "Zanesville." The first Roseville artwork pieces were marked either Rozane or RPCO, both impressed or ink-stamped on the bottom.

In 1902, a line was developed called Azurean. Some pieces were marked Azurean,

Pine Cone umbrella stand in blue, shape number 777, impressed "Roseville 777-20" on bottom with old Cincinnati Art Galleries label from Rookwood VII, excellent original condition, uncrazed, 20 1/4" high. **$1,150**

Courtesy of Mark Mussio, Humler & Nolan, humlernolan.com

Experimental Geranium vase with pink flowers on front and incised "Geranium Flowers white pink rose" on back, marked "Flower 58 washed 168 8-34-103" in black grease pencil on bottom, excellent original condition, 9" high. **$2,400**

Courtesy of Mark Mussio, Humler & Nolan, humlernolan.com

Dealer advertising sign, 1940s, Roseville script mark in yellow matte against pink matte background, excellent original condition, 4 5/8" x 7 3/4". **$1,000**

Courtesy of Mark Mussio, Humler & Nolan, humlernolan.com

but more often RPCO. In 1904 at the St. Louis Exposition, Roseville's Rozane Mongol, a high-gloss oxblood red line, captured first prize, gaining recognition for the firm and its creator, John Herold.

Many Roseville lines were a response to the innovations of Weller Pottery, and in 1904 Frederick Rhead was hired away from Weller as artistic director. He created the Olympic and Della Robbia lines for Roseville. His brother Harry took over as artistic director in 1908, and in 1915 he introduced the popular Donatello line.

By 1908, all handcrafting ended except for Rozane Royal. Roseville was the first pottery in Ohio to install a tunnel kiln, which increased its production capacity.

Frank Ferrell, who was a top decorator at Weller Pottery by 1904, was Roseville's artistic director from 1917 until 1954. This Zanesville native created many of the most popular lines, including Pine Cone, which had scores of individual pieces.

Many collectors believe Roseville's circa 1925 glazes were the best of any Zanesville pottery. George Krause, who in 1915 became Roseville's technical supervisor responsible for glaze, remained with Roseville until the 1950s.

Company sales declined after World War II, especially in the early 1950s when cheap Japanese imports began to replace American wares, and a simpler, more modern style made many of Roseville's elaborate floral designs seem old-fashioned.

In the late 1940s Roseville began to issue lines with glossy glazes. Then the company tried to offset its flagging artware sales by launching a dinnerware line – Raymor – in 1953. The line was a commercial failure.

Roseville issued its last new designs in 1953. On Nov. 29, 1954, the facilities of Roseville were sold to the Mosaic Tile Co.

For more information on Roseville, see *Warman's Roseville Pottery,* 2nd edition, by Denise Rago.

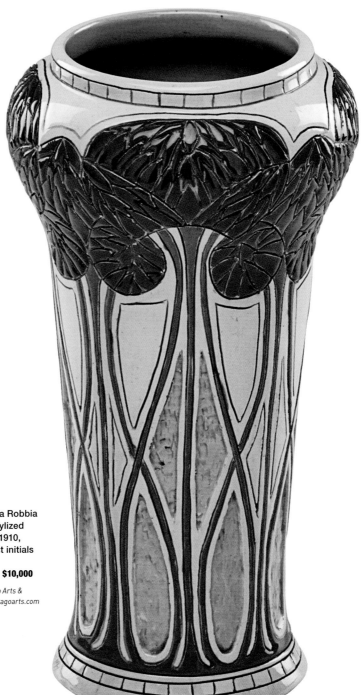

Rozane Della Robbia
vase with stylized
trees, circa 1910,
incised artist initials
to body,
10" x 5 1/2". **$10,000**

*Courtesy of Rago Arts &
Auction Center, ragoarts.com*

Pair of green Baneda candlesticks, 1087-5", foil labels. **$450-$650**

Rare Egypto oil lamp base consisting of three elephants with riders providing support for font area, marked with Rozane Ware Egypto wafer seal on bottom, older restoration to large chip on flat base, 10 1/2" high. **$1,000**

Courtesy of Mark Mussio, Humler & Nolan, humlernolan.com

Blackberry hanging basket, 348-5", unmarked, 5" x 7". **$850-$1,250**

Roseville dealer advertising sign made during 1940s, Roseville script in white against blue background, excellent original condition with light crazing, 4 1/2" high x 8" wide. **$650**

Courtesy of Mark Mussio, Humler & Nolan, humlernolan.com

Olympic tankard titled "Triptolemos and the Grain of Wheat," three classic Greek figures with repeating bands at top and base, marked in black on bottom "Rozane Pottery Triptolemos and the Grain of Wheat," excellent condition with minor scratches, 11" high. **$2,000**

Courtesy of Mark Mussio, Humler & Nolan, humlernolan.com

Olympic vase on three feet, three full-length classical women with repeating bands around rim and foot, unmarked, red color with overspray, 13 1/8" high. **$1,200**

Courtesy of Mark Mussio, Humler & Nolan, humlernolan.com

Chloron pattern "Knight" wall sconce, shape number E-61 in listing of Chloron pattern forms, thick leathery Egypto-like glaze, unmarked, minor edge nicks and restoration to small chip at top edge of sconce, 17 1/4" high. **$1,800**

Courtesy of Mark Mussio, Humler & Nolan, humlernolan.com

Tourist vase depicting tourists on country road in red car, wide dark bands, unmarked, some crazing and two glaze bubbles, fine original condition, 12 3/8" high. **$1,100**

Courtesy of Mark Mussio, Humler & Nolan, humlernolan.com

Crystalis oil lamp vase on Egypto form of three elephants with riders that form support for oil font holder, reddish orange Crystalis glaze covers inside and outside of vase, large crystals visible on flatter surfaces, marked with Rozane Ware Egypto wafer seal, restoration to small base chip, 10 5/8" high. **$2,900**

Courtesy of Mark Mussio, Humler & Nolan, humlernolan.com

Large Sunflower jardinière on pedestal, marked with shape number and size 619-10 in red crayon beneath, pedestal with factory firing separation inside base rim, excellent condition, jardinière 10 1/8" x 10 1/2" across rim, pedestal 18 1/2" high, 28 1/2" high combined. **$3,025**

Courtesy of Mark Mussio, Humler & Nolan, humlernolan.com

Large Blackberry pattern jardinière on pedestal, unmarked, excellent original condition, minor black glaze runs, jardinière 10 1/4" high x 13 1/2" handle to handle, pedestal 18" high, 28 1/4" high combined. **$1,300**

Courtesy of Mark Mussio, Humler & Nolan, humlernolan.com

Fine and rare Imperial II bowl embossed with banded snail-like design around body, covered in a pale dripping green glaze over a pink ground, 202-6", a very fine example of this form, unmarked, 4 1/2". **$2,250-$3,250**

Rare Aztec jardinière and pedestal, circa 1915, artist's cipher on pedestal, 35 1/2" x 16" overall. **$1,875**

Courtesy of Rago Arts & Auction Center, ragoarts.com

Green Freesia teapot, 6-T, sugar, 6-S, and a creamer, 6-C, raised marks. **$200-$400**

Chloron pattern "Woman's Head" wall pocket in Egypto-like glaze with leathery texture, shape number 345 in listing of Chloron pattern pieces, unmarked, back side appears to have had major restoration, 9 3/8" high. **$1,300**

Courtesy of Mark Mussio, Humler & Nolan, humlernolan.com

Della Robbia vase with stylized poppies done by artisan with initials "KO," four carved flowers and many seed pods encircle vase, marked with artist's initials on side, shape 27 in Della Robbia line, light overall crazing, excellent original condition, 14 1/4" high. **$9,750**

Courtesy of Mark Mussio, Humler & Nolan, humlernolan.com

Fudji vase in several shades of blue, unmarked, excellent original condition, 7 3/4" high. **$2,600**

Courtesy of Mark Mussio, Humler & Nolan, humlernolan.com

Tall rare Della Robbia vase with wild roses and cut-out rim, circa 1910, raised Rozane Ware seal, incised artist's signature on bottom and initials on side, 15 1/2" x 6". **$43,750**

Courtesy of Rago Arts & Auction Center, ragoarts.com

Oversize Baneda vase, shape number 600, in mottled green glaze with flow of blue glaze extending from wide decorative band to dribbles of color on foot, marked with Roseville Pottery Rv foil sticker, excellent original condition, 15 1/4" high. **$1,573**

Courtesy of Mark Mussio, Humler & Nolan, humlernolan.com

Weller Pottery

Weller Pottery was made from 1872 to 1945 at a pottery established originally by Samuel A. Weller at Fultonham, Ohio and moved in 1882 to Zanesville, Ohio.

Weller's famous pottery slugged it out with several other important Zanesville potteries for decades. Cross-town rivals such as Roseville, Owens, La Moro, and McCoy were all serious fish in a fairly small and well-stocked lake. While Weller occasionally landed some solid body punches with many of his better art lines, the prevailing thought was that his later production ware just wasn't up to snuff.

Samuel Weller was a notorious copier and, it is said, a bit of a scallywag. He paid designers such as William Long to bring their famous discoveries to Zanesville. He then attempted to steal their secrets, and, when successful, renamed them and made them his own.

After World War I, when the cost of materials became less expensive than the cost of labor, many companies, including the famous Rookwood Pottery, increased their output of less expensive production ware. Weller Pottery followed along in the trend of production ware by introducing scores of interesting and unique lines, the likes of which have never been created anywhere else, before or since.

In addition to a number of noteworthy production lines, Weller continued in the creation of hand-painted ware long after Roseville abandoned them. Some of the more interesting Hudson pieces, for example, are post-World War I pieces. Even later lines, such as Bonito, were hand painted and often signed by important artists such as Hester Pillsbury. The closer you look at Weller's output after 1920, the more obvious the fact that it was the only Zanesville company still producing both quality art ware and quality production ware.

For more information on Weller pottery, see *Warman's Weller Pottery Identification and Price Guide* by Denise Rago and David Rago.

Sicard candlestick in green and gold with shamrock designs, signed Weller and Sicard on opposite sides near base, excellent condition, 7 1/2" high. **$450**

Courtesy of Mark Mussio, Humler & Nolan, humlernolan.com

Coppertone helmet-shaped bowl with frog seated on edge and trio of fish cast on outer portion of bowl, marked with Weller Pottery half kiln ink stamp and either 3B or 38 on bottom, excellent original condition, 5 1/2" high x 10" long. **$425**

Courtesy of Mark Mussio, Humler & Nolan, humlernolan.com

Jewell footed dresser box with cover, embossed face of maiden, mermaids/fish around base portion, cosmetic repair to nose of maiden, very good condition, 4 1/2" high x 5 1/2" diameter. **$400**

Courtesy of Mark Mussio, Humler & Nolan, humlernolan.com

Sicard candlestick with swirls of green, gold, and purple, signed Weller and Sicard on opposite sides of base, excellent condition, 6 1/2". **$500**

Courtesy of Mark Mussio, Humler & Nolan, humlernolan.com

▲ Flemish hanging shade with garlands embossed in surface, impressed Weller inside, brass hanging hooks attached, electrical fixture inside with opaque globe in center of shade, wiring not operative, excellent original condition with minor rubs, 17 1/2" diameter. **$550**

Courtesy of Mark Mussio, Humler & Nolan, humlernolan.com

◄ Roma hanging chandelier, impressed "Weller" inside shade, fine overall crazing, 17 1/2" dia. **$500**

Courtesy of Mark Mussio, Humler & Nolan, humlernolan.com

C

Ewer, Dickensware II, rare and unusual, shows a golfer and caddy along a deeply incised line of trees. Impressed mark, 11" x 5". **$3,000-$4,000**

▲ Jar, Selma, lidded, decorated with swans, impressed mark, 4 1/4". **$650-$950**

◄ Selma covered jar with repeating pattern of bluebirds in apple tree, impressed with WELLER on bottom, restoration to small chip on lid and fine overall crazing, 7 7/8" high. **$650**

Courtesy of Mark Mussio, Humler & Nolan, humlernolan.com

Coppertone Gardenware Pan with Rabbit figure, impressed on bottom with Weller Pottery script logo, excellent original condition, 13 5/8" high. **$3,000**

Courtesy of Mark Mussio, Humler & Nolan, humlernolan.com

Gardenware rooster, naturalistic mat tones, incised Weller logo, fine crazing, professional restoration to comb, some small chips at base, 12 7/8" high x 13" long. **$1,000**

Courtesy of Mark Mussio, Humler & Nolan, humlernolan.com

Rare Majolica-style jardinière and pedestal with flora, fauna, and scenes under high glaze, design by Rudolph Lorber, rim with great horned owl perched in branch before full moon, opposing side with landscape and Dutch windmill; lug handles on either side of jardiniere in shape of owl's head, pedestal with squirrel holding acorn, opposing side with night scene with castle and full moon; both pieces with molded surround of leaves, pinecones, and acorns bordering each vignette, conjoined initials of designer molded into pedestal, both pieces hand-incised; excellent original condition, jardinière 12" x 14 1/2" wide, pedestal 22 1/2" high, 34" high combined. **$3,630**

Courtesy of Mark Mussio, Humler & Nolan, humlernolan.com

Jardinière and pedestal set, Flemish, with birds and flowers on an ivory ground, unmarked, 30" overall, **$1,000-$2,000**

Tankard, Woodcraft, embossed with foxes in their den, impressed mark, 13" x 7". **$800-$1,200**

Courtesy of Mark Mussio, Humler & Nolan, humlernolan.com

Rare Minerva pitcher with two dancing satyrs on one side and autumnal forest on other, impressed "Weller" in large block letters on bottom, excellent original condition, 9 7/8" high. Provenance: Pitcher comes with 1977 warrant card from White Pillars Museum in Zanesville, Ohio, signed by Louise Purviance and Harold Nichols. **$2,000**

Courtesy of Mark Mussio, Humler & Nolan, humlernolan.com

Rare monumental Hudson vase by Mae Timberlake, pair of birds perched among branches of fruit tree, marked on bottom with circular Weller Ware ink stamp and signed by artist in blue slip near base, excellent condition, 29 3/8" high. **$8,500**

Courtesy of Mark Mussio, Humler & Nolan, humlernolan.com

Umbrella stand, Forest, 22". **$1,000-$1,500**

Rare etched mat scenic tankard showing swans in wooded pond, work of Albert Wilson, swans and water are incised, trees in background are painted, typical Weller numbers on bottom, signed A. Wilson on side in white slip, uncrazed with small glaze chip on spout and pinhead nick at base, 16 5/8" high. **$600**

Courtesy of Mark Mussio, Humler & Nolan, humlernolan.com

Rare Coppertone "Two Fish" vase, marked with Weller half-kiln ink stamp and marked with 2 and H in black slip, small chip to dorsal fin of smaller fish, good mold and color, 8". **$1,300**

Courtesy of Mark Mussio, Humler & Nolan, humlernolan.com

Rare large mat green vase with snake and bird, circa 1905, stamped WELLER, 18" x 8 1/2". **$8,125**

Courtesy of Rago Arts and Auctions, ragoarts.com

Tall Sicard vase with berry-filled branches, unsigned, shape number 472 on bottom, fine overall crazing and minor glaze rubs, 13 1/4" high. **$1,573**

Courtesy of Mark Mussio, Humler & Nolan, humlernolan.com

Etched mat vase decorated by Frank Ferrell, incised yellow flower and green leaves against tan ground, signed Ferrell on side with incised Weller and White Pillars Museum label on bottom, overall crazing, 10 3/4" high. **$1,331**

Courtesy of Mark Mussio, Humler & Nolan, humlernolan.com

Coppertone trumpet vase with quatrain of frogs surrounding base, Weller half kiln ink stamp with numbers 2 and 11 in green slip, excellent original condition, 11 1/2" high. **$1,600**

Courtesy of Mark Mussio, Humler & Nolan, humlernolan.com

Woodcraft wall pocket with two bluebirds, one in nest, one on branch, with red flowers and leaves, impressed Weller in block letters on rear, fine crazing with restoration to beak of bird on branch, minor firing separation to vine, 14 3/4" x 12". **$700**

Courtesy of Mark Mussio, Humler & Nolan, humlernolan.com

Hudson vase by Hester Pillsbury, two hummingbirds among honeysuckle flowers, incised "Weller Pottery" on bottom and signed "Pillsbury" above foot, fine overall crazing, 12 7/8" high. **$1,700**

Courtesy of Mark Mussio, Humler & Nolan, humlernolan.com

Sicard vase with floral pattern, signed Weller Sicard on side, fine overall crazing, 7 3/8" high. **$1,694**

Courtesy of Mark Mussio, Humler & Nolan, humlernolan.com

Clewell copper-clad corn vase on Weller L'Art Nouveau blank, Canton, Ohio, stamped L'ART NOUVEAU WELLER, 10" x 4". **$1,625**

Courtesy of Rago Arts and Auction, ragoarts.com

Hudson twin-handled vase decorated with robin perched among blooms on tree branch, artist's initials, LBM, are at base of piece in black slip, bottom marked with Weller Pottery half-kiln stamp and possibly the letter "A" in green slip, light overall crazing, 7 3/4" high. **$2,200**

Courtesy of Mark Mussio, Humler & Nolan, humlernolan.com

Woodcraft apple tree stump vase with black-faced owl perched at entrance of knothole with built-in floral arranger inside rim, impressed Weller and incised A, excellent condition, 15 1/2" high. **$1,331**

Courtesy of Mark Mussio, Humler & Nolan, humlernolan.com

Clocks

The clock is one of the oldest human inventions. The word "clock" (from the Latin word *clocca*, "bell") suggests that it was the sound of bells that also characterized early timepieces.

The first mechanical clocks to be driven by weights and gears were invented by medieval Muslim engineers. The first geared mechanical clock was invented by an 11th century Arab engineer in Islamic Spain. The knowledge of weight-driven mechanical clocks produced by Muslim engineers was transmitted to other parts of Europe through Latin translations of Arabic and Spanish texts.

In the early 14th century, existing clock mechanisms that used waterpower were being adapted to take their driving power from falling weights. Some form of oscillating mechanism controlled this power. The controlled release of power – the escapement – marks the beginning of the true mechanical clock.

The Dutch are credited with inventing the first pendulum clock in the mid-17th century. French clockmakers of the 17th and 18th centuries expanded on the Dutch pendulum concept by focusing on the cases of their clocks. Ornately lacquered bracket clocks in oak, marble, tortoiseshell, brass and gilt

bronze were typical, as were larger pedestal clocks sporting similarly Rococo details.

The English improved the pendulum by inventing a recoil, or anchor, escapement. This allowed for a longer pendulum, resulting a slower swing and less stress on the clock. Tall, walnut, long-case clocks were common in the 18th century.

The Austrian wall clock, or Vienna regulator, emerged at the end of the 18th century. These rectangular clocks were designed to reveal the slowly swinging pendulum. Most of these regulators ran for eight days between windings, while some could run for as long as six weeks.

Meanwhile, Colonial clockmakers flourished in Pennsylvania and New England. Prominent clockmakers included David Rittenhouse, the first director of the U.S. Mint. So accomplished was Rittenhouse that he was known as the king of Pennsylvania clockmakers. Others of note include Jacob Godchalk, his brother-in-law, Griffith Owen and John Paul, Jr., whose German-style tall clocks were marvels of maple, walnut and ivory.

In 1802, brothers Simon and Aaron Willard of Massachusetts invented the banjo clock. Although wildly popular, it would be Connecticut that would become known as the center of clock

Cartier diamond, jade, pearl, coral and rock crystal "Mystery Clock," No. 202085. Case: upper mother-of pearl, coral and rock crystal case measuring 6" diameter with gold-set diamonds at the hour positions, silver and gold framework, atop a diamond-set, onyx and jade Oriental motif pedestal, jade and pearl base measuring 6" by 4 1/2" with coral-set silver feet, bottom sterling movement cover, 14 3/8". Dial: tapered yellow gold and black enamel hands with diamond-encrusted center. Movement: base-mounted 3/4-plate eight-day lever movement, 15 jewels, wound and set through the base, mono-metallic balance with circular gear-toothed regulator, gold finish to the plates. Signed, with original red and gold fitted box, movement signed Cartier, base signed Cartier N. 202085. (The mystery effect achieved by this timepiece has the clock hands seemingly floating in space without any connection to the movement. The hands are set on two clear revolving discs with toothed metal outer rims that are propelled by gears hidden in the outer clock frame.) **$155,350**

Courtesy of Heritage Auctions, www.ha.com

making in the U.S. thanks to the likes of Eli Terry, Seth Thomas, Joseph Ives and others. Terry created decorative pillar-and-scroll shelf clocks in the early 19th century. Mass-produced and modestly priced, Terry's clocks became wildly popular.

With the introduction of the first spring-driven clocks in the mid 19th century, clocks became smaller and lighter. Balance wheels replaced pendulums, allowing greater portability, further expanding markets. Other manufacturers of note are Brewster & Ingrahams, the Ansonia Clock Company, Waterbury Clock Company, and the Sessions Clock Company.

Clock styles and clock technology advanced dramatically in the 1900s. Arts & Crafts design took hold, giving way to Art Deco, which in turn surrendered to Mid-century Modern. Clocks became strikingly utilitarian when Westclox introduced Big Ben, Baby Ben and Tiny Tim alarm clocks that fit nicely on cluttered nightstands. Even so, while technology and design leap forward, collectors find the craftsmanship, beauty and mechanical ingenuity of clocks made long ago timeless.

For more information checkout the National Association of Watch & Clock Collectors (www.nawcc.org).

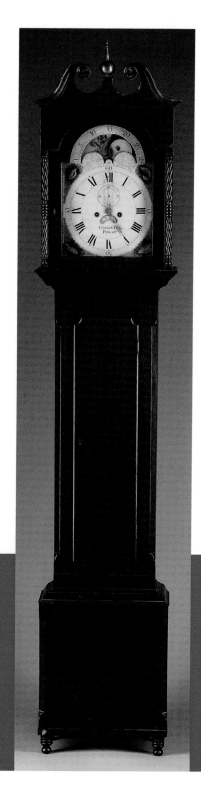

▶ Philadelphia Sheraton tall case clock, Crowley & Farr. Circa 1823-1825. Figured mahogany example with molded swan's neck pediment terminating in rosettes centering a ball-and-spire brass finial, the astragal-glazed door flanked by free-standing rope-twist colonnettes, opening to the painted dial with moon phase aperture, the dial with paint-decorated and gilt Nautilus spandrels and shells, centering a Roman numeral dial marked with minutes, further centering a calendar aperture and subsidiary seconds dial, marked "Crowley & Farr / PHILAD,a". With winder, door keys, single brass finial, pendulum, and two weights, 8'4" h. x 15" throat w. x 9 1/2" d. **$2,875**

Courtesy James D. Julia Auctioneers, www.JuliaAuctions.com

English painted and gilt wood tall-case clock, late 18th century; dial signed "John Burges Gosport", 86" x 19 1/2" x 10". The bonnet with shaped and arched crown over glazed door flanked by colonettes, waist with shaped door, raised on bracket feet, decorated all over in black paint with gilt chinoiserie motifs. **$4,182**

Courtesy of Heritage Auctions, www. ha.com

Rare American Federal inlaid mahogany dwarf clock with alarm, signed R. Tower, Kingston, case attributed to Henry Willard, circa 1821-1824, forward sliding hood with fretwork between three brass finials over arched cornice supported by plain columns, sides pierced with lozenge array of circular holes, trunk with crossbanded long door, crossbanded plinth with applied bead molding above French feet, finely painted white dial with foliage, urn and drapery in arch, gilt spandrels enclosing roman chapter ring, blued steel arrow hands, two barrel weight driven brass movement with rectangular plates joined by four pillars, anchor escapement, iron rod pendulum with brass bob, separately wound alarm train planted on side of movement, 50 1/2" high. **$91,500**

Courtesy of Bonhams, www.bonhams. com

New Jersey Federal inlaid mahogany tall-case clock, unsigned, painted iron moon-phase dial and eight-day brass works, hood with broken-arch pediment, brass finials and reeded columns, waist with reeded quarter columns and inlaid ovals, string-inlaid base raised on replaced bracket feet. First quarter 19th century, 100" overall, base 9 1/2" x 20 1/2", top 10" x 20 7/8", with some small repairs to case. **$4,600**

Courtesy of Jeffrey S. Evans & Associates, www.jeffreyevans.com

Arts & Crafts oak tall clock with Regina musical box, circa 1900, chamfered edge crown molding above glazed door opening to composite brass dial with Arabic numerals and cast brass spandrels, eight-day time and gong strike movement marked Seth Thomas, chain driven with two brass-cased weights, beveled glass waist door and side glass, all above Regina musical box playing six different tunes on single disc, with 14 bells, 90" high. **$7,110**

Courtesy of Skinner, Inc., www. skinnerinc.com

E. Howard No. 12 wall regulator, E. Howard & Company, Boston, circa 1875, black walnut case with turned molded bezel over 15" diameter painted zinc Roman numeral dial inscribed E. Howard & Company, Boston, lower door with black, gold and maroon painted tablet, eight-day damascened brass plate, time-only movement with dead-beat escapement, maintaining power and Geneva stop, iron weight and four jar etched glass mercury temperature compensating pendulum and looking glass behind, 62" high. **$26,070**

Courtesy of Skinner, Inc., www. skinnerinc.com

James Arthur Regulator with Remontoir, New York, 1901, maple case with molded top, glazed dial and waist doors and mirrored back, skeletonized movement stamped with maker's name and date with three front mounted dials, seconds at top, hours object lower right and minutes, lower left, dead-beat escapement with adjustable pallet faces, lever activated one minute remontoir rewound by large brass cased weight and internal "ball" pulley all regulated by steel grid iron pendulum and cylindrical bob, 81" high. **$15,405**

Courtesy of Skinner, Inc., www. skinnerinc.com

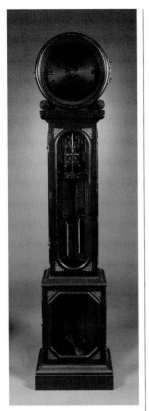

James Arthur drum-head tall clock, James Arthur, New York City, 1903, mahogany case with 14" brass Roman numeral dial stamped by maker, glazed waist door with eight-day time, wooden and brass wheeled skeletonized movement with dead-beat escapement, signed "James Arthur 1903" and "James Arthur Co. New York," transfer gearing to transmit power to hands, applied plaque stating "To Bessie Humphrey Arthur, From her Father James Arthur, October 24th, 1904," powered by two brass-cased weights and regulated by a brass bob, wooden rod pendulum, 87". **$4,444**

Courtesy of Skinner, Inc.,
www.skinnerinc.com

Jan Gobels burl walnut marquetry tall clock, Amsterdam, circa 1760, case with blind sound fret in crest, flat fluted columns with Corinthian capitals flanking composite brass dial with silvered Roman numeral chapter ring engraved "Jan Gobels Amsterdam," engraved and matted center with calendar, cast brass four seasons spandrels, moon's age in arch with lunar and tidal calibrations, tombstone-shaped waist door with oval lentical and floral and scroll marquetry pattern inlays, bombe base with similar decoration all on hairy paw feet, eight-day time and Dutch striking movement with two bells, two iron cased weights and pendulum, 100 1/2" high. **$6,518**

Courtesy of Skinner, Inc.,
www.skinnerinc.com

Benjamin Willard tall clock, Roxbury, Massachusetts, no. 207, circa 1780, silvered sheet brass dial engraved "Benja. Willard Roxbury, No. 207," and "Ab Hoc Momento Pendet Eternitas" with phoenix in arch, fret-top maple case with fan-carved waist door flanked by thumbnail corners, all on two-stage molded bracket foot base, eight-day time and strike movement with rack and snail strike regulated by wooden pendulum rod and brass-faced bob all powered by two period iron weights, 87 1/2" high. **$23,700**

Courtesy of Skinner, Inc.,
www.skinnerinc.com

Empire-style green marble, patinated and gilt bronze figural mantle clock with Cupid and Psyche, early 20th century, 30 1/2" x 19 1/2" x 8". **$9,375**

Courtesy of Heritage Auctions, www.ha.com

French empire-style marble and gilt bronze mounted figural mantle clock, 20th century, marks to mechanism: TIFFANY & CO, A1 (encircled), 16 1/2" high. **$1,625**

Courtesy of Heritage Auctions, www.ha.com

R. Lalique topaz glass le jour et la nuit clock, circa 1926, France, M p. 372, No. 728, 14 3/4" tall. **$47,000**

Courtesy of Heritage Auctions, www.ha.com

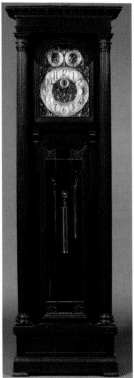

Bigelow, Kennard & Co. mahogany nine tubular bell chime clock, London, circa 1890, flat-top case with dentil and scrolled molding, fluted columns with carved capitols flanking tombstone upper door, composite brass dial with Arabic numerals marked Bigelow Kennard & Co., subsidiary dials tune selection and chime silent, glazed waist door, eight-day quarter-chiming movement on nine tubular bells, marked "J.J.E. Made in England," pendulum and three brass cased weights, 92" high. **$2,160**

Courtesy of Skinner, Inc., www.skinnerinc.com

Ephraim Willard rocking ship tall clock, Boston, circa 1800, mahogany case with inlaid scroll-top hood and vase-shape classical brass finials, applied handles, brass stop-fluted freestanding columns flanking 13" painted iron Roman numeral dial inscribed "Warranted for Mr. James Gardner, E. Willard, Boston," with painted rocking American ship automaton in arch and gilt scroll spandrels, rectangular waist door with line and marquetry inlays flanked by brass stop fluted quarter columns and marquetry plinths, base with line and fan inlay on French feet, eight-day time, hour striking movement with iron weights and seconds beating pendulum, 95" high. **$42,000**

Courtesy of Skinner, Inc., www.skinnerinc.com

Simon Willard rocking ship tall clock, Roxbury, circa 1810, mahogany case with fret top, brass, stop-fluted, freestanding columns flanking 12" painted iron Roman numeral dial inscribed Simon Willard, floral spandrels and painted arch with American coastal scene, rocking ship automaton and ship in background, both flying American flags, inlaid rectangular waist door flanked by brass stop fluted quarter columns, inlaid base and tall bracket feet, eight-day, time and hour strike movement with two tin-cased weights, period pendulum and key, 91" high. **$31,200**

Courtesy of Skinner, Inc., www.skinnerinc.com

Father Time statue clock, France, circa 1880, eight-day, spring-powered, time and count-wheel strike movement, 3 1/2" black dial with applied brass Roman numerals, serpent hands, ouroboros bezel, brass crescent moon pendulum bob, carried by patinated brass statue of winged, bearded man with scythe, black slate plinth, 16" high. **$2,214**

Courtesy of Skinner, Inc., www.skinnerinc.com

Dutch Rococo ormolu-mounted red and gilt japanned musical clock, circa 1740, with matching later bracket, 24 1/4" high x 14 1/4" wide x 9 1/4" deep. **$12,500**

Courtesy of Sotheby's, www.sothebys.com

Large Black Forest carved wood and ivory mantle clock, 19th century, minor restoration to elk's removable antlers, scuffing at anchor for clock key, 57 3/4" x 27" x 15". **$23,750**

Courtesy of Heritage Auctions, www.ha.com

▶ Rare directoire ormolu and patinated bronze "Bon Savage" mantel clock, circa 1795, dial signed "Piel À Paris," 21 1/2" high x 16 3/4" wide x 5 3/4 " deep. **$62,500**

Courtesy of Sotheby's, www.sothebys.com

Louis XIV-style ormolu-mounted brass and tortoiseshell-inlaid bracket clock, late 19th century, signed "E. Gübelin Lucerne," 48" high x 17" wide x 8 1/2" deep. **$5,000**

Courtesy of Sotheby's, www.sothebys.com

Oak calendar wall clock, Prentiss Clock Improvement Co., 36 1/2" high. **$1,230**

Courtesy of Pook & Pook, Inc., www.pookandpook.com

Uncommon George Nelson & Associates wall clock, model 2241, by Howard Miller Clock Co., circa 1957, brass, lacquered wood, and enameled aluminum, signed with manufacturer's mark to reverse, "Howard Miller Clock Company Zeeland, Michigan 2241," 27 1/4" deep x 40 1/2" high. **$11,520**

Courtesy of Wright, www.wright20.com

Lemerle Charpentier & Cie French gilt bronze figural mantle clock and thermometer, 19th century, pomegranate finial flanked by rooster heads, floral garland held aloft by two allegorical robed women, central harp-style standard with thermometer and porcelain clock face, decorated on sides with foliate swag, gilt pedestal on red marble pedestal, wear to gilt, with original key and pendulum, 33" x 18 1/2" x 11". **$25,000**

Courtesy of Heritage Auctions, www.ha.com

▲ Union Depot train station clock, originally in Troy, New York, as part of renovation to third version of terminal completed in early 1900s, white terracotta glazed in green with Grecian-style relief, locomotive breaking through tunnel of steam, same design concepts were used by Reed & Stern in their development of Grand Central Station, 88" high x 122" wide x 18" deep. **$43,750**

Courtesy of Guernsey's, www.guernseys.com

Ormolu skeleton clock, circa 1830, dial signed Berthold Hger. Du Roi, 14" high x 9 1/4" wide x 3 3/4" deep. **$17,500**

Courtesy of Sotheby's, www.sothebys.com

ALLAN PETRETTI is one of the world's top authorities on Coca-Cola memorabilia. He conducts seminars for Coca-Cola collector groups and has been interviewed by the Wall Street Journal, USA TODAY, London Times and The New York Times, and has appeared on many television shows, including "History Detectives."

Coca-Cola

By Allan Petretti

Organized Coca-Cola collecting began in the early 1970s. The advertising art of the Coca-Cola Co., which used to be thought of as a simple area of collecting, has reached a whole new level of appreciation. Because of their artistic quality, these images deserve to be considered true Americana.

Coca-Cola art is more than bottles and trays, more than calendars and signage, more than trinkets, giveaways, and displays. It incorporates all the best that America has to offer. The Coca-Cola Co., since its inception in 1886, has taken advertising to a whole new level. So much so that it has been studied and dissected by scholars as to why it has proved to be so successful for more than 130 years.

Can soda pop advertising be considered true art? Without a doubt! The very best artists in America were an integral part of that honorary place in art history. Renowned artists like Rockwell, Sundblom, Elvgren, and Wyeth helped take a quality product and advance it to the status of an American icon and all that exemplifies the very best about America.

This beautiful advertising directly reflects the history of our country: its styles and fashion, patriotism, family life, the best of times, and the worst of times. Everything this country has gone through since 1886 can be seen in these wonderful images.

For more information on Coca-Cola collectibles, see *Petretti's Coca-Cola Collectibles Price Guide*, 12th edition, by Allan Petretti.

Red countertop porthole clock on swivel base, "Drink Coca Cola 5 [cent symbol], Delicious, Refreshing," 15" diameter x 17" high. **$200**

Courtesy of Victorian Casino Antiques

1910 Coca-Cola embossed tin sign. **$2,400**

Courtesy of Morphy Auctions

1899 sign, 20" x 28", Hilda Clark, embossed tin, rare. **$30,000**

"Drink Coca-Cola" vending machine, Vendo Co., No. 5352, 53" high x 27" wide x 22" deep. **$185**

Courtesy of Kaminski Auctions, kaminskiauctions.com

1920s cardboard bottle cutout, 10" x 14", "Boy with Weiner." **$4,000**

Vintage "Refresh, Drink Coca-Cola" advertisement sign in gold-painted Art Deco Coca-Cola wood and metal frame, with bowling girl with bottle of Cok, copyright 1946 The Coca-Cola Co., lithograph produced in United States by Niagara Lith. Co., 35" x 56". **$850**

Courtesy of Victorian Casino Auctions

▲ Sprite boy tin sign, circular with embossed edge and mounting/hanging holes and rope, circa 1947, 12 3/4" diameter. **$325**

Courtesy of Mosby & Co. Auctions

Two-sided porcelain sign, circa 1938, produced by Tennessee Enamel Manufacturing Co., one small surface flake to lower right corner and two small chips to lower center on one side. **$2,400**

Courtesy of Mosby & Co. Auctions

▶ Neon clock by Neon Products Inc., Lima, Ohio, fine working condition, 18 1/4" high x 18 1/4" wide x 6 3/4" deep. **$4,000**

Courtesy of Mosby & Co. Auctions

Rare rotation light-up sign showing Sprite boy, late 1940s, excellent working condition, 18" diameter. **$2,000-$4,000**

Courtesy of Showtime Auction Service

Smith Miller truck, die-cast aluminum and wood, 1940s, includes original crates, minor surface wear, 14" long x 7 1/2" high. **$475**

Courtesy of Mosby & Co. Auctions

▲ Coca-Cola Route Truck, 1950s, Sanyo, Japan, battery-operated tin truck in original box, scarce, 12 1/2". **$453**

Courtesy of Serious Toyz Auctions

"Drink Coca-Cola" child's pedal car with matching trailer with cooler, Gearbox Pedal Car Co., Cedar Rapids, Iowa, "refresh yourself" yellow and red motif, excellent condition. **$200-$800**

Courtesy of Victorian Casino Auctions

◄ Sonja Henie Coca-Cola advertising sign, circa mid-1930s, one of only two known, heavy lithographed cardboard with added graphic, lettering printed in French, 40" high x 36" wide. **$11,500**

Courtesy of Bertoia Auctions

Double-sided "Drink Coca-Cola" tin drug store sign, excellent condition, 63" x 42". **$2,000-$3,000**

Courtesy of Ron Garrett

Embossed tin sign, 1933, good color and appearance, very good condition, 27 1/4" x 19 1/4". **$1,920**

Courtesy of Morphy Auctions

Pick up 12 sign, 1956, near mint-plus condition, 54 1/4" x 16". **$14,400**

Courtesy of Courtesy of Morphy Auctions

1927-1929 die-cut sign, 7 3/4" x 30". **$1,000**

Cardboard sign, 1940s-1950s, excellent condition, 15" x 12". **$210**

Courtesy of Morphy Auctions

Early Baird clock, "Coca-Cola / The Ideal Brain Tonic / Relieves / Exhaustion." **$3,000**

Courtesy of Morphy Auctions

1930s Coca-Cola lamp. **$4,200**

Courtesy of Morphy Auctions

Neon building clock and sign, circa mid-to-late 1930s, once adorned Piqua, Ohio, bottling plant, metal and neon tubing, 14' x 7'. **$50,000**

1898 calendar, 7 1/4" x 12 3/4". **$25,000**

1957 serving tray. **$300**

Can soda pop advertising be considered true art? Without a doubt! "

1919 classic calendar, with bottle, near mint condition. **$7,000**

1956 cardboard sign, 20" x 36". **$450**

"Drink Coca-Cola" tin serving tray, 1927, with soda jerk artwork, made by American Art Works Inc., 10" x 13". **$390**

Courtesy of Morphy Auctions, www.morphyauctions.com

Porcelain double-sided sign, circa 1950s, original base and brackets, never used, planned for use outdoors at service stations, outstanding condition. **$16,000**

Courtesy of Richard Opfer Auctioneering, Inc.

1964 tin sign, 18" x 54". **$450**

Lighted counter sign, 1930, made by Brunhoff, very good condition, 14" high. **$20,400**

Courtesy of Morphy Auctions

1900 calendar with actress Hilda Clark, near mint condition. **$210,000**

Courtesy of Morphy Auctions

1934 4 1/2' Wallace Beery and Jackie Cooper foldout. **$4,800**

"Happy Holidays" light-up
Christmas floor/lawn display
with Coca-Cola bottle, snow,
and thermometer, 36" high. **$90**

Courtesy of Victorian Casino Auctions

Cardboard sign, 1952,
featuring Sugar Ray
Robinson, 12" x 15". **$896**

Courtesy of Heritage Auctions

▶ Tin sign, 1936, bold
graphic with bottle,
excellent condition, 45
1/2" diameter. **$540**

Courtesy of Morphy Auctions

Circa 1929 Glascock
cooler, single case, junior
size, all original choice
condition. **$1,600**

Porcelain double-sided triangle
sign, strong unfaded color,
strong shine and no surface
scratches, near mint condition,
22" x 24". **$16,000**

Courtesy of Richard Opfer Auctioneering, Inc.

Coin-Operated Devices

Coin-operated devices fall into three main categories: amusement or arcade games, trade stimulators, and vending machines.

Vending machines have been around longer than any other kind of coin-op, and the 1880s witnessed the invention of many varieties. Gambling devices and amusement machines soon followed suit. The industry swelled during the 1890s and early 1900s but slowed during World War I. It rebounded in the 1920s and 1930s, which is considered the "Golden Age" of coin-ops.

Coin-ops reflect the prevailing art form of the era in which they were produced. Early machines exhibit designs ranging from Victorian to Art Nouveau and Art Deco, while later devices manufactured from 1940 on feature Modernism.

For more information on coin-operated devices, visit the website of the Coin Operated Collectors Association (www. coinopclub.org).

Caille Ben Hur counter wheel slot machine, 1908, 16" x 10" x 25".
$1,020

Courtesy of Morphy Auctions, www.morphyauctions.com

Mills 10¢ floor model slot machine, bird's-eye maple cabinet, castings and cabinet have been restored, 59" tall. **$2,040**

Courtesy of Morphy Auctions, www.morphyauctions.com

French crane digger machine, mahogany case with beveled front door glass, 66" high x 22" wide x 21" deep. **$605**

Courtesy of Fontaines Auction Gallery, www.fontainesauction.com

Caille's Centaur upright slot machine, overall exceptional restoration to the quarter sewn oak cabinet with black oxidized finish, retains original oak back door, plays nickels, marquee is probably a replacement, 65" tall. **$24,000**

Courtesy of Morphy Auctions, www.morphyauctions.com

Ride the Champion 10¢ horse ride, 57" high x 71" long x 25 1/2" wide. **$1,180**

Courtesy of Bright Star Antiques Co., www.brightstarantiques.com

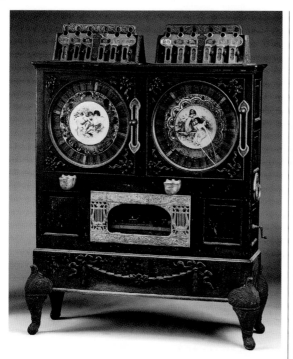

5-Cent/25-Cent Caille Double with original music. All the original linkage is intact except wire rods to trip music. The crank on the side and the lever to deactivate music are still present. The original iron castings have substantial nickel plating and painted highlighting to head is almost all intact. The iron legs have little nickel left, which is typical and often times the legs were painted silver. Dials are intact and in fine condition, original reverse glasses are present; one has three cracks, the others are intact and are flaking to blue background paint. Back doors are present with original locks; one door missing section of wood. Musical containment area is present including rear containment door. Approximately 47" x 14" x 63". Left-side handle plate is intact; handle missing. Mechanisms appear to be complete. Iron castings are intact and the only visible damage is a hairline crack in iron plate surrounding the right side coin head. **$80,500**

Courtesy of James D. Julia Auctioneers,
www.jamesdjulia.com

Mills 10¢ floor model, original wood finish and older paint restoration to castings, 59" tall. **$1,800**

Courtesy of Morphy Auctions,
www.morphyauctions.com

Pink elephant
kiddie ride. **$1,440**

Courtesy of Morphy Auctions,
www.morphyauctions.com

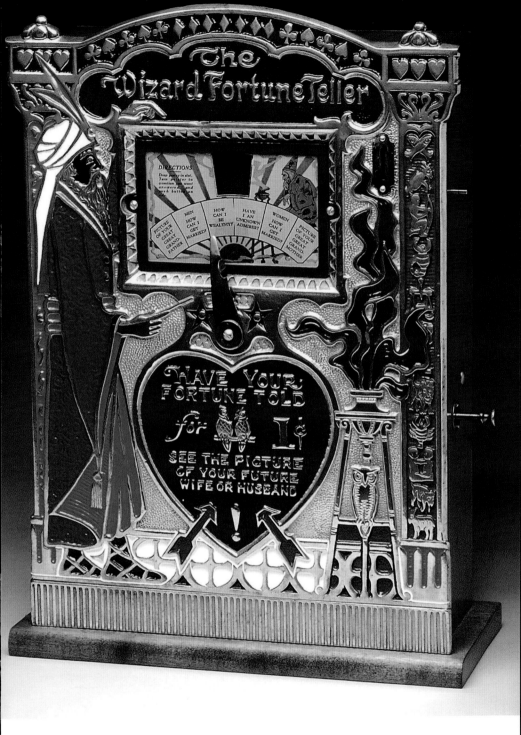

Mills Wizard Fortune Teller, Mills trademark owl on the front casting, which is covered in card symbols, signs of the Zodiac, flaming urn and a wise man/wizard. Customer selected the question; upon depositing a penny and plunging the lever on the right of the machine, the answer would appear. Professionally restored, 13 1/2" x 6" x 18 1/2". **$2,070**

Courtesy of James D. Julia Auctioneers, www.jamesdjulia.com

Superior Confection Company 5¢ trade stimulator, working, all original, includes gum vendor, 18" tall. **$1,920**

Courtesy of Morphy Auctions, www.morphyauctions.com

Electric baseball 1¢ arcade game, working, all original, nice labels on both sides, 17" tall. **$3,000**

Courtesy of Morphy Auctions, www.morphyauctions.com

Smilin' Sam from Alabam' / The Salted Peanut Man vending machine manufactured by General Merchandising Co. of Chicago, 13" high. **$720**

Courtesy of Morphy Auctions, www.morphyauctions.com

10¢ American Coin Rol-A-Top machine, with castle board top, restored, 27" tall. **$3,300**

Courtesy of Morphy Auctions, www.morphyauctions.com

Jennings Peacock Escalator model, all original, as-found and untouched, 26" tall. **$2,280**

Courtesy of Morphy Auctions, www.morphyauctions.com

Jennings Monte Carlo 5¢ prospector slot machine, working, rare and desirable machine in overall very fine, restored condition, 60 1/2" tall. **$3,600**

Courtesy of Morphy Auctions, www.morphyauctions.com

Mills 25¢ floor model, brown paint, appears to be in as-found all original condition, 59" tall. **$3,900**

Courtesy of Morphy Auctions, www.morphyauctions.com

Mills floor model golf ball vendor, working original 25-cent slot machine, motor for golf ball dispenser is intact and functional, restored castings, 59" tall. **$8,400**

Courtesy of Morphy Auctions, www.morphyauctions.com

Superior Confection Company 1¢ trade stimulator, working, all original, includes gum vendor, 18" tall. **$1,320**

Courtesy of Morphy Auctions, www.morphyauctions.com

Ohio Blue Tip Matches vending machine, red-painted metal with blue decal, 12 1/2" high x 6" wide. **$366**

Courtesy of Clars Auction Gallery, www.clars.com

U.S. Postage Stamps machine, original, with keys. **$108**

Courtesy of Milestone Auctions, Inc., www.milestoneauctions.com

Nevada Club 25¢ four-reel Buckaroo machine, with red plastic light-ups and hand low jackpot, features the Lake Tahoe Reno figure on jackpot cover, castings have been re-plated, 27" tall. **$4,500**

Courtesy of Morphy Auctions, www.morphyauctions.com

▲ Countertop trade stimulator, 5¢ skill test with fox hunt scene on back panel, pine case, 26" high x 17 3/4" wide x 9" deep, 25.25 pounds. **$363**

Courtesy of Fontaines Auction Gallery, www.fontainesauction.com

◄ Roll Out the Barrel countertop reel trade stimulator vendor, 18" x 9" x 24". **$1,680**

Courtesy of Morphy Auctions, www.morphyauctions.com

Mills 10¢ melon bell machine, all original, very fine condition, 26 1/2" tall. **$2,700**

Courtesy of Morphy Auctions, www.morphyauctions.com

Mills 5¢ QT twin jackpot slot machine, working, brown spatter finish, 19" tall. **$3,000**

Courtesy of Morphy Auctions, www.morphyauctions.com

Jennings $1 Nevada Club machine, open front model with green light up plastics, 27 1/2" tall. **$5,400**

Courtesy of Morphy Auctions, www.morphyauctions.com

Two tabletop game vendors, both working, Booster machine and Select'em machine with dice and ball game, each 17" long. **$570**

Courtesy of Morphy Auctions, www.morphyauctions.com

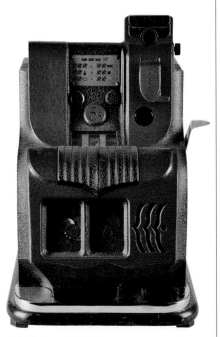

Mills 5¢ Hash Mark QT slot machine, working, all original, includes twin jackpot, 19" tall. **$1,560**

Courtesy of Morphy Auctions, www.morphyauctions.com

Jennings 10¢ Standard Chief machine, reel strips are original, machine has been restored with a hammered gold finish and refinishing to wood cabinet, 27" tall. **$1,440**

Courtesy of Morphy Auctions, www.morphyauctions.com

Mills jockey machine, turn-of-the-century, early fancy cabinet, machine appears to be original except for cash drawer on right side, 21" tall. **$9,600**

Courtesy of Morphy Auctions, www.morphyauctions.com

Groetchen "Poison This Rat" arcade machine, 1940s, featuring Hitler on the front facade. A penny is deposited and the player gets five "poison" pills to be dispensed to the Fuhrer in hopes of killing him. The game uses slopes and runways to get the small red balls into Hitler's mouth. Game retains much of its original finish and in working order, 16 1/2" x 11" x 24". Couple of minor splits to wooden cabinet. Original directions on interior panel. **$7,475**

Courtesy of James D. Julia Auctioneers, www.jamesdjulia.com

▲ Miniature Baseball World Champion arcade game, working, original with nice labels on both sides of machine, includes a small sampling of tokens to be won, two small skulls and one Popeye charm, 16 1/2" tall. **$750-$1,250**

Courtesy of Morphy Auctions, www.morphyauctions.com

◀ Encore coin-operated automated banjo. Features a banjo inside an elaborate oak case. When a coin is deposited, the banjo would play a tune. A paper roll similar to those used on player pianos is responsible for the action of the banjo. Curved metal "fingers" pluck the banjo. The cabinetry is oak with detailed inset panels, fancy trims and moldings, serpentine opening front, and cast-metal grilles in place on front and sides. Extremely rare, 83" x 26" x 24". Machine has had total overall restoration inside and out. Internal wood barrel covering the mechanics and music roll has been replaced. Wood panel at the rear of the machine is also of newer vintage. **$54,625**

Courtesy of James D. Julia Auctioneers, www.jamesdjulia.com

Comic Books

By Barry Sandoval

BARRY SANDOVAL is
Director of Operations
for Comics at Heritage
Auctions. In addition to
managing Heritage's
Comics division, which
sells some $45 million
worth of comics and
original comic art each
year, Sandoval is a noted
comic book evaluator and
serves as an advisor to
the *Overstreet Comic Book
Price Guide*.

In 1993, Sotheby's auctioned a copy of *Fantastic Four #1* (1961) that was said to be the finest copy known to exist. It sold for $27,600, which at the time was considered an unheard-of price for a 1960s comic. A few years ago, Heritage Auctions sold that same copy for $203,000 … and it's not even the finest known copy anymore.

It used to be that only comics from the 1930s or 1940s could be worth thousands of dollars. Now, truly high-grade copies of comics from the Silver Age (1956-1969 by most people's reckoning) can sell for four, five, or even six figures. Note I said truly high-grade. Long gone are the days when a near mint condition copy was only worth triple the price of a good condition copy. Now near mint is more like 10-20 times good, and sometimes it's as much as a factor of 1,000.

A trend of recent years has been that the "key" issues have separated even further from the pack, value-wise. Note that not every key is a "#1" issue – if you have *Amazing Fantasy #15, Tales of Suspense #39*, and *Journey into Mystery #83*, you've got the first appearances of Spider-Man, Iron Man, and Thor. (Beware of reprints and replica editions, however.)

The most expensive comics of all remain the Golden Age (1938-1949) first appearances, like Superman's 1938 debut in *Action Comics #1*, several copies of which have sold for $1 million or more. However, not every single comic from the old days is going up in value. Take western-themed comics. Values are actually going down in this genre as the generation that grew up watching westerns is at the age where they're looking to sell, and there are more sellers than potential buyers.

Comics from the 1970s and later, while increasing in value, rarely garner anywhere near the same value as 1960s issues, primarily because in the 1970s comics were increasingly seen as a potentially valuable

Archie Comics #1 (1942), CGC-graded 8.5 (very fine+). **$167,300**

collectible. People took better care of them, and in many cases hoarded multiple copies.

What about 1980s favorites like *The Dark Knight Returns* and *Watchmen*? Here the demand is high, but the supply is really high. These series were heavily hyped at the time and were done by well-known creators, so copies were socked away in great quantities. We've come across more than one dealer who has 20-30 mint copies of every single 1980s comic socked away in a warehouse, waiting for the day when they're worth selling.

If you've bought comics at an auction house or on eBay, you might have seen some in CGC holders. Certified Guaranty Co., or CGC, is a third-party grading service that grades a comic book on a scale from 0.5 to 10. These numbers correspond with traditional descriptive grades of good, very fine, near mint, and mint, with the higher numbers indicating a better grade. Once graded, CGC encapsulates the comic book in plastic. The grade remains valid as long as the plastic holder is not broken open. CGC has been a boon to the hobby, allowing people to buy comics with more confidence and with the subjectivity of grading taken out of the equation. Unless

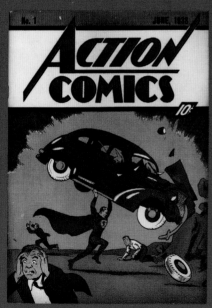

Action Comics #1 (1938), CGC-graded 9.0 (very fine/near mint), pristine copy of the first appearance of Superman, issue by Jerry Siegel and Joe Shuster, the most valuable comic book in the world. **$3,207,852**

Courtesy of eBay/Pristine Comics

Adventure Comics #40 (1939), CGC-graded 8.0 (very fine), from the Billy Wright Collection. **$59,750**

Courtesy of Heritage Auctions, www.ha.com

extremely rare, it's usually only high-grade comics that are worth certifying.

One aspect of collecting that has exploded in the last 20 years has been original comic art, and not just art for the vintage stuff. It's not unusual for a page that was bought for $20 in the 1980s to be worth $5,000 now.

If you want to get into collecting original comic art, McFarlane would not be the place to start unless you've got a really fat wallet. I suggest picking a current comic artist you like who isn't yet a major name. Chances are his originals will be a lot more affordable. Another idea is to collect the original art for comic strips. You can find originals for as little as $20, as long as you're not expecting a Peanuts or a Prince Valiant.

As expensive as both comic books and comic art can be at the high end of the spectrum, in many ways this is a buyer's market. In the old days you might search for years to find a given issue of a comic; now you can often search eBay and see 10 different copies for sale. Also, comic book conventions seem to be thriving in almost every major city – and while the people in crazy costumes get all the publicity, you can also find plenty of vintage comics dealers at these shows. From that point of view, it's a great time to be a comic book collector.

All-American Comics #16 (1940), CGC-graded 8.0 (very fine). **$203,150**

Courtesy of Heritage Auctions, www.ha.com

All-Star Comics #8 (1942), CGC-graded 8.0 (very fine), from the Empire Comics Collection. **$56,763**

Courtesy of Heritage Auctions, www.ha.com

Amazing Fantasy #15 (1962), the first appearance of Spider-Man, CGC-graded 7.5 (very fine-). **$49,294**

Courtesy of Heritage Auctions, www.ha.com

The Amazing Spider-Man #50 (1967), CGC-graded 9.8 (near mint/mint). **$26,290**

Courtesy of Heritage Auctions, www.ha.com

Avengers #1 (1963), CGC-graded 9.6 (near mint+), cover by Jack Kirby, Pacific Coast pedigree copy from the Doug Schmeel Collection. **$274,850**

Courtesy of Heritage Auctions, www.ha.com

The Avengers #4 (1964), CGC-graded 9.6 (near mint). **$31,070**

Courtesy of Heritage Auctions, www.ha.com

Batman #1 (1940), CGC-graded 8.5 (very fine+), from the Billy Wright Collection. **$274,850**

Courtesy of Heritage Auctions, www.ha.com

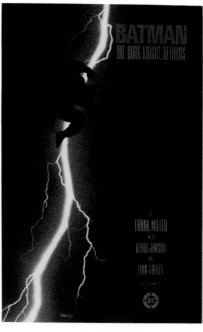

Batman: The Dark Knight Returns #1 (1986), CGC-graded 9.6 (near mint+). **$143**

Courtesy of Heritage Auctions, www.ha.com

Brave and the Bold #29 (1960), CGC-graded 8.0 (very fine). **$5,975**

Courtesy of Heritage Auctions, www.ha.com

Captain America Comics #1 (1941), CGC-graded 7.0 (fine/very fine). **$89,625**

Courtesy of Heritage Auctions, www.ha.com

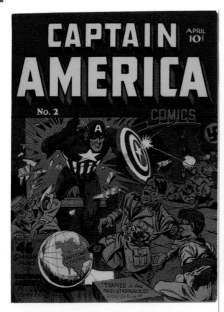

Captain America Comics #2 (1941), CGC-graded 9.4 (near mint), from the Billy Wright Collection. **$113,525**

Courtesy of Heritage Auctions, www.ha.com

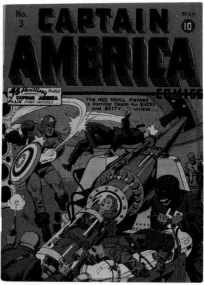

Captain America Comics #3 (1941), CGC-graded 9.2 (near mint-), from the Billy Wright Collection. **$50,788**

Courtesy of Heritage Auctions, www.ha.com

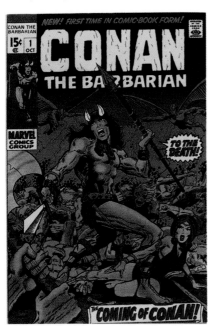

Conan the Barbarian #1 (1970), CGC-graded 9.8 (near mint/mint), from the Empire Comics Collection. **$3,884**

Courtesy of Heritage Auctions, www.ha.com

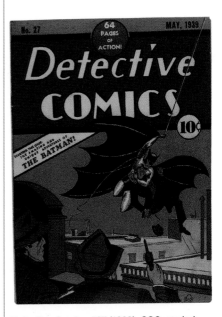

Detective Comics #27 (1939), CGC-graded 6.5 (fine+), from the Billy Wright Collection. **$522,813**

Courtesy of Heritage Auctions, www.ha.com

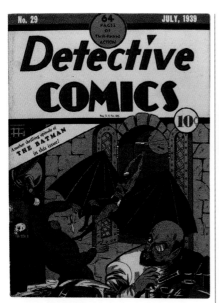

Detective Comics #29 (1939), CGC-graded
7.0 (fine/very fine), from the Billy Wright
Collection. **$83,650**

Courtesy of Heritage Auctions, www.ha.com

Detective Comics #359 (1967), CGC-graded
9.2 (near mint-). **$1,613**

Courtesy of Heritage Auctions, www.ha.com

Fantastic Four #1 (1961), CGC-graded 9.2
(near mint-), White Mountain pedigree copy
from the Doug Schmeel Collection. **$203,150**

Courtesy of Heritage Auctions, www.ha.com

Fantastic Four #48 (1966), CGC-graded 9.8
(near mint/mint). **$13,145**

Courtesy of Heritage Auctions, www.ha.com

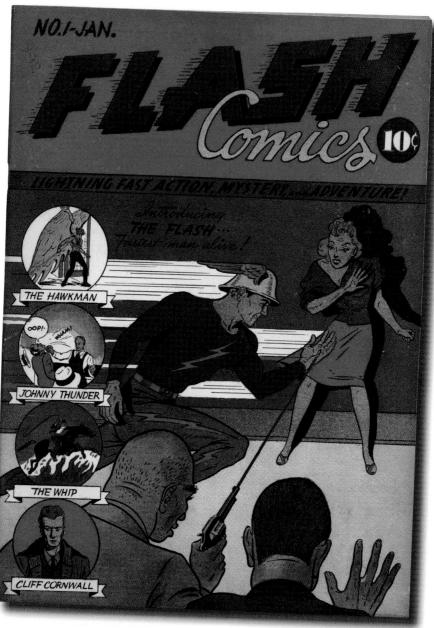

Flash Comics #1 (1940), the introduction of
Flash, CGC-rated 9.6 (near mint). **$273,125**

Courtesy of Heritage Auctions, www.ha.com

Green Hornet Comics #1 (1940), CGC-graded
8.5 (very fine). **$14,375**

Courtesy of Heritage Auctions, www.ha.com

Green Lantern #76 (1970), CGC-rated 9.8 (near
mint/mint). **$37,343**

Courtesy of Heritage Auctions, www.ha.com

The Incredible Hulk #1 (1962), CGC-graded 9.2
(near mint). **$125,475**

Courtesy of Heritage Auctions, www.ha.com

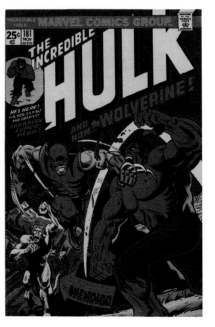

Incredible Hulk #181 (1974), CGC-graded 9.8
(near mint/mint). **$9,560**

Courtesy of Heritage Auctions, www.ha.com

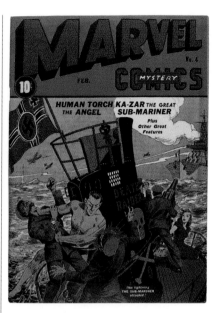

Marvel Comics #1 (1939), CGC-graded 7.5
(very fine-), from the Billy Wright Collection.
$113,525

Courtesy of Heritage Auctions, www.ha.com

Marvel Mystery Comics #4 (1940), CGC-
graded 9.2 (near mint-), from the Billy Wright
Collection. **$50,788**

Courtesy of Heritage Auctions, www.ha.com

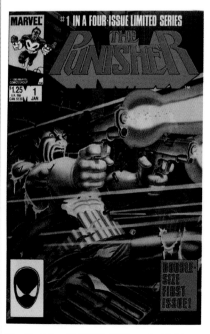

Nick Fury, Agent of S.H.I.E.L.D. #4 (1968),
CGC-graded 9.8 (near mint/mint). **$1,135**

Courtesy of Heritage Auctions, www.ha.com

The Punisher #1 (1986), CGC-graded 9.8 (near
mint/mint). **$286**

Courtesy of Heritage Auctions, www.ha.com

Marvel Feature #1 Red Sonja (1975), CGC-graded 9.8 (near mint/mint). **$430**

The Savage She-Hulk #1 (1980), CGC-graded 9.8 (near mint/mint). **$131**

Courtesy of Heritage Auctions, www.ha.com

Showcase #22 (1959), CGC-graded 7.5 (very fine-). **$14,340**

Courtesy of Heritage Auctions, www.ha.com

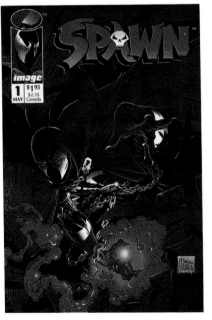

Spawn #1 (1992), CGC-graded 9.8 (near mint/mint). **$42**

Courtesy of Heritage Auctions, www.ha.com

Star Wars #1 (1977), CGC-graded 9.2 (near mint-). **$508**

Courtesy of Heritage Auctions, www.ha.com

Tales of Suspense #39 (1963), CGC-graded 9.6 (near mint+), Pacific Coast pedigree copy from the Doug Schmeel Collection. **$262,900**

Courtesy of Heritage Auctions, www.ha.com

Teenage Mutant Ninja Turtles #1 (1984), CGC-graded 9.4 (near mint). **$5,378**

Courtesy of Heritage Auctions, www.ha.com

Journey into Mystery #83 (1962), the introduction of Thor, CGC-graded 9.2 (near mint-). **$83,650**

Courtesy of Heritage Auctions, www.ha.com

X-Men #1 (1963), the introduction of the
X-Men, CGC-graded 9.8 (near mint/mint), from
the Doug Schmeel Collection. **$492,938**

Courtesy of Heritage Auctions, www.ha.com

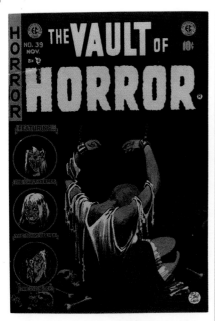

Vault of Horror #39 (1954), CGC-graded 9.8 (near mint/mint), Gaines File Copy #1. **$3,585**

Courtesy of Heritage Auctions, www.ha.com

Walking Dead #1 (2003), CGC-graded 9.8 (near mint/mint). **$1,434**

Courtesy of Heritage Auctions, www.ha.com

Watchmen #1 (1986), CGC-graded 9.8 (near mint/mint). **$478**

Courtesy of Heritage Auctions, www.ha.com

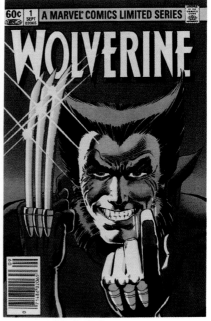

Wolverine (Limited Series) #1 (1982), CGC-graded 10 (mint). **$15,535**

Courtesy of Heritage Auctions, www.ha.com

Wonder Woman #1 (1942), the introduction of Wonder Woman, CGC-graded 8.5 (very fine+). **$53,775**

Courtesy of Heritage Auctions, www.ha.com

X-Men #3 (1964), CGC-graded 9.8 (near mint/mint). **$16,730**

Courtesy of Heritage Auctions, www.ha.com

Cookie Jars

Cookie jars, colorful and often whimsical, are popular with collectors. They were made by almost every manufacturer in all types of materials. Figural character cookie jars are the most popular with collectors.

Cookie jars often were redesigned to reflect newer tastes. Hence, the same jar may be found in several different variations, and these variations can affect the price.

Many cookie-jar shapes were manufactured by more than one company and, as a result, can be found with different marks. This often happened because of mergers. Molds also were traded and sold among companies.

Some cookie jars by American Bisque were enhanced with flashers – a plastic piece, technically known as a lenticular image, that changes when the item is moved back and forth.

For more information on cookie jars, see *Warman's Cookie Jars Identification and Price Guide* by Mark F. Moran.

◄ Pinocchio, two versions, by California Originals, impressed marks on bottom, "Calif. Orig. G-131 USA," both 12 1/4" h. Also found unmarked or with only an impressed "USA." Unlike some other older jars, the color variations in these Pinocchios do not affect value. **$1,200+ each**

◄ Watermelon by Metlox, 1960s, impressed mark on bottom, "Made in Poppytrail Calif." with gold and brown foil label, "Metlox Manufacturing Co.," 10 1/8" h. **$1,000+**

Abingdon Halloween-themed china cookie jar with relief image on each side of witch flying on broomstick by light of crescent moon with bat nearby, jar lid handle of cat with arched back, circa 1950s, incised "692" on underside, with Abingdon stamp, handle with professional repair at both feet, 8 1/4" x 11 1/4" x 4 1/2". **$494**

Courtesy of Hake's Americana & Collectibles

Buick convertible cookie jar, Glenn Appleman, Appleman Autoworks, Inc., signed by artist, near mint condition, 15" l. **$540**

Courtesy of Morphy Auctions, morphyauctions.com

American Bisque Herman & Katnip with A.B. Co. paper label under lid, marked "Herman & Katnip – USA," not stamped on bottom, very good condition with some crazing, rarest of all American Bisque jars, only six known to exist. **$1,560**

Courtesy of Victorian Casino Antiques

Little Boy Blue marked "Hull-Ware Boy Blue U.S.A. 971-122" with cold paint. This jar was not produced, and there are only a few known to exist. **$5,000**

American Bisque Baby Huey, marked "USA" near bottom, "Baby Huey" on front, rarer black-haired version, hard to find, some crazing and small chip on back of neck. **$978**

Courtesy of Victorian Casino Antiques

Brush Pottery Pink Elephant with Monkey finial, marked "Brush USA" on bottom, good condition, very rare, only 10-12 made. **$1,020**

Courtesy of Victorian Casino Antiques

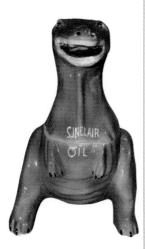

Green painted and glazed ceramic tyrannosaurus rex cookie jar with "Sinclair Oil" etched on front, marked "1942 USA" on bottom, excellent condition, 13" high. **$1,200**

Courtesy of Morphy Auctions, morphyauctions.com

Flintstones cookie jar with Barney and Betty Rubble, American Bisque, circa 1960s, bird head on top repaired, near mint-plus condition, 10" x 7" x 6". **$83**

Courtesy of Morphy Auctions, morphyauctions.com

Mammy figural cookie jar by McCoy, marked on underside, loss to paint, 11" high. **$50**

Courtesy of Thomaston Place Auction Galleries

Leprechaun (in red) by McCoy, 1950s, unmarked, never put into wide production, not known many were made, 12" h (widely reproduced slightly smaller). **$3,000+**

Little Red Riding Hood cookie jar, Hull. **$104**

Courtesy of Strawser Auctions, strawserauctions.com

Water Lily blue cookie jar (1-8") by Roseville, raised mark, 9" x 10 1/4". **$400-$500**

Bisque cookie jar designed as classic flying saucer, 1960s, underside with sticker reading "Handmade Exclusively For Silvestri, Chicago Ill.," top of saucer lifts off, underside of base with scuffs, very fine condition, all-over even aging with light scattered wear to gold paint accent on saucer's rim edge, scarce and desirable, 12 1/2" diameter x 6" high. **$316**

Courtesy of Hake's Americana & Collectibles

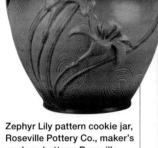

Zephyr Lily pattern cookie jar, Roseville Pottery Co., maker's mark on bottom: Roseville, USA 5-8", very good condition, 10 1/2" high. **$210**

Courtesy of Morphy Auctions, morphyauctions.com

Superman in Phone Booth cookie jar, 1978, rectangular, removable top, excellent condition, approximately 13 1/4" high (with lid) x 6 1/2" wide. Provenance: From the Kirk Alyn Archives Collection. This was the "Superman" actor's personal cookie jar, as seen in a snapshot taken of his office with the porcelain jar sitting on a shelf. **$313**

Courtesy of Heritage Auctions

Warner Bros. Champ Kangaroo, sculpted and designed by Don Winton for DeForest, yellow sweater version, unmarked, some crazing, very rare. **$780**

Courtesy of Victorian Casino Antiques

American Bisque Olive Oyl with removable plastic flower in hat, marked "USA" near bottom, thin-neck version was the prototype for Olive Oyl cookie jars, good condition with minor crazing, very rare. **$960**

Courtesy of Victorian Casino Antiques

Carousel by Red Wing, with distinct color and decorating styles, 1950s, marked with two styles of ink stamp, each 8" h. **$800 each**

Furniture Styles
AMERICAN

PILGRIM CENTURY 1620–1700

MAJOR WOOD: Oak

GENERAL CHARACTERISTICS:

- **Case pieces:** Rectilinear low-relief carved panels; blocky and bulbous turnings; splint-spindle trim

- **Seating pieces:** Shallow carved panels; spindle turnings

WILLIAM AND MARY 1685–1720

MAJOR WOODS: Maple and walnut

GENERAL CHARACTERISTICS:

- **Case pieces:** Paint-decorated chests on ball feet; chests on frames; chests with two-part construction; trumpet-turned legs; slant-front desks

- **Seating pieces:** Molded, carved crest rails; banister backs; cane, rush (leather) seats; baluster, ball and block turnings; ball and Spanish feet

QUEEN ANNE 1720–1750

MAJOR WOOD: Walnut

GENERAL CHARACTERISTICS:

- **Case pieces:** Mathematical proportions of elements; use of the cyma or S-curve broken-arch pediments; arched panels, shell carving, star inlay; blocked fronts; cabriole legs and pad feet

- **Seating pieces:** Molded yoke-shaped crest rails; solid vase-shaped splats; rush or upholstered seats; cabriole legs; baluster, ring, ball and block-turned stretchers; pad and slipper feet

CHIPPENDALE 1750–1785

MAJOR WOODS: Mahogany and walnut

GENERAL CHARACTERISTICS:

- **Case pieces:** Relief-carved broken-arch pediments; foliate, scroll, shell, fretwork carving; straight, bow or serpentine fronts; carved cabriole legs; claw and ball, bracket or ogee feet

- **Seating pieces:** Carved, shaped crest rails with out-turned ears; pierced, shaped splats; ladder (ribbon) backs; upholstered seats; scrolled arms; carved cabriole legs or straight (Marlboro) legs; claw and ball feet

FURNITURE

F

FEDERAL (HEPPLEWHITE) 1785–1800

MAJOR WOODS: Mahogany and light inlays

GENERAL CHARACTERISTICS:

- **Case pieces:** More delicate rectilinear forms; inlay with eagle and classical motifs; bow, serpentine or tambour fronts; reeded quarter columns at sides; flared bracket feet

- **Seating pieces:** Shield backs; upholstered seats; tapered square legs

FEDERAL (SHERATON) 1800–1820

MAJOR WOODS: Mahogany, mahogany veneer, and maple

GENERAL CHARACTERISTICS:

- **Case pieces:** Architectural pediments; acanthus carving; outset (cookie or ovolu) corners and reeded columns; paneled sides; tapered, turned, reeded or spiral-turned legs; bow or tambour fronts; mirrors on dressing tables

- **Seating pieces:** Rectangular or square backs; slender carved banisters; tapered, turned or reeded legs

CLASSICAL (AMERICAN EMPIRE) 1815–1850

MAJOR WOODS: Mahogany, mahogany veneer, and rosewood

GENERAL CHARACTERISTICS:

- **Case pieces:** Increasingly heavy proportions; pillar and scroll construction; lyre, eagle, Greco-Roman and Egyptian motifs; marble tops; projecting top drawer; large ball feet, tapered fluted feet or hairy paw feet; brass, ormolu decoration

- **Seating pieces:** High-relief carving; curved backs; out-scrolled arms; ring turnings; sabre legs, curule (scrolled-S) legs; brass-capped feet, casters

VICTORIAN – EARLY VICTORIAN 1840–1850

MAJOR WOODS: Mahogany veneer, black walnut, and rosewood

GENERAL CHARACTERISTICS:

- **Case pieces:** Pieces tend to carry over the Classical style with the beginnings of the Rococo substyle, especially in seating pieces.

VICTORIAN – GOTHIC REVIVAL 1840–1890

MAJOR WOODS: Black walnut, mahogany, and rosewood

GENERAL CHARACTERISTICS:

- **Case pieces:** Architectural motifs; triangular arched pediments; arched panels; marble tops; paneled or molded drawer fronts; cluster columns; bracket feet, block feet or plinth bases

- **Seating pieces:** Tall backs; pierced arabesque backs with trefoils or quatrefoils; spool turning; drop pendants

VICTORIAN – ROCOCO (LOUIS XV) 1845–1870

MAJOR WOODS: Black walnut, mahogany, and rosewood

GENERAL CHARACTERISTICS:

- **Case pieces:** Arched carved pediments; high-relief carving, S- and C-scrolls, floral, fruit motifs, busts and cartouches; mirror panels; carved slender cabriole legs; scroll feet; bedroom suites (bed, dresser, commode)

- **Seating pieces:** High-relief carved crest rails; balloon-shaped backs; urn-shaped splats; upholstery (tufting); demi-cabriole legs; laminated, pierced and carved construction (Belter and Meeks); parlor suites (sets of chairs, love seats, sofas)

VICTORIAN – RENAISSANCE REVIVAL 1860–1885

MAJOR WOODS: Black walnut, burl veneer, painted and grained pine

GENERAL CHARACTERISTICS:

- **Case pieces:** Rectilinear arched pediments; arched panels; burl veneer; applied moldings; bracket feet, block feet, plinth bases; medium and high-relief carving, floral and fruit, cartouches, masks and animal heads; cyma-curve brackets; Wooton patent desks

- **Seating pieces:** Oval or rectangular backs with floral or figural cresting; upholstery outlined with brass tacks; padded armrests; tapered turned front legs, flared square rear legs

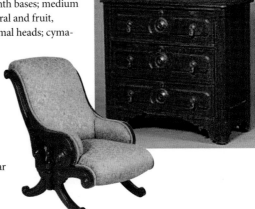

VICTORIAN – LOUIS XVI 1865–1875

MAJOR WOODS: Black walnut and ebonized maple

GENERAL CHARACTERISTICS:

- **Case pieces:** Gilt decoration, marquetry, inlay; egg and dart carving; tapered turned legs, fluted

- **Seating pieces:** Molded, slightly arched crest rails; keystone-shaped backs; circular seats; fluted tapered legs

VICTORIAN – EASTLAKE 1870-1895

MAJOR WOODS: Black walnut, burl veneer, cherry, and oak

GENERAL CHARACTERISTICS:

- **Case pieces:** Flat cornices; stile and rail construction; burl veneer panels; low-relief geometric and floral machine carving; incised horizontal lines

- **Seating pieces:** Rectilinear; spindles; tapered, turned legs, trumpet-shaped legs

VICTORIAN JACOBEAN AND TURKISH REVIVAL 1870-1890

MAJOR WOODS: Black walnut and maple

GENERAL CHARACTERISTICS:

- **Case pieces:** A revival of some heavy 17th century forms, most commonly in dining room pieces

- **Seating pieces:** Turkish Revival style features: oversized, low forms; overstuffed upholstery; padded arms; short baluster, vase-turned legs; ottomans, circular sofas

- **Jacobean Revival style features:** heavy bold carving; spool and spiral turnings

VICTORIAN – AESTHETIC MOVEMENT 1880–1900

MAJOR WOODS: Painted hardwoods, black walnut, ebonized finishes

GENERAL CHARACTERISTICS:

- **Case pieces:** Rectilinear forms; bamboo turnings, spaced ball turnings; incised stylized geometric and floral designs, sometimes highlighted with gilt

- **Seating pieces:** Bamboo turning; rectangular backs; patented folding chairs

ART NOUVEAU 1895–1918

MAJOR WOODS: Ebonized hardwoods, fruitwoods

GENERAL CHARACTERISTICS:

- **Case pieces:** Curvilinear shapes; floral marquetry; whiplash curves

- **Seating pieces:** Elongated forms; relief-carved floral decoration; spindle backs, pierced floral backs; cabriole legs

TURN-OF-THE-CENTURY (EARLY 20TH CENTURY) 1895–1910

MAJOR WOODS: Golden (quarter-sawn) oak, mahogany, hardwood stained to resemble mahogany

GENERAL CHARACTERISTICS:

- **Case pieces:** Rectilinear and bulky forms; applied scroll carving or machine-pressed designs; some Colonial and Classical Revival detailing

- **Seating pieces:** Heavy framing or high spindle-trimmed backs; applied carved or machine-pressed back designs; heavy scrolled or slender turned legs; Colonial Revival or Classical Revival detailing such as claw and ball feet

MISSION (ARTS & CRAFTS MOVEMENT) 1900–1915

MAJOR WOODS: Oak

GENERAL CHARACTERISTICS:

- **Case pieces:** Rectilinear through-tenon construction; copper decoration, hand-hammered hardware; square legs

- **Seating pieces:** Rectangular splats; medial and side stretchers; exposed pegs; corbel supports

COLONIAL REVIVAL 1890-1930

MAJOR WOODS: Oak, walnut and walnut veneer, mahogany veneer

GENERAL CHARACTERISTICS:

- **Case pieces:** Forms generally following designs of the 17th, 18th, and early 19th centuries; details for the styles such as William and Mary, Federal, Queen Anne, Chippendale, or early Classical were used but often in a simplified or stylized form; mass-production in the early 20th century flooded the market with pieces that often mixed and matched design details and used a great deal of thin veneering to dress up designs; dining room and bedroom suites were especially popular.

- **Seating pieces:** Designs again generally followed early period designs with some mixing of design elements.

ART DECO 1925-1940

MAJOR WOODS: Bleached woods, exotic woods, steel, and chrome

GENERAL CHARACTERISTICS:

- **Case pieces:** Heavy geometric forms

- **Seating pieces:** Streamlined, attenuated geometric forms; overstuffed upholstery

MODERNIST OR MID-CENTURY 1945-1970

MAJOR WOODS: Plywood, hardwood, or metal frames

GENERAL CHARACTERISTICS: Modernistic designers such as the Eames, Vladimir Kagan, George Nelson, and Isamu Noguchi led the way in post-war design. Carrying on the tradition of Modernist designers of the 1920s and 1930s, they focused on designs for the machine age that could be mass-produced for the popular market. By the late 1950s many of their pieces were used in commercial office spaces and schools as well as in private homes.

- **Case pieces:** Streamlined or curvilinear abstract designs with simple detailing; plain round or flattened legs and arms; mixed materials including wood, plywood, metal, glass, and molded plastics

- **Seating pieces:** Streamlined or abstract curvilinear designs generally using newer materials such as plywood or simple hardwood framing; fabric and synthetics such as vinyl used for upholstery with finer fabrics and real leather featured on more expensive pieces; seating made of molded plastic shells on metal frames and legs used on many mass-produced designs

DANISH MODERN 1950-1970

MAJOR WOOD: Teak

GENERAL CHARACTERISTICS:

- **Case and seating pieces:** This variation of Modernistic post-war design originated in Scandinavia, hence the name; designs were simple and restrained with case pieces often having simple boxy forms with short rounded tapering legs; seating pieces have a simple teak framework with lines coordinating with case pieces; vinyl or natural fabric were most often used for upholstery; in the United States dining room suites were the most popular use for this style although some bedroom suites and general seating pieces were available.

ENGLISH

JACOBEAN MID-17TH CENTURY

MAJOR WOODS: Oak, walnut

GENERAL CHARACTERISTICS:

- **Case pieces:** Low-relief carving; geometrics and florals; panel, rail and stile construction; applied split balusters

- **Seating pieces:** Rectangular backs; carved and pierced crests; spiral turnings ball feet

WILLIAM AND MARY 1689–1702

MAJOR WOODS: Walnut, burl walnut veneer

GENERAL CHARACTERISTICS:

- **Case pieces:** Marquetry, veneering; shaped aprons; 6-8 trumpet-form legs; curved flat stretchers

- **Seating pieces:** Carved, pierced crests; tall caned backs and seats; trumpet-form legs; Spanish feet

QUEEN ANNE 1702–1714

MAJOR WOODS: Walnut, mahogany, veneer

GENERAL CHARACTERISTICS:

- **Case pieces:** Cyma curves; broken arch pediments and finials; bracket feet

- **Seating pieces:** Carved crest rails; high, rounded backs; solid vase-shaped splats; cabriole legs; pad feet

GEORGE I 1714–1727

MAJOR WOODS: Walnut, mahogany, veneer, and yew wood

GENERAL CHARACTERISTICS:

- **Case pieces:** Broken arch pediments; gilt decoration, japanning; bracket feet

- **Seating pieces:** Curvilinear forms; yoke-shaped crests; shaped solid splats; shell carving; upholstered seats; carved cabriole legs; claw and ball feet, pad feet

GEORGE II 1727–1760

MAJOR WOODS: Mahogany

GENERAL CHARACTERISTICS:

- **Case pieces:** Broken arch pedaiments; relief-carved foliate, scroll and shell carving; carved cabriole legs; claw and ball feet, bracket feet, ogee bracket feet

- **Seating pieces:** Carved, shaped crest rails, out-turned ears; pierced shaped splats; ladder (ribbon) backs; upholstered seats; scrolled arms; carved cabriole legs or straight (Marlboro) legs; claw and ball feet

GEORGE III 1760–1820

MAJOR WOODS: Mahogany, veneer, satinwood

GENERAL CHARACTERISTICS:

- **Case pieces:** Rectilinear forms; parcel gilt decoration; inlaid ovals, circles, banding or marquetry; carved columns, urns; tambour fronts or bow fronts; plinth bases

- **Seating pieces:** Shield backs; upholstered seats; tapered square legs, square legs

REGENCY 1811–1820

MAJOR WOODS: Mahogany, mahogany veneer, satinwood, and rosewood

GENERAL CHARACTERISTICS:

- **Case pieces:** Greco-Roman and Egyptian motifs; inlay, ormolu mounts; marble tops; round columns, pilasters; mirrored backs; scroll feet

- **Seating pieces:** Straight backs; latticework; caned seats; sabre legs, tapered turned legs, flared turned legs; parcel gilt, ebonizing

GEORGE IV 1820–1830

MAJOR WOODS: Mahogany, mahogany veneer, and rosewood

GENERAL CHARACTERISTICS: Continuation of Regency designs

WILLIAM IV 1830–1837

MAJOR WOODS: Mahogany, mahogany veneer

GENERAL CHARACTERISTICS:

- **Case pieces:** Rectilinear; brass mounts, grillwork; carved moldings; plinth bases

- **Seating pieces:** Rectangular backs; carved straight crest rails; acanthus, animal carving; carved cabriole legs; paw feet

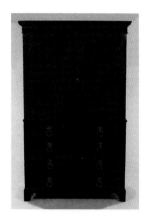

VICTORIAN 1837–1901

MAJOR WOODS: Black walnut, mahogany, veneers, and rosewood

GENERAL CHARACTERISTICS:

- **Case pieces:** Applied floral carving; surmounting mirrors, drawers, candle shelves; marble tops

- **Seating pieces:** High-relief carved crest rails; floral and fruit carving; balloon backs, oval backs; upholstered seats, backs; spool, spiral turnings; cabriole legs, fluted tapered legs; scrolled feet

EDWARDIAN 1901–1910

MAJOR WOODS: Mahogany, mahogany veneer, and satinwood

GENERAL CHARACTERISTICS: Neo-Classical motifs and revivals of earlier 18th century and early 19th century styles

Antique Furniture

Cherry one-drawer stand, possibly New England, early 19th century, the square scratch-beaded top above a drawer and ring-turned tapering legs, old refinish, 25 1/2" high x 15 3/4" wide x 16" deep. **$444**

Courtesy of Skinner Auctioneers, www.skinnerinc.com

▲ Painted pine chest over two drawers, New England, early 18th century, the hinged top on a single arch-molded case of two false drawers and two working drawers below, with applied molding at base, on turned feet, with three original brass escutcheons, old surface, 39" high, case 37 1/2" wide, top 19" deep. **$2,844**

Courtesy of Skinner Auctioneers, www.skinnerinc.com

◄ Pennsylvania painted pine spice chest, 19th century, retaining a smoke decoration on a red ground, 16 1/2" high, 17" wide. **$1,778**

Courtesy of Pook & Pook, Inc., www.pookandpook.com

Federal mahogany slant-lid desk, probably
Massachusetts, circa 1790-1800, the molded
lid opens to an interior of three central
drawers inlaid with an arch of stringing
centering a diamond escutcheon, with flanking
long drawer, short drawers, and valanced
compartments, on a case of four scratch-
beaded graduated drawers and dovetailed
bracket base, old brasses, refinished, 44 1/4"
high x 41" wide x 20 1/2" deep. **$1,185**

Courtesy of Skinner Auctioneers, www.skinnerinc.com

Windsor braced bow-back side chair, partial
brand of I. ALWAYS, New York, late 18th
century, with swelled spindles and bulbous
vase and ring-turnings, refinished, 37" high,
seat 17" high. **$429**

Courtesy of Skinner Auctioneers, www.skinnerinc.com

Federal inlaid mahogany demilune card table,
possibly Charlestown, Massachusetts, circa
1800, old refinish, 29" high x 34 1/2" wide x
17" deep. **$2,133**

Courtesy of Skinner Auctioneers, www.skinnerinc.com

Mid Atlantic classical mahogany card table,
circa 1815, 28 3/4" high, 37 1/2" wide. **$2,133**

Courtesy of Pook & Pook, Inc., www.pookandpook.com

New England Federal mahogany
lyre pedestal card table, circa
1810, 30" high, 36" wide. **$516**

Courtesy of Pook & Pook, Inc.,
www.pookandpook.com

Unusual painted pine bench with four
drawers and boot jack ends, 18" high,
71" long, 13" deep. **$3,081**

Courtesy of Pook & Pook, Inc., www.pookandpook.com

New England pine sawbuck table, 19th century, retaining an old stained surface, 28 1/4" high, 80" wide, 28" deep. **$668**

Courtesy of Pook & Pook, Inc., www.pookandpook.com

Pine wall cupboard with two raised panel doors, circa 1790, 67 1/2" high, 33" wide. **$563**

Courtesy of Pook & Pook, Inc., www.pookandpook.com

Pennsylvania Federal cherry two-part secretary, circa 1805, with unusual chamfered corners with single flute, 87" high, 39 1/2" wide. **$3,555**

Courtesy of Pook & Pook, Inc., www.pookandpook.com

Federal tiger maple and cherry inlaid chest of drawers, Asa Loomis, Shaftsbury, Vermont, 1816, the case of cockbeaded drawers and flanking bird's-eye maple panels, refinished, replaced brass pulls, inscribed on the underside of the top by the cabinetmaker "Made by Asa Loomis in the year 1816," 45 1/4" high, case 42 1/2" wide x 20 3/4" deep. **$6,518**

Courtesy of Skinner Auctioneers, www.skinnerinc.com

Federal cherry and bird's-eye maple and mahogany veneer half sideboard, made in the shop of Hastings Warren (1779-1845), Middlebury, Vermont, 1814, 39 1/2" high, case 40 1/2" wide x 19" deep. **$5,629**

Courtesy of Skinner Auctioneers, www.skinnerinc.com

Federal tiger maple and mahogany, flame birch and bird's-eye maple veneer inlaid bureau, Rutland, Vermont, 1805-1815, rare, refinished, 41 1/2" high, case 42" wide, top 20 1/4" deep. Provenance: Nathan Liverant and Son; Israel Sack, Inc.; Christie's New York, Important American Furniture, Silver, Folk Art and Decorative Arts, June 23, 1993, lot 204, pp. 132-33. **$65,175**

Courtesy of Skinner Auctioneers, www.skinnerinc.com

Red-painted sack-back Windsor chair, Newport, Rhode Island, area, late 18th century, with curved arm supports and carved seat, old red-painted surface over earlier green, 36 1/2" high, seat 16 1/4" high. Consigned by descendant of John Goddard, 18th century Newport, Rhode Island, cabinetmaker. **$7,703**

Courtesy of Skinner Auctioneers, www.skinnerinc.com

Pennsylvania two-piece walnut Dutch cupboard, circa1820, the upper section with glazed doors and candle drawers, 89" high, 59 1/2" wide. **$1,778**

Courtesy of Pook & Pook, Inc., www.pookandpook.com

New England Chippendale figured maple chest on chest, circa 1770, 75" high, 39" wide. **$7,703**

Courtesy of Pook & Pook, Inc., www.pookandpook.com

Federal mahogany inlaid card table, Rhode Island, circa 1795, hinged top with string-inlaid edge, four square tapering legs old surface, 29" high, 34 1/2" wide, 17" deep. **$533**

Courtesy of Skinner Auctioneers, www.skinnerinc.com

Chippendale carved mahogany oxbow slant-lid desk, Massachusetts, circa 1770-1780, old replaced brasses, refinished, 44" high, 42 1/2" wide, 22" deep. **$1,422**

Courtesy of Skinner Auctioneers, www.skinnerinc.com

Queen Anne carved maple and cherry slant-lid desk, Massachusetts or New Hampshire, late 18th century, fitted with an elaborate interior of blocked and shaped drawers, old refinish, 44 1/2" high, case 37 1/2" wide, 18 1/2" deep. **$5,036**

Courtesy of Skinner Auctioneers, www.skinnerinc.com

Federal carved cherry and mahogany veneer inlaid swell-front chest of drawers, probably southeastern New England, circa 1810, the top with reeded edge on four cockbeaded drawers and base of flaring French feet with inlaid crossbanding, old oval brasses, refinished, 37" high, case 40" wide, 21 1/2" deep. **$1,185**

Courtesy of Skinner Auctioneers, www.skinnerinc.com

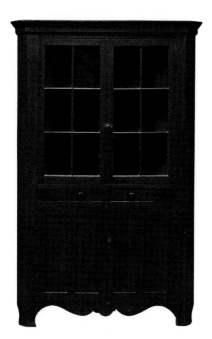

Glazed cherry corner cupboard, possibly Ohio, circa 1830, the doors opening to three shelves with plate grooves, 86" high, 53 1/2" wide. **$770**

Courtesy of Skinner Auctioneers, www.skinnerinc.com

Federal maple carved and inlaid one-drawer stand, possibly Vermont, circa 1825, with contrasting inlay in drawer front, and vase- and ring-turned spiral-carved legs, pulls appear to be original, refinished, 29 3/4" high x 18" wide x 17 3/4" deep. **$889**

Courtesy of Skinner Auctioneers, www.skinnerinc.com

Mustard yellow-painted maple glazed two-part step-back cupboard, Pennsylvania, circa 1830-1840, upper section with hinged doors open to a three-shelf interior with plate grooves, above projecting lower section with two shelves, 81" high, 49" wide, 20" deep. **$2,252**

Courtesy of Skinner Auctioneers, www.skinnerinc.com

Southern Furniture

Regional furniture is highly desirable in today's fractured antique and collectible furniture market. It seems collectors are specializing and becoming more focused in their pursuits of both functional and artistic pieces of furniture. Few areas are as dynamic as Southern furniture. According to the Journal of Early Southern Decorative Arts, interest in Southern furniture is comparatively recent.

Antiquarians began collecting furniture from the North as early as the 1820s, but there was almost no awareness of its southern counterparts before the 1930s. Many of the northern prestigious museums outright shunned Southern furniture in favor of New England craftsmen. In many cases it was also misidentified as from New England or the Middle Atlantic states. Dismissal of the Southern furniture history is but one by-product of differences that reached fever pitch during and after the Civil War.

Today's collectors have long put these slights in their rearview mirror. Values continue to climb for artworks by Thomas Day, Virginia joiner John Shearer, carvers William Buckland and William Bernard Sears. Recently, a circa 1780 Virginia Chippendale walnut sideboard table sold for $87,750 against a $10,000 estimate.

Cupboard, late 18th century, Eastern Virginia, corner cupboard, yellow pine with teal painted field and red trim, 102" h. x 47" w. x 27" d. **$2,400**

Courtesy Leland Little Auctions

Cupboard, circa 1840-1850, mahogany, mahogany veneer, white pine, poplar and oak secondary, one piece form, beveled flared cornice above two cabinet doors with astragal moldings, 86" h. x 44" w. x 32" d., **$850**

Courtesy Leland Little Auctions

Press, late 18th century, Chippendale, china press, Roanoke River Basin, walnut, yellow pine secondary, three part form, upper broken arched cove molded pediment rests on the case and features a central plinth, important, 100" h. x 46" w. x 22" d. **$38,000**

Courtesy Leland Little Auctions

The table had been deaccessioned by the Thomas Jefferson Foundation at Monticello. The museum made clear that this particular table is not directly related to either Thomas Jefferson or Monticello.

The buyer felt that the table closely resembled two related pieces – one of which is held by the Virginia Historical Society. It seems Thomas Jefferson was acquainted with furniture makers in the region. With a little work, it's possible to discover whether or not Jefferson worked with the same craftsmen at the time the table was made. And so the research into the mottled history of Southern furniture continues.

Chest, 1840s, Chatham County, North Carolina, six board yellow pine case with right side open till, dark green ground centered with hand-painted floral and fruit urn with initials for its owner, Mary Jane Pearson (1820-1904), exceptional example of paint decoration and Southern folk art, 20-3/4" h. x 38" w. x 16-1/2" d., **$70,000**

Courtesy Leland Little Auctions

Chest, early 19th century, Rowan County, North Carolina, walnut with yellow pine secondary, early 19th century, two over three scratch beaded drawers, the case set into the original frame having a high arched skirt with pendant drops and cabriole legs terminating in trifid feet, 48" h. x 40" w. x 19-1/5" d., **$15,000**

Courtesy Leland Little Auctions

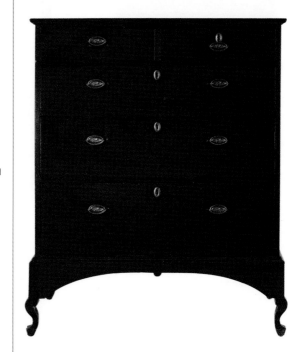

Chest, circa 1830, Washington County, Tennessee painted poplar blanket chest, "sugar chest form," retaining most of the original salmon color paint, 27" h. x 33 1/4" w. x 19-3/4" d. **$475**

Courtesy Case Antiques, Inc. Auctions & Appraisals

Chest, mid-19th century, attributed to Thomas Day, North Carolina, mahogany, mahogany veneers over poplar and yellow pine, tall arched mirror frame centered with a carved finial, 97" h. x 43-1/2" w. x 22" d. **$5,500**

Courtesy Leland Little Auctions

Chest, circa 1780, Chippendale, Roanoke River Valley, yellow pine dovetailed case, allover original blue - green paint, lid with snipe hinges and breadboard ends with battens, open interior, molded base with half blind, dove tailed shaped bracket feet, 24-3/4" h. x 56" w. x 22" d. **$1,300**

Courtesy Leland Little Auctions

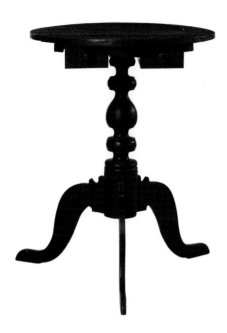

Stand, mid-19th century, Moore Country, N.C., painted candle stand, "Plain Style," poplar with old original red painted surface, 26 3/4" h. x 20 1/8" w. x 19 7/8" d. **$2,200**

Courtesy Leland Little Auctions

Cupboard, circa 1800-1820, Federal, probably Virginia, walnut, poplar secondary, one piece form, pronounced cove molded cornice above a stylized dentil molded frieze, single hinged door with twelve mullioned lights, 88" h. x 43" w. x 28" d. **$3,800**

Courtesy Leland Little Auctions

Table, circa 1770, Eastern North Carolina, Chippendale drop leaf dining, mahogany, oak and yellow pine secondary, rectangular table with drop leaves supported by a single gate leg, 27-3/4 h. x 48" w. x 18-1/2" d. **$18,000**

Courtesy Leland Little Auctions

▲ Desk, early 19th century, possibly Virginia or Tennessee, poplar secondary, dove tailed case, hinged lid with breadboard ends, molded edge, and light wood line inlay, 43-1/4" h. x 39-1/5" w. x 20" d., **$750**

Courtesy Leland Little Auctions

◄ Side table, late 18th century, Southern, one-drawer, walnut, yellow pine secondary, rectangular form, single lipped drawer, scalloped skirt, turned legs with stretcher base, suppressed ball foot, 26" h. x 15" w. x 211/2" d. **$2,300**

Courtesy Leland Little Auctions

Chair, circa 1780, Chippendale, eastern Virginia or North Carolina, yellow pine corner blocks, stiles and crest rail with molded edge, central shaped splat with pierced heart cut-out, molded straight legs with inside chamfer, stretcher base, 37" h. x 26" w. x 21-1/5 d. **$950**

Courtesy Leland Little Auctions

Wash stand, mid-19th century, attributed to craftsman Thomas Day, Caswell County, NC., mahogany veneers, white pine secondary, rectangular marble top with back splash above a single convex drawer, scrolled front supports, shaped lower shelf, 33-1/2" h. x 29" w. x 17" d. **$2,500**

Courtesy Leland Little Auctions

Side table, circa 1800, bald cypress secondary, beveled molded top, three molded lipped drawers with escutcheon and lock, flush side panels, shaped skirt, on tall cabriole legs with hoof foot, 26-3/4" h. x 18" w. x 15-1/4" d. **$9,000**

Courtesy Leland Little Auctions

Sofa, 19th century, Morovian School, Forsyth County
NC, mahogany with yellow pine, the form features
outwardly curved arms, ogee seat rail, and out swept legs,
upholstered, 35" h. x 80" w. x 25" d. **$3,000**

Courtesy Leland Little Auctions

Bed, by Henkel Harris Rice, carved,
tall post bed, mahogany, unsigned, urn finial,
reeded tapered posts with tobacco leaf
terminating in a marlborough foot, bolt rails,
87" h. x 87" w. x 67" d. **$3,000**

Courtesy Leland Little Auctions

Modern Furniture

Although it is often associated with the 1950s, Modern design didn't just one day emerge, say January 1, 1950, fully realized, from the mind of its remote creators.

It is the stuff of the 1933 Chicago World's Fair "Century of Progress," the boundless optimism of post-World War II America, the sleek comic lines and manic music of Tex Avery's MGM 1949 "House of Tomorrow" cartoons, and the ever-present acres of the suburban ranch house that subsequently spread endlessly across the nation.

That form, those colors, the unbridled enthusiasm and audacious hope represented therein … It all hearkens back to post-War 1950s America, when the West was ready to embrace the new realities of easy living and convenience.

The fact is that Modernism has never gone out of style. Its reach into the present day is as deep as its roots in the past. Just as it can be seen and felt ubiquitously in the mass media of today – on film, television, in magazines and department stores – it can be traced to the mid-1800s post-Empire non-conformity of the Biedermeier Movement, the turn of the 20th century anti-Victorianism of the Vienna Secessionists, the radical reductionism of Frank Lloyd Wright and the revolutionary post-Depression thinking of Walter Gropius and the Bauhaus school in Germany. There is no end to the ways in which the movement of Modernism, its evolution and continuing influence, can be parsed. To that end, there is more than a little irony in the fact that, in the world of collecting, Modern has a retro connotation.

In today's economic climate, Modern is as close to a sure bet as collectors – experienced and neophyte alike – are going to get. From there, however, it's a game of names and taste. Do you gravitate to Scandinavian design? American? Chairs or tables? Loveseats or sofas? Lighting?

More than perhaps any other genre, Modernism is open ended, providing a plethora of options and opportunities depending on your taste. Ask the experts where to put your money and energy when it comes to buying Modern and you'll invariably get two answers: Put your energy into what you love, and your money into the best that you can afford. What that means on an individual basis is as varied, however, as the Modern movement itself.

No discussion of Modern can be complete, however, without examining its genesis and enduring influence. There can be no denying that the post-World War II manufacturing techniques, and subsequent boom led to the widespread acceptance of plastic and bent plywood chairs along with low-sitting coffee tables, couches and recliners.

Richard Wright, president and namesake of Wright20 Auctions, one of the leading modern design auction houses in the county, speaks of Modernism's appeal on an individual basis, despite its mass-production origins.

"The Modern aesthetic is the culture of our times," he said. "We live in a post-Modern world that freely borrows from all past styles. In addition, art and design have become signifiers to a large group of the upper-middle class. We are increasingly individually designing our world. Technology fuels this and the wide range of choices available."

"The modern aesthetic grew out of a perfect storm of post-war optimism, innovative materials and an incredible crop of designers," said Lisanne Dickson of John Toomey Gallery. "The wide availability of the designs has made them accessible to the general public at reasonable prices."

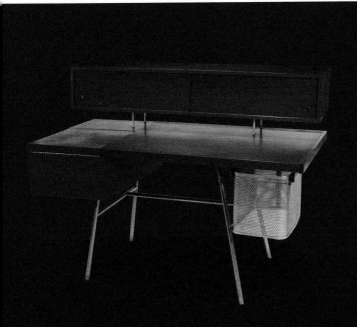

"Home Office" desk, George Nelson design, 1946, manufactured by Herman Miller, Model Nos. 4658 & 601. This example contains the original Pendaflex file basket, which was a special order, 40 1/2" x 54 1/2" x 28". **$6,875**

Courtesy of Rago Arts and Auction, www.ragoarts.com

George Nakashima, Japanese-American woodworker, furniture maker and architect in a warehouse with raw planks of exotic woods. He sits on a Conoid chair of his own design.

Photo by Nathan Benn/ Corbis via Getty Images

George Nakashima
Nature's Architect and Craftsman

George Nakashima (1905-1990) was often called "The Father of the American Crafts Movement." His designs resonated in their day and have grown even more so today, commanding substantial attention at auction. He is famous for his tables – made of huge wooden slabs with unfinished sides and joined by butterfly joins – and his Conoid chairs and benches. His work is treasured at any auction, or at any show, especially if provenance ties the pieces directly back to the hand of Nakashima himself. Prices on the best original Nakashima pieces routinely reach into the high five figures.

Nakashima, born in Spokane, Wash., is an example of the great international melding that symbolizes so much of Modern design. He was deeply influenced by his home in America's Northwest, yet the time he spent in Japan – as well as being interred in a work camp in Idaho during World War II – were as deeply influential on his work as anything he saw or studied in his travels around the world. Nakashima was a master craftsman and woodworker, and he insisted on perfection in every step of the creation of his tables and chairs. His work was not mass-produced; it was one-of-a-kind, lovingly crafted art that doubled as furniture.

Nakashima's home, studio and workshop near New Hope, Pennsylvania, are listed on the U.S. National Register of Historic Places in August 2008; six years later the property was designated a National Historic Landmark. It was in his studio and workshop where Nakashima explored the organic expressiveness of wood and choosing boards with knots and burls and figured grain. He designed furniture lines for Knoll, including the Straight Back Chair (which is still in production), and Widdicomb-Mueller as he continued his private commissions. The studio grew incrementally until Nelson Rockefeller commissioned 200 pieces for his house in Pocantico Hills, New York, in 1973. Demand for his work was fierce after that.

George Nakashima sideboard, circa 1960, American black walnut and pandanus cloth, 31 1/2" x 70 1/2" x 22". **$15,000**

Courtesy of Rago Arts and Auction, www.ragoarts.com

George Nakashima, walnut Conoid dining table with four rosewood keys on book-matched top, signed with client's name, 28 3/4" x 46 1/2" x 72". **$25,620**

Courtesy of Rago Arts and Auction, www.ragoarts.com

Custom bench with drawers, New Hope, Pennsylvania, 1962, Persian walnut, walnut, designed by George Nakashima, manufactured by Nakashima Studios, signed with client's name, 16 1/2" x 108" x 22". Provenance: Copy of original drawing, order card, and evaluation from Mira Nakashima. **$22,500**

Courtesy of Rago Arts and Auction, www.ragoarts.com

Pair of three-drawer bedside tables, New Hope, Pennsylvania, before 1954, walnut, unmarked, designed by George Nakashima, manufactured by Nakashima Studios, 25 1/2" x 15 1/2" x 19". Provenance: Letter of authentication from Mira Nakashima. **$12,500**

Courtesy of Rago Arts and Auction, www.ragoarts.com

Pair of Conoid chairs, New Hope, Pennsylvania, 1969, walnut, hickory, designed by George Nakashima, manufactured by Nakashima Studios, signed with client's name, 35 1/2" x 20" x 21 1/2". **$13,750**

Courtesy of Rago Arts and Auction, www.ragoarts.com

▲ George Nakashima, figured walnut Conoid bench with hickory spindles, unmarked, 30" x 83" x 39". **$21,960**

Courtesy of Rago Arts and Auction, www.ragoarts.com

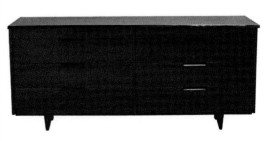

Walnut double dresser, New Hope, Pennsylvania, 1959, designed by George Nakashima, manufactured by Nakashima Studios, signed with client name, 31 3/4" x 60" x 20". **$18,750**

Courtesy of Rago Arts and Auction, www.ragoarts.com

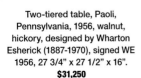

Two-tiered table, Paoli, Pennsylvania, 1956, walnut, hickory, designed by Wharton Esherick (1887-1970), signed WE 1956, 27 3/4" x 27 1/2" x 16". **$31,250**

Courtesy of Rago Arts and Auction, www.ragoarts.com

Double dresser, New Hope, Pennsylvania, 1967-1968, Persian walnut, walnut, unmarked, designed by George Nakashima, manufactured by Nakashima Studios, 32" x 72" x 23 1/2". **$20,000**

Courtesy of Rago Arts and Auction, www.ragoarts.com

For a 1959 Vogue magazine story, Charles Eames, architect and designer, sits with his wife Ray on the floor in their living room, with Eames' furniture and designs in background.

Photo by John Bryson/ Condé Nast via Getty Images

Charles and Ray Eames
A Modern Love Affair

If ever there was a first couple of design, any period, then it was Charles (1907-1978) and Ray (1912-1988) Eames. Lucky for us it happened to be Modernism where the two made their most significant influence. It's challenging to think of another name more synonymous with the form than this husband-and-wife duo. Some designers would have given just about anything to have a single piece of furniture they created be referred to as iconic, but for the Eameses you can choose from a dozen. Charles has even been credited with having single-handedly introducing the Modern era of design with his molded plywood leg braces, developed for the War Department during World War II. While not the most famous design with the Eames name on it, the braces certainly marked a unique moment when the esoteric machine-age philosophy and the practical concerns of Americans melded.

The couple met in 1940, married in 1941, and spent the rest of their lives designing together. In the 1950s, working for the legendary design firm Herman Miller, the couple introduced even more revolutionary techniques than their molded plywood. They engineered new plastic resins and wire mesh chairs that captured the attention of the world. Their methods were easy to reproduce and many other designers quickly picked up on them. For four decades the couple produced a prodigious amount, always working the same way, with the same precision and focus on process. Mention an Eames lounge chair or sofa and even the uninitiated will have an idea of what you mean. While prices for Eames skyrocketed in the 1990s, and dropped back in the early 2000s, decent examples can still be found at auction, for relatively reasonable prices. For original, prime examples in excellent condition, expect to pay five figures and up.

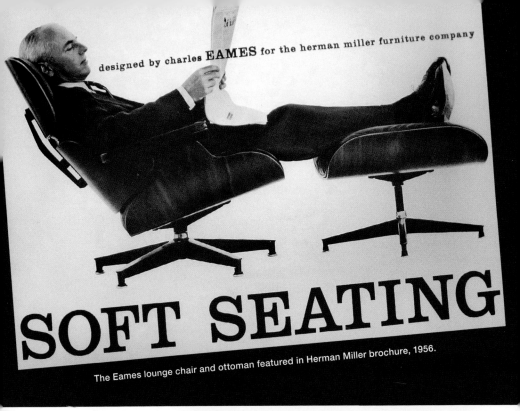

designed by charles **EAMES** for the herman miller furniture company

SOFT SEATING

The Eames lounge chair and ottoman featured in Herman Miller brochure, 1956.

Charles and Ray Eames lounge chair, model no. 670, and ottoman, model no. 671, walnut, leather, enameled aluminum, steel, rubber, black-tufted leather and bent plywood construction, chair with silver Herman Miller label, ottoman with black label, chair 30" high, ottoman 17". **$2,400**

Courtesy of Skinner, Inc.; www.skinnerinc.com

◀ Charles and Ray Eames special-order lounge chair, model no. 670, and ottoman, model no. 671, circa 1956, with firm's foil label, rosewood, enameled aluminum, rubber, original leather upholstery, chair 32 1/2" x 33 1/4" x 34 3/4", ottoman 16 1/8" x 26" x 21 1/2". **$12,500**

Courtesy of Sotheby's, www.southebys.com

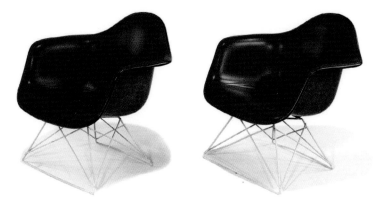

Pair of armchairs, Charles and Ray Eames design, 1950,
manufactured by Zenith Plastics Company for Herman Miller,
molded fiberglass with wire rod base and red Naugahyde pad,
Model No. LAR-6, each 24" x 24 3/4" x 24". **$4,063**

Courtesy of Rago Arts and Auction, www.ragoarts.com

Charles and Ray Eames ESU 270-C birch plywood desk, enameled steel,
lacquered Masonite, laminate, rubber, circa 1950, three drawers in red, black, and
white case panels over perforated metal screen and black laminate shelf, 32 1/2"
high x 24" wide x 16" deep. **$9,600**

Courtesy of Skinner, Inc.; www.skinnerinc.com

Charles and Ray Eames, Evans
Plywood, Herman Miller, walnut
LCW chair, late 1940s, remnants
of an Evans Plywood Co. label,
26 1/4" x 22" x 23 1/2". **$1,586**

Courtesy of Rago Arts and Auction,
www.ragoarts.com

▲ Eames-era "Cloud" sofa, metal and upholstery,
32" high x 96" wide x 44" deep. **$1,700**

Courtesy of Palm Beach Modern Auctions

Wire mesh (Eiffel Tower) chair, Charles and Ray
Eames design, 1951-1953, manufactured by Herman
Miller, Model No. DKR, 32" x 18 1/2" x 17". **$1,250**

Courtesy of Rago Arts and Auction, www.ragoarts.com

▲ Osvaldo Borsani, Tecno, P40 lounge chair, marked, 31" x 27 3/4" x 58". **$2,928**

Courtesy of Rago Arts and Auction, www.ragoarts.com

◄ Pedro Friedeberg, acrylic, pen and ink and carved wood wall relief sculpture, ink signature, 30" x 30" x 1". **$17,080**

Courtesy of Rago Arts and Auction, www.ragoarts.com

▼ Pair of club chairs, United States, 1960s, oak, distressed leather, unmarked, designed by James Mont, manufactured by James Mont Design, 30" x 32" x 42 1/2". **$12,500**

Courtesy of Rago Arts and Auction, www.ragoarts.com

T.H. Robsjohn-Gibbings, Widdicomb, large Mesa walnut veneer coffee table, Widdicomb label, stenciled numbers "3-53, 1760-6", 16 3/4" x 72 1/2" x 49". **$42,700**

Courtesy of Rago Arts and Auction, www.ragoarts.com

Side table, Carl Aubock design, circa 1950, manufactured by Aubock, 16 1/2" x 29" x 21 1/2". **$2,000-$3,000**

Courtesy of Rago Arts and Auction, www.ragoarts.com

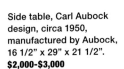

Isamu Noguchi, Herman Miller, rare birch and aluminum Rudder coffee table (no. IN-52), circa 1949, unmarked, 15 1/4" x 50" x 35 1/2". **$7,930**

Courtesy of Rago Arts and Auction, www.ragoarts.com

Sleeper sofa, Marco Zanuso design, 1954, manufactured by Arflex, 32" high x 74" long x 35" deep. **$1,750**

Courtesy of Rago Arts and Auction, www.ragoarts.com

John Lewis, cast glass
Medusa table, 1997,
unmarked, 16" x 60". **$6,100**

Courtesy of Rago Arts and Auction,
www.ragoarts.com

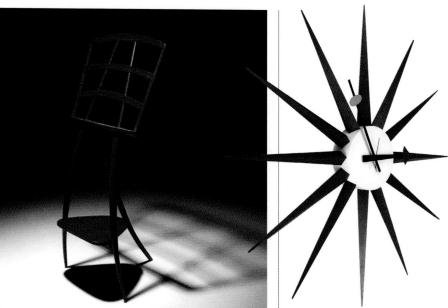

Wharton Esherick, cherry sheet-music stand, 1962, carved
"WE 1962", 43 1/2" x 19 1/2" x 20 1/2". (An identical example
is owned by the Metropolitan Museum of Art, New York.)
$48,800

Courtesy of Rago Arts and Auction, www.ragoarts.com

George Nelson, Howard
Miller, large walnut "Spike"
clock, Howard Miller label,
30" diameter. **$732**

Courtesy of Rago Arts and Auction,
www.ragoarts.com

Non Stop Sofa, Ueli Berger design, 1972, manufactured by de Sede, Ueli Berger, Eleonore Peduzzi-Riva and Heinz Ulrich, Model No. DS-600, approximately 30" x 174" x 39 1/2". **$8,750**

Courtesy of Rago Arts and Auction, www.ragoarts.com

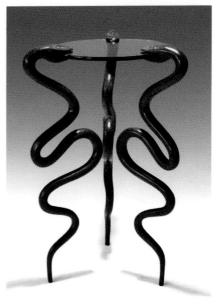

Judy Kensley McKie, patinated bronze and glass Serpent side table, 1997, Inscribed "15 of 16", each snake engraved "JKM 97" and copyright, 31" x 21". **$31,720**

Courtesy of Rago Arts and Auction, www.ragoarts.com

Wing lounge chair (no. 503), United States, 1970s, sculpted walnut, wool, unmarked, designed by Vladimir Kagan, manufactured by Vladimir Kagan Designs, Inc., 42" x 31" x 33". **$10,000**

Courtesy of Rago Arts and Auction, www.ragoarts.com

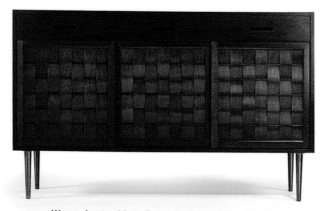

Woven-front cabinet, Berne, Indiana, 1950s, bleached
mahogany, brass, brass label, designed by Edward
Wormley, manufactured by Dunbar, 38" x 61 1/2" x 18 1/4".
$10,000

Courtesy of Rago Arts and Auction, www.ragoarts.com

Console table, New
Hope, Pennsylvania,
1960s, sculpted walnut,
inlaid marble, holly,
unmarked, designed by
Phil Powell, 28" x 80 3/4"
x 20 1/2". **$15,000**

*Courtesy of Rago Arts and
Auction, www.ragoarts.com*

Station wagon desk,
United States, 1940s,
painted cork, stained
and lacquered
mahogany, brass,
branded, designed
by Paul Frankl,
manufactured by
Johnson Furniture Co.,
28" x 60 1/4" x 27".
$10,000

*Courtesy of Rago Arts and
Auction, www.ragoarts.com*

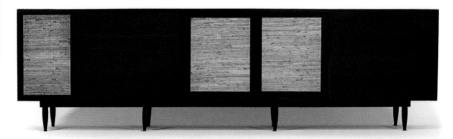

▲ Long cabinet, New Hope, Pennsylvania, circa 1959, walnut, cherry, woven grass cloth, unmarked, designed by Phil Powell, 33" x 21" x 114". **$11,250**

Courtesy of Rago Arts and Auction, www.ragoarts.com

▶ Dressers (2), Edward Wormley design, circa 1955, manufactured by Dunbar, retains Dunbar label in one drawer, each 38" x 41 1/2" x 18". **$2,500**

Courtesy of Rago Arts and Auction, www.ragoarts.com

Oval drop-leaf dining table, Edward Wormley design, circa1950, manufactured by Dunbar, from the "Career Group," Model No. 4913, Dunbar Berne Indiana label, closed: 29" x 72" x 18 1/4"; open: 29" x 72" x 72". **$3,125**

Courtesy of Rago Arts and Auction,

Six-drawer dresser, United States, 1950s, lacquered wood, brass, designed by Tommi Parzinger, manufactured by Parzinger Originals, unmarked, 32" x 85 1/2" x 18 1/2". **$15,000**

Courtesy of Rago Arts and Auction, www.ragoarts.com

Bookcase, Wilhelm Lutjens design, 1953, manufactured by Den Boer, Netherlands, bent plywood with beech veneer, 52" x 58 1/2" x 11 1/2". **$3,125**

Courtesy of Rago Arts and Auction, www.ragoarts.com

Pair of two-drawer side tables (no. 464-393), United States, 1940s, lacquered cork, mahogany, brass, branded and stenciled, designed by Paul Frankl, manufactured by Johnson Furniture Co., 24 1/4" x 24" x 19". **$10,000**

Courtesy of Rago Arts and Auction, www.ragoarts.com

Vladimir Kagan, pair of barrel chairs with painted wood legs, unmarked, 31" x 30" x 36". **$6,100 pair**

Courtesy of Rago Arts and Auction, www.ragoarts.com

Hans J. Wegner
A Danish Modern Master

Hans Jorgen Wegner (1914-2007) helped change the course of design history in the 1950s and '60s. His Danish Modern furniture — most famously his chairs — was elegant and comfortable, making the style all the rage among cosmopolitan Americans of the era.

Wegner learned woodworking as a boy, the son of a cobbler, in Tondern, in southern Denmark. Wegner (pronounced VEG-ner in English and VAY-ner in Danish) rose to international prominence as one of a handful of Danes who seized the design world's attention with a fresh aesthetic of sculptural and organic modern furniture. Others were Arne Jacobsen, Finn Juhl, Borge Mogensen and Poul Kjaerholm.

Their work, often made in warm blond wood, domesticated the cold chrome shine of the Bauhaus-influenced International style. In the process, they found a way to dovetail the words "Danish" and "modern" for the first time, joining cabinetmaker-guild traditions of high craftsmanship, quality and comfort with modernist principles of simplicity and graphic beauty.

Wegner also earned a footnote in political history, when, in 1960, Vice President Richard M. Nixon and Senator John F. Kennedy were seated on Wegner chairs during the first nationally televised presidential debate.

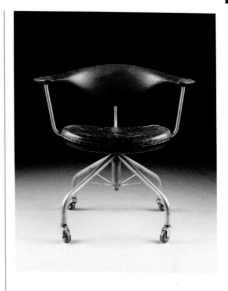

Hans J. Wegner teak and brass Valet Chair, manufactured by Johannes Hansen, Copenhagen, Denmark, designed 1953, 37-1/2 x 19-1/8 x 19-1/2 inches, three-legged with vasiform back and hanger shape crest rail; the saddle form seat is hinged in front by two brass rings, opening to a storage box with leather strip protectors. **$7,767**

Courtesy of Heritage Auctions, www.ha.com

Johannes Hansen swivel arm chair, Copenhagen, Denmark, circa 1955, designed by Hans J. Wegner, wide wood carved backrest with conforming elbow rests, held to seat on chrome armature, distressed black leather seat, four chrome rolling legs on casters, one of the most sought-after pieces of furniture produced during the golden era of mid-century Danish design, 28 3/4" high x 28 3/4" wide x 21 1/2" deep. **$12,000**

Courtesy of Simpson Galleries, www.simpsongalleries.com

Hans Wegner Wishbone Chairs, circa 1950, Carl Hansen & Son, oak and cord, 29-3/4 x 21-1/2 x 19-3/4 inches, applied Hansen label to the underside. **$550**

Courtesy of Heritage Auctions, www.ha.com

Hans J. Wegner contemporary Ox Chair, leather and metal, designed in 1960. **$8,000-$10,000**

Courtesy of Rago Arts and Auction, www.ragoarts.com

Shell sofa, teak plywood, beech, Denmark, Hans J. Wegner (1914-2007), circa 1948, model 1936, original paper label and faded manufacturer's stamp, 27 1/2" high x 48" wide x 21" deep. **$5,535**

Courtesy of Skinner, Inc.; www.skinnerinc.com

Hans J. Wegner, Sawbuck Chair (lounge), designed circa 1952, oak with newer faux leather upholstery, 30-1/4 x 29 x 21-1/4 inches. **$1,065**

Courtesy of Heritage Auctions, www.ha.com

Bellevue chair, France, 1950s,
enameled plywood, enameled steel,
chromed steel, unmarked, designed
by Andre Bloc, 32 1/2" x 16" x 19".
$11,875

Courtesy of Rago Arts and Auction,
www.ragoarts.com

Danish Modern sideboard, rosewood, case with two sliding doors fitted over two outer compartments each with interior adjustable shelf, central compartment fitted with five drawers, tapered legs, unmarked, 31 1/2" high x 86" wide x 18 1/2" deep. **$2,706**

Courtesy of Skinner, Inc.;
www.skinnerinc.com

Sideboard, teak, circa 1950, case with lip to back edge and fitted with central bank of two shallow and two deep drawers flanked by two cabinets each with single adjustable shelf, all with recessed lozenge pulls, turned legs, back and base with branded mark Made in Denmark, George Tanier Selection, Sibast Møbler, 30" high x 72" wide x 19 1/2" deep. **$3,690**

Courtesy of Skinner, Inc.;
www.skinnerinc.com

Pair of lounge chairs (NV 45), Denmark, 1940s, teak, wool, leather, one branded, by cabinetmaker Niels Vodder, Copenhagen, Denmark, designed by Finn Juhl, 32 3/4" x 27 1/2" x 30". **$22,500**

Courtesy of Rago Arts and Auction, www.ragoarts.com

Grasshopper lounge chair, Denmark, 1960s, chrome-plated steel, leather, canvas, unmarked, Preben Fabricius, Jorgen Kastholm, Alfred Kill, 32 1/2" x 28 1/4" x 57". **$13,750**

Courtesy of Rago Arts and Auction, www.ragoarts.com

Grasshopper chair, Eero Saarinen design, 1945, manufactured by Knoll, Model No. 61U, 35 1/2" x 26 1/2" x 33". **$1,800-$2,500**

Courtesy of Rago Arts and Auction, www.ragoarts.com

Chieftain chair, Denmark, 1949, teak, leather, leatherette, branded, cabinetmaker Niels Vodder, Copenhagen, designed by Finn Juhl, 37" x 40 1/2" x 35". **$27,500**

Courtesy of Rago Arts and Auction, www.ragoarts.com

Art Glass

Art glass is artistic novelty glassware created for decorative purposes. Types of art glass include leaded glass, molded glass, blown glass, and sandblasted glass. Tiffany, Lalique, and Steuben are some of the best-known types of art glass. Daum Nancy, Baccarat, Gallé, Moser, Mt. Washington, Fenton,and Quezal are a few others.

▲ Steuben gold Aurene classic vase in yellow with magenta on shoulder, engraved "Steuben" beneath, excellent condition, light surface scratches mainly to one area, 8" high. **$400**

Courtesy of Mark Musio, Humler & Nolan, www.humlernolan.com

◄ Murano glass tall bandiere vase, Anzolo Fuga (attr.), possible A.V.E.M., Murano, Italy, second half 20th century, polychrome and lattimo glass, 18 3/4" high x 8 1/2" diameter. **$5,000**

Courtesy of Rago Arts

Loetz art glass vase, bulbous form shouldered with short neck and flared rim, decoration of wave pattern in blues, purples, and platinum on background of purple with copper iridescent finish, signed Loetz Austria, 7" high. **$2,552**

Courtesy of James D. Julia Auctioneers, www.jamesdjulia.com

Mosaico vase internally decorated with murrines and rods, circa 1925, Vetreria Artistica Barovier, Italy, incised signature "E. Barovier Murano" to lower edge, 13 3/4" high, 8" diameter. **$258,300**

Courtesy of Wright, www.wright20.com

"Wizard Teapot" vase in blown glass, paint, and murrine, circa 1987, Richard Marquis, for Washington State, signed and dated with copyright, 18" x 8 1/2". **$24,320**

Courtesy of Rago Arts and Auctions, www.ragoarts.com

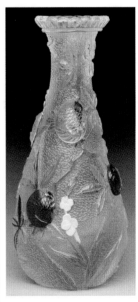

Webb carved and applied vase, cameo carved clear glass flowers surrounding vase against acid-carved background, decorated with applied oval cabochons with colored glass inclusions and wheel carved decorations, decorated with random padded light blue wheel-carved flowers, unsigned, very good to excellent condition, 7" high. **$18,368**

Courtesy of James D. Julia Auctioneers, www.jamesdjulia.com

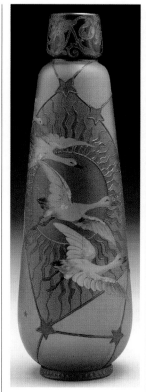

Mt. Washington Peach Blow jack-in-the-pulpit vase, shading from pink to pale blue with crimped top and matte finish, 13" high. **$1,659**

Courtesy of James D. Julia Auctioneers, www.jamesdjulia.com

Mt. Washington Royal Flemish vase decorated with snow geese in flight against large sunburst with surrounding panels of blue and teal separated by raised gold gilding and stars, 14 1/4" high. **$4,859**

Courtesy of James D. Julia Auctioneers, www.jamesdjulia.com

Moser mercury glass pokal, clear glass with mercury lining, decorated with enameled stylized flowers and leaves with two center cartouches with gilded paintings of castles, applied rigaree around top and bottom as well as lid, applied snail-like cabochons on foot and lid, applied cabochons and rigaree are all gilded, 20 1/2" high. **$8,295**

Courtesy of James D. Julia Auctioneers, www.jamesdjulia.com

Gallé vase with purple marquetry iris flowers with yellow and red centers set against mottled yellow and white background, wheel-carved flowers in background encircling entire vase, signed on side with engraved signature Gallé, 8" high. **$21,330**

Courtesy of James D. Julia Auctioneers, www.jamesdjulia.com

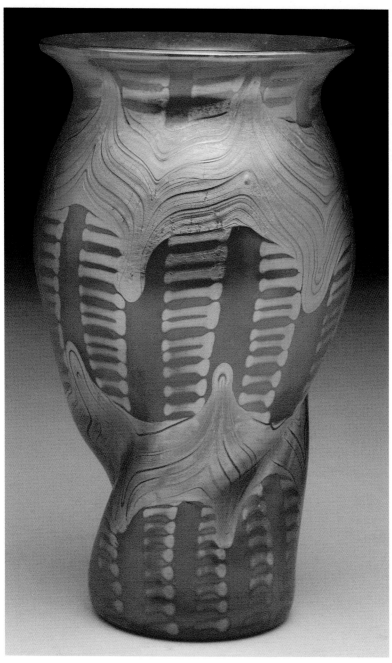

Loetz Phanomen vase with twisted gold body and platinum iridescent
wavy pulled bands at shoulder and waist with platinum iridescent
vertical zipper designs, blue and purple highlights, unsigned, very good
to excellent condition, 7" high. **$7,110**

Courtesy of James D. Julia Auctioneers, www.jamesdjulia.com

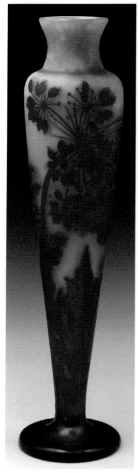

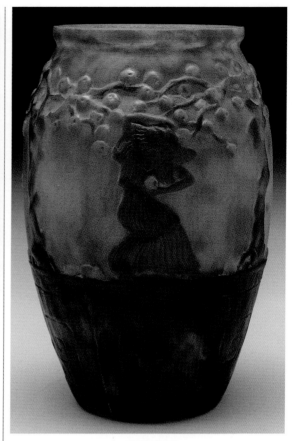

Argy-Rousseau Pate de Verre vase titled "The Garden of Hesperides" (sometimes called the "Apple Picker"), red-orange maidens picking yellow fruit, background of yellow, peach, and frost in upper half, yellows, oranges, and browns to lower geometric portion; signed G. ARGY-ROUSSEAU on side, marked "France" on bottom, 9" high. **$18,960**

Courtesy of James D. Julia Auctioneers, www.jamesdjulia.com

Gallé glass vase with translucent amber cameo leaves, stems and flowers against frosted background of green and cream shading to pink at top, signed on top of foot with engraved signature "Gallé," 17" high. **$1,185**

Courtesy of James D. Julia Auctioneers, www.jamesdjulia.com

"Bursting Chaos" fillet-de-verre sculptural glass bowl with multicolored fused and slumped glass threads, exhibited in "Calido! Contemporary Warm Glass, Tucson Museum of Art Arizona" traveling exhibition, 11" x 21" x 13 1/2". **$22,610**

Courtesy of Mroczek Brothers Seattle Auction House, www.mroczek.com

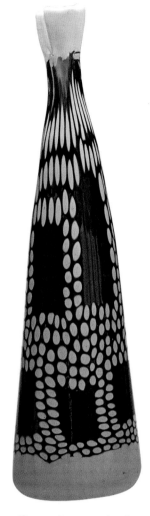

Rare Loetz vase in Phanomen pattern with blue iridescent waves against gold iridescent background, strong purple highlights, gold iridescent stylized leaves extending vertically up body, unsigned, very good to excellent condition, 7" high. **$11,258**

Courtesy of James D. Julia Auctioneers, www.jamesdjulia.com

Murano glass vase, Anzolo Fuga (attr.), possible A.V.E.M., with lattimo glass, Murano, Italy, second half 20th century, unmarked, 21" high x 6" diameter. **$5,000**

Courtesy of Rago Arts

Austrian fan vase, iridescent orange shading to gold with green highlights, slightly ruffled top, ground pontil, unsigned, very good to excellent condition, 12" high x 11 1/2" wide. **$790**

Courtesy of James D. Julia Auctioneers, www.jamesdjulia.com

Alexandrite pedestal-form trumpet vase, gently ribbed, purple flared rim receding to topaz and ending in blue foot, very good to excellent condition, 5" high. **$2,103**

Courtesy of James D. Julia Auctioneers, www.jamesdjulia.com

Loetz vase with pale green body and reddish-brown Cytisus pattern shading to light amber at top with random spots of gold iridescence, five indentations around shoulder, unsigned, very good to excellent condition,
8" high. **$4,444**

Courtesy of James D. Julia Auctioneers, www.jamesdjulia.com

Gallé French cameo vase, wheel-carved iris in purple and green set against mottled green, blue, and purple ground with internal bubble decoration, accented with white and purple vertical ribbing, finished with circular pedestal foot in complimentary colors, signed on side with engraved elaborate Gallé, very good to excellent condition, 6 1/2" high. **$9,480**

Courtesy of James D. Julia Auctioneers, www.jamesdjulia.com

Intarsio vase with alternating orange and green glass tesserae, circa 1963, Ercole Barovier for Barovier & Toso, Italy, 10 1/2" wide x 13 1/2" high. **$56,320**

Courtesy of Wright, www.wright20.com

Thomas Webb & Sons
English cameo art glass vase, cranberry background with blue and white floral decor carved overlay, two butterflies on reverse, signed "Thomas Webb & Sons," good condition, 9 1/2" high. **$19,000**

Courtesy of Woody Auction

Carnival Glass

By Ellen T. Schroy

Carnival glass is what is fondly called mass-produced iridescent glassware. The term "carnival glass" has evolved through the years as glass collectors have responded to the idea that much of this beautiful glassware was made as giveaway glass at local carnivals and fairs. However, more of it was made and sold through the same channels as pattern glass and Depression glass. Some patterns were indeed giveaways, and others were used as advertising premiums, souvenirs, etc. Whatever the origin, the term "carnival glass" today encompasses glassware that is usually pattern molded and treated with metallic salts, creating that unique coloration that is so desirable to collectors.

Early names for iridescent glassware, which early 20th century consumers believed to have all come from foreign manufacturers, include Pompeiian Iridescent, Venetian Art, and Mexican Aurora. Another popular early name was "Nancy Glass" as some patterns were believed to have come from the Daum, Nancy, glassmaking area in France. This was at a time when the artistic cameo glass was enjoying great success. While the iridescent glassware being made by such European glassmakers as Loetz influenced the American market place, it was Louis Tiffany's Favrile glass that really caught the eye of glass consumers of the early 1900s. It seems an easy leap to transform Tiffany's shimmering glassware to something that could be mass-produced, allowing what we call carnival glass today to become "poor man's" Tiffany.

Carnival glass is iridized glassware that is created by pressing hot molten glass into molds, just as pattern glass had evolved. Some forms are hand finished, while others are completely formed by molds. To achieve the marvelous iridescent colors that carnival glass collectors seek, a process was developed where a liquid solution of metallic salts was put onto the still hot glass form after it was unmolded. As the liquid evaporated, a fine metallic surface was left which refracts light into wonderful colors. The name given to the iridescent spray by early glassmakers was "dope".

ELLEN T. SCHROY one of the leading experts in her field, is the author of *Warman's Carnival Glass Identification and Price Guide* and other books on collectible glass. Her books are the definitive references for glass collectors.

▲ Northwood Grape and Cable bonbon, stippled, aqua opalescent. **$4,000**

◀ Little Stars ice cream shaped bowl, marigold, made by Millersburg, 9" diameter, rare size. **$850**

Many of the forms created by carnival glass manufacturers were accessories to the china American housewives so loved. By the early 1900s, consumers could find carnival glassware at such popular stores as F. W. Woolworth and McCrory's. To capitalize on the popular fancy for these colored wares, some other industries bought large quantities of carnival glass and turned them into "packers". This term reflects the practice where baking powder, mustard, or other household products were packed into a special piece of glass that could take on another life after the original product was used. Lee Manufacturing Co. used iridized carnival glass as premiums for its baking powder and other products, causing some early carnival glass to be known by the generic term "Baking Powder Glass".

Classic carnival glass production began in the early 1900s and continued for about 20 years. Fenton Art Glass became the top producer with more than 150 patterns. No one really documented or researched production until the first collecting wave struck in 1960.

It is important to remember that carnival glasswares were sold in department stores as well as mass merchants rather than through the general store often associated with a young America. Glassware by this time was mass-produced and sold in large quantities by such enterprising companies as Butler Brothers. When the economics of the country soured in the 1920s, those interested in purchasing iridized glassware were not spared. Many of the leftover inventories of glasshouses that hoped to sell this mass-produced glassware found their way to wholesalers who, in turn, sold the wares to those who offered the glittering glass as prizes at carnivals, fairs, circuses, etc. Possibly because this was the last venue people associated with the iridized glassware, it became known as "carnival glass."

For more information on carnival glass, see *Warman's Carnival Glass Identification and Price Guide,* 2nd edition, by Ellen T. Schroy.

Acanthus pattern deep round bowl, emerald green, Imperial Glass Co., rare. **$650**

Courtesy of Seeck Auctions, www.seeckauction.com

Grape and Cable pattern exterior/Persian Medallion pattern interior orange bowl, emerald green iridescent, circa 1911, ruffled and scalloped rim, three ball feet, Fenton Art Glass Co., 5 1/2" high overall, 9 3/4" diameter overall. **$108**

Courtesy of Jeffrey S. Evans & Associates, www.jeffreysevans.com

Farmyard pattern ruffled bowl, purple, base. **$2,100**

Courtesy of Seeck Auctions, www.seeckauction.com

Rare Cherry Chain pattern chop plate, marigold, Fenton Art Glass Co., good condition, 11". **$944**

Courtesy of Woody Auction, www.woodyauction.com

Daisy and Drape pattern vase, aqua opalescent, three feet, first quarter 20th century, H. Northwood Co., 6 1/4" high. **$360**

Courtesy of Jeffrey S. Evans & Associates, www.jeffreysevans.com

◀ Northwood Daisy and Plume rose bowl, aqua opalescent, footed, one of three known, possibly only butterscotch. **$7,000**

▲ Peacock at the Fountain master berry bowl, ice blue, straight up. **$650**

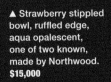

▲ Strawberry stippled bowl, ruffled edge, aqua opalescent, one of two known, made by Northwood. **$15,000**

Leaf and Beads pattern rose bowl, ice green, Northwood Glass Co. **$2,000**

Courtesy of Seeck Auctions, www.seeckauction.com

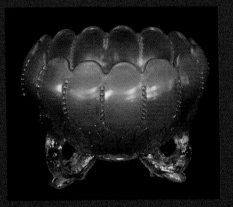

Raspberry water pitcher and five tumblers (four shown), ice blue, made by Northwood. **$1,400**

Blackberry Spray ruffled hat, red opalescent, made by Fenton. **$650**

Cherry Chain bonbon, large size, red, made by Fenton. **$5,000**

▲ Good Luck bowl, enameled, only one known, blue, made by Northwood. **$800**

◄ Holly ruffled bowl, red, made by Fenton, 9" diameter. **$1,200**

Grape Arbor water pitcher and one tumbler, ice green, one of three known, made by Northwood. **$10,000**

Fashion compote, smoke, made by Imperial. **$900**

Acorn Burrs punch bowl,
base and six cups, ice green,
made by Northwood, very few
known. **$23,000**

Heavy Iris water pitcher,
tankard, peach opalescent,
made by Dugan. **$2,000**

Daisy and Drape vase,
turned in, ice green, made by
Northwood. **$4,000**

Rose Show plate, ice green opalescent,
made by Northwood. **$10,000**

Three Fruits bowl, sapphire,
made by Northwood. **$2,200**

Multi-Fruits
and Flowers
water pitcher,
green, made
by Millersburg.
$15,000

Feather and Heart water pitcher and six tumblers, dark marigold, made by Millersburg. **$875**

Frolicking Bears water pitcher and one tumbler, green, one of three known, made by U.S. Glass. **$42,000**

Gay Nineties water pitcher and one tumbler, green, made by Millersburg. Only one perfect known, second known pitcher, second known tumbler. **$24,000**

▲ Inverted Feather water pitcher, marigold, made by Cambridge. **$8,100**

◄ Palm Beach vase, whimsy, marigold, made by U.S. Glass, 6 1/2" high, 3 1/2" base. **$800**

Daum Nancy

Daum Nancy fine glass, much of it cameo, was made by Auguste and Antonin Daum, who founded a factory in 1875 in Nancy, France. Most of their cameo and enameled glass was made from the 1890s into the early 20th century.

Cameo glass is made by carving into multiple layers of colored glass to create a design in relief. It is at least as old as the Romans.

Rib-optic decanter and two wine glasses, pink and colorless with gilt decorations, decanter with applied handle and original cut stopper, each wine with thistle-shape bowl engraved with fleur-de-lis, ribbed stem and foot with polished pontil mark, circa 1891, wines undamaged, decanter with small chip and associated short crack to rim at upper handle terminal, 9 1/2" high and 4 7/8" high. **$173**

Courtesy of Jeffrey S. Evans & Associates, jeffreysevans.com

◄ "Monnaie du Pape" lamp with glass shades, circa 1903, gilt metal cameo, two sockets, base molded "L. Majorelle, DAUM NANCY" and Cross of Lorraine etched on shades, excellent condition, light oxidation to base, 26 1/2" high x 10" wide. **$45,312**

Courtesy of Rago Arts and Auctions, ragoarts.com

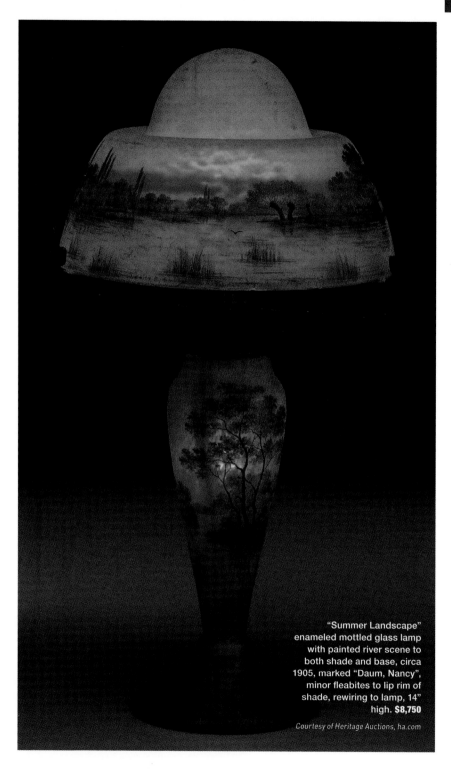

"Summer Landscape"
enameled mottled glass lamp
with painted river scene to
both shade and base, circa
1905, marked "Daum, Nancy",
minor fleabites to lip rim of
shade, rewiring to lamp, 14"
high. **$8,750**

Courtesy of Heritage Auctions, ha.com

Rectangular winter scene vase decorated with cameo trees on all four sides with enameled tree bark and snow on trees and covering ground, yellow shading to orange background, signed on underside in black enamel "Daum Nancy" with Cross of Lorraine, very good to excellent condition, 7 1/4" high. **$7,110**

Courtesy of James D. Julia, Inc., jamesdjulia.com

Vase with enameled cameo glass autumn scene, signed "Daum Nancy" with Cross of Lorraine, circa 1900, excellent condition, 13 1/4" high x 5 3/4" wide. **$14,844**

Courtesy of Rago Arts and Auctions, ragoarts.com

Cameo cabinet vase, yellow and purple mottled background with carved floral, wasp, and spiderweb design, signed, no chips, cracks or repairs, 4" high x 4 1/2" wide. **$3,835**

Courtesy of Woody Auction, woodyauction.com

Lamp with cameo and enameled winter scene of barren trees
on snow-covered ground, trees enameled in brown, shade in
triangular shape with flared apron, with original hammered
iron collar and spider, signed on underside of base with
enamel signature "Daum Nancy" with Cross of Lorraine,
very good to excellent condition, some wear to finish on iron
spider and replacement socket, rewired, 18" high. **$16,590**

Courtesy of James D. Julia, Inc., jamesdjulia.com

Quadrefoil-shaped bowl with violets in various stages of bloom in purple with green stems and foliage set against purple and white frosted ground, signed "Daum Nancy" with Cross of Lorraine on side of bowl, very good to excellent condition, 3" high x 8" diameter. **$4,740**

Courtesy of James D. Julia, Inc., jamesdjulia.com

Autumn leaf box decorated with vitrified glass cameo leaves surrounding body and lid of box in green, yellow, orange and red against mottled frosted background, signed on side with engraved signature "Daum Nancy" with Cross of Lorraine, very good to excellent condition, 5 1/2 diameter x 3" high. **$3,555**

Courtesy of James D. Julia, jamesdjulia.com

Large French cameo lamp with domical-shaped shade decorated in earthen hues with pattern of grape clusters and vines on mottled yellow and peach ground, shade supported by three-armed base with same grape cluster and leaf decoration and background coloration, signed in cameo on shade "Daum Nancy" with Cross of Lorraine, signed in cameo "DN" with Cross of Lorraine on base, very good to excellent condition with single socket replaced and painted, shade 15" diameter, lamp 24" high. **$5,333**

Courtesy of James D. Julia, Inc., jamesdjulia.com

▲ "Apres L' Amour" pate-de-verre glass sculpture, late 20th century, marked "SL, Daum, France, 027/375", with original retail tag on underside, good condition, 27" long. **$4,500**

Courtesy of Heritage Auctions, ha.com

▶ Handled pitcher in ovoid shape with cameo winter scene decoration, signed "Daum Nancy", 5 3/4" high. **$5,900**

Courtesy of Woody Auction, woodyauction.com

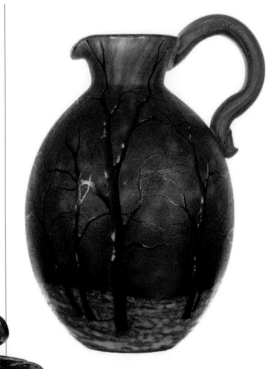

◀ Cameo and applied glass jar with layered autumnal-colored cameo oak leaves and background, decorated with applied acorns and insect, one oak leaf decorated with faceted cabochon with foil backing, matching lid with carved and applied insect, signed on underside with incised signature "Daum Nancy" with Cross of Lorraine, very good to excellent condition, 4" square x 4 1/2" high. **$3,555**

Courtesy of James D. Julia, Inc., jamesdjulia.com

French cameo tray of vitrified glass depicting grapes with leaves in purple, green, russet, and brown on molten ground of green, purple, and frost, scalloped border, signed "Daum Nancy" with Cross of Lorraine in cameo, very good to excellent condition, 8 1/4" diameter. **$948**

Courtesy of James D. Julia, Inc., jamesdjulia.com

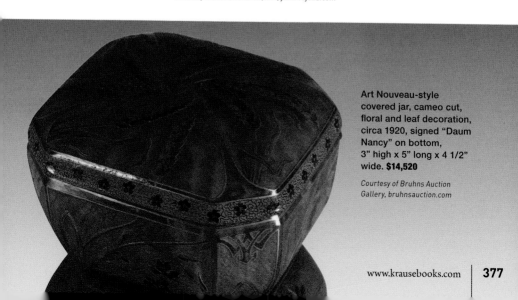

Art Nouveau-style covered jar, cameo cut, floral and leaf decoration, circa 1920, signed "Daum Nancy" on bottom, 3" high x 5" long x 4 1/2" wide. **$14,520**

Courtesy of Bruhns Auction Gallery, bruhnsauction.com

Table lamp with cameo decoration of large green leaves encircling shade and base with orange cameo oranges or peaches against mottled pink shading to orange background, lamp base with hammered metal collar and four-arm spider, shade signed on side in cameo "Daum Nancy" with Cross of Lorraine, base signed near bottom "DN," very good to excellent condition, rewired, 10 1/2" wide x 19 3/4" high. **$9,480**

Courtesy of James D. Julia, Inc., jamesdjulia.com

Applied glass covered jar, rare, one green-gold applied cabochon, one green applied insect, and one red applied leaf on body with acid etched maple leaves, lid has applied and wheel-carved handle with red applied insect on top, signed on underside with remnants of engraved and gilded "Daum Nancy" with Cross of Lorraine, very good to excellent condition, 4 1/2" high. **$2,844**

Courtesy of James D. Julia, Inc., jamesdjulia.com

Vase with red cameo leaves, stems, and flowers extending from foot against frosted amber background, flowers and some leaves detailed with wheel carving, background near foot with wheel-carved texture, signed on side of foot with engraved signature "Daum Nancy France" with Cross of Lorraine, very good to excellent condition, 9 1/2" high. **$8,295**

Courtesy of James D. Julia, Inc., jamesdjulia.com

Cameo and enameled footed vase decorated with cameo violets enameled in purple with gilded outline of stylized leaves around foot, finished with three applied blue glass loop feet, signed on underside with engraved signature "Daum Nancy," very good to excellent condition, 4 5/8" diameter x 4" high. **$9,480**

Courtesy of James D. Julia, Inc., jamesdjulia.com

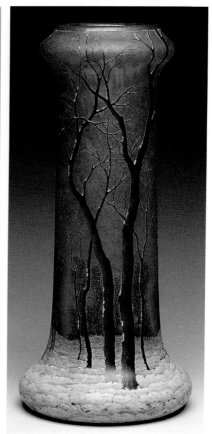

▲ Large vase with cameo and enameled winter scene with barren trees rising from enameled snowy ground, tree trunks enameled in brown, cameo decoration set against mottled yellow shading to orange background, signed on underside in black enamel "Daum Nancy" with Cross of Lorraine, very good to excellent condition, 14" high. **$10,665**

Courtesy of James D. Julia, Inc., jamesdjulia.com

◄ Vase with cameo decoration of various colored mushrooms with pine tree limbs, needles and pinecones near top of vase against mottled yellow and cream background, wheel-carved detailing to grasses at bottom of vase and underside of mushrooms, mushrooms enameled in orange, green, brown, and tan, signed on underside with etched signature "Daum Nancy" with Cross of Lorraine, very good to excellent condition, small grind mark to outside lip and small acid burn on lip from manufacture, 15 3/4" high. **$11,850**

Courtesy of James D. Julia, Inc., jamesdjulia.com

Vase of silver-mounted cameo glass with wheel-carved azaleas, circa 1900, silver stamped with hallmarks, "Daum Nancy" with Cross of Lorraine acid-etched to bottom, excellent condition, 7 1/4" high x 4 1/2" wide. **$12,500**

Courtesy of Rago Arts and Auctions, www.ragoarts.com

Vase with cameo flowers, stems and leaves extending from applied stem upward, stems and leaves enameled in shaded green, flowers enameled in shaded red, cameo spiderwebs throughout flowers, applied foot and stem with brown cameo stylized leaves against frosted brown background, signed on side in cameo "Daum Nancy" with Cross of Lorraine, very good to excellent condition, 8 1/8" high. **$7,703**

Courtesy of James D. Julia, Inc., jamesdjulia.com

Cameo and enameled vase with cameo decoration of barren trees rising from snowy ground against light blue frosted background sky with snow in air, trees enameled in mottled gray with four enameled blackbirds perched on tree limbs with three blackbirds in flight, signed on underside in black enamel "Daum Nancy" with Cross of Lorraine, very good to excellent condition, 2 3/4" high. **$10,665**

Courtesy of James D. Julia, Inc., jamesdjulia.com

Vase with cameo and enameled seagulls flying over ocean with setting
sun in background, sea turtle looking at a seagull, gray enameled details
to feathers and turtle shell, cameo decoration set against opalescent
shading to white background, gilded lip, foot and sun rays, signed on
underside in gold "Daum Nancy" with Cross of Lorraine, very good to
excellent condition, 7 1/2" high. **$11,850**

Courtesy of James D. Julia, Inc., jamesdjulia.com

◄ Vase with mottled green and orange cameo leaves and stems leading to large cameo flowers in red, purple, lavender, and yellow against frosted background of mottled purple shading to yellow shading to cream, signed on underside with lightly etched signature "Daum Nancy" with Cross of Lorraine, very good to excellent condition, 10" high. **$5,558**

Courtesy of James D. Julia, Inc., jamesdjulia.com

Vase with tall oval body decorated with white cameo swan in pond with white cameo trees and grasses extending around to back of vase, cameo with gray enamel shading with white cameo leaves and grasses with random green spattering, signed on underside in black enamel "Daum Nancy" with Cross of Lorraine, very good to excellent condition, 8 3/4" high. **$11,850**

Courtesy of James D. Julia, Inc., jamesdjulia.com

Depression Glass

By Ellen T. Schroy

Depression glass is the name of the colorful glassware manufactured during the years surrounding the Great Depression in America. Homemakers of the era enjoyed this new, inexpensive dinnerware because they received pieces of their favorite patterns and colors packed in boxes of soap or as premiums on "dish night" at the local movie theater. Merchandisers, such as Sears & Roebuck and F. W. Woolworth, enticed young brides with the colorful wares that they could afford even when economic times were harsh.

Because of advancements in glassware technology, Depression-era patterns were mass-produced and could be purchased for a fraction of what cut glass or lead crystal cost. As one manufacturer found a pattern that was pleasing to the buying public, other companies soon followed with their adaptations of a similar design. Hundreds of patterns exist and include several design motifs, such as florals, geometrics, and even patterns that looked back to Early American patterns like Sandwich glass.

As America emerged from the Great Depression and life became more leisure-oriented again, new glassware patterns were created to reflect the new tastes of this generation. More elegant shapes and forms were designed, leading to what is sometimes called "Elegant Glass." Today's collectors often include these more elegant patterns when they talk about Depression glass.

Depression glass researchers have many accurate sources, including company records, catalogs, magazine advertisements, and oral and written histories from sales staff, factory workers, etc. It is one of the best-researched collecting areas available to the American marketplace. This is due in large part to the careful research of several people, including Hazel Marie Weatherman, Gene Florence, Barbara Mauzy, Carl F. Luckey, and Kent Washburn, whose books are held in

ELLEN T. SCHROY, one of the leading experts in her field, is the author of *Warman's Depression Glass Identification and Price Guide* and *Warman's Depression Glass Handbook.* Her books are the definitive references for Depression glass collectors.

Floral, pink
dinner plate.
$22.50

high regard by researchers and collectors today.

Regarding values for Depression glass, rarity does not always equate to a high dollar amount. Some more readily found items command lofty prices because of high demand or other factors, not because they are necessarily rare. As collectors' tastes range from the simple patterns to the more elaborate patterns, so does the ability of their budget to invest in inexpensive patterns to multi-hundreds of dollars per form patterns.

For more information on Depression glass, see *Warman's Depression Glass Handbook: Identification, Values, Pattern Guide, Warman's Depression Glass Identification and Price Guide*, 6th Edition, or *Warman's Depression Glass Field Guide*, 5th Edition, all by Ellen T. Schroy.

PATTERN SILHOUETTE Identification Guide

Depression-era glassware can be confusing. Many times a manufacturer came up with a neat new design, and as soon as it was successful, other companies started to make patterns that were similar. To help you figure out what pattern you might be trying to research, here's a quick identification guide. The patterns are broken down into several different classifications by design elements.

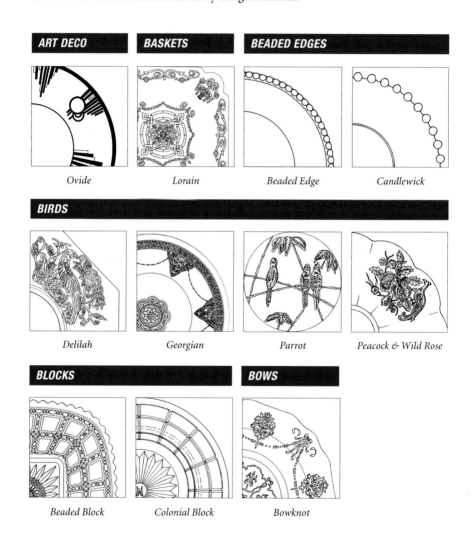

ART DECO

Ovide

BASKETS

Lorain

BEADED EDGES

Beaded Edge

Candlewick

BIRDS

Delilah

Georgian

Parrot

Peacock & Wild Rose

BLOCKS

Beaded Block

Colonial Block

BOWS

Bowknot

COINS

Coin

CUBES

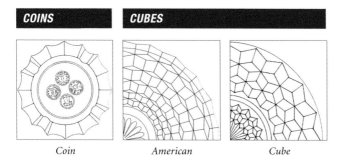

American   *Cube*

DIAMONDS

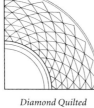

Cape Cod   *Diamond Quilted*   *English Hobnail*   *Holiday*

Laced Edge   *Miss America*   *Peanut Butter*   *Waterford*

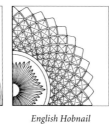

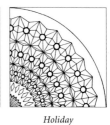

Windsor

ELLIPSES (FANS)

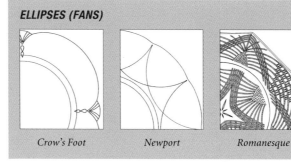

Crow's Foot   *Newport*   *Romanesque*

FIGURES

Cameo

Cupid

FLORALS

Alice

Cherry Blossom

Cloverleaf

Daisy

Dogwood

Doric

Doric & Pansy

Floragold

Floral

Floral and
Diamond Band

Flower Garden with
Butterflies

Indiana Custard

Iris

Jubilee

FLORALS *continued*

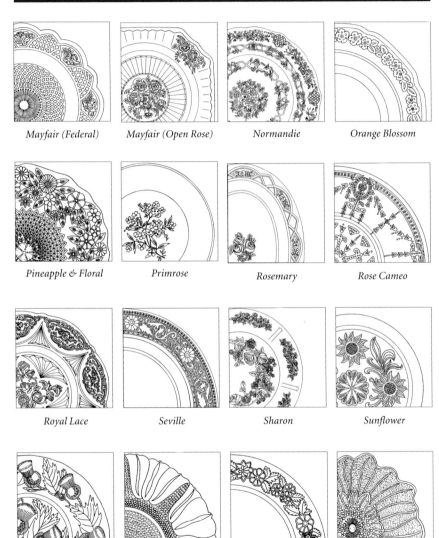

Mayfair (Federal) Mayfair (Open Rose) Normandie Orange Blossom

Pineapple & Floral Primrose Rosemary Rose Cameo

Royal Lace Seville Sharon Sunflower

Thistle Tulip Vitrock Wild Rose

FRUITS

Avocado

Cherryberry

Della Robbia

Fruits

Paneled Grape

Strawberry

GEOMETIC & LINE DESIGNS

Cracked Ice

Cape Cod

Cremax

Early American Prescut

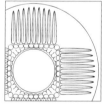

Park Avenue

Pioneer

Sierra

Star

Starlight

Tea Room

HONEYCOMB

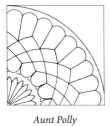

Aunt Polly

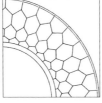

Hex Optic

HORSESHOE

Horseshoe

LEAVES

Laurel Leaf

Sunburst

LACY DESIGNS

Harp

Heritage

S-Pattern

Sandwich (Duncan Miller)

Sandwich (Hocking)

Sandwich (Indiana)

LOOPS

Christmas Candy

Crocheted Crystal

Pretzel

PETALS

Aurora

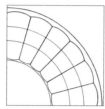

Block Optic

Circle

Colonial

National

New Century

Old Café

Ribbon

Roulette

Round Robin

Victory

PETALS/RIDGES WITH DIAMOND ACCENTS

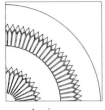

Anniversary

Coronation

Fortune

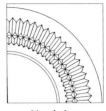

Lincoln Inn

Petalware

Queen Mary

PLAIN

Charm

Mt. Pleasant

PYRAMIDS

Pyramid

RAISED BAND

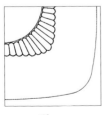

Charm

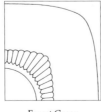

Forest Green

Jane Ray

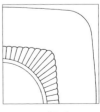

Royal Ruby

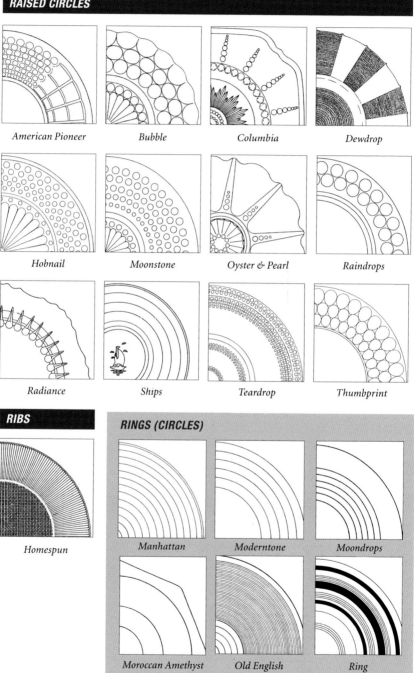

RAISED CIRCLES

American Pioneer

Bubble

Columbia

Dewdrop

Hobnail

Moonstone

Oyster & Pearl

Raindrops

Radiance

Ships

Teardrop

Thumbprint

RIBS

Homespun

RINGS (CIRCLES)

Manhattan

Moderntone

Moondrops

Moroccan Amethyst

Old English

Ring

SCENES

Chinex Classic

Lake Como

SCROLLING DESIGNS

Adam

American Sweetheart

Florentine No. 1

Florentine No. 2

Madrid

Patrick

Philbe

Primo

Princess

Rock Crystal

Roxana

Vernon

SWIRLS

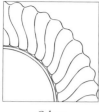
Colony

Diana

Fairfax

Jamestown

Spiral

Swirl

Swirl (Fire King)

Twisted Optic

TEXTURED

U.S. Swirl

By Cracky

Twiggy

Adam pattern pink butter dish, Jeannette Glass Co., 1932-1934.
$40

Courtesy of Specialists of the South, specialistsofthesouth.com

Adam, green ashtray. **$28**
Pink pitcher. **$65**

▲ Aurora pattern cobalt blue tumbler, Hazel Atlas Glass Co., late 1930s. **$22**

▲ Coin, red candy dish with cover. **$120**

◄ Bubble pattern royal ruby two-tier tidbit tray, Hocking Glass Co./Anchor Hocking Glass Co., 1937-1965. **$35**

Cameo pattern sandwich server with center handle in green, one of only four recorded examples, Hocking Glass Co., 1930-1934, undamaged, 4" high overall, 10" diameter. **$5,000-$6,000**

Courtesy of Jeffrey S. Evans & Associates, jeffreysevans.com

Colony pattern pink candlesticks, Fostoria Glass Co., 1930s-1983, excellent condition, 8" high. **$48**

Courtesy of Milestone Auctions, milestoneauctions.com

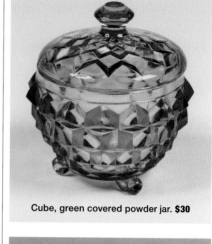

Cube, green covered powder jar. **$30**

Daisy, amber creamer. **$10**

Early American Prescut, crystal cake plate. **$25**

Fire King Charm, Azur-ite cup and saucer. **$12**

▲ English Hobnail pattern pink covered puff box, Westmoreland Glass Co., 1920s-1983, 6" diameter. **$80**

Holiday/Buttons and Bows pink covered butter dish, Jeannette Glass Co., 1947-1950s, 6" diameter. **$40**

Courtesy of Specialists of the South, specialistsofthesouth.com

Iris, iridescent vase, 9". **$25**

Jubilee, yellow goblet. **$150**

Newport pattern cobalt blue pitcher with ice lip, creamer, sugar, five cups, four saucers, four plates, and sherbet, plates 8 1/4" diameter. **$34**

Courtesy of Specialists of the South, specialistsofthesouth.com

Old Café, royal ruby bowl with handles and original label. **$15**

Parrot, amber jam dish. **$35**
Green sherbet plate. **$35**

Patrician, amber pitcher, molded handle, 75 oz, 8" high. **$110**

Princess, green octagonal salad bowl. **$40**
Cookie jar. **$65**

Queen Mary, pink oval open sugar. **$12.**
Oval creamer. **$14**

Royal Ruby, tilted ball pitcher, 5 1/2". **$45**

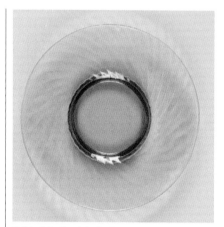

Twisted Optic, pink sherbet plate, 6" diameter. **$3**

Swirl, ultramarine sugar. **$15**
Creamer. **$12**

Fenton

The Fenton Art Glass Co. was founded in 1905 by Frank L. Fenton and his brother, John W., in Martins Ferry, Ohio. They initially sold hand-painted glass made by other manufacturers, but it wasn't long before they decided to produce their own glass.

The new Fenton factory in Williamstown, West Virginia, opened on Jan. 2, 1907. From that point on, the company expanded by developing unusual colors and continued to decorate glassware in innovative ways. Two more brothers, James and Robert, joined the firm.

But despite the company's initial success, John W. left to establish the Millersburg Glass Co. of Millersburg, Ohio, in 1909. The first months of the new operation were devoted to the production of crystal glass only. Later iridized glass was called "Radium Glass." After only two years, Millersburg filed for bankruptcy.

Fenton's iridescent glass had a metallic luster over a colored, pressed pattern, and sold in dime stores. It was only after the sales of this glass decreased and it was sold in bulk as carnival prizes that it came to be known as carnival glass.

Fenton became the top producer of carnival glass, with more than 150 patterns. The quality of the glass, and its popularity with the public, enabled the new company to be profitable through the late 1920s.

As interest in carnival glass subsided, Fenton moved on to stretch glass and opalescent patterns. A line of

Karnak red-footed bowl with Hanging Vine decoration and random threading, cobalt blue edge and cobalt blue stem and foot, iridescent finish, mid-1920s, 8 1/2" diameter. $2,630

Courtesy of Randy Clark/Dexter City Auction Gallery

Karnak red No. 3024 vase
with applied Hanging Vine
decoration, 18 1/2" high.
$16,500

*Courtesy of Randy Clark/Dexter City
Auction Gallery*

Mosaic inlaid No. 3051 vase,
ground and polished pontil,
shiny finish, mid-1920s,
10 1/2" high. **$2,750**

*Courtesy of Randy Clark/
Dexter City Auction Gallery*

colorful blown glass (called "off-hand" by Fenton) was also produced in the mid-1920s.

During the Great Depression, Fenton survived by producing functional colored glass tableware and other household items, including water sets, table sets, bowls, mugs, plates, perfume bottles, and vases.

Restrictions on European imports during World War II ushered in the arrival of Fenton's opaque colored glass, and the lines of "Crest" pieces soon followed.

In the 1950s, production continued to diversify with a focus on milk glass, particularly in Hobnail patterns.

In the third quarter of Fenton's history, the company returned to themes that had proved popular to preceding generations, and began adding special lines, such as the Bicentennial series.

Innovations included the line of Colonial colors that debuted in 1963, including amber, blue, green, orange and ruby. Based on a special order for an Ohio museum, Fenton in 1969 revisited its early success with "Original Formula Carnival Glass." Fenton also started marking its glass in the molds for the first time.

The star of the 1970s was the yellow and blushing pink creation known as Burmese, which remains popular today, followed closely by a menagerie of animals, birds, and children.

In 1975, Robert Barber was hired by Fenton to begin an artist-in-residence program, producing a limited line of art-glass vases in a return to the off-hand, blown-glass creations of the mid-1920s.

In August 2007, Fenton discontinued all but a few of its more popular lines, and in 2011 ceased production entirely.

For more information on Fenton Art Glass, see *Warman's Fenton Glass Identification and Price Guide*, 2nd edition, by Mark F. Moran.

Turquoise vase with applied
Hanging Vine decoration,
mid-1920s, 11" high. **$2,750**

*Courtesy of Randy Clark/
Dexter City Auction Gallery*

▲ Twelve-piece hobnail drink set in blue opalescent, possibly Fenton, large pitcher with ruffled rim, 7 3/4" high, 7 1/2" diameter, and 11 tumblers with slightly rounded bodies, 4 3/4" high, 2 1/2" diameter. **$423**

Courtesy of Austin Auction Gallery, www.austinauction.com

◄ Pulled Feather offhand vase in rainbow colors, Fenton oval logo on underside, designed by Robert Barber, circa 1975, 7 1/4" high. **$880**

Courtesy of Randy Clark/Dexter City Auction Gallery

Mulberry Diamond Optic pitcher and matching tumbler, circa 1942. **$358**

Courtesy of Randy Clark/ Dexter City Auction Gallery

Mosaic footed vase, shouldered form in dark iridescent amethyst with randomly applied threading, spurious Tiffany signature, 6 1/2" high. **$1,150**

Courtesy of Early Auction Co., www.earlyauctionco.com

Karnak red vase, cylindrical expanded body with random wine-colored decorations and deep blue circular disc foot, 7" high. **$3,872**

Courtesy of Early Auction Co., www.earlyauctionco.com

Rare Amberina No. 222 ice tea set: pitcher with applied cobalt blue handle, four matching tumblers (one shown) and four cobalt blue coasters (one shown), circa mid-1920s. **$2,750**

Courtesy of Randy Clark/Dexter City Auction Gallery

Vase with blue Aurene glass foot and red overall vine motif, unmarked, 12" high. **$5,700**

Courtesy of John McInnis Auctioneers, www.mcinnisauctions.com

Victoria topaz Drapery Optic
ice tea pitcher with applied
topaz handle, circa mid-
1920s. **$1,320**

*Courtesy of Randy Clark/Dexter City
Auction Gallery*

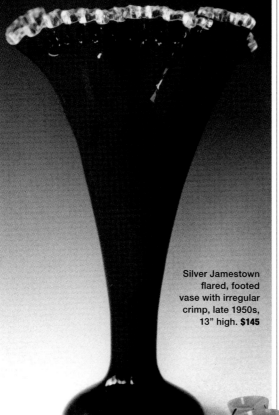

Silver Jamestown
flared, footed
vase with irregular
crimp, late 1950s,
13" high. **$145**

Hanging Hearts pattern
seven-piece custard glass
water set by Robert Barber,
#8964 pitcher and six #8940
10-oz. tumblers, produced
only one year. **$464**

Courtesy of Strawser Auction Group,

Mosaic inlaid long oval comport with threading
and applied cobalt blue foot and shiny
iridescent finish, mid-1920s, 7" high. **$2,310**

Courtesy of Randy Clark/Dexter City Auction Gallery

▲ Jade Green pieces in Wide Rib, early 1930s. Left: creamer and sugar, each 3 3/4" high. $80+ pair Center and right: jug with crimped ice lip, 7 1/2" high, and tumbler, 4 1/4" high. **$125**

Cranberry opalescent Coin Dot two-handled vase, circa 1948, 11" high. **$303**

Courtesy of Randy Clark/Dexter City Auction Gallery

Blue Opalescent hanging shade in Coin Dot, early 1960s, 13" high. **$250**

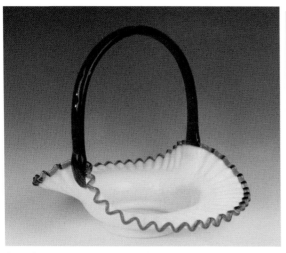

Aqua Crest large basket, 1940s, 14 1/2" wide, 13" high. **$500**

Two pairs of New World shakers in Cranberry Opalescent and Green Opalescent Rib Optic, 1950s, sold in pairs of two sizes, 4" high and 5" high. Cranberry. **$175 pair;** Green, rare. **$300 pair**

Nymph Ruby console set including figurine in flower frog, flared petal bowl, ebony base and footed candleholders, early 1930s; nymph, frog, bowl and stand, 9" high; candleholders, 4 1/2" diameter. **$225 for set**

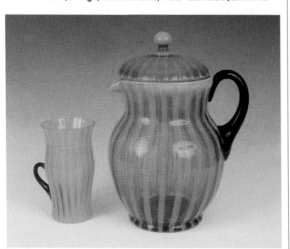

Blue Opalescent covered jug and tumbler in Rib Optic with cobalt handles, part of a lemonade set that would have included six tumblers, 1920s; jug, 10" high; tumbler, 5" high. **$700+** for complete set

Celeste Blue bud vase, 1920s, 11 1/2" high. **$55+**

Lalique

René Jules Lalique was born on April 6, 1860, in the village of Ay, in the Champagne region of France. In 1862, his family moved to the suburbs of Paris.

In 1872, Lalique attended College Turgot, where he studied drawing with Justin-Marie Lequien. After the death of his father in 1876, Lalique began working as an apprentice to Louis Aucoc, who was a prominent jeweler and goldsmith in Paris.

Lalique moved to London in 1878 to continue his studies. He spent two years attending Sydenham College, developing his graphic design skills. He returned to Paris in 1880 and worked as an illustrator of jewelry, creating designs for Cartier, among others. In 1884, Lalique's drawings were displayed at the National Exhibition of Industrial Arts, organized at the Louvre.

At the end of 1885, Lalique took over Jules Destapes' jewelry workshop. Lalique's designs incorporated translucent enamels, semiprecious stones, ivory, and hard stones. In 1889, at the Universal

Clear and frosted tapering rectangular crystal bottle relief-decorated with fruits and foliage with black enameled highlights, flanked by outset green tassels and surmounted by oval-shaped foliate-decorated stopper, circa 1919, with molded signature "R. Lalique" to one face and "Volnay Paris" to other, etched to underside "50," 5 3/8" high x 1 5/8" wide x 1 1/8" deep. **$7,995**

Courtesy of John Moran Auctioneers, johnmoran.com

Amethyst glass buckle, three sections with stag in center and curling fern bows encircling stag and adorning two outside panels, housed in brass backing with matching fern-type design in repose, original satin-covered and lined box marked on interior of lid "Lalique Place Vendome 24 Paris," very good to excellent condition, 4 1/4" long. **$8,888**

Courtesy of James D. Julia Auctioneers, jamesdjulia.com

Exhibition in Paris, the jewelry firms of Vever and Boucheron included collaborative works by Lalique in their displays.

In the early 1890s, Lalique began to incorporate glass into his jewelry, and in 1893 he took part in a competition organized by the Union Centrale des Arts Decoratifs to design a drinking vessel. He won second prize.

Lalique opened his first Paris retail shop in 1905, near the perfume business of François Coty, who commissioned Lalique to design his perfume labels in 1907. In the first decade of the 20th century, Lalique continued to experiment with glass manufacturing techniques and mounted his first show devoted entirely to glass in 1911.

During World War I, Lalique's first factory was forced to close, but the construction of a new factory was soon begun in Wingen-sur-Moder in the Alsace region. It was completed in 1921 and still produces Lalique crystal today.

In 1925, Lalique designed the first car mascot (hood ornament) for Citroën, the French automobile company. For the next six years, Lalique designed 29 models for automotive companies such as Bentley, Bugatti, Delage, Hispano-Suiza, Rolls Royce, and Voisin.

Lalique's second boutique opened in 1931, and this location continues to serve as the main Lalique showroom today.

René Lalique died on May 5, 1945, at the age of 85. His son, Marc, took over the business at that time, and when Marc died in 1977, his daughter, Marie-Claude Lalique Dedouvre, assumed control of the company. She sold her interest in the firm and retired in 1994.

For more information on Lalique, see *Warman's Lalique Identification and Price Guide* by Mark F. Moran.

Inkwell impressed with entwined serpents, original domed glass lid, light brown patination, signed on side with engraved block letters "R. Lalique," very good to excellent condition with slight roughness to bottom inside edge of foot, 6 1/4" diameter. **$9,113**

Courtesy of James D. Julia Auctioneers, jamesdjulia.com

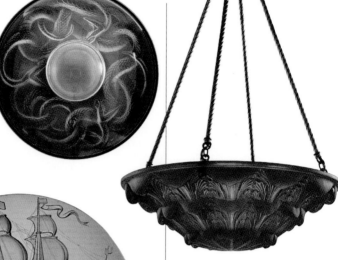

Scarce Caravelle centerpiece in clear and frosted smoky topaz glass with illuminating metal base (model later modified and given as a gift by the city of Paris to King George VI and Queen Elizabeth during their royal visit in 1928), circa 1930, etched "R. Lalique France", light surface scratches on both sides, light wear to metal base, 18" high x 28" wide, 6" diameter. **$59,375**

Courtesy of Rago Arts and Auctions, ragoarts.com

Gaillon plafonnier, frosted and patinated glass, circa 1927, engraved "R. LALIQUE," glass only 5" x 17 3/4" diameter. **$4,375**

Courtesy of Rago Arts and Auctions, ragoarts.com

Pair of crystal swans on etched plateau, signed Lalique, good condition, light surface scuffs, swans 13" long x 10" high x 8" wide (head up), 14" long x 7 1/2" high x 8" wide (head down), plateau 33" long x 22" wide. **$6,820**

Courtesy of Bruce Kodner Galleries, brucekodner.com

Seville chandelier in glass and chrome, circa 1947, marked "Lalique, France", repaired chip on lower rim of ceiling cap near standard, minor surface wear to glass and metal expected with age, 33" high, 20" diameter. **$11,875**

Courtesy of Heritage Auctions, ha.com

La Belle Saison perfume bottle in clear and frosted glass with sepia patina, circa 1925, made for Houbigant, marked "MADE IN FRANCE, R LALIQUE, 5011", light residue in interior, putty on underside, lid in place, light rubbing of patina, 3 7/8" high. **$1,625**

Courtesy of Heritage Auctions, ha.com

Ronces lamp base covered with pattern of intertwining thorny stems in green glass with gray patination, glass supported by stepped metal base with Greek key pattern, upper hardware has acanthus leaves and is finished with single socket, very good to excellent condition with wear to hardware commensurate with age, overall 21" high. **$1,422**

Courtesy of James D. Julia Auctioneers, jamesdjulia.com

Mascot in Victoire pattern in light amethyst tinted glass with frosted head and neck and clear headdress, signed on side in raised block letters "R. Lalique," contemporary stand marked "Breves Galleries Knightsbridge S.W.3 Pat. No. 309301," very good to excellent condition, 10" long x 8 7/8" high in stand. **$23,700**

Courtesy of James D. Julia Auctioneers, jamesdjulia.com

"Le Jade" perfume bottle for Roger et Gallet, molded flask-form green glass body relief-decorated with bird-of-paradise among scrolling vines, surmounted by vine-molded domed stopper, circa 1926, molded signature to underside "R.L. France," impressed verso "Roger et Gallet / Paris," 3 1/4" high x 2 3/8" wide x 1 1/8" deep. **$2,337**

Courtesy of John Moran Auctioneers, johnmoran.com

"L'Elegance" perfume bottle, frosted and clear glass with amber patina, after 1914, (M p. 934, No. 10), etched "R. Lalique France 850," stopper etched "850," 3 3/4" x 2 3/4" x 3/4". **$4,375**

Courtesy of Rago Arts and Auctions, ragoarts.com

Frosted glass "Mask De Femme" plaque with maiden surrounded by fish-form relief-decorated reserves on silvered stand, with original double box and original stand, signed with script "Lalique France" mark, purchased at Shreve & Co., San Francisco, 12 1/2" square. **$4,880**

Courtesy of Clars Auction Gallery, clars.com

Libellule mascot of perched dragonfly with folded wings, frosted body, clear wings with frosted texture, contemporary chrome stand marked "Breves Galleries Knightsbridge S.W.3 Pat. No. 309301," very good to excellent condition, 6 1/4" long x 4" high, including stand. **$7,110**

Courtesy of James D. Julia Auctioneers, jamesdjulia.com

Rare Chrysis mascot in fiery opalescent glass, signed on base with engraved block letters "R. Lalique France," in contemporary holder marked "Breves Galleries Knightsbridge S.W.3 Pat. No. 309301," very good to excellent condition, figure 5" high, 9" high with stand. **$41,000**

Courtesy of James D. Julia Auctioneers, jamesdjulia.com

Grande Nue Socle Lierre statuette, frosted glass with brown patina on wood base, circa 1919, etched "R. Lalique France no. 836," 16 1/4" x 6 1/4". **$17,500**

Courtesy of Rago Arts and Auctions, ragoarts.com

Coq Nain mascot in form of rooster with tail raised high in green glass, signed on underside in etched block letters "R. Lalique France," contemporary stand marked "Breves Galleries Knightsbridge S.W.3 Pat. No. 309301," very good to excellent condition with one fleabite on edge of top tail feather, mascot 8 1/4" high, 11 1/2" high with stand. **$5,000-$7,000**

Courtesy of James D. Julia Auctioneers, jamesdjulia.com

Pair of amethyst-tinted glass Grandes Feuilles torchiers on French Art Deco wrought iron bases, circa 1927, bases fitted with European bulbs, marked "R. Lalique, France", scratching on globe exteriors, chipping on rims from hardware contact, fleabites and flaking on rims, globes 17" high, base with globes 92" high. **$20,000**

Courtesy of Heritage Auctions, ha.com

Covered tumbler of slightly tapering cylindrical clear and frosted art glass molded with scrolling grapevines and roosters with trailing tails, inset with removable strainer with fruiting grapevines, surmounted by similarly molded domed cover, designed in 1928, tumbler signed "R. Lalique France," model no. 3879, 8 3/4" high, 3 3/4" diameter. **$4,200**

Courtesy of John Moran Auctioneers, johnmoran.com

Perdrix plateau tray, post-1945, rectangular-form with frosted partridges against foliage to verso, marks: Lalique, France (engraved), 1" x 18" x 12". **$2,500**

Courtesy of Heritage Auctions, ha.com

Poissons pattern vase, allover pressed design of swimming fish, blue glass with iridescent finish, signed on underside in block letters R. Lalique, very good to excellent condition with hole drilled in bottom center, 9" high. **$4,860**

Courtesy of James D. Julia Auctioneers, jamesdjulia.com

Cluny vase in smoky topaz glass with patinated bronze handles, circa 1925, etched "R. Lalique, France," excellent condition, 10 1/2" high x 12" wide. **$125,000**

Courtesy of Rago Arts and Auctions, ragoarts.com

Perruches vase, circa 1919, clear glass with green patina, marks:
R. LALIQUE (molded), 10 1/2" high. **$6,875**

Courtesy of Heritage Auctions, ha.com

Oran vase in monumental form in frosted glass with opalescent tinting, circa 1927, flowers and leaves in deep relief, engraved signature "R. Lalique France No. 999" on base, good condition overall, base with typical scratches and wear, scattered bubbles and inclusions and other anomalies, as made, 10 1/2" high x 10 5/8" wide. **$19,680**

Courtesy of Brunk Auctions, www.brunk.com

Vessel of clear and frosted glass with tapering cylindrical body decorated in high relief with continuous scene of dancing bacchantes, third quarter 20th century, numbered "F016" and etched in script "Lalique France" with copyright symbol to foot, "Lalique / Paris" sticker to underside, with original box, 9 3/4" high, 8 3/4"diameter. **$2,160**

Courtesy of John Moran Auctioneers, johnmoran.com

Quezal

The Quezal Art Glass Decorating Co., named for the quetzal – a bird with brilliantly colored feathers found in tropical regions of the Americas – was organized in 1901 in Brooklyn, New York, by Martin Bach and Thomas Johnson, two disgruntled Tiffany workers. They soon hired Percy Britton and William Wiedebine, two more former Tiffany employees. The first products, unmarked, were exact Tiffany imitations.

Johnson left in 1905. T. Conrad Vahlsing, Bach's son-in-law, joined the firm in 1918, but left with Paul Frank in 1920 to form Lustre Art Glass Co., which in turn copied Quezal pieces. Martin Bach died in 1924, and by 1925, Quezal had ceased operations.

The "Quezal" trademark was first used in 1902 and was placed on the base of vases and bowls and the rims of shades. The acid-etched or engraved letters vary in size and may be found in amber, black, or gold. A printed label that includes an illustration of a quetzal was used briefly in 1907.

Quezal pieces differ from Tiffany pieces in that they are more defined and the decorations are more visible and brighter. No new techniques were developed by Quezal.

Perfume bottle made for Melba
Perfume Co., Chicago, early 20th
century, bottom marked "Quezal/
Melba," matching stopper, light wear
to base, good condition,
5 3/4" high. **$1,240**

Courtesy of Brunk Auctions, brunkauctions.com

Compote with white pulled feather design on exterior against white opalescent background, interior in gold iridescence with stretched rim, applied inverted saucer foot with white pulled feather design and blue iridescent zipper design against slightly iridescent clear shading to opalescent background, signed in polished pontil "Quezal P 523," very good to excellent condition, 6 1/4" high. **$1,896**

Courtesy of James D. Julia Auctioneers, jamesdjulia.com

Covered jar with orange/gold iridescent finish on body and lid with three applied gold iridescent loop feet, signed in polished pontil "Quezal," very good to excellent condition, 12" high. **$1,701**

Courtesy of James D. Julia Auctioneers, jamesdjulia.com

◄ Hanging lamps with bronze ceiling caps with single turned stem leading to flowerform shade holders that house long flaring vertically ribs, shades with gold iridescent hooked feather design descending from fitter against cream-colored background, each shade finished in interior with light gold iridescence and signed on inside of fitter "Quezal," brown-shaded patina, unsigned, one shade with long tight hairline in fitter, otherwise very good to excellent condition, shades 7 3/4" long, with hangers 21" long. **$4,740**

Courtesy of James D. Julia Auctioneers, jamesdjulia.com

Mantel lamps with shades decorated with gold iridescent fishnet design against cream-colored background, sterling silver circular stepped foot finished with sterling silver lip stamped "Sterling," very good to excellent condition, each 7 1/2" high. **$1,067**

Courtesy of James D. Julia Auctioneers, jamesdjulia.com

Torchiere morning glory shade with snakeskin design in purple, Aurene blue, green, and magenta with gold interior, engraved "Quezal" on fitter, excellent original condition, 7" high x 8 1/2" wide, 2 1/4" fitter. **$2,600**

Courtesy of Mark Musio, Humler & Nolan, humlernolan.com

Helmet shade with gold iridescent fishnet design against cream-colored background with platinum iridescent zipper design running vertically over fishnet, interior in gold iridescence, signed on inside of fitter "Quezal," very good to excellent condition, 10 1/4" diameter, 2 1/4" fitter. **$2,133**

Courtesy of James D. Julia Auctioneers, jamesdjulia.com

Helmet shade with white pulled feather design descending from fitter rim against gold iridescent background, each feather outlined in green, interior in gold iridescence with stretched rim, signed on inside of fitter "Quezal," very good to excellent condition, 10 1/4" diameter. **$1,896**

Courtesy of James D. Julia Auctioneers, jamesdjulia.com

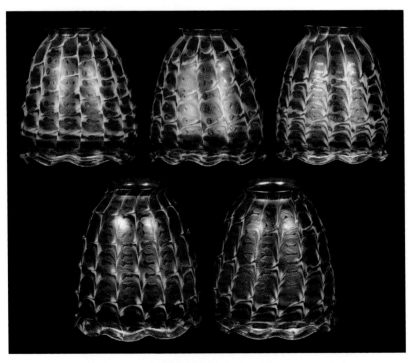

Five signed lampshades, gold iridescent with white spiderweb design, no chips, cracks, or repairs, 4 1/2". **$1,121**

Courtesy of Woody Auction, woodyauction.com

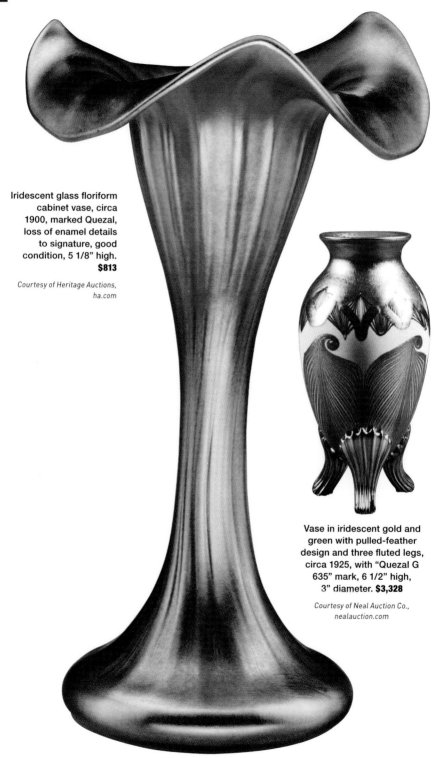

Iridescent glass floriform cabinet vase, circa 1900, marked Quezal, loss of enamel details to signature, good condition, 5 1/8" high. **$813**

Courtesy of Heritage Auctions, ha.com

Vase in iridescent gold and green with pulled-feather design and three fluted legs, circa 1925, with "Quezal G 635" mark, 6 1/2" high, 3" diameter. **$3,328**

Courtesy of Neal Auction Co., nealauction.com

Iridescent glass cabinet vase, circa 1910, marked Quezal, minor scuffing to underside, good condition, 3 7/8" high. **$213**

Courtesy of Heritage Auctions, ha.com

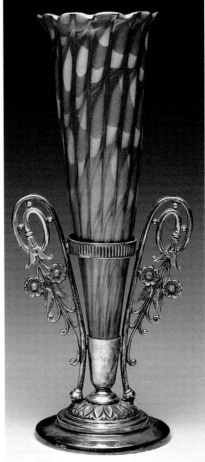

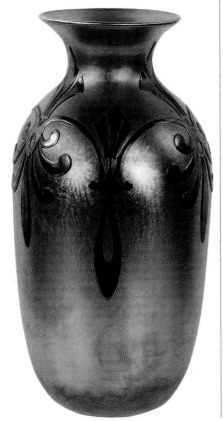

Vase decorated with green and gold iridescent random pattern against light green background, interior in gold iridescence, silver-plated holder with floral design handles, vase marked on side at bottom "Quezal," holder marked "James W. Tufts Boston Quadruple Plate," very good condition, 8 1/2" high. **$2,066**

Courtesy of James D. Julia Auctioneers, jamesdjulia.com

◀ Art Nouveau vase with gold iridescent and ornate silver overlay, signed on base, 9" high x 4 1/2" wide. **$1,722**

Courtesy of Kaminski Auctions, kaminskiauctions.com

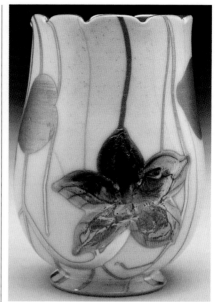

Green tulip shade decorated with three large iridescent purple flowers and iridescent gold hearts and vines on opal ground, gold lined, signed with early engraved signature, one of four matching shades, very good to excellent condition, 5" high with 2 1/4" fitter. **$3,259**

Courtesy of James D. Julia Auctioneers, jamesdjulia.com

Vase with blue and gold iridescent King Tut design against white background, interior of mouth in gold iridescence, signed in polished pontil "Quezal," very good to excellent condition, 12 3/4" high. **$2,074**

Courtesy of James D. Julia Auctioneers, jamesdjulia.com

▶ Vase with Alvin Silver overlay, circa 1900, iridescent blue and violet glass with silver overlay in chased floral motif, marked to glass "Quezal, 13," marked to silver "A, 999-1000 FINE, PATENTED, 15," 5 1/2" high. **$1,125**

Courtesy of Heritage Auctions, ha.com

Iridescent glass footed vase, circa 1900, marked Quezal, rubbing to lip rim, light scuffing and label residue to underside, 7 3/8" high. **$475**

Courtesy of Heritage Auctions, ha.com

Blue iridescent glass vase, circa 1915, enameled Quezal, fleabite and minor rubbing of iridescence to base, good condition, 7" high. **$906**

Courtesy of Heritage Auctions, ha.com

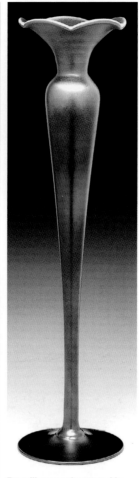

Rare lily vase decorated in blue with iridescent finish in green, yellow, and purple on exterior, gold interior, signed Quezal on underside, very good to excellent condition, 11" high. **$1,580**

Courtesy of James D. Julia Auctioneers, jamesdjulia.com

Vase with flower-form base and pulled-feather design, circa 1920, "Quezal 774" mark, light scuffing to underside, 8 3/8" high. **$1,125**

Courtesy of Heritage Auctions, ha.com

Vase with gold and purple coiled swirl design with Quezal attributes, unsigned, 6" high. **$1,599**

Courtesy of Tremont Auctions, tremontauctions.com

Vase with opal and green ground and gold iridescent pulled-feather design, "Quezal B753" signature, 6 3/4" high, 2 5/8" diameter. **$3,840**

Courtesy of Neal Auction Co., nealauction.com

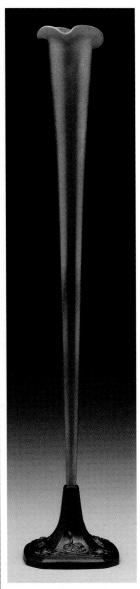

Jack-in-the-pulpit vase, diminutive size with stretched gold face, decorated with green pulled feather design, back of face is ivory color with green pulled feather design and platinum iridescent border, signed Quezal 875 on underside, very good to excellent condition, 9" high. **$4,148**

Courtesy of James D. Julia Auctioneers, jamesdjulia.com

Tall slender lily vase with ruffled and rolled rim with gold iridescence showing bands of pink, blue and green highlights, signed on bottom side "Quezal," cast bronze foot with swans and pond lilies surrounding bottom, foot unsigned, very good to excellent condition, 20" high. **$668**

Courtesy of James D. Julia Auctioneers, jamesdjulia.com

Tiffany Glass

Tiffany & Co. was founded by Charles Lewis Tiffany (1812-1902) and Teddy Young in New York City in 1837 as a "stationery and fancy goods emporium." The store initially sold a wide variety of stationery items, and operated as Tiffany, Young and Ellis in lower Manhattan. The name was shortened to Tiffany & Co. in 1853, and the firm's emphasis on jewelry was established.

The first Tiffany catalog, known as the "Blue Book," was published in 1845. It is still being published today.

In 1862 Tiffany & Co. supplied the Union Army with swords, flags and surgical implements.

Charles' son, Louis Comfort Tiffany (1848-1933), was an American artist and designer who worked in the decorative arts and is best known for his work in stained glass. Louis established Tiffany Glass Co. in 1885, and in 1902 it became known as Tiffany Studios. America's outstanding glass designer of the Art Nouveau period produced glass from the last quarter of the 19th century until the early 1930s. Tiffany revived early techniques and devised many new ones.

More Information on Tiffany is Located in Lamps & Lighting.

Tiffany Studios Rambling Rose table lamp mounted on rare bronze base that features green Favrile glass blown into openings in bronze from just above lower section up to light cluster, shade unsigned, base impressed TIFFANY STUDIOS NEW YORK 25873, with Tiffany Glass and Decorating Co. logo, 25" h, shade 16" diameter. **$141,600**

Courtesy of Michaan's Auctions, michaans.com

Tiffany Studios red tulip table lamp, shade depicts the tulip n every stage of bloom, colors used encompass the entire range of the red family from pink to purple, pattern also shows the foliage in most every color of green, glass used is also of a wide variety from striated to cat's paw to rippled and finally granular, shade is completed with three geometric bands of rippled glass in earthen hues of fiery orange with hints of green and supported by a mock-turtleback base, three-socket base is complete with riser, wheel and top cap all in a rich patina finish, shade is signed "Tiffany Studios New York 1596," base is signed "Tiffany Studios New York 587," shade is 18" diameter, overall 22 1/2" h. **$109,250**

Courtesy of James D. Julia Auctioneers, jamesdjulia.com

Two candelabras with jeweled feet and stylized leaf design leading to four curved arms supporting reticulated glass candle cups with bobeches, bronze with reddish-brown patina with green highlights, one candelabra signed on underside "Tiffany Studios New York 22324" with Tiffany Glass & Decorating logo, other signed "Tiffany Studios New York D886" with Tiffany Glass & Decorating logo, 12" h. **$4,010**

Courtesy of James D. Julia Auctioneers, jamesdjulia.com

Tiffany Studios turtle back tile clock, iridescent blue, green, and purple turtle back tiles set in bronze, case unsigned, enamel dial signed Tiffany & Co., 13" h. **$76,700**

Courtesy of Michaan's Auctions, michaans.com

Tiffany Studios Pine Needle card case, constructed of green slag panels with darker striations, panels are set in a bronze frame with decorative pine-needle decoration overall, signed on underside "Tiffany Studios New York 875," 4" x 3" x 1". **$1,495**

Courtesy of James D. Julia Auctioneers, jamesdjulia.com

▲ Rare inkwell with wide squat body with impressed waves with koi swimming among waves, brown patina with green highlights, signed on underside "Tiffany Studios New York 854," very good to excellent condition, missing original insert, small blue iridescent insert glued into opening as replacement, small professional repair on lip beneath lid, 7" diameter x 3 3/4" h. **$3,555**

Courtesy of James D. Julia Auctioneers, jamesdjulia.com

▲ Tiffany Studios Grapevine carriage clock, signed "Tiffany & Co." on the face and "Tiffany Studios New York 877" on underside as well as "Made in France" on the mechanism, 5" h. **$6,900**

Courtesy of James D. Julia Auctioneers, jamesdjulia.com

▶ Rare scarab inkwell, 1900s, patinated bronze, Favrile glass, clear glass, stamped "TIFFANY STUDIOS NEW YORK 1501," 2 1/4" x 3 1/2". **$25,000**

Courtesy of Rago Arts and Auction Center, ragoarts.com

Tiffany Studios calendar-style bronze frame in the Abalone pattern with gold finish, design originally created to represent a grape pattern and an abalone disc was used to form the design, signed on the underside "Tiffany Studios New York 1166," 6 1/2" x 5 3/4", opening: 3 1/4" x 2 1/4" h. **$1,680**

Courtesy of James D. Julia Auctioneers, jamesdjulia.com

Tiffany Studios picture frame, circa 1906, in the Grapevine pattern with green and white opalescent glass, easel back, 7 3/8" x 8 3/4". **$1,673**

Courtesy of Heritage Auctions, ha.com

Tiffany Studios mosaic pentray, inlaid blue decorated Favrile glass, impressed on the underside "TIFFANY STUDIOS NEW YORK 24336" together with the monogram of the Tiffany Glass & Decorating Co., 7 3/4" l. **$8,000**

Courtesy of James D. Julia Auctioneers, jamesdjulia.com

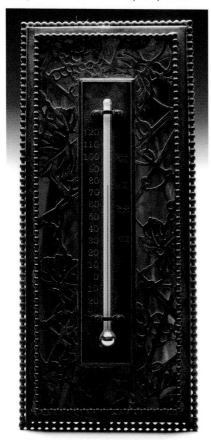

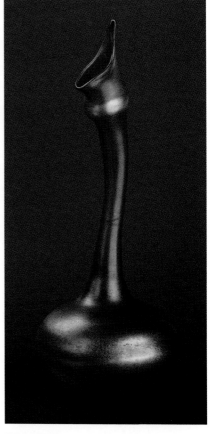

Grapevine thermometer with acid-etched design with double row of beaded trim backed with brown, blue, green and purple glass, brown patina and strong green highlights, signed on backside with small applied tag "Tiffany Studios New York," very good to excellent condition, 3 3/4" x 8 1/4". **$2,133**

Courtesy of James D. Julia Auctioneers, jamesdjulia.com

Tiffany Studios rose-water sprinkler, circa 1900, goose-neck form in iridescent Favrile glass with pink undertones, marked "L.C. Tiffany - Favrile W2714," 10" x 4". **$5,078**

Courtesy of Heritage Auctions, ha.com

Four wine glasses with opalescent inverted saucer foot, clear stem and pastel lavender bowls with vertical bands of white opalescence and white opalescent lip, each wine signed "LC Tiffany Favrile," very good to excellent condition, 7 3/4" h. **$2,248**

Courtesy of James D. Julia Auctioneers, jamesdjulia.com

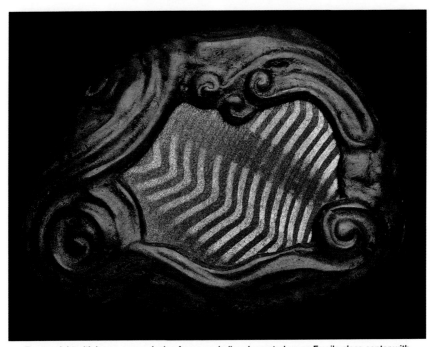

Paperweight with bronze wave design frame encircling decorated green Favrile glass center with iridescent wavy lines in platinum to purple against green background, bronze with brown patina with green highlights, signed on underside "Tiffany Studios New York 932" with Tiffany Glass & Decorating Co. logo, very good to excellent condition, 3 5/8" l x 2 3/4" w. **$3,555**

Courtesy of James D. Julia Auctioneers, jamesdjulia.com

Tiffany Studios flower-form vase, pulled-feather vase on opalescent ground with everted rim and decorated foot, engraved signature "L.C. Tiffany Favrile 539A," 11 1/4" h. **$3,680**

Courtesy of James D. Julia Auctioneers, jamesdjulia.com

Tiffany Studios Apple Blossom window depicting apple tree in full bloom with limbs covered in flowers, cloud-streaked sky, and body of water, circa 1915, panel with metal tag impressed Tiffany Studios New York, 50" h x 20 1/2" w, 60 1/4" h x 30 1/2" w with museum frame. **$118,000**

Courtesy of Michaan's Auctions, michaans.com

Tiffany Studios Tel El Amarna Vase, with applied and decorated collar, engraved "Exhibition Piece" and "6340N L.C. Tiffany – Favrile" on the underside, 5 3/4" h. **$5,750**

Courtesy of James D. Julia Auctioneers, jamesdjulia.com

Tiffany Studios Magnolia
landscape window depicting
flowering magnolia tree in
foreground of landscape with
a river meandering down from
a mountainous pass to a lake,
setting sun behind mountains
sending rays of light up into
the sky, effect achieved by
selective acid etching on rear
layers of glass, circa 1912,
unsigned, 44 1/4" h x 30 1/4"
w, 55" h x 40" w with frame.
$177,000

*Courtesy of Michaan's Auctions,
michaans.com*

▼ Tiffany Studios
Aquamarine vase, inscribed
L.C. Tiffany-Favrile 5202G,
9 7/8" h. **$65,000**

*Courtesy of Michaan's Auctions,
michaans.com*

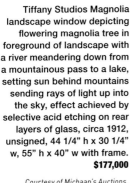

◄ Tiffany Studios scent
bottle-on-stand, circa
1900-1905, inscribed mark
Ex. identifies piece as one
displayed at an international
exhibition, glass with plique-
a-jour and champleve
enameled gold mount,
collar and cover impressed
TIFFANY & CO. and 18K
(twice), bottle inscribed L.C.T
9270, stand inscribed Louis
C. Tiffany Ex., impressed
TIFFANY & CO., Art Nouveau
foliate mount suggests it
was designed specifically
for display in Paris, 7 1/16"
h on stand, bottle 6 15/16" l.
$70,800

*Courtesy of Michaan's Auctions,
michaans.com*

Tiffany Studios Alamander chandelier depicting blossoms against background of mottled confetti glass, shade impressed Tiffany Studios, New York, 28 1/4" diameter. **$212,400**

Courtesy of Michaan's Auctions, michaans.com

Three Byzantine desk pieces, stamp box, letter scale, and ashtray, letter scale and stamp box inset with gold Favrile glass, stamp box marked "Tiffany Studios New York," letter scale stamped "Tiffany Studios New York 870," ashtray not marked, overall very good condition, stamp box missing its four ball feet, ashtray 4 1/4" x 2 3/4". **$3,645**

Courtesy of James D. Julia Auctioneers, jamesdjulia.com

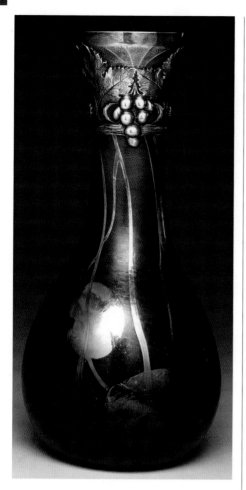

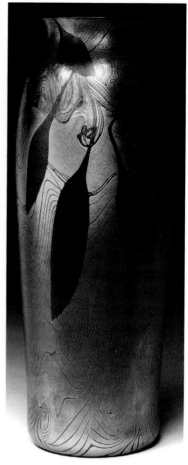

Vase with blue iridescent heart and vine decoration against bronze iridescent shading to green swirled background, purple and green highlights, silver collar of grape leaves and grape clusters, vase signed on underside with original paper label "Tiffany Favrile Glass Registered Trademark" with Tiffany Glass & Decorating Co. logo, silver collar signed "Tiffany & Co. Makers Sterling Silver C," very good to excellent condition, 14 1/2" h. **$25,478**

Courtesy of James D. Julia Auctioneers, jamesdjulia.com

Monumental vase with gold iridescent body shading to blue at shoulder, blue and green iridescent swirling lines and green leaf and vine pattern descending from lip, blue iridescence at top with purple flashes, gold iridescence at bottom with pink highlights, interior with iridescent exterior atop amber glass body shading to red at top, signed in polished pontil "Louis C. Tiffany 0454" with remnants of original paper label with Tiffany Glass & Decorating Co. logo, very good to excellent condition, 19" h. **$18,664**

Courtesy of James D. Julia Auctioneers, jamesdjulia.com

Tiffany Studios blown-glass six-arm candelabra, made of bronze, has patina finish of brown with hints of green and red, from the oval-shaped platform base arises a single center stem with three candle cups on either side, each of these candle cups has green blown-glass ornamentation and a bobeche, in the center stem of the candlestick rests a Tiffany snuffer that is concealed when in place, signed on the underside "Tiffany Studios New York 1648," 15" x 21". **$6,900**

Courtesy of James D. Julia Auctioneers, jamesdjulia.com

Favrile center bowl with green leaf and vine design in interior, green leaves intaglio carved, decoration set against gold iridescence with pink and green highlights, bowl finished with gold iridescent double row flower frog insert and signed on underside "6354L L.C. Tiffany Favrile," frog signed "9894K L.C. Tiffany Favrile," bowl 12 1/2" diameter. **$3,555**

Courtesy of James D. Julia Auctioneers, jamesdjulia.com

Halloween Collectibles

By Mark B. Ledenbach

Halloween became quite the event in the first decade of the 1900s, mainly through the exchange of festive postcards. Those cards, with the art drawn by such luminaries as Winsch and Clapsaddle, typically accented the agricultural roots of Halloween, then branched out into the more whimsical realm of witches, black cats, blazing jack-o'-lanterns, bats, cavorting devils, and the like.

As Halloween became an event to be celebrated with parties – primarily given by and for adults through the 1920s – the imagery began to change. From about 1909 through 1913, manufacturers of party supplies like Dennison of Framingham, Massachusetts, simply offered an array of seasonally decorated crepe papers from which the host would fashion decorations and party favors. The imagery from this period tends to be more subdued and somewhat pedestrian. However, as the manufacturers became more entranced by the business possibilities of offering finished goods for sale, the lines of available products exploded into a dazzling array of seals, silhouettes, tally cards, place cards, invitations, die-cuts, aprons, and costumes. To keep up with the seemingly endless kinds of products to be sold to adults, the imagery became more complex, scary, and perhaps sometimes chilling.

The most innovative purveyor of such complex Halloween imagery was the Beistle Co. of Shippensburg, Pennsylvania. It provided nut cups, die-cuts, lanterns, games, table decorations, and other small paper decorations that are especially coveted by collectors today. The firm's design sensibilities are easily recognized today for their ingenuity in extending Halloween imagery beyond what was offered previously

MARK B. LEDENBACH, longtime collector and expert on all things Halloween, is the author of *Vintage Halloween Collectibles, 3rd edition.* His website: www.halloweencollector.com

"Sacred Be Ye Fire O Halloween," mechanical, United States, 1910-1917, non-embossed with easel for use as table decoration, 9 3/4" x 7 1/4". **$475**

by other manufacturers. Examples of this would be Beistle's 1930-1931 identical dual-sided lantern and 1923 fairy clock.

Imagery through about 1940 tends to be more adult-focused. However, as trick-or-treating become more of an entrenched feature of Halloween celebrations, the target market segment for parties ceased to be adults and moved inexorably toward juveniles. The impact on Halloween imagery was profound. Out were the more complex and scary images of devils, witches, and black cats to be replaced by less threatening, less interesting, and less memorable imagery of apple-cheeked witches; grinning, plump devils; and friendly black cats. The air of implied menace, so evocative of early Halloween imagery, had been replaced by a sugar-high-inducing cuteness that any retailer could carry without censure.

Through the present day, cuteness has been dethroned by goriness. One can shop at any mass retailer and find die-cuts of skulls with worms wriggling through eye sockets, costumes complete with wretch-inducing masks trumpeting various deformities or tortures, and other horrors meant to shock and dismay. The sense of subtlety and artistry so apparent in the majority of decorations made prior to 1940 is nowhere in evidence today.

Fairy honeycomb band hat, United States, Beistle, printed name, 1923, 6" x 11 1/2" long. **$250**

As with many hobbies, certain sub-categories have done better than others. Hotter categories are embossed German die-cuts; U.S. die-cuts, especially those made by Dennison and Gibson; Beistle paper products; boxed seals, silhouettes, and cut-outs from Dennison; tin tambourines; and German candy containers and figurals as well as Halloween-themed games. Colder categories include tin noisemakers, U.S. pulp, and hard plastic.

Collecting vintage Halloween memorabilia became a red-hot hobby complete with skyrocketing prices and scarce supply in the early 1990s. Even with all of the economic cycles since and the rise of more efficient supply channels like eBay, prices continue to climb for nearly all genres of near-mint condition or better items. For example, embossed German die-cuts sold then for $30-$75. Today many examples bring $100-$400, with the rarest items, like a winged bat devil and a large fireplace screen, topping $2,250. Even ephemera like a 1932 Beistle grandfather clock mechanical invitation bring astronomical prices.

Not all categories have benefited. The garish hard plastic made in huge quantities during the 1950s used to command head-scratching prices of $40-$1,000. Today prices have decreased to about half of the market's height given more collector awareness of the ubiquity of these items.

Unlike Christmas items, Halloween decorations were purchased with the intention of using them once, then tossing them out after the event. This is the primary supply driver behind the rapid escalation of prices today. The primary demand driver is the large number of new collectors entering this fun field as each Halloween season comes around.

As with all hobbies where values have risen, reproductions and fantasy pieces are a problem. Consult other collectors and buy the right references before plunking down cash. Get in the habit of asking a lot of questions. Don't be shy.

SUGGESTED READING: *Vintage Halloween Collectibles*, 3rd edition, contains nearly 550 photographs showing over 600 new Halloween items, all in full color. **www.HalloweenCollector.com.**

1616

1616

1616

1616

1616

1616

1616

1616

1616

Nut cup, Gibson Art Co., Cincinnati, Ohio, 1920s, 1 3/4" x 1 3/4" x 3". **$35**

Hallowe'en Decorations box for German die-cuts, Germany, 1920s, 8 3/4" x 1 3/4" x 9 1/2". **$350**

Jack-o'-lantern with raccoon eyes, Germany, 1920s, 7 1/4" x 7", heavily embossed. **$165**

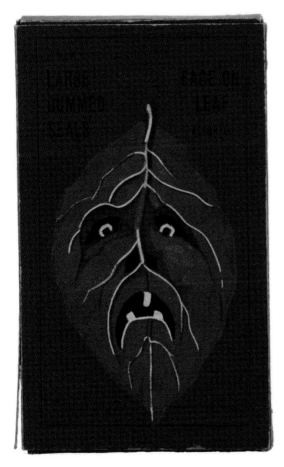

Box of six assorted face-on-leaf seals, United States, Dennison, first appeared in its 1924 Bogie Book, 3 3/4" x 2 1/4", sold with stock number H684. **$250**

Composition witch candy container, bottom plug, Germany, early 1920s, 4 3/4" high. **$300**

Bux – The Hallowe'en
Owl, United States,
Beistle, HE Luhrs mark,
1940s, patent number
1593646, 9" x 14". **$165**

Winged ghost table
decoration, United States,
Beistle, no mark, 1925-1931,
11 1/2" x 20". **$375**

Softcover Bogie Book, United
States, Dennison, 1921, 7 3/4"
x 5 1/4", 32 numbered pages.
$200

Black cat centerpiece, United States, Gibson Art Co.,
Cincinnati, Ohio, late 1920s, each side is different, detached
sides are often mistakenly sold as individual die-cuts, 6 1/4" x
3 3/4". **$200**

Place card with flip-out base, United States, Beistle, diamond mark, 1930-1931, marked with patent number 1616568, lightly embossed (unusual for Beistle place card), 3" x 4" x 4". **$100**

Green-faced broomed witch, United States, Beistle, no mark, late 1950s, 21" x 9", non-embossed. **$300**

Full-bodied cardboard witch centerpiece, United States, Beistle, no mark, mid-1950s, 24" x 13 1/2" wide. This superbly detailed item was made for no more than two seasons. Because of a flawed design, the piece would generally bend and then rip at the waist. Therefore, these typically have tape or some other sort of repair at this juncture. The art is interesting in that the witch is anything but a crone, whereas her cat looks quite fearsome. This is a definite transitional piece away from the more challenging earlier designs toward the typically more banal ones seen later. **$275**

Porcelain
children's lidded
teapot, Germany,
1913-1932,
4" x 5". **$600**

Candle table decoration, United
States, Dennison, late 1920s,
note cat face in the flames,
candle's expression, cats along
base skew to give effect of
rounded base, 6 1/4" x 5 3/4"
wide. **$185**

Place card with running mice along bottom
border, United States, Whitney Co. of Worcester,
Massachusetts, 1920s, 4 1/4" x 3". **$85**

Box of 25 boy and spook seals, #H636, United States,
Dennison, 1922-1924, 1 1/2" x 2 1/2. **$140**

Tin clicker, Germany, 1930s,
3 3/4" high. **$65**

Placecard with witch at cauldron, bats, and cat atop chair, U.S.A., Dennison, sold with stock number H8, first appeared in 1920 Bogie Book, 3" high x 5" wide. **$125**

Boxed set of 20 cat with bowtie seals, U.S.A., Gibson Art Co., Cincinnati, Ohio, 1920s, 1 3/4" high x 1 1/4" wide. **$70**

▼ Pumpkin house invitation, U.S.A., Dennison, sold with stock number H87, first appeared in 1924 Bogie Book, 4" high x 3 1/2" wide. **$125**

Celluloid jack-o-lantern-headed boy with owl and squirrel on stump, U.S.A., Viscoloid Co. of Leominster, Massachusetts, early 1920s, 3 1/4" high x 2" wide. Provenance: From the collection of Barry Koester and Tammy Martin. **$600**

Slot and tab candy container, owl on stump, U.S.A., Fibro toy manufactured by Dolly Toy Co. of Dayton, Ohio, mid-1930s, 5 1/2" high x 2" diameter. **$20**

◄ Candy holder, skeleton pushing jack-o-lantern in wheelbarrow, U.S.A., G.M. Co., 1950s, heavy cardboard, marked RH-6A, 7 1/2" high x 3" wide x 10 3/4" long. **$195**

► Here's Your Fate game, U.S.A., Whitney Co., Worcester, Massachusetts, 1920s, 10" high x 7 3/4" wide. Spin the center arrow to discover the name of your future spouse and his or her occupation and background. Your spin would also direct you to a listing of 24 fortunes on the reverse. A typical fortune reads, "You will soon receive news of great importance by telephone on a rainy evening." The instructions include this admonishment: "It is bad luck to try this more than one time in 24 hours." **$200**

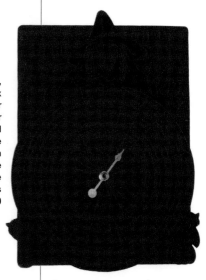

◄ Tri-fold invitation with stooped witch, U.S.A., Dennison, sold with stock number H82, first appeared in 1922 Bogie Book, 3 1/4" square, closed. **$135**

◄ Crawling baby boy, Germany, late 1920s, heavily embossed, back legs with perforated hinge giving 3-D effect, 8 1/4" high x 7 1/2" wide. **$500**

Composition candy container, jester creature playing lute, opens at neck, Germany, pre-1920s, jester's conical blue and white hat rests on ground between his legs, 6 1/4" high. **$725**

Candy container, jack-o-lantern-headed woman with cat, complex and well-made in Germany between 1910-1914, opens at neck, green circular wood base, 8" high. **$1,000-$1,200**

Enveloped set of five pumpkin head cut-outs, U.S.A., Beistle, no mark, early 1920s, envelope 12 1/4" high x 9 1/2" wide, contents 5" to 8" diameter. **$350**

Blow mold, orange slanted haunted house, U.S.A., Empire Plastic Corp. of New York, 1969, 13 1/4" high. **$65**

Spook Cat Game, U.S.A., Beistle, no mark, 1928, 11" high x 6 1/2" wide; pieces include main body, four legs and one tail, all made from black construction paper – variation of a standard "pin-the-tail" game; the envelope is the most compelling aspect because it does not rise to the design standard Beistle typically produced during the late 1920s. **$275**

Skull and crossbones, U.S.A., Hallmark, early 1950s, glossy-stock light cardboard, plain reverse side typically colored red, non-embossed, 8 1/4" high x 6 1/4" wide. **$60**

Dual-sided jack-o-lantern shade with different expressions, U.S.A., Beistle, no mark, late 1930s, 6 1/4" high x 3 1/4" wide x 8 1/2" long. **$165**

Tin clanger, U.S.A., T. Cohn, 1950s, 3 3/4" diameter. **$85**

Suitcase candy container, 1910-1914, marked "Made in Saxony," lithographed paper, thicker cardboard slide box to hold hard candies, covered with stickers saying Black Cat Hotel, Oct 31st, Pumpkin Hotel, Great Witch Railway, and Halloween Express, 1 1/4" high x 1/2" wide x 1 3/4" long. **$900-$1,000**

Candy container, jack-o-lantern-faced book, Germany, 1916-1921, made from lithographed paper over cardboard with simulated leather corners and spine, yellow string extends from back to small metal clasp at front, front lid opens, 3" high x 3/4" wide x 2 1/4" long. **$1,500**

Surprised moon with attached witch on broom, U.S.A., Beistle, no mark, mid-1950s, non-embossed, witch separately attached to die-cut, unusual, 12" high x 12" wide. **$200**

Soft cover Bogie Book, U.S.A., Dennison,
1917, 36 numbered pages, very best
wraparound cover art of all editions with
such covers, 7 1/2" high x 5" wide. **$400**

Bogie Book envelope, U.S.A., Dennison,
1917, 5 1/2" high x 8 1/4" wide. **$375**

Harry Potter Collectibles

By Eric Bradley

After making his debut in the June 1997 book, *Harry Potter and the Philosopher's Stone*, by J.K. Rowling, Harry Potter has become the favorite wizard of millions of Muggles all over the world.

Twenty years on, Harry Potter has also become one of the most successful franchises in the world and continues to expand with new films, books, plays, amusement parks, and more on the horizon. Whenever there's fan frenzy about a new book, movie or any other development, it boosts the franchise across the board and one of the areas that continues to rapidly grow is the collectibles market of items associated with the books and movies.

Some of these items often have no trouble auctioning for hundreds of thousands of dollars, such as Rowling's writing chair that sold for almost $400,000 - or even millions, like a handwritten copy of *The Tales of Beedle the Bard* that Amazon paid $4 million for. Many movie props like wands and quidditch brooms, and books, particularly first editions, also sell for five figures or more.

Values for early *Harry Potter* first edition books continue to climb. As if written in the stars, the first edition, first printing is the rarest and most

ERIC BRADLEY is the author of *Harry Potter - The Unofficial Guide to The Collectibles of Our Favorite Wizard* (Krause Publications, $22.99). Featuring hundreds of color images, the book showcases rare, extraordinary and even magical treasures from the Harry Potter books and movies, as well as from the imaginations of fans. Highlights include first-edition books, original art, movie posters, film props, exclusives, autographs and other wonders to behold. Bradley is the Public Relations Director at Heritage Auctions.

When Jeff Bezos, founder and CEO of Amazon, purchased the chair used by J.K. Rowling while writing the first two Harry Potter books for **$394,000** he raised the ceiling on such collectibles. The sale refocused collector attention on a wide world of unique items relating to the books and movies.

Courtesy of Heritage Auctions, ha.com

valuable of all editions. Securing an original copy is extremely difficult and even former library copies fly through auction houses like a seeker during a quiddich match.

Just seven years ago, a first edition, first printing copy (signed and inscribed by Rowling) with solid provenance to her early years as a writer sold for $23,900. Now standard copies from the late 1990s routinely sell between $10,000 and $16,000 on up. Condition makes all the difference: A copy "virtually as new" sold for an astounding $43,750 at auction. The former owner knew the book had value and wrapped it inside a first edition, later printing dust jacket.

With the books a near instant hit with children and later adults, it was only natural for them to be adapted into motion pictures. Assorted collectibles produced in 2001 in conjunction with the first eight Harry Potter movies are deep and diverse and among

the most valuable and rare items, including limited edition original movie posters, baseball caps, movie props, LEGO sets, lamps, holiday ornaments, first edition book sets, and even period bronze sculptures that are increasing in value on the secondary market.

Demand is so strong that items with even peripheral ties to the films and books are seeing an up-tick in interest and values. The market for "mystical-looking" flags made 70 years ago and other antique, vintage, and retro round eye glasses similar to those worn by Harry, yet produced decades before the original book series, are now sought after by adult cosplayers. These fans are seeking more collectibles and new ideas for more elaborate costumes and collections. Movie props continue to soar in value and successful replica companies have opened to meet demand for movie prop weapons and

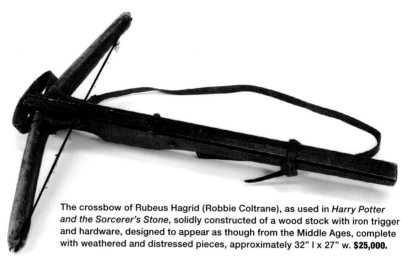

The crossbow of Rubeus Hagrid (Robbie Coltrane), as used in *Harry Potter and the Sorcerer's Stone*, solidly constructed of a wood stock with iron trigger and hardware, designed to appear as though from the Middle Ages, complete with weathered and distressed pieces, approximately 32" l x 27" w. **$25,000.**

Courtesy of Julien's Auctions, juliensauctions.com

wands and even these items have begun increasing between collectors ... but there is no replacement for the real thing.

"The world of Harry Potter is one that reaches all ages," said John Lohmann, owner at Harry Potter prop seller Animation Ink Archives, which has been selling animation art and movie prop for 25 years. "They were not just books for kids, but for everyone. With the movies, when they could actually see the world of Harry Potter, everyone wants a piece of it - not a toy or a theme park replica, but the real thing. Something when watching the movies, they can point to and say, 'Hey, that's mine!'

"To some collectors, having a robe worn by Daniel Radcliffe in the films is almost like having Darth Vader's black cape from the *Star Wars* films."

Despite this demand, there exists very little Harry Potter film props available to the public, making the material that is available all the more valuable. The challenge with collecting prop items is that Warner Brothers has only ever officially released a very limited amount of them from the productions.

"Hero wands, robes, and broom sticks are highly collectible and sought-after," Lohmann said. He should know.

His company once sold a single wand for $16,000.

Take the gray linen overcoat worn by Gary Oldman (Sirius Black) in *Harry Potter and the Prisoner of Azkaban*. The famous coat was expected to sell for around $5,000, but ultimately fetched a staggering $30,082 by the auction's end.

For the earlier films, some items were rented to the production or given away for marketing purposes and they can be legally owned and sold. This is the case with Hagrid's crossbow from *Harry Potter and the Sorcerer's Stone*. It was acquired from Bapty Armory in England, which rented the piece to production for filming. The massive crossbow was made to look like it was from the Middle Ages, but it is really fashioned from aluminum bow limbs wrapped in leather and included a leather carrying shoulder and hand straps. It was sold in a Hollywood prop auction for $25,000.

The most obvious prop from the films might be Harry's own eyeglasses, a pair of which, from the collection of Simon Murray, spectacle maker, were sold at auction. The iconic glasses were first described by author J.K. Rowling and became an integral part of Harry's signature look and persona.

"Props from the first film are generally

most desired," said Lohmann. "It's such a joy to see people's faces when we can offer them a piece of film and animation history. Even to see them get a piece of their childhood back."

Movie posters can be bought be for much obtainable prices because of their size. Framing and displaying a poster of gigantic proportions is expensive and requires custom frames. Without framing, the posters risk being damaged every time the owner unrolls them to enjoy the artwork. You could say that big posters are like Godric Gryffindor's Sword – double edged. Many can be bought for under $50 and upward to $150+. One of the rarest and most valuable posters is a lenticular one sheet prototype for *Harry Potter and the Prisoner of Azkaban* (Warner Brothers, 2004) that was never issued by Warner Brothers. It depicts Harry Potter's long suffering Uncle Sirius Black (Gary Oldman) and in a brilliant marketing ploy, Warner's created this poster to mimic the "Wanted" posters used in the movie itself. What's exciting about these wanted posters is that you can see Sirius laughing with insanity on the poster and Warner's tried to duplicate a motion effect with the lenticular posters. As you move back and forth before this poster, the image of Black actually begins to disappear. After creating six of these full-size prototypes at a facility in Michigan, Warner Bros decided that it was too expensive to put them into full production and so the project was dropped. They are valued between $3,800 and $4,000.

For more information on Harry Potter collectibles, see *Harry Potter: The Unofficial Guide to the Collectibles of Our Favorite Wizard* by Eric Bradley.

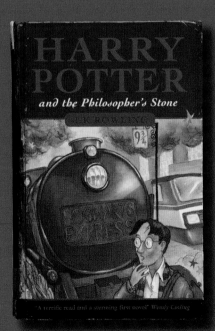

First edition, first printing, one of 500 copies of the first and rarest of the *Harry Potter* books, and one of approximately 300 copies sent to British libraries. Featuring "Copyright © Text Joanne Rowling 1997" (rather than "J. K. Rowling"), and "Taylor1997" (rather than "Taylor 1997") on the copyright page. This particular copy was once the property of the West Sussex Libraries, evidenced by the circular library stamp on the front pastedown. **$15,535**

Courtesy of Heritage Auctions, ha.com

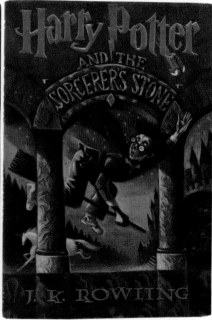

For the astute fans of the *Harry Potter* series, a complete set of seven large octavo volumes of the first American editions of the series can be worth thousands. This set, including *The Sorcerer's Stone, Chamber of Secrets, Prisoner of Azkaban, Goblet of Fire, Order of the Phoenix, Half Blood Prince, and Deathly Hallows*, was published in New York by Arthur A. Levine / Scholastic Press, 1998-2007. **$2,987.**

Courtesy of Heritage Auctions, ha.com

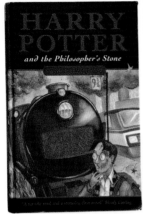

A rare, first edition, first printing of *Harry Potter and the Philosopher's Stone* (as published in England) is the pinnacle of Harry Pottery. This copy from the Portsmouth City Library was sold in a custom 19th century-style morocco leather box. **$33,460.**

Courtesy of Heritage Auctions, ha.com

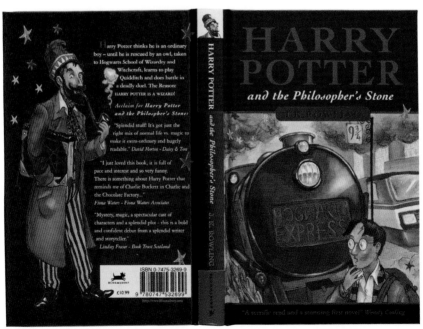

A first edition, first printing of *Harry Potter and the Philosopher's Stone*, 1997, in like new condition, has surpassed the ranks of first edition *James Bond* titles and first edition copies of *Lord of the Rings* by J. R. R. Tolkien in terms of collector worth. **$43,750.**

Courtesy of Bonhams, Bonhams.com

A rare copy of J.K. Rowling's hand-written and illustrated *The Tales of Beedle the Bard* edition was given to the publisher who launched her career. Rowling gave the edition to mark the publication of the final book in the *Harry Potter* series. **$467,000**

Courtesy of Sotheby's, sothebys.com

Signed twice by J. K. Rowling and 15 members of the film *Harry Potter and the Deathly Hallows*, a first American, first printing copy features a rare collection of principal cast members such as Ralph Fiennes (Lord Voldemort), Richard Griffith (Vernon Dursley), Tom Fenton (Draco Malfoy), Helena Bonham Carter (Bellatrix Lestrange), Rupert Grint (Ron Weasley), Daniel Radcliffe (Harry Potter), Bonnie Wright (Ginny Weasley), Fiona Shaw (Petunia Dursley), Michael Gambon (Albus Dumbledore), Emma Watson (Hermione Granger), Alan Rickman (Severus Snape), Evana Lynch (Luna Lovegood), and six others. **$3,500**

Courtesy of Heritage Auctions, ha.com

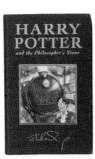
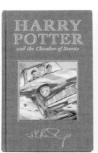
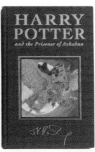

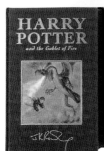

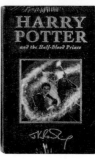

A complete set of the Bloomsbury deluxe limited editions, first printings. Comprises: *Harry Potter and the Philosopher's Stone*, Deluxe First Printing [1999]; *Harry Potter and the Chamber of Secrets*, Deluxe First Printing [1999]; *Harry Potter and the Prisoner of Azkaban*, Deluxe First Printing [1999]; *Harry Potter and the Goblet of Fire*, Deluxe First Printing [2000]; *Harry Potter and the Order of the Phoenix*, Deluxe First Printing [2003]; *Harry Potter and the Half-Blood Prince*, Deluxe First Printing [2005]; *Harry Potter and the Deathly Hallows*, Deluxe First Printing [2007]. Seven octavo volumes, all in the original cloth, final three titles still in publisher's shrinkwrap. Also included are first editions of two companion paperback volumes: *Quidditch Through the Ages* and *Fantastic Beasts & Where to Find Them*. **$2,700.**

Courtesy of PBA Galleries, PBAGalleries.com

Copies do not need to be signed to be valuable. This photo signed by Rowling was simply sold along with a first edition, first printing copy. The image is signed, "To Kevin with best wishes J K Rowling." Accompanied by a certificate of authenticity by Kevin Reynor of BOOKSKCR, a bookstore based in Cromer, Norfolk, in England. Rowling-signed photos are rare, especially combined with a fine first printing copy of Philosopher's Stone. **$15,535**

Courtesy of Heritage Auctions, ha.com

This English-made wool-nylon blend sweater was worn by an actor in one of the later *Harry Potter* movies. It is gray with scarlet-and-gold piping of the Gryffindor house on the hem and cuffs, and bears a "Property of Hogwarts" tag sewn inside the collar. The sweaters in the first two films in the series were of a lighter gray color, with additional piping around the collar. **$286.**

Courtesy of Heritage Auctions, ha.com

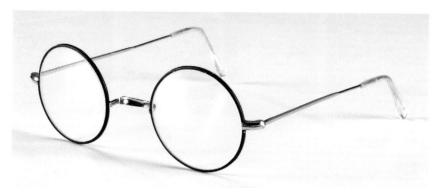

A pair of silver metal wire frame glasses with round clear lenses, worn by Daniel Radcliffe in his role as *Harry Potter in Harry Potter and the Sorcerer's Stone* is one of several pairs of glasses made for the film. **$20,000.**

Courtesy of Julien's Auctions, juliensauctions.com

A detailed prop production-used broomstick, constructed of fiberglass GRP material, purchased from a crew member before the release of the first movie. **$2,860.**

Courtesy of Eubanks Auctions, ewbankauctions.co.uk

▲ Original ink and watercolor cover art by Cliff Wright (British, born 1963) for *Harry Potter and the Chamber of Secrets* (Bloomsbury, 1998). **$13,000.**

Courtesy of Heritage Auctions, ha.com

◄ This antique Welsh dragon flag from the 1920s is an example of "Potter-like" items used for Harry Potter décor. **$150.**

Courtesy of eBay, ebay.com

Harry Potter and the Sorcerer's Stone (Warner Brothers, 2001), one sheet DS advance movie poster, artwork by Drew Struzan, rolled, Near Mint. **$150-$300.**

Courtesy of Heritage Auctions, ha.com

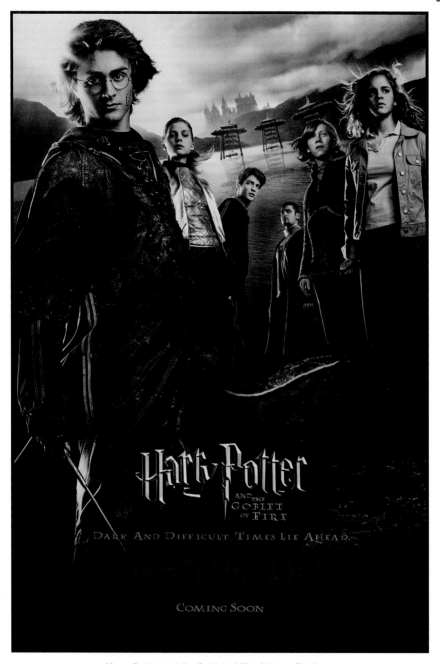

Harry Potter and the Goblet of Fire (Warner Brothers, 2005), one sheet DS Advance movie poster, has never been used or displayed, rolled, Mint, 27" x 40". **$131.**

Courtesy of Heritage Auctions, ha.com

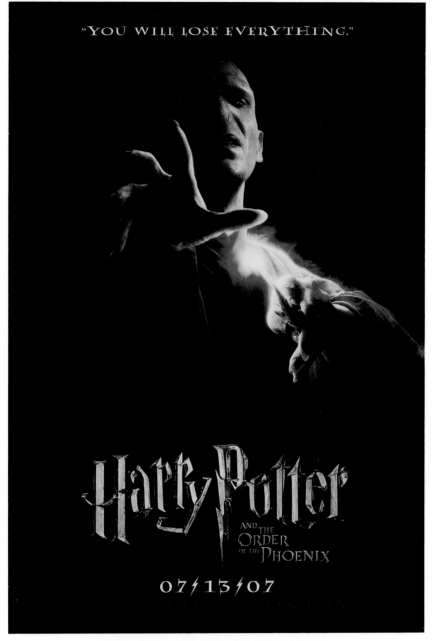

Harry Potter and the Order of the Phoenix (Warner Brothers, 2007), one sheet DS Advance movie poster with Voldemort image, rolled, Very Fine-, 27" x 40".
$26.

Courtesy of Heritage Auctions, ha.com

Harry Potter's long suffering godfather Sirius Black (Gary Oldman) is depicted on this amazing one sheet prototype for *Harry Potter and the Prisoner of Azkaban* (Warner Brothers, 2004) that was never issued by Warner Brothers. In a brilliant marketing ploy, Warner's created this poster to mimic the "Wanted" posters used in the movie and tried to duplicate a motion effect. As you move back and forth before this poster, the image of Black begins to disappear. After creating six of these full-size prototypes, Warner Bros decided that it was too expensive to put them into full production and so the project was dropped. This is probably the most rare of all the lenticular posters ever produced, near mint/mint, 25-3/4" x 40". **$3,800-$4,000.**

Courtesy of Heritage Auctions, ha.com

Hollywood Memorabilia

Entertainment and movie props are big business in Hollywood.

Studios are doing a better job at controlling their props from big-budget films. Props are now being sold by the studio itself or through small companies owned by the studio. It has turned the entertainment collecting world on its head as quality material gets more difficult to find for traditional brick and mortar dealers and auctioneers.

By cutting out the middleman, studios can make a healthy profit on expenses they write off to produce a feature or a program. This trend shows the market for entertainment and movie props is stronger than ever and will continue to grow in the future.

According to Julien's Auctions, one of the world's largest auctioneers of entertainment and film props, the market has been growing steadily for the last three decades. "In the past 35 years, the Entertainment Memorabilia auction market has gradually emerged to become an important and unequivocal collecting category," according to the company.

Collectors can pinpoint the exact year entertainment prop collecting became a mainstream collecting category. The seminal MGM Studios auction in 1970 was a watershed moment for film scholars and the auction business, which essentiality created a new market for an area of collecting that previously only existed among a few film enthusiasts. The studio's objective was to simply consolidate space on an already overcrowded lot by creating a three-day film memorabilia auction to clear seven soundstages. A vast assortment of costumes, film props and related property from the studios beginnings dating from the 1920s were cataloged, tagged and placed on the auction block.

Costume, "Superman III" (1983), Superman's bodysuit, screen-worn suit as used by actor Christopher Reeve, the only original Superman costume to be released to the public with full Warner Brothers Archives sanctioning, accompanied by Certificate of Authenticity direct from Warner Bros., rare. **$120,000**

Courtesy ScreenUsed

Prop, "Back to the Future Part III" (1990), Mr. Fusion, screen-used prop in Doc Brown's upgraded DeLorean Time Machine, 9-1/2" h. x 6" w. x 3-1/4" d. **$33,000**

Courtesy ScreenUsed

Highlights recall the full size sailing ship from *Mutiny on the Bounty* (1935), Elizabeth Taylor's wedding gown worn in *Father of the Bride* (1950), Clark Gable's trench coat worn in several films, a group of swimsuits worn by Esther Williams and Johnny Weissmuller's loin cloth worn in *Tarzan* films of the 1940s. However, the most coveted pieces sold were from *The Wizard of Oz* (1939), including a pair of ruby red slippers worn by Judy Garland that hammered on the auction block for $15,000 ($94,252 in today's dollars).

"With the auction's blockbuster success, film enthusiasts and collectors soon recognized film memorabilia as a fertile and profitable area of collecting. In the following years, small boutique shops, specialty companies and private brokering businesses began to crop up and thrive selling recognized film props and screen-seen objects," according to Julien.

Since then, studios have recognized and embraced this booming market on their own.

One thing is for certain, the market for mid-range and high-value entertainment memorabilia and props will continue to grow as movie production studios and smaller producers, such as Netflix and Amazon, continue creating captivating content.

Marilyn Monroe

Marilyn Monroe stands between Robert Kennedy (left) and John F. Kennedy at a party following her performance of "Happy Birthday" for the president.

Cecil Stoughton/The LIFE Images Collection/Getty Images

Marilyn Monroe singing "Happy Birthday" to President Kennedy at Madison Square Garden.

Bettman/Getty Images

The provocative "Happy Birthday, Mr. President" dress worn by Marilyn Monroe while serenading President John F. Kennedy, sold at auction for **$4.8 million.** Monroe wore the figure-hugging gown, embellished with hand-sewn crystals, while cooing the most memorable rendition of Happy Birthday ever sung at a Democratic fundraiser held at Madison Square Garden on May 19, 1962, ten days before Kennedy's 45th birthday. The flesh-colored dress features 2,500 hand-stitched crystals and was designed and made by Academy Award-winning costume designer Jean Louis. Legend has it the dress was so tight that Louis had to sew it while Monroe was wearing it. The birthday celebration was one of Monroe's final public appearances before her August 1962 death. Ripley's Believe It or Not bought the gown well beyond the pre-auction estimate of $3 million. "We believe this is the most iconic piece of pop culture that there is," Ripley's vice president Edward Meyer said after the museum chain won the auction. "In the 20th century I cannot think of one single item that tells the story of the 1960s as well as this dress." The "Happy Birthday, Mr. President" dress previously hit the Christie's auction block in 1999, where it sold for a then-record $1.27 million. "This dress, this story, this momentous occasion represents a defining moment in history," Julien's Auctions executive director Martin Nolan said.

Dress photo courtesy of Julien's Auctions

Television prop, CBS
Television, "I Love Lucy,"
1951-1957, made of Styrofoam
and fiberglass, painted gray
to simulate concrete, with
text reading "John Wayne"
used in the first and second
episodes of Season 5 - titled
"Lucy Visits Grauman's" and
"Lucy & John Wayne," original
air dates October 3 and 10,
1955 - when Lucy steals
the Duke's footprints from
Grauman's Chinese Theatre,
24" x 36". **$22,500**

Courtesy Heritage Auctions, ha.com

Prop, "Captain America: The First Avenger" (2011), screen-used by actor Chris Evans, Captain America's stunt shield, hard polyurethane, rubber with airbrushed darkened patina, scoring and scuffing, 24" dia. **$16,520**

Costume, "Terminator 2: Judgment Day" (1991), T-1000 costume as worn by actor Robert Patrick. **$6,000**

Courtesy ScreenUsed

Prop, "The Mask" (1994), Loki's Mask as screen used and worn by Jim Carrey as "Stanley Ipkiss," made of resin and painted to look like wood, autographed by Jim Carrey. **$45,000**

Courtesy ScreenUsed

Prop, "X-Men Origins: Wolverine" (2009), pair of "Adamantium Claws" were custom-made by the production for use by Hugh Jackman as Logan/Wolverine, made from resin, with cast-in-place metal posts that are attached to the base grips, 10-1/2" l. **$17,700**

Courtesy ScreenUsed

Silver Screen Collection/Getty Images

Prop, "I Dream of Jeannie" (NBC, 1965-1970), Jim Bean decanter that served as the original prop genie bottle used on the set, from the collection of Gene Nelson, who worked on the development of the program and directed eight episodes of the first season. Actress Barbara Eden played Jeannie in the title role. **$34,375**

Courtesy Julien's Auction

Grave marker, circa 1990s, from actress Marilyn Monroe's
crypt, bronze, raised lettering on front reads "Marilyn
Monroe / 1926-1962," 4 1/2" h. x 15" w. **$35,000**

Courtesy of Heritage Auctions, www.ha.com

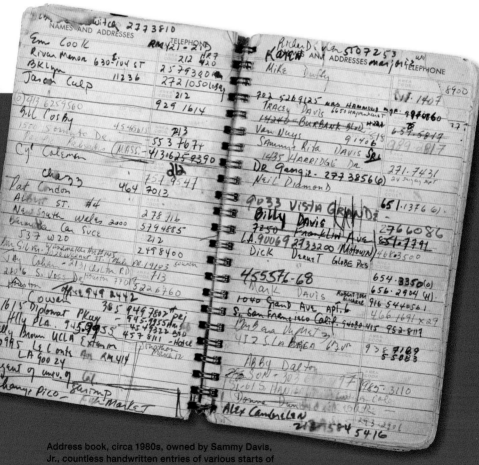

Address book, circa 1980s, owned by Sammy Davis,
Jr., countless handwritten entries of various starts of
movies, television, and music, 8" h. x 5" w. **$687**

Courtesy of Heritage Auctions, www.ha.com

Photograph, "The Ten Commandments," Paramount Pictures, 1956, original test exposure proof photograph from the 1955 hit movie, showing Yul Brenner and Anne Baxter. **$200**

PremiereProps, www.premiereprops.com

Costume, "Gone With The Wind" (1939), screen-worn by actress Vivien Leigh, two-piece ensemble; the jacket slate blue-gray ribbed cotton (now faded to light gray), black 'zig zag' applique and cord adornment on the collar, shoulders, front, and cuffs, nine decorative buttons on front, hidden hook-and-eye front closure. **$137,000**

Courtesy of Heritage Auctions, www.ha.com

Equipment, "Star Wars: The Empire Strikes Back (1980), clapperboard was used during filming of the second of George Lucas' original trilogy. **$23,600**

Courtesy ScreenUsed

Prop, "Star Trek: The Original Series" (1966-1969), Phaser pistol, one of two known to still exist, featured in an opening scene in the 2nd season episode "Assignment: Earth", where it is seen in a close-up view on-screen in the hand of a security officer in the Transporter Room. **$20,000**

Courtesy Propworx

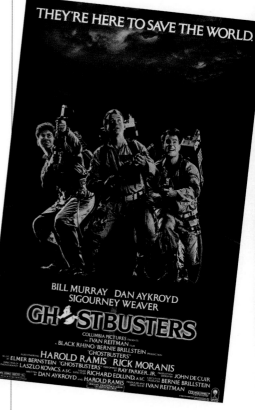

Prop, "Ghostbusters" (1984), proton pack, screen-used, fiberglass, aluminum, lights, rubber tubing, and computer parts, designed by Stephen Dane and Ivan Reitman. **$169,000**

Courtesy Profiles in History

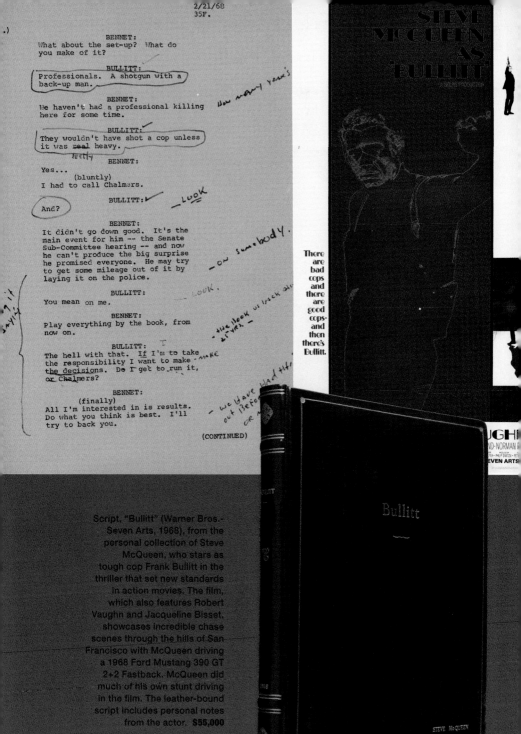

Script, "Bullitt" (Warner Bros.-Seven Arts, 1968), from the personal collection of Steve McQueen, who stars as tough cop Frank Bullitt in the thriller that set new standards in action movies. The film, which also features Robert Vaughn and Jacqueline Bisset, showcases incredible chase scenes through the hills of San Francisco with McQueen driving a 1968 Ford Mustang 390 GT 2+2 Fastback. McQueen did much of his own stunt driving in the film. The leather-bound script includes personal notes from the actor. $55,000

Courtesy of Heritage Auctions, www.ha.com

His whole life was a million-to-one shot.

ROCKY

A ROBERT CHARTOFF · IRWIN WINKLER PRODUCTION · A JOHN G. AVILDSEN FILM · STARRING SYLVESTER STALLONE IN "ROCKY"

ALSO STARRING TALIA SHIRE · BURT YOUNG · CARL WEATHERS · AND BURGESS MEREDITH AS MICKEY · WRITTEN BY SYLVESTER STALLONE

PRODUCED BY IRWIN WINKLER AND ROBERT CHARTOFF · DIRECTED BY JOHN G. AVILDSEN · EXECUTIVE PRODUCER GENE KIRKWOOD · MUSIC BY BILL CONTI

PG PARENTAL GUIDANCE SUGGESTED
SOME MATERIAL MAY NOT BE SUITABLE FOR PRE-TEENAGERS

ORIGINAL MOTION PICTURE SOUNDTRACK ALBUM AND TAPE AVAILABLE ON UNITED ARTISTS **UA** RECORDS

United Artists
A Transamerica Company

Movie Prop, "Rocky" and "Rocky II," United Artists, 1976 and 1979, black rubber handball, side stamped with blue text reading "Official / Seamless / 555;" kept by Stallone as "Rocky Balboa" in his pocket in many memorable scenes throughout both films. From the personal collection of Sylvester Stallone. **$32,500**

Heritage Auctions, www.ha.com

Long before Sylvester Stallone scored his first major movie success he cruised the streets of Philadelphia in a black leather jacket. Little did Stallone know that both he and the jacket had a bright future. "I remember when I bought this jacket in Philadelphia. It was obviously quite a few years before I ever even thought about Rocky, before Rocky was even an idea," Stallone said of his now famous jacket. "This is what I would wear in my everyday life. And when the time came to do the movie, we didn't have a budget where we could afford an original wardrobe so I thought, Why don't I just wear the things that I think Rocky would wear, clothes from my real life?" The jacket, which Stallone wore throughout Rocky, the surprise movie hit from 1976 that launched a movie franchise and Stallone's superstar career, sold at auction for **$149,000.** The leather jacket and other movie memorabilia from Stallone's career earned more than $3 million during a three-day sale in Los Angeles by Heritage Auctions. The auction featured 600 one-of-a-kind costumes, movie props, scripts, documents and other items from the actor-director's storied career.

Images courtesy Heritage Auctions, www.ha.com

Jewelry Styles

Jewelry has been a part of every culture throughout time, reflecting the times as well as social and aesthetic movements. Jewelry is usually divided into periods and styles. Each period may have several styles, with some of the same styles and types of jewelry being made in both precious and non-precious materials. Elements of one period may also overlap into others.

Georgian, 1760-1837: Fine jewelry from this period is quite desirable, but few good-quality pieces have found their way to auction in recent years. Sadly, much jewelry from this period has been lost.

Victorian, 1837-1901: Queen Victoria of England ascended the throne in 1837 and remained queen until her death in 1901. The Victorian period is a long and prolific one, abundant with many styles of jewelry. It warrants being divided into three sub-periods: Early or Romantic period dating from 1837-1860; Mid or Grand period dating from 1860-1880; and Late or Aesthetic period dating from 1880-1901.

Sentiment and romance were significant factors in Victorian jewelry. Often, jewelry and clothing represented love and affection, with symbolic motifs hearts, crosses, hands, flowers, anchors, es, crowns, knots, stars, thistles, wheat, arlands, horseshoes and moons. The materials of the time were also abundant

Platinum, diamond and sapphire ring, circa 1930s, with approximately 3.0 carat synthetic sapphire, 3.5 dwt, size 5. **$363**

Courtesy of Elite Decorative Arts, eliteauction.com

and varied. They included silver, gold, diamonds, onyx, glass, cameo, paste, carnelian, agate, coral, amber, garnet, emeralds, opals, pearls, peridot, rubies, sapphires, marcasites, cut steel, enameling, tortoise shell, topaz, turquoise, bog oak, ivory, jet, hair, gutta percha and vulcanite.

Sentiments of love were often expressed in miniatures. Sometimes they were representative of deceased loved ones, but often the miniatures were of the living. Occasionally, the miniatures depicted landscapes, cherubs or religious themes.

Hair jewelry was a popular expression of love and sentiment. The hair of a loved one was placed in a special compartment in a brooch or a locket, or used to form a picture under a glass compartment. Later in the mid-19th century, pieces of jewelry were made completely of woven hair. Individual strands of hair would be woven together to create necklaces, watch chains, brooches, earrings and rings.

In 1861, Queen Victoria's husband, Prince Albert, died. The queen went into mourning for the rest of her life, and Victoria required that the royal court wear

Pink topaz and gold jewelry suite, French; demi parure includes necklace with oval and pear-shaped pink topaz, approximately 34.40 carats, set in textured 15k gold, with pendant wires and clasp; matching earrings made for pierced ears, detachable drops with oval and pear-shaped pink topaz, approximately 11.10 carats, set in 15k gold ear wires; French hallmarks; necklace 18" x 1 1/4", earrings with drop, 2 7/8" x 7/8", without drop, 3/4" x 5/8". **$7,170**

Courtesy of Heritage Auctions, ha.com

black. This atmosphere spread to the populace and created a demand for mourning jewelry, which is typically black. When it first came into fashion, it was made from jet, fossilized wood. By 1850, there were dozens of English workshops making jet brooches, lockets, bracelets and necklaces. As the supply of jet dwindled, other materials were used such as vulcanite, gutta percha, bog oak and French jet.

By the 1880s, somber mourning jewelry was losing popularity. Fashions had changed and the clothing was simpler and had an air of delicacy. The Industrial Revolution, which had begun in the early part of the century, was now in full swing and machine-manufactured jewelry was affordable to the working class.

Edwardian, 1890-1920: The Edwardian period takes its name from England's King Edward VII. Though he ascended the throne in 1901, he and his wife, Alexandria of Denmark, exerted influence over the period before and after his ascension. The 1890s were known as La Belle Epoque. This was a time known for ostentation and extravagance. As the years passed, jewelry became simpler and smaller. Instead of wearing one large brooch, women were often found wearing several small lapel pins.

In the early 1900s, platinum, diamonds and pearls were prevalent in the jewelry of the wealthy, while paste was being used by the masses to imitate the real thing. The styles were reminiscent of the neo-classical and rococo motifs. The jewelry was lacy and ornate, feminine and delicate.

Arts & Crafts, 1890-1920: The Arts & Crafts movement was focused on artisans and craftsmanship. There was a simplification of form where the material was secondary to the design. Guilds of artisans banded together. Some jewelry was mass-produced, but the most highly prized examples of this period are handmade and signed by their makers. The pieces were simple and at times abstract. They could be hammered, patinated and acid etched. Common materials were brass, bronze, copper, silver, blister pearls, freshwater pearls, turquoise, agate, opals, moonstones, coral, horn, ivory, base metals, amber, cabochon-cut garnets and amethysts.

Art Nouveau, 1895-1910: In 1895, Samuel Bing opened a shop called "Maison de l'Art Nouveau" at 22 Rue de Provence in Paris. Art Nouveau designs in the jewelry were characterized by a sensuality that took on the forms of the female figure, butterflies, dragonflies, peacocks, snakes, wasps, swans, bats, orchids, irises and other exotic flowers. The

Art Nouveau hair comb, gold, tortoiseshell, opal and enamel, Georges Fouquet, France, circa 1905-1908, carved tortoiseshell comb of Egyptian inspiration with lotus and papyrus motifs, set with opal cabochons, black and green enamel, signed G. Fouquet, numbered 4680, with signed box. **$22,500**

Sotheby's

lines used whiplash curves to create a feeling of lushness and opulence.

1920s-1930s: Costume jewelry began its steady ascent to popularity in the 1920s. Since it was relatively inexpensive to produce, it was mass-produced. The sizes and designs of the jewelry varied. Often, it was worn a few times, disposed of and then replaced with a new piece. It was thought of as expendable, a cheap throwaway to dress up an outfit. Costume jewelry became so popular that it was sold in both upscale and "five and dime" stores.

During the 1920s, fashions were often accompanied by jewelry that drew on the Art Deco movement, which got its beginning in Paris at the "Exposition Internationale des Arts Décoratifs et Industriels Modernes" held in 1925. The idea behind this movement was that form follows function. The style was characterized by simple, straight, clean lines, stylized motifs and geometric shapes. Favored materials included chrome, rhodium, pot metal, glass, rhinestones, Bakelite and celluloid.

One designer who played an important role was Coco Chanel. Though previously reserved for evening wear, the jewelry was worn by Chanel during the day, making it fashionable for millions of other women to do so, too.

With the 1930s came the Depression and the advent of World War II. Perhaps in response to the gloom, designers began using enameling and brightly colored rhinestones to create whimsical birds, flowers, circus animals, bows, dogs and just about every other figural form imaginable.

Retro Modern, 1939-1950: Other jewelry designs of the 1940s were big and bold. Retro Modern had a more substantial feel to it and designers began using larger stones to enhance the dramatic pieces. The jewelry was stylized and exaggerated. Common motifs included flowing scrolls, bows, ribbons, birds, animals, snakes, flowers and knots.

KTF bracelet, circa 1937, rhodium-plated base metal, prong-set emerald-cut faux emeralds with bezel-set rhinestones, channel-set baguettes, and pavé-set round rhinestones, fold-over clasp integrated into design, marked KTF, 1 1/4" w, central element 3/4" h.
$5,000-$6,000

Courtesy of Robin Deutsch Collection

Hamilton Heritage diamond bracelet with radiant-cut fancy yellow and colorless diamonds. $79,000

Courtesy of Hamilton Jewelers of Natural Color Diamond Association

Sterling silver now became the metal of choice, often dipped in a gold wash known as vermeil.

Designers often incorporated patriotic themes of American flags, the V-sign, Uncle Sam's hat, airplanes, anchors and eagles.

Post-War Modern, 1945-1965: This was a movement that emphasized the artistic approach to jewelry making. It is also referred to as Mid-Century Modern. This approach was occurring at a time when the Beat Generation was prevalent. These avant-garde designers created jewelry that was handcrafted to illustrate the artist's own concepts and ideas. The materials often used were sterling, gold, copper, brass, enamel, cabochons, wood, quartz and amber.

1950s-1960s: The 1950s saw the rise of jewelry that was made purely of rhinestones: necklaces, bracelets, earrings and pins. The focus of the early 1960s was on clean lines: Pillbox hats and A-line dresses with short jackets were a mainstay for the conservative woman. The large, bold rhinestone pieces were no longer the must-have accessory. They were now replaced with smaller, more delicate gold-tone metal and faux pearls with only a hint of rhinestones.

At the other end of the spectrum were psychedelic-colored clothing, Nehru jackets, thigh-high miniskirts and go-go boots. These clothes were accessorized with beads, large metal pendants and occasionally big, bold rhinestones. By the late 1960s, there was a movement back to Mother Nature and the "hippie" look was born. Ethnic clothing, tie-dye, long skirts, fringe and jeans were the prevalent style, and the rhinestone had, for the most part, been left behind.

Architectural Revival-themed
necklace with micromosaics
in malachite frames, set in
18k gold, good condition,
gross weight 44.30 grams,
14" l. **$5,313**

Courtesy of Heritage Auctions, ha.com

American costume
jewelry designer
Kenneth Jay Lane.

*Photo by RonGalella/
WireImage/Getty Images*

Jewelry World Loses
Iconic Designer

Unlike the "fakes" he was famous for designing, the jewelry world lost a true
gem in July 2017 with the death of Kenneth Jay Lane, 85.

The American costume-jewelry designer was known for using unusual color
combinations of sapphire and topaz, amber and turquoise, and amethyst
and coral, and early in his career, he came up with such innovations as
embroidered earrings. Lane was also known for costume jewelry animals,
including rhinestone-studded Scottie dog brooches, bangles ending in pairs of
animal heads, and pins in the shapes of faux-emerald-eyed lions.

Lane's creations caught the eye of some of the most glamorous women for
more than 50 years, including Jacqueline Kennedy Onassis, Elizabeth Taylor,
Audrey Hepburn, Madonna, and Lady Gaga, and his pieces are now as sought
after and collectible as precious gems, with vintage pieces selling at auction
houses around the world, including Christies and Sothebys.

A documentary film about him, Fabulously Fake: The Real Life of Kenneth Jay
Lane, is expected to be released in 2018.

This vintage multi-strand bead necklace created by iconic costume-jewelry designer Kenneth Jay Lane can be worn casually or complemented with other gold pieces. In shades of red and blue beads with gold settings in between, a gold Indian-style charm hangs from the end as the centerpiece. The necklace, 19" long, sold at auction for **$312.50.**

Courtesy of Heritage Auctions, ha.com

Costume-jewelry pioneer Kenneth Jay Lane was known for his bangles that end in pairs of animal heads, such as this zebra bracelet. It sold at auction for **$102.**

Courtesy of Heritage Auctions, ha.com

Turquoise bracelet with oval-shaped clasp with center oval cabochon with 16 3.5-mm round cabochon turquoises, set in 18k yellow gold mount, four stands of 5-mm round beads, three separator bars set with nine 2.5-mm round turquoise beads, gross weight 36 grams, 6 1/2". **$1,054**

Courtesy of Brunk Auctions, brunkauctions.com

Gold cannetille and amethyst bracelet, early 19th century, hand-wrought cannetille work surrounding six graduated amethysts, three at 7.45 carats and two at 9.12 carats, 18k, with later fitted case by Garrard & Co., with appraisal, minor bends to some of the outer loops in cannetille work, minute wear to crown surfaces of amethysts, missing safety chain, 41.7 grams, 7" l. **$9,300**

Courtesy of Brunk Auctions, brunkauctions.com

▼ KTF "invisibly" set faux ruby bracelet, circa 1936, made of rhodium-plated base metal with 10 bead-set rhinestone pavé links and channel-set baguettes running down center, and invisibly set simulated rubies, fully articulated links slightly curved to mold to wrist, fold-over clasp integrates into design, marked KTF and 53 for stonesetter, 7" l x 3/4" w. **$1,650-$1,850**

Courtesy of Robin Deutsch Collection

Chanel cuff bracelet, circa 1980s, red and green Gripoix glass surrounded by faux pearl accents on gold-tone base, marked Chanel 2 CC 5 Made in France, 2 1/2" wide at front. **$6,000-$6,500**

Courtesy of ChicAntiques.com

Dior garland necklace, circa 1962, collar necklace with sapphire blue navette and pear-shaped rhinestones along with red accents, marked Chr. Dior © 1962, 16 3/4" l, front centerpiece 3 3/4". **$850-$1,000**

Courtesy of Pamela Y. Wiggins

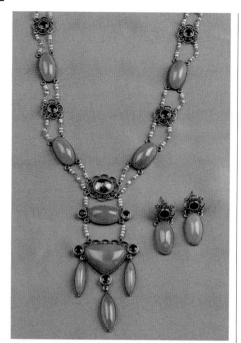

Arts & Crafts 14k gold and serpentine necklace, set with shaped and oval cabochons, cabochon sapphire accent, quatrefoil motifs centering blue stones, seed pearls, ear studs en suite, 13 3/4" long, 2 7/8" drop. **$4,622**

Courtesy of Skinner, Inc., www.skinnerinc.com

Art Nouveau 18k gold and plique à jour enamel gem-set pendant, L. Gautrait, France, designed as maiden with plique à jour enamel tresses wearing diamond and rose-cut diamond diadem, opal accents, diamond and pearl drop, suspended from fancy link chain, pendant signed L. Gautrait, chain with partial maker's mark for Leon Gariod, guarantee stamps, 2" x 2 1/2"; chain 20" long. **$21,600**

Courtesy of Skinner, Inc., skinnerinc.com

Ruby, diamond, and platinum-topped gold ring with oval-shaped ruby measuring 8.60 mm x 6.90 mm x 4.45 mm and weighing approximately 2.20 carats, European- and single-cut diamonds weighing approximately 2.60 carats, set in platinum-topped 14k gold, gross weight 9 grams, size 6 1/4. **$3,750**

Courtesy of Heritage Auctions, ha.com

Diamond ring, platinum and vertically set European-cut diamonds, approximately 4.25 carats, elongated pierced openwork mount set throughout with numerous single-cut diamonds, circa 1915, approximately 4 dwt, 1 3/16" l. **$12,000**

Courtesy of Doyle New York

Late Victorian enamel, ruby, diamond and gold snake bracelet, round-shaped rubies, approximately 3.50 carats, rose-cut diamonds, approximately 0.50 carat, green enamel applied on 18k gold, articulated gold tongue, 83.37 grams, 6 1/2" x 3/4". **$7,187**

Courtesy of Heritage Auctions, ha.com

Ruby, sapphire and diamond brooch, Oscar Heyman & Brothers, waving American flag composed of fancy-cut sapphires, calibré-cut rubies, round brilliant, baguette and pear-shaped diamonds, maker's mark for Oscar Heyman & Brothers, no. 75239, estimated total diamond weight 3.30 carats, mounted in platinum, 2" l. **$31,250**

Courtesy of Bonhams

Pink sapphire and black diamond spider brooch, articulated legs, estimated total diamond weight 3.50 carats, mounted in blackened 18k gold, 2" long. **$1,875**

Courtesy of Bonhams

Blister pearl, diamond, ruby, emerald, and gold bird-shaped pendant-brooch, pearl measuring 23.00 mm x 14.00 mm, with rose-cut yellow and colorless diamonds weighing approximately 0.95 carat, with marquise and round-cut rubies weighing approximately 0.25 carat, with triangle-shaped emerald, set in 14k gold, very good condition, 2" x 7/8", gross weight 10.20 grams. **$1,250**

Courtesy of Heritage Auctions, ha.com

Agate cameo brooch, Russian, depicting Cupid and Psyche, Russian assay mark, mounted in 14k gold, 2 9/16" x 2 1/4". **$3,125**

Courtesy of Bonhams

Cartier Art Deco platinum and gemstone ear or dress clips set with hand-carved green chrysoprase flowers, with rose-cut and single-cut diamonds weighing approximately 0.25 carats, and square-cut blue sapphires weighing approximately 2 carats, platinum and 18k white gold mounts, marked "Cartier 3519897" on each clip, with appraisal and Cartier box, 19.6 mm x 16.5 mm, 12.5 grams. **$44,640**

Courtesy of Brunk Auctions, brunkauctions.com

Eisenberg Original fur clip, circa 1940, glass opalescent blue stones with simulated sapphire bullet cabochon accents and clear rhinestones with simulated pearls in heavy cast setting, marked Eisenberg Original, 4" l. **$1,100-$1,300**

Courtesy of LinsyJsJewels.com

Cultured pearl, diamond, sapphire, coral, emerald, and aquamarine ear clips, Italy hallmark, 3/4" x 1". **$2,000**

Courtesy of Doyle New York, doylenewyork.com

Emerald, ruby and diamond pendant/brooch, central oval-shaped emerald cabochon weighing approximately 30 carats, estimated total diamond weight 7.30 carats, gross weight approximately 51.6 g., mounted in 18k gold and platinum; 2 1/4" l. **$23,750**

Courtesy of Bonhams

Edwardian set of necklace, bracelet and pair of earrings, Tiffany
& Co., designed by Louis Comfort Tiffany, circa 1910, formed of
sculpted gold links of foliate and scroll design, set with variety of
colored stones, including sapphires in multiple hues, blue and purple
spinel, pink tourmaline, amethyst and zircon, in round, cushion and
various fancy shapes, necklace 18 1/2" long, bracelet 6 7/8", earrings
with later-added backs, signed Tiffany & Co. **$121,000**

Courtesy of Sotheby's, sothebys.com

Lamps & Lighting

By Martin Willis

MARTIN WILLIS has been appraising antiques and fine art for more than 40 years. He comes from a family of auctioneers: His father, Morgan Willis, developed and ran the Seaboard Auction Gallery, Maine. Martin has served in the antique auction business with companies in Maine, New Hampshire, Massachusetts, Colorado and California. He spent six years with Clars Auction Gallery of Oakland, California, as senior appraiser, cataloger and auctioneer, handling the estate of TV mogul Merv Griffin as well as talk show host Tom Snyder. In 2009, Martin launched Antique Auction Forum, a biweekly podcast on the art and antiques trade with followers across North America and throughout the world.

A fine lamp provides illumination as well as a decorative focal point for a room. This dual-purpose trend had its origins in the mid-to-late 1800s with American lighting. As with most game-changing style movements, timing was key in this evolution.

Arguably, the vanguard name of decorative lighting was Louis Comfort Tiffany (1848-1933) of New York City. Urban homes became electrified on a wide scale near the end of the 19th century; it was then that Tiffany was becoming recognized as a designer as well as a commercial success.

Tiffany's first stained glass shade for an electric lamp was designed by Clara Driscoll around 1895. Since their introduction over a century ago, Tiffany's shades have always had a unique, glowing quality to them due to their masterful designs and chemically compounded stained glass colors. Today, Tiffany Studios lamps remain collectors' favorites. Rare and unusual designs – including the Hanging Head Dragonfly, Peony, Apple Blossom, and Wisteria patterns – generate the most interest and dollars; outstanding examples have commanded up to $2 million.

Tiffany's commercial success catalyzed the creation of many new stained glass lamp companies. Contemporaries included Duffner & Kimberly, *Suess*, Chicago Mosaic, and Wilkinson. See *Mosaic Shades II* by Paul Crist for more information.

There were several other companies in the United States making fine glass lamps at the turn of last century. These included Handel from Meriden, Connecticut, and Pairpoint from New Bedford, Massachusetts. Handel was known primarily for its reverse-painted shades. Fine examples of the company's landscape, aquarium, and other unusual motifs have garnered prices up to $85,000. Pairpoint opened in 1880 and soon merged with Mt. Washington Glass of Boston. They created reverse-painted shades as well, the most

Daum cameo glass
ceiling fixture, Nancy,
France, 1900s, glass,
iron, single socket,
marked Daum Nancy,
bowl 7" x 16", 31" tall
total. **$6,250**

Courtesy of Rago Arts &
Auction Center, ragoarts.com

popular being their "Puffy" shade. Prices for Pairpoint lamps start around
$1,000 and peak at about $25,000 for top examples.

Perhaps the most notable European glass lamp manufacturer from the
late 19th century was Daum, founded by Jean Daum in France in 1878. The
company is still in business today, manufacturing crystal art glass. Daum's
lamps were made of cameo glass, produced through a proprietary technique
of using acid to cut through layers of fused glass. This creates dramatic color
reliefs. During its heyday, 1895-1914, Daum produced beautiful cameo
glass lamp bases and shades. Today, early examples can be
purchased starting at $1,000. Exceptional pieces may
garner up to $80,000.

It is important to note that when it comes to
vintage lamps, reproductions and fakes dominate
the secondary market. If a price seems too good
to be true, it probably is. It is imperative to buy
from a reputable dealer or an auction house
that will stand behind an item's authenticity. If
a piece has the word "style" as part of its description,
i.e., a "Tiffany style" lamp, this indicates that it is either
a reproduction or that the seller is uncertain of its origins.
Always ask plenty of questions before investing in a fine art lamp.

As always, anything is worth whatever someone will pay, and there are
often good buys available, even from top manufacturers. With the exception
of rare examples, enthusiasts should be able to find and afford a nice
authentic vintage lamp to admire and enjoy.

Austrian Art Nouveau lamp with bronze base with
organic lines and maiden's head on front, single
arching arm supports shade ring, mushroom shade
with amber mottled decoration against light yellow
background; very good to excellent condition;
shade 10" diameter, lamp 18" high. **$2,844**

Courtesy of James D. Julia, Inc., jamesdjulia.com

Rare pair of gilt bronze Argand lamps, early 19th century, probably English, each with Classical amphora font, navette-shaped acanthine bowl, on bed of acanthus with scrolled feet, etched and frosted shades, with antique presentation cases, 13 1/2" high x 11" wide. **$15,625**

Courtesy of Neal Auction Co., nealauction.com

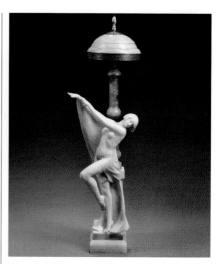

Figural alabaster lamp, Italy, early 20th century, with green shade and stem mounted to base with carved female dancer, incised "Prof. G. Bessi Italy," 34 1/4" high overall. **$923**

Courtesy of Skinner, Inc.; skinnerinc.com

Rare hanging cast iron miniature triple-arm chandelier lamp fitted with three colorless glass tapered fonts, each embossed "FIRE FLY" and with correct opaque glass chimney-shade, frame 10 1/4" high. **$8,625**

Courtesy of Jeffrey S. Evans & Associates, jeffreysevans.com

Daum etched and enameled glass lamp with trees in rain, circa 1900, enameled DAUM, NANCY, with cross of Lorraine, good condition, 14 1/4" high. **$43,750**

Courtesy of Heritage Auctions, ha.com

Daum Nancy ribbed table lamp with purple-blue raised vertical ribs against a shaded green to raspberry ground on shade and maize-yellow to powdered blue mottled on base. **$13,800**

Courtesy of James D. Julia, Inc., jamesdjulia.com

Gallé French cameo boudoir lamp with creamy ground and purple and blue floral and foliage pattern overall, layer of chartreuse green glass behind pattern, shade supported by three-armed base with cast iron supports and single socket in identical pattern, signed "Gallé" in cameo to shade and base, very good to excellent condition with base having slight rub to finish, 14" high. **$7,703**

Courtesy of James D. Julia, Inc., jamesdjulia.com

Rookwood Arts & Crafts-style lamp with hand-carved thistle by Rose Fechheimer, circa 1905, heavy form with original electrical fittings done in two-tone mat finish, marks include mostly obscured company logo, date and shape number, artist's initials carved inside base, pale green shade is appropriate but not original; excellent original condition; ceramic portion 15 3/4" high. **$2,800**

Courtesy of Mark Mussio, Humler & Nolan, humlernolan.com

Handel Wisteria table lamp with massive leaded shade, recurring design of 12 wisteria flowers in purple, lavender, amethyst, and blue with yellow centers, set against foliage in green hues, hanging wisteria vines in earthen hues, accentuated irregular border gives the shade a three-dimensional affect. **$17,500**

Courtesy of James D. Julia, Inc., jamesdjulia.com

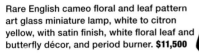

Rare English cameo floral and leaf pattern art glass miniature lamp, white to citron yellow, with satin finish, white floral leaf and butterfly décor, and period burner. **$11,500**

Courtesy Jeffrey S. Evans & Associates, jeffreysevans.com

Metal overlay lamp, Handel Lamp Co., early 20th century, slag glass shade with metal overlay in landscape motif, three sockets with three acorn finial pull chains, bronze base marked "Handel Lamps" and decorated with flowers and foliates, both base and shade are property signed, 23" high. **$2,430**

Courtesy of Louis J. Dianni, LLC, louisjdianni.com

Pairpoint owl table lamp, rarest and most desirable of all Pairpoint lamps made and only eighth example known to exist. Exaggerated, blown out, molded owl shade, white feathers with light brown, yellow, and gray highlights, brown and gold eyes and beak, border decorated with green foliage, pine needles, and tree limbs; owl-shaped metal base with original patina and glass eyes, single socket, and original shade ring; shade signed on outside edge in gold "Pat. Applied For"; shade in very good condition with small chip and 2" sliver to inside rim, base in very good to excellent condition; shade 12" diameter with 10" fitter, 20 1/2" high overall. **$77,025**

Courtesy of James D. Julia, Inc., jamesdjulia.com

Tiffany Studios leaded glass peony border bronze floor lamp, circa 1910, marks to shade: TIFFANY STUDIOS, NEW YORK, 1374, overall fine condition, no evidence of damage to shade or base, 74 1/2" high, 24" diameter. **$131,000**

Courtesy of Heritage Auctions, ha.com

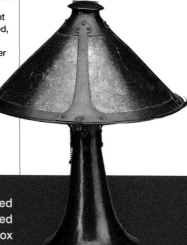

Dirk van Erp early trumpet lamp with vented cap, San Francisco, 1911-1915, hammered copper, mica, single socket, closed box windmill stamp, 19 1/2" x 16" diameter. **$10,625**

Courtesy of Rago Arts & Auction Center, ragoarts.com

Tiffany prism student lamp with artichoke foot and adjustable single arm that supports shade consisting of 12 Tiffany amber glass prisms, brown patina with green highlights, base signed "Tiffany Studios New York 10914"; very good to excellent condition; 26" high. **$11,258**

Courtesy of James D. Julia, Inc., jamesdjulia.com

Tiffany Studios Moorish double student lamp with twisted wire Moorish decoration on bronze base that supports two bronze overlay shades with blown out green glass inserts. **$12,000**

Courtesy of James D. Julia, Inc., jamesdjulia.com

Pairpoint Puffy apple tree lamp with background of green leaves with bluish highlights and pink apple blossoms surrounding green and red apples, pair of bumblebees on one side and two butterflies on opposing side. **$23,575**

Courtesy of James D. Julia, Inc., jamesdjulia.com

Tiffany Studios loaded glass and turtleback tile bronze floor lamp, circa 1910, tapering standard issued from squat base supporting shade in mottled green glass and turtleback tile border, marks to lamp base: Tiffany Studios, NEW YORK, 377, marks to shade: TIFFANY STUDIOS, NEW YORK, 1511-2, overall very fine and original condition, pigtail finial appears original, 72" high, 21 1/4" diameter. **$106,250**

Courtesy of Heritage Auctions, ha.com

Unusual Tiffany Studios turtleback lamp with bronze base, ribbed inverted saucer foot, and simple turned stem. **$12,075**

Courtesy of James D. Julia, Inc., jamesdjulia.com

Tiffany Studios Daffodil table lamp with yellow daffodils, centers created with heavily ribbed glass with dark green stems and leaves against a light green background shading to creamy white. **$39,100**

Courtesy of James D. Julia, Inc., jamesdjulia.com

Tiffany Studios Venetian desk lamp, circa 1910, multicolored shade in blue and green with red accents, shade signed Tiffany Studios New York 515, surmounting three-socket cluster above cast gilt bronze jeweled standard on graduated base, marked Tiffany Studios, New York 515, 20" high x 13" wide. **$57,750**

Courtesy of Clars Auction Gallery, clars.com

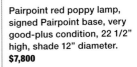

Coca-Cola bottle lamp, 1930s, with original embossed bronze-colored iron base and metal display cap with wear and patch, excellent condition, small touched rubs or paint nicks, light soiling, factory paint irregularities, 20 1/4" high. **$4,200**

Courtesy of Morphy Auctions, morphyauctions.com

Pairpoint red poppy lamp, signed Pairpoint base, very good-plus condition, 22 1/2" high, shade 12" diameter. **$7,800**

Courtesy of Morphy Auctions, morphyauctions.com

Cold-painted bronze and metal lamp, Austria, early 20th century, faint impressed Bergman mark, modeled as cottage with minstrel at one side, doors opening to reveal cobbler at work, 11 3/8" high. **$3,120**

Courtesy of Skinner, Inc., skinnerinc.com

Pair of Walter von Nessen Space Age aluminum lamps, tiered, with inset bands of brass and Bakelite, designed for Pattyn Products, Detroit, circa 1935-1936, marked Model 310, 19 1/4" high. **$5,322**

Courtesy of Heritage Auctions, ha.com

Rare Handel Peacock floor lamp, domical glass shade decorated and acid etched on exterior with two peacocks being the central focus, surrounded by a floral and foliage pattern. **$23,575**

Courtesy of James D. Julia, Inc., jamesdjulia.com

Luxury Items

By Noah Fleisher

The market for vintage, high-end luxury accessories is one of the hottest markets in the world right now and, even more important, it's brought an entirely new and non-traditional clientele to the world of high-end collectible auctions.

Matt Rubinger, who heads the Luxury Accessories category for Heritage Auctions, is the foremost authority on handbags, has been in the business since he was 13 years old, and is largely responsible for driving this upswing in attention to the market. He has been profiled by the Associated Press, *The Wall Street Journal* and *The Washington Post,* among others.

"Collectibles and collecting have traditionally been male-dominated pursuits," Rubinger said. "No one in the business was looking at these very high quality pieces of enduring *haute couture* as having value beyond being arm candy. This assumption effectively dismissed half the potential population of collectors, that is, women."

Via his work with innovative websites like Portero.com and Moda Operandi, and for the last three years running his department at Heritage, Rubinger has more than succeeded in establishing his category's brand. He's focused the attention of all collectors, men and women, on the category as an important and viable investment-grade tangible and drawn international mainstream attention at the same time via huge sales, including the highest price ever paid at auction for a handbag, in December 2011, when he sold an Hermès Diamond Birkin for more than $203,000.

"That was the moment when the luxury accessories market really matured," said Rubinger. "A price realized like that legitimized the pursuit in the broader public imagination. Suddenly, what savvy women have known for years – that a great handbag

Writer and author
NOAH FLEISHER has 20 years of experience in the antiques and collectibles field. He is the author of *The Beatles: Fab Finds of the Fab Four*, *Warman's Modern Furniture*, and *Collecting Children's Books.*

is an investment as well as a collectible and a fashion statement – was recognized by the rest of the collecting world, the men, many of whom were married to these women. Now, when we have an auction and a collector is considering their options on a $50,000 handbag, their husband is right there with them discussing the possibility."

It's an exciting thing to see a market being born and to be conscious of the fact that you are seeing, right in front of you, the birth of a powerhouse. For Rubinger, however, it's not a surprise. He just does the math and looks at the market objectively.

"You can walk into a high-end retail outlet and buy a bag for a few hundred or a few thousand dollars and it loses a good deal of value the minute you walk out of the store, and it will never get that value back," he said. "However, if you spend, say, $20,000 on an Hermès bag, or $5,000 on a Louis Vuitton, that bag will hold its value five, 10 and 20 years later and, in many cases, will have risen and will return a significant amount on that initial investment."

Handbags are not graded like coins, cards or comics – though do not be surprised if this happens in the future – though there are criteria they are judged on:

Pristine – The piece is in perfect condition and appears to have never been used. It is in as-new condition.

Excellent – The piece is in nearly perfect condition, with only very slight signs of use.

Very good – The piece has been used but well cared for with no major flaws or wear.

Good – The piece has been used and shows wear. It is in as-is condition.

Fair – The piece exhibits condition issues that may or may not be repairable, but is still wearable as purchased.

Now, unless you are a veteran buyer in the market and a true aficionado of the form, these criteria will not mean a tremendous amount to the untrained eye.

Birkin Bag with palladium hardware, pristine condition, 14" wide x 10" high x 7" deep. This bag is one of the rarest and most sought-after bags in the world; produced once or twice per year, this color is known as bubblegum pink.
$104,500

Courtesy of Heritage Auctions, www.ha.com

They are, nonetheless, the standard by which the objects are measured, and the main reason that neophyte handbag collectors needs to educate themselves, studying auction records and sales on business websites and, perhaps most importantly, consulting experts like Rubinger.

"It's not difficult to look at a handbag and assess its beauty and style relative to its intended purpose," said Rubinger, "but unless you know what is good, and what is not good, it's very easy to overpay for something that does not warrant it."

As with anything of great value, there's a significant market in fakes. Handbags are no exception, as evidenced by the sheer number of fake Hermès, Chanel, and Vuitton bags you buy on the street in Chinatown. Move up the ladder of fakes a rung or two and you have very well-crafted fakes that can be sold in stores, online or even by fly-by-night "dealers" who will not be

there the next time you call.

Experts like Rubinger have the institutional knowledge and the expertise writ hard in their DNA and can spot a fake across the room. If you are interested in the market and want to get into it, then it is imperative that you do your homework and talk to an expert, like Rubinger, who will be more than happy to share his expertise with you, regardless of your price point.

"This is an emerging market and there are tremendous opportunities for collectors of all levels and all ages," said Rubinger. "Know what you want, know where to find it, and go after the very best examples you can afford, whether it's $100 or $100,000."

The good news is that there are great examples available in those price ranges, and everywhere in between. All they are waiting for are the right stylish collectors.

Handbag, Gucci, "Dionysus Bag," red suede and leather, featuring one shoulder chain, 10-1/5" w. x 6-1/5" h. x 2.5" d. **$2,000**

Courtesy of Heritage Auctions, www.ha.com

◄ Handbag, 2016, Hermes, shiny cactus alligator and feather Stromboli Bag with sterling silver hardware, multicolor feather detailing, interior is done in matching Cactus Chevre Leather, 5-1/5" w. x 5-1/5" h. x 3" d. **$38,750**

Courtesy of Heritage Auctions, www.ha.com

▲ Handbag, deisgned by Judith Leiber, full bead gray and multicolor crystal Liberty Minaudiere evening bag, interior in metallic silver leather, 6" w. x 4-1/5" h. x 1-1/2" d. **$1,187**

Courtesy of Heritage Auctions, www.ha.com

◄ Handbag, Prada, "Lux Tote Bag," purple saffiano leather, featuring two rolled handles, gold hardware, and a magnetic clasp closure, 14-1/5" w. x 10-1/5" h. x 7" d. **$1,000**

Courtesy of Heritage Auctions, www.ha.com

▼ Handbag, Chanel, limited edition, blue, pink, and white beaded satin, featuring one woven satin and silver tone shoulder chain, CC turnlock closure, interior in blue satin. **$7,812**

Courtesy of Heritage Auctions, www.ha.com

Hermès

▲ Handbag, 2013, Hermes, 25cm Matte White Himalayan Nilo Crocodile Birkin Bag with Palladium Hardware. Q Square, 10" w. x 8" h. x 5" d., **$68,750**

Courtesy of Heritage Auctions, www.ha.com

◄ Handbag, 2012, Hermes, Matte Cactus Alligator, featuring two rolled handles, Palladium Hardware, and a flap top with a turnlock closure, 14" w. x 10" h. x 7" d. **$50,000**

Courtesy of Heritage Auctions, www.ha.com

Hermès Extraordinary Collection 35cm diamond, Shiny Black porosus crocodile Birkin Bag with 18k white gold hardware, excellent condition, 14" wide x 10" high x 7" deep.
$122,500

Courtesy of Heritage Auctions, www.ha.com

Hermès rare 30cm Shiny Violet porosus crocodile Birkin Bag with palladium hardware, excellent to pristine condition, 12" wide x 8" high x 6" deep. **$74,500**

Courtesy of Heritage Auctions, www.ha.com

Hermès 35cm Shiny Braise Red porosus crocodile Birkin Bag with palladium hardware, pristine condition, 14" wide x 10" high x 7" deep. **$95,600**

Courtesy of Heritage Auctions, www.ha.com

Hermès 35cm Matte Brighton Blue porosus crocodile Birkin Bag with palladium hardware , pristine condition, 14" wide x 11" high x 7" deep. **$113,525**

Courtesy of Heritage Auctions, www.ha.com

Hermès 35cm Shiny Rouge H porosus crocodile Birkin Bag with palladium hardware, pristine condition, 14" wide x 10" high x 7" deep. **$59,000**

Courtesy of Heritage Auctions, www.ha.com

Hermès 35cm Shiny Gris Elephant porosus crocodile Birkin Bag with palladium hardware, pristine condition, 14" wide x 10" high x 7" deep. **$86,500**

Courtesy of Heritage Auctions, www.ha.com

Clutch bag, 2013, Hermes, Shiny Violet Alligator, featuring palladium hardware, and a flap top with a slide lock closure, 9" w. x 4-1/2" h. x 1-1/2" d. **$23,750**

Courtesy of Heritage Auctions, www.ha.com

Tote, Salvatore Ferragamo, brown ponyhair and black leather, two shoulder straps, gold tone brass hardware, two zip pockets, and a zip closure, 13-1/5" w. x 12" h. x 5" d. **$812**

Courtesy of Heritage Auctions, www.ha.com

> **What savvy women have known for years – that a great handbag is an investment as well as a collectible and a fashion statement – was recognized by the rest of the collecting world.**

Tote, Michael Kors, white python leather, gold tone hardware, two shoulder straps, a snap and drawstring closure, and four exterior pockets, 22" w. x 15" h. x 6" d. **$325**

Courtesy of Heritage Auctions, www.ha.com

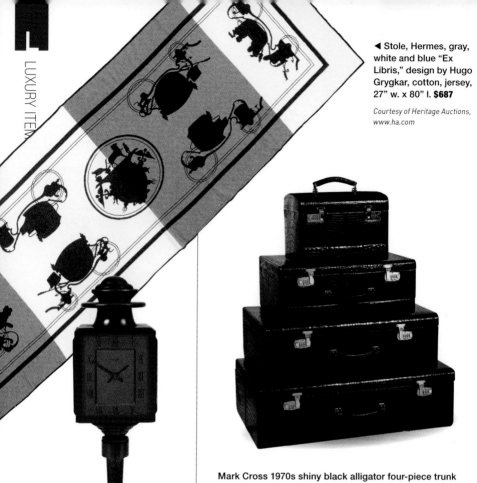

◀ Stole, Hermes, gray, white and blue "Ex Libris," design by Hugo Grygkar, cotton, jersey, 27" w. x 80" l. **$687**

Courtesy of Heritage Auctions, www.ha.com

Mark Cross 1970s shiny black alligator four-piece trunk set with beige leather and red velvet interior, pristine condition; piece 1, 30" wide x 18" high x 9" deep; piece 2, 26" wide x 16" high x 8" deep; piece 3, 20" wide x 14" high x 8" deep; piece 4, 13" wide x 9" high x 8.5" deep. **$28,680**

Courtesy of Heritage Auctions, www.ha.com

Clock, 20th century, French, marked Hermes, Paris, with Roman numerals on a U-form stand, 10-1/8" h. **$2,300**

Courtesy Auction Gallery of the Palm Beaches Inc.

▶ Pillbox, 20th century, Hermes, gold and silver, unusual pillbox by Hermes features a 1709 French silver coin featuring a likeness of King Louis XIV and a triple crown on the reverse, coin has been split to make the top and bottom of this pillbox, joined in the center by gilt metal, 1-1/5" w., x 1/5" h. **$450**

Courtesy of Heritage Auctions, www.ha.com

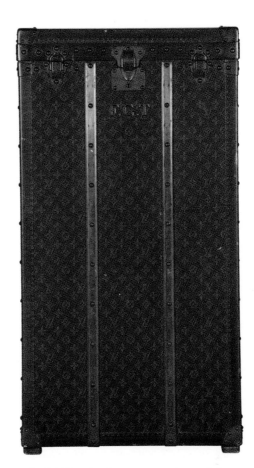

▲ Louis Vuitton Damier canvas oversize wardrobe trunk with burnt orange Alcantara interior, pristine condition, 43" wide x 25.5" high x 21.5" deep. **$13,750**

Courtesy of Heritage Auctions, www.ha.com

▼ Trunk, circa 1940s, Louis Vuitton, classic monogram coated canvas, 40" w. x 21" h. x 18" d. **$15,000**

Courtesy of Heritage Auctions, www.ha.com

Maps & Globes

Throughout the ages, pictorial maps have been used to show the industries of a city, the attractions of a tourist town, the history of a region, or its holy shrines. Ancient artifacts suggest that pictorial mapping has been around since recorded history began. "Here be dragons" is a mapping phrase used to denote dangerous or unexplored territories, in imitation of the medieval practice of putting sea serpents and other mythological creatures in blank areas of maps.

Our fascination with maps and globes expanded dramatically in the 15th and 16th centuries. with advances in shipbuilding and the growing desire for expansion, exploration and trade. Emboldened by improved sailing and enticed by the dream of riches to be found in far-off lands, Portuguese exploration and trade along the West African coast and to Atlantic islands opened new oportunities for expansion. Portugal's Prince Henry the Navigator encouraged and directed an international team of experts who paved the way for revolutionary advances in geography, navigation and cartography.

The European worldview in the late 15th century wavered between bizarre imaginings about the unknown and scientific observation. While technological advances have removed the mystery early cartographers dealt with, the early work remains historically captivating, adventurously romantic and highly collectible. A well-executed map, no matter the subject, remains an artistic treasure and monument to our sense of exploration.

Weber Costello Company 12" terrestrial globe, early 20th century, cartouche reads, "Made by Weber Costello Co., Chicago Heights, Illinois," on a turned wooden pedestal, 20" high. **$700**

Courtesy of Neal Auction Co., www.nealauction.com

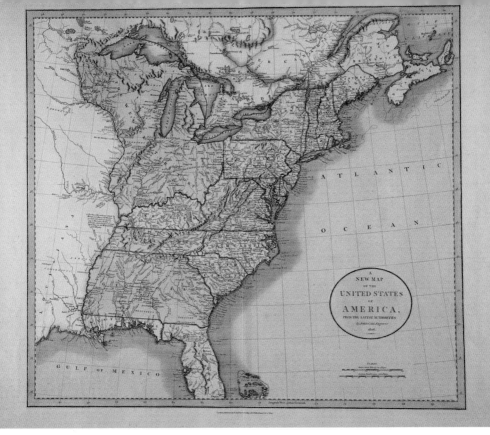

▲ Map, United States, 1806, "A New Map of the United States of America, from the Latest Authorities," London, John Cary, 1806. First edition taken from Cary's New Universal Atlas from 1808, contemporary hand coloring, 20 1/4" x 26 1/4". Cary (1754-1835) was one of the finest and most prolific English cartographers of the 19th century; also became the foremost globe maker of his day. **$1,375**

Courtesy of Heritage Auctions, Inc., www.ha.com

◀ Terrestrial table globe, George Philip and Son, London, early 20th century, annotated with principal towns, cities, rivers, mountain ranges, and transcontinental railway routes, oceans with principal steamship routes annotated in nautical miles, 19" maximum diameter, 22" high, globe 4". **$1,630**

Courtesy of Dreweatts & Bloomsbury Auctions, www.dreweatts.com

W. & A. K. Johnston, Ltd. 18" terrestrial library globe, Edinburgh, Scotland, circa 1900, printed gores with states and countries highlighted in different colors, all on turned and carved walnut base with central carved shaft support and four supporting legs, 40" high. **$2,252**

Courtesy of Skinner Auctioneers, Inc., www.skinnerinc.com

Cary's 14" terrestrial table globe on stand, London, published by G & J Cary, St. James's, Jan. 4, 1826, Alaska labeled "Russian America," the American southwest labeled "Mexico," South Africa shown as "Unknown Parts," the oceans marked with tracks of various explorers, on three turned mahogany legs, 22 3/4" high. **$3,851**

Courtesy of Skinner Auctioneers, Inc., www.skinnerinc.com

Pair of similar globes, mid-19th century, one with compass inlaid to base, loss of information to areas, otherwise surface wear commensurate with age, taller globe 24" high. **$1,875**

Courtesy of Heritage Auctions, Inc., www.ha.com

Illuminated electric globe, maker unknown, French, circa 1930, on stepped chromed metal base, labeled in French, 9 3/8" high. **$300**

Courtesy of Heritage Auctions, Inc., www.ha.com

Weber Costello Co. terrestrial 16" floor globe on stand, 38" high. **$225**

Courtesy of Michaans Auctions, www.michaans.com

American cast iron terrestrial floor globe, Gilman Joslin, Boston, third quarter 19th century, 15" globe raised on a painted foliate and scroll cast iron standard, 42" high, 21 1/2" diameter. **$6,875**

Courtesy of Bonhams, www.bonhams.com

Woodblock map, hand-colored, decorated paper over boards, paper cover label with title "Keisei bankoku zenzu," copy of Matteo Ricci's "World Map" on oval projection translated into Japanese, 36" x 65" folding to 11 1/4" x 6 1/2". **$4,920**

Courtesy of PBA Galleries, www.pbagalleries.com

▲ Original Cocomalt
premium Buck Rogers
Solar System map, R. B.
Davis Co., 1933, part of
rare Solar Scouts campaign
available only by mail order,
fine condition, 18" x 25",
professionally matted and
framed with glass to 30" x
23". **$598**

*Courtesy of Heritage Auctions, Inc.,
www.ha.com*

Atlas, New York and vicinity,
New York, F. W. Beers, A. D.
Ellis & G. G. Soule, 1867. First
edition of Beers' atlas, 17 1/2"
x 14 1/4", 12 lithographic maps
printed on onionskin paper
inserted throughout, 61 hand-
colored lithographic maps and
uncolored lithographic views,
publisher's quarter brown
morocco over cloth boards.
$625

*Courtesy of Heritage Auctions, Inc.,
www.ha.com*

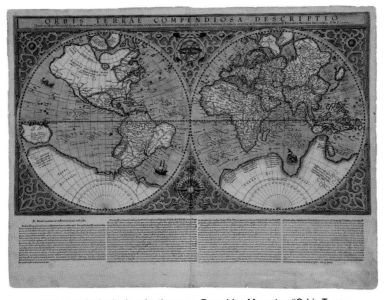

World hemispherical projection map, Rumoldus Mercator, "Orbis Terrae Compendiosa Descriptio," 1587 [actually 1595]. Gerardus Mercator (1512-1594) was the most important and influential cartographer of the 16th century, famous for producing the most accurate maps of his day and for the invention of the Mercator Projection, in which the world is pictured in a cylindrical-like fashion, showing the entire globe in a single map. This map is by his youngest son, Rumoldus (1545-1599), who based it on his father's designs of the original map of 1567. The Mercators are considered the most important cartographers after Ptolemy. **$4,750**

Courtesy of Heritage Auctions, Inc., www.ha.com

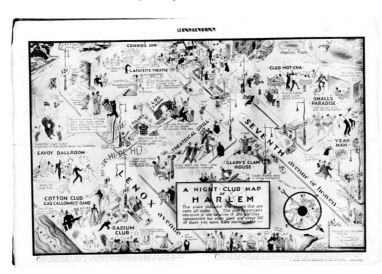

A Night-Club Map of Harlem, 1932, first and only printing, 16 pages, 12" x 16", unfolding to 16" x 24", centerfold by E. Simms Campbell, "The stars indicate the places that are open all night…" numerous small cartoon vignettes illustrating Harlem street scenes, map considered a rarity of Harlem Jazz age in last days of Prohibition. **$12,300**

Courtesy of PBA Galleries, www.pbagalleries.com

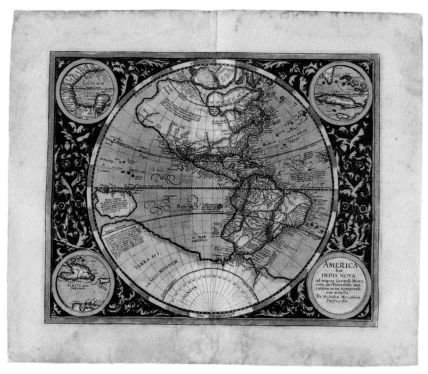

Copper-engraved, hand-colored map of Western Hemisphere as known at end of 16th century, coloring is early, if not original, French text on verso with folio no. 69 and signature mark S, a feature of editions published in 1633, 1635 and 1639, 14 1/2" x 18". **$3,382**

Courtesy of PBA Galleries, www.pbagalleries.com

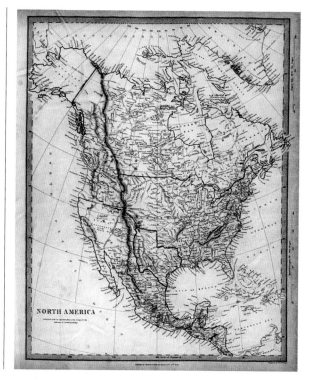

Early map of North America, London: Chapman and Hall, 1843, with hand-colored borders, fine condition, 16" x 13 1/4". **$688**

Courtesy of Heritage Auctions, Inc., www.ha.com

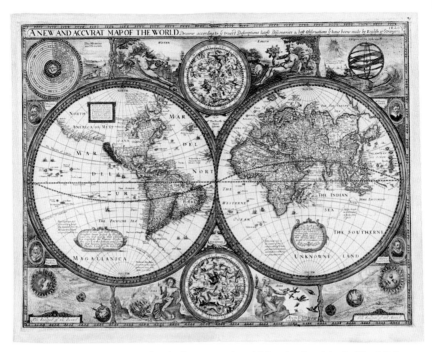

Copper-engraved double-hemisphere map of world, hand-colored, in double-sided archival mat, based on William Grent's rare, separately issued map of 1625, one of the earliest published world maps to be printed in English, first atlas map to show cartographic curiosity of California as an island, one of first to show settlement of New Plymouth; engraver unknown but most likely Abraham Goos, 15 1/2" x 20 1/4". **$15,990**

Courtesy of PBA Galleries, www.pbagalleries.com

Beatles signed Pan Am Airways route map obtained on their flight to America, Feb. 7, 1964; 15 ¾" x 9", signed in blue ink: "John Lennon", "Paul McCartney", "George Harrison", and "Ringo Starr" in the Pacific Ocean area where there was room for all four to sign together. The Beatles performed on The Ed Sullivan Show Feb. 9, 1964, before some 73 million television viewers, changing forever the course of pop music history. **$23,750**

Courtesy of Heritage Auctions, Inc., www.ha.com

Movie Posters

By Noah Fleisher

There is little that can connect us to our last century of shared history like a great movie poster. Think of the very best movies of all time, whatever genre you love, and you likely associate the image of the movie poster with the film itself. A great movie poster not only encapsulates the film it represents, it captures the era in which it was produced and reflects the state of the world at its time of production.

Few people are as well situated as Grey Smith, Heritage Auctions' Director of Rare & Vintage Movie Posters. Over the last 20 years, and throughout his life as a collector, he has handled the greatest movie posters of all time, including the 2017 sale of a First Post-War Release Italian 4-Fogli movie poster for *Casablanca* (Warner Brother, 1946), a never-before-sold poster from what is widely considered one of the best films ever made. The poster sold for $478,000.

"The buyer has just set a world record and acquired what we in the poster collecting world would equate to a masterpiece," Smith said. "The stunning artistry put into this poster makes it stand head and shoulders above any paper produced for the film."

The poster, measuring 55-1/2 inches by 78-1/4 inches, was produced in 1946. The film, starring Humphrey Bogart and Ingrid Bergman, opened in Italy on Nov. 21 that year, almost four years after its U.S. premiere. Featuring artwork by Luigi Martinati, the poster is considered the best of the picture's numerous advertisements, Smith said.

Previous Italian-issue posters for the film have sold for as much as $203,000. A U.S.-issue of the poster has sold for $191,200.

After a few years in which the poster market looked

GREY SMITH
Director of Rare &
Vintage Movie Posters
Heritage Auctions, Dallas

Casablanca (Warner Brothers, 1946): First Post-War Release
Italian 4 - Fogli (55.5" X 78.25") Luigi Martinati Artwork. **$478,000.**

Courtesy of Heritage Auctions, www.HA.com.

a little bit thin, it has come roaring back in the last few, as collectors look to pay top dollar for the best possible posters of their respective collecting genres.

A few truisms hold in the market, currently, such as the old Universal Horror movie posters are always the top of the heap, but we are also seeing that great examples of hit movies, from all decades, are selling well and bringing top dollar. If it is rare, and it is quality, then it will be highly collectible.

Below, Grey shares a few of his insights with Warman's:

Warman's: What is the current state of the Movie Poster market?
Grey Smith (GS): The market seems very healthy as prices seem to grow yearly for the majority of the more scarce higher end pieces. Good and rare titles are also bringing record prices. Some of the more common material of the last 40 years has not held up as well due to the quantity found in today's Internet market.

Warman's: What makes something a great Movie Poster?
GS: First and foremost, the film title. The scarcity of that title is what really drives this hobby. Second is the star power of the title and, finally, the graphic appeal.

Warman's: Is there still great film art being produced?
GS: I'm fairly jaded and believe the older material is great, especially pre-1960s posters. These outshine newer posters in all respects. There are some very well done posters produced today, such as "Walk the Line" 2005 or "The Dark Knight" 2008, not to mention the "alternate" posters of such companies as Mondo, which is brilliantly rethinking movie posters today. That said, I think the majority of current posters are all a photo shop jobs done on a formulaic premise. It keeps going back to the desirability of the title or star, but in my opinion, there is little great poster art being produced anymore by the studios.

Walk The Line
(20th Century Fox, 2005):
One Sheet (27" X 40").
$203

*Courtesy of Heritage Auctions,
HA.com.*

Warman's: What are some of the top genres selling right now – besides Horror, which seems to always be the top?

GS: The top selling posters now are the great and scarce titles, not necessarily genres. If the title or poster is scarce in the market, it sells. For example, a Lady Eve one sheet sold for more than $80,000 in Heritage's July 2017 auction – a very scarce one sheet and from a classic film that exceeded our previous sale of the poster by five-fold.

Warman's: Any advice for the starting collector?

GS: Collect what you love, from the films you appreciate and what you can afford. By educating yourself you will find your way in this fascinating hobby. Very good posters can be found at reasonable prices if one is willing to put in the time and effort.

Metropolis (UFA-Cinema Art Ltd., 1928):
Australian Pre-War Daybill (15" X 40")
Robotrix Style, Bernie Bragg Artwork.
$215,100.

Image courtesy of Heritage Auctions, HA.com.

The Great White Way (First National,
1924): Australian Pre-War Daybill
(14.75" X 39.5"). **$109.**

Courtesy of Heritage Auctions, www.HA.com.

Dumbo (RKO, 1941):
Three Sheet (41" X 79.75"), Style B. **$7,170.**

Courtesy of Heritage Auctions, www.HA.com.

Kiss Me Deadly (United Artists, 1955):
Three Sheet (41" X 79"). **$776.**

Courtesy of Heritage Auctions, www.HA.com.

Goldfinger (United Artists, 1964): 24 Sheet (104" X 232"). **$3,824.**

Courtesy of Heritage Auctions, www.HA.com.

The Night Ride (Universal, 1930): One Sheet
(27" X 41"). **$2,868.**

Courtesy of Heritage Auctions, www.HA.com.

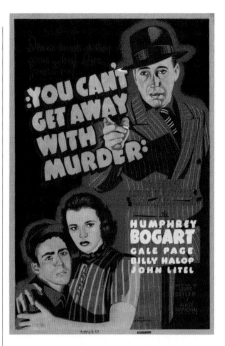

You Can't Get Away with Murder (Warner
Brothers-First National, 1939): Silk Screen
Poster (40" X 60"). **$4,182.**

Courtesy of Heritage Auctions, www.HA.com.

The Lady Eve (Paramount, 1941): One Sheet
(27" X 41"). **$83,650.**

Courtesy of Heritage Auctions, www.HA.com.

Supernatural (Paramount, 1933): One Sheet
(27.5" X 41"). **$107,550.**

Courtesy of Heritage Auctions, www.HA.com.

Let's Fall in Love (Columbia, 1933): One Sheet (27" X 41"). **$4,302.**

Courtesy of Heritage Auctions, www.HA.com.

It Came from Outer Space (Universal International, 1953): One Sheet (27" X 41"). 3-D Style. **$1,135.**

Courtesy of Heritage Auctions, www.IIA.com.

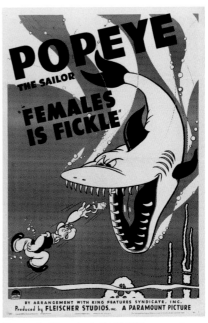

Popeye in "Females is Fickle" (Paramount, 1940): One Sheet (27" X 41"). **$2,629.**

Courtesy of Heritage Auctions, www.HA.com.

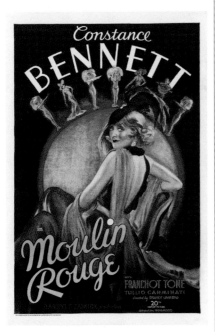

Moulin Rouge (United Artists, 1934): One Sheet (27" X 41"). **$2,390.**

Courtesy of Heritage Auctions, www.HA.com.

A Night at the Opera (MGM, R-1948): One Sheet (27" X 41"). Al Hirschfeld Artwork. **$2,629.**

Courtesy of Heritage Auctions, www.HA.com.

The Invisible Man (Universal, 1933): One Sheet (27"
X 41") Style A, Teaser, Karoly Grosz Art. **$274,850.**

Courtesy of Heritage Auctions, www.HA.com.

Woman (Hiller & Wilk, 1918): One Sheet (27" X
41"). Burton Rice Artwork. **$430.**

Courtesy of Heritage Auctions, www.HA.com.

Swing Shift Cinderella (MGM, 1945): One Sheet
(27" X 41"). **$5,019.**

Courtesy of Heritage Auctions, www.HA.com.

The Lawless Legion (First National, 1929): One
Sheet (27.5" X 41"), Style B. **$3,107.**

Courtesy of Heritage Auctions, www.HA.com.

Barbarella (Paramount, 1968): One Sheet (27" X 41"), Style B. **$2,509.**

Courtesy of Heritage Auctions, www.HA.com.

The Memphis Belle (Paramount, 1944): One Sheet (27" X 41"). **$4,063.**

Courtesy of Heritage Auctions, www.HA.com.

Devil Girl from Mars (Spartan, 1955): British One Sheet (27" X 40"). **$3,346.**

Courtesy of Heritage Auctions, www.HA.com.

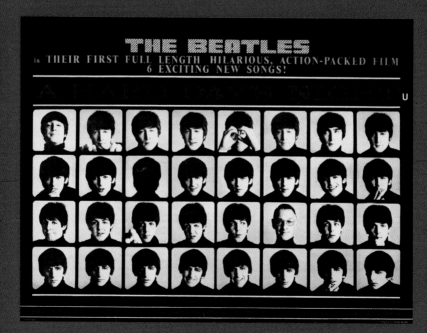

A Hard Day's Night (United Artists, 1964): British Quad (30" X 40"). **$4,182.**

Courtesy of Heritage Auctions, www.HA.com.

The Wizard of Oz (MGM, 1939): Half Sheet
(22" X 28"), Style A. **$71,700.**

Courtesy of Heritage Auctions, www.HA.com.

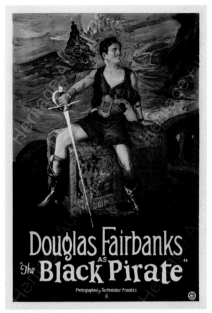

The Black Pirate (United Artists, 1926):
One Sheet (27" X 41"). **$6,572.**

Courtesy of Heritage Auctions, www.HA.com.

▲ The Seven Samurai (Toho, 1954): Japanese
B2 (20" X 28.5"). **$13,145.**

Courtesy of Heritage Auctions, www.HA.com.

◀ Top Hat (RKO, R-1953): Insert (14" X 36"). **$475.**

Courtesy of Heritage Auctions, www.HA.com.

The Ghost of Frankenstein (Realart, R-1948): One Sheet (27" X 41"). **$5,019.**

Courtesy of Heritage Auctions, www.HA.com.

Petroliana

Petroliana covers a broad range of gas station collectibles from containers and globes to signs and pumps and everything in between.

As with all advertising items, factors such as brand name, intricacy of design, color, age, condition, and rarity drastically affect value.

Beware of reproduction and fantasy pieces. For collectors of vintage gas and oil items, the only way to avoid reproductions is experience: making mistakes and learning from them; talking with other collectors and dealers; finding reputable resources (including books and websites), and learning to invest wisely, buying the best examples one can afford.

Marks can be deceiving, paper labels and tags are often missing, and those that remain may be spurious. Adding to the confusion are "fantasy" pieces, globes that have no vintage counterpart and are often made more for visual impact than deception.

How does one know whether a given piece is authentic? Does it look old, and to what degree can age be simulated? What is the difference between high-quality vintage advertising and modern mass-produced examples? Even experts are fooled when trying to assess qualities that have subtle distinctions.

There is another important factor to consider. A contemporary maker may create a "reproduction" sign or gas globe in tribute

◄ Gasoline double-sided oval porcelain porcelain sign, scratches throughout, chip at bottom of field, large chip in word "Clipper," 60" high x 30" wide.
$30,000-$40,000

Matthews Auctions

Chevron Supreme Gasoline single-sided tin sign, minor paint loss on bottom edge, 24" diameter. **$2,600+**

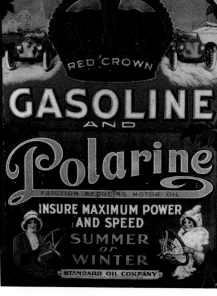

Red Crown Gasoline and Polarine self-framed beveled edge tin over cardboard sign, copyright 1913, Standard Oil Co., depicting women drivers, repaired nail hole at top and some scratches otherwise very good condition, 19 1/4" wide x 27 1/2" high. **$14,000**

Showtime Auction Services

Large Shell Oil embossed die-cut seashell porcelain sign, 48" high x 48" wide. **$1,000-$4,000**

of the original, and sell it for what it is: a legitimate copy. Many of these are dated and signed by the artist or manufacturer, and these legitimate copies are highly collectible today. Such items are not intended to be frauds.

But a contemporary piece may pass through many hands between the time it leaves the maker and wind up in a collection. When profit is the only motive of a reseller, details about origin, ownership, and age can become a slippery slope of guesses, attribution, and

– unfortunately – fabrication.

As the collector's eye sharpens, and the approach to inspecting and assessing petroliana improves, it will become easier to buy with confidence. And a knowledgeable collecting public should be the goal of all sellers, if for no other reason than the willingness to invest in quality.

For more information about petroliana, consult *Warman's Gas Station Collectibles Identification and Price Guide* by Mark Moran.

Fleet-Wing Gasoline Motor Oil tin sign, M.C.A. 5-47 with wood framing, one of the earliest examples of promotions used by this company since it was established in 1956, 71" high x 35" wide. **$500-$1,500**

Victorian Casino Auctions

Sign, circa 1950s, electrical, neon, die cut, manufactured by Flexlume Corp., Buffalo. **$6,000**

Courtesy Rich Penn Auction

Phillips 66-Battery Service vertical embossed self-framed tin sign with wood backing, 18" high x 72" wide. **$500-$1,800**

Victorian Casino Auctions

United Motors Service neon and porcelain oval sign, includes original crate, circa 1950s, sign 37" long x 24" wide. **$1,600-$3,000**

Victorian Casino Auctions

Vintage gas/service station island metal Mobloil display with six glass oil bottles with spouts, pre-1938, with original porcelain sign. **$500-$1,200**

Victorian Casino Auctions

◀ Wolf's Head Motor Oil, founded in 1879, oil can graphics, round thermometer with glass face, slightly soiled, marked Pam Clock Co., 12" diameter. **$210-$500**

Matthews Auctions

Mohawk Gasoline single-sided tombstone-shaped neon sign, mounted on new can, neon in working condition, 52" high x 44" wide. **$20,000-$30,000**

Matthews Auctions

◀ Standard's Supreme (with Ethyl) Gasoline globe, 15" lenses in a high-profile metal body. **$2,300+**

Vintage electric Imperial Mobiloil metal and glass wall mount clock by C.J. Hug Co., Inc., Highland, Illinois, 15" diameter. **$350**

Victorian Casino Auctions

Sunoco Motor Oil light-up store display stand, original spout bottles in carriers, "Mercury Made" motto, company formed in 1890, carrier circa mid-1940s, holes in porcelain sides for light to show through. **$1,000-$2,500**

Victorian Casino Auctions

Sign, Texaco Gasoline & Motor Oil, in original iron hanger, made by The Texas Company, 42-1/2" dia. **$1,900**

Courtesy Rich Penn Auctions

Wyeth Tires single-sided porcelain curved shield-shaped sign, marked "Wyeth Hdw. & Mfg. Co. / St. Joseph, Mo. U.S.A." and "Burdick Consumer building. Chicago and Beaver Falls, Pa.," small chips along top edge, 22" high x 18" wide. **$20,000-$25,000**

Matthews Auctions

Sign, enamel on porcelain, Musgo Gasoline, Michigan's Mile Marker, (sign is one of the known "Septic Tank Cap" finds) 48" dia., **$55,000**

Courtesy Dan Morphy Auctions, morphyauctions.com

Oilzum Motor Oils, "The Cream of Pure Pennsylvania Oil" with logo display sign, light paper marks, reverse has chip in lower field, 24" diameter. **$2,100-$4,300**

Matthews Auctions

Sign, enamel on porcelain, circa 1950s, Red Hat Motor Oil & Gasoline, maker Marked Reliance Adv. Co. Milwaukee, best known example of this sign, 32" dia., **$21,000**

Courtesy Dan Morphy Auctions

Wil-Flo Motor Oil double-sided tin oval sign, 17" x 23", display side restored, reverse total loss. **$3,100+**

Union 76 single-sided porcelain die-cut truck door sign, minor edge chip, 7" x 7". **$2,900+**

Sav'n Sam's Regular Gasoline with logo, station's operated primarily in Northern California, die-cut sign, 10" diameter. **$1,600-$2,500**

Matthews Auctions

Koolmotor jewel-body globe,
15" lenses, 19 1/2" tall overall,
circa 1930s. **$5,000+**

Gurney Seed globe 13 1/2"
lenses, showing radio station,
Yankton, S.D., in a wide white
glass body. **$1,500+**

Co-op Gasoline globe single lens
in a narrow glass body. **$2,000+**

Mobiloil Gargoyle large oval
globe, one-piece body, probably
new old stock. **$2,900+**

Blue Crown one-piece, possibly
original paint, 17" tall, metal collar.
(The blue Crown is the rarest color,
followed by gold and red.) **$800+**

Texaco leaded stained-
glass metal body globe,
slight fading, smaller size.
$4,500+

PHOTOGRAPHY

P

Photography

The world of Photography collecting is a fascinating and rewarding pursuit. There are as many styles as there are tastes and, with the explosion of online auction accessibility and e-commerce, now more than ever collectors can gain access to the art and artists that make their hearts flutter.

Rachel Peart, a Photography Specialist at Phillips in New York City – one of the world's leading art auction houses – has more than a decade of professional experience in the photography market, first at Heritage Auctions in Dallas, and for the last few with Phillips, where she has brought fresh works of photography to auction and has influenced collectors across genres, impressing everyone with her eye for a great picture and her ability to express exactly what makes a photograph compelling.

Below, Rachel shares some of her considerable insight with Warman's.

Warman's: What is the current state of the Photography market?
Rachel Peart (RP): Photography has always been relatively stable, in some part due to the more accessible price point for new collectors and the inherently democratic nature of the medium that captures an array of subject matter. However, it continues evolving; there's continued and growing interest in both classic and contemporary photography. The prices for certain contemporary photographers and exceptional classic works continues to rise, which is exciting to see at the top end of the marketplace. The growing global photo market also contributes – people can buy at auction around the world more easily than ever before. We've seen a great deal of participation from Asia in recent seasons, as collectors there have been more and more interested in works of Western art.

Warman's: What makes a great photograph?
RP: Great photographs are best viewed in person, where you can truly appreciate the beauty of the image and the object itself – how it resonates, how the artist's process informs your experience. Beyond that it is the artist's importance and place in the history of the medium and significance of that particular piece: is it from a specific period or series? Was it printed earlier in a special process? Is it a seminal image from their oeuvre? Does it carry special provenance or exhibition history? These are key elements in defining a great photograph.

Warman's: Has digital changed the definition of "great" photograph?

RP: The constant evolution of technology has always changed how we take and view photographs; digital has most certainly altered the accessibility to cameras and images. However, that hasn't changed how we view and define "great" photography. Conversely, I think the general awareness of today's technical capabilities help us gauge a great work of art vs. one that's only aesthetically pleasing. It's wonderful that the digital world has expanded the interest and vocabulary for imaging making, but a person can take one amazing photo, though if that's their only

"Girls in the Windows, New York City, 1960" by Ormond Gigli (American, b. 1925): Oversized dye coupler, printed later, 46" x 46". **$35,000.**

Courtesy Heritage Auctions, ha.com.

"Dusek Brothers" by Irving Penn (American, 1917-2009), New York, 1948: gelatin silver, 6-3/4" x 8-3/4". **$13,750.**

Courtesy of Heritage Auctions, ha.com.

contribution, it's unlikely their work is going to be marked in a similar way as an artist who devoted their life to the medium, or fine art in general. Collectors, curators, gallerists and auction specialists are still looking at the various hallmarks that make someone an important artist or that make certain photographs an important body of work.

Warman's: Who are some of the top names selling right now and why?
RP: Artists like Cindy Sherman and John Baldessari, who straddle and blur the line between photographs and contemporary collecting categories achieve strong prices for their work, along with setting top records for prices realized for photographs. Other

top selling works tend to be more of a reflection of the quality and rarity of a piece regardless of when it was taken, print type or scale. An auction that offers a rare and beautifully preserved 19th century print can bring as much attention as a contemporary work from a series created within the last five years.

Warman's: Where can you get a great deal?
RP: Do your homework and know what you're looking for – this will guide you to the most reasonable prices. Increasingly, auctions are where many photographs are offered and can present great opportunities to buy works at a better price than you might elsewhere.

Warman's: If I was just starting, what advice would you give me?

RP: Get out and see as much as you can. Attending auction viewings open to the public, an excellent opportunity to see works of various price points and to see works up close with a Specialist. Get acquainted with galleries that show works you like, get to know the owners and directors. Mark Photo Fair dates on your calendar, like the annual Aipad (Association of International Photography Art Dealers) Fair in New York each spring. Fairs present an opportunity to see a lot in one location, giving you a better idea of what "speaks to you," while also getting a chance to meet gallerists from all over the world. Taking time to see museum exhibitions is also incredibly helpful and really fun. I also highly recommend monographs and photobooks by artists you enjoy, or are considering purchasing. The more you can see and experience, the better you will be to find what you love.

"Wheelbarrow with Flower Pots" by Edward Steichen (American, 1879-1973), 1920: gelatin silver contact print, printed 1930's, 7-5/8" x 9-5/8". $7,500.

Courtesy of Heritage Auctions, ha.com.

"Nastassja Kinski and the Serpent, Los
Angeles, California, 1981" by Richard
Avedon (American, 1923-2004): gelatin
silver, 28-3/4" x 43-1/4". **$42,500.**

Courtesy of Heritage Auctions, ha.com.

▲ "American Soldier,
El Guettar, Tunisia" by Robert
Capa, March 1943: gelatin
silver print, with pencil
inscription to verso (possibly
by Capa's hand). This is one of
a series of photographs Capa
took during World War II as
Allied forces opened a front in
Tunisia in an effort to liberate
Italy from Fascism, 7-1/2" x
7-1/2". **$700.**

Courtesy of Leland Little, lelandlittle.com.

▶ Ambbrotype: 1/9th plate,
scroll pattern in a thermoplastic
case, subject identified as
Confederate soldier Matthew
McCauley, Pittsylvania County,
Danville Va. **$2,100.**
*Courtesy of Philip Weiss Auctions,
weissauctions.com.*

▲ "Ironwoods, Molokai, Hawaii, 1992" by Elaine Mayes (American, b. 1938): dye coupler, 32" x 48". **$2,000**

Courtesy of Heritage Auctions, ha.com.

◄ "Tunisian Youth, circa 1920" by Rudolf Franz Lehnert (Czech, 1878-1948) and Ernst Heinrick Landrock (Swiss, 1878-1966): photogravure, 11-3/8" x 9". **$350.**

Courtesy of Heritage Auctions, ha.com.

"Coleman's Café" by William Christenberry (Am., 1936-2016), 1971: photographic paper, depicting rural Greensboro, Alabama, restaurant, 8" x 10". **$1,500.**

Courtesy of Bruneau & Co. Auctioneers, bruneauandco.com.

Gelatin silver print photograph of Yale University's men's outdoor track and field circa 1903: Two, matted and mounted on board, 22 1/2" x 30 3/4". **$1,500**

Courtesy of University Archives, universityarchives.com.

"Transform (Lipstick)" by
John Baldessari, 1990:
unique work comprised of
two chromogenic prints with
vinyl paint, flush-mounted,
73-3/8" x 67-1/2". **$528,359.**

Courtesy of PHILLIPS, phillips.com.

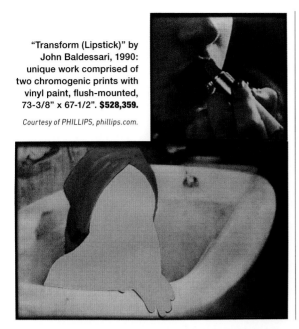

"Boy & Girl" by Ruud Van Empel,
2008: dye destruction print,
face-mounted to Plexiglas and
flush-mounted, signed, titled,
dated and numbered 1/7 in ink
on an artist label affixed to the
reverse of the flush-mount 95" x
67-1/2". **$93,379.**

Courtesy of PHILLIPS, phillips.com.

"At the time of the flood, Louisville, Kentucky," Margaret Bourke-White
(1904-1971). Silver print, 8 3/4" x 11 3/4", 1937; printed 1998. **$32,500**

Courtesy of Swann Auction Galleries, swanngalleries.com

"Safety-man coming up on mooring mast, Empire State Building," Lewis W. Hine (1874-1940). Silver print, 9 1/2 x 7 1/2 inches, 1930. **$21,250**

Courtesy of Swann Auction Galleries, swanngalleries.com

Cleora Wheeler, (American, 20th century), Capistrano, Redwoods, Gulls, Near Monterey (a group of 4 works): photographs with hand coloring, each signed and titled in pencil, largest 4" x 3". **$150.**

Courtesy of Treadway Toomey Auctions, treadwaygallery.com.

"Untitled" by Wingate Paine, circa 1970: chromogenic print, 21" x 17". Realized **$300.**

Courtesy Wright: Auctions of Art and Design, wright20.com.

"Suzy Parker and Robin Tattersall, evening dress by Grès, Moulin Rouge," Richard Avedon, 1957, oversized silver print, 17 3/4" x 14 3/4", with Avedon's signature and edition notation 7/25, in pencil, and his hand stamp, on verso. **$35,000**

Courtesy of Swann Auction Galleries, swanngalleries.com.

"New York City, 1974" by Elliott Erwitt (American, b. 1928): gelatin silver Lambda, 2016, 25-1/4" x 38". **$6,600.**

Courtesy of Heritage Auctions, ha.com.

"Route 66, Albuquerque, New Mexico" by Alexander Haas (Ernst): chromogenic print, printed later, signed by Alexander Haas, titled and editioned 5/50 in black ink on accompanying Haas Studio label, 1969, 17-1/4" x 26". **$2,000**

Courtesy of Bloomsbury Auctions, dreweatt s.com.

"Untitled (teenagers), 1964" by Edwin Roseberry (American, b. 1925): gelatin silver, 13-3/8" x 10-1/2". **$20.**

Courtesy of Heritage Auctions, ha.com.

▲ "Child in Window, 105th St., New York, 1952" by Walter Rosenblum (American, b. 1919): gelatin silver, 7-1/4" x 9-3/8". **$325.**

Courtesy of Heritage Auctions, ha.com.

◄ "Walk to Paradise Garden, 1946" by W. Eugene Smith (American, 1918-1978): gelatin silver, printed late 1960s to 1971, photographer's credit limitation stamp on verso. With signed provenance letter from Takeshi Ishikawa, Smith's assistant, 15-1/4" x 13-1/8". **$23,750.**

Courtesy of Heritage Auctions, ha.com.

Quilts

Each generation made quilts, comforters and coverlets, all intended to be used. Many were used into oblivion and rest in quilt heaven, but for myriad reasons, some have survived. Many of them remain because they were not used but stored, often forgotten, in trunks and linen cabinets.

A quilt is made up of three layers: the top, which can be a solid piece of fabric, appliquéd, pieced, or a combination; the back, which can be another solid piece of fabric or pieced; and the batting, which is the center layer, which can be cotton, wool, polyester, a blend of poly and cotton, or even silk. Many vintage quilts are batted with an old blanket or even another old, worn quilt.

The fabrics are usually cotton or wool, or fine fancy fabrics like silk, velvet, satin, and taffeta. The layers of a true quilt are held together by the stitching, or quilting, that goes through all three layers and is usually worked in a design or pattern that enhances the piece overall. The term "quilt" has become synonymous with bedcover to many people; tied quilts, comforters, and quilt tops are included in this category, though none is a true quilt in the technical description.

Quilts made from a seemingly single solid piece of fabric are known as wholecloth quilts, or if they are white, as whitework quilts. Usually such quilts are constructed from two or more pieces of the same fabric joined to make up the necessary width. They are often quilted quite elaborately, and the seams virtually disappear within the decorative stitching. Most wholecloth quilts are solid-colored, but prints were also used. Whitework quilts were often made as bridal quilts and many were kept for "best", which means that they have survived in reasonable numbers.

Wholecloth quilts were among the earliest type of quilted bedcovers made in Britain, and the colonists brought examples with them according to inventory

For more information on quilts, see *Warman's Vintage Quilts Identification and Price Guide* by Maggi McCormick Gordon.

Appliqué Pride of Iowa
variation quilt, circa 1880,
74" x 77". **$1,067**

Courtesy of Pook & Pook, Inc.,
pookandpook.com

lists that exist from Colonial times. American
quiltmakers used the patterns early in the nation's
history, and some were carried with settlers moving
west across the Appalachians.

Appliqué quilts are made from shapes cut from
fabric and applied, or appliquéd, to a background,
usually solid-colored on vintage quilts, to make a
design. Early appliqué quilts dating back to the 18th
century were often worked in a technique called
broderie perse, or Persian embroidery, in which
printed motifs were cut from a piece of fabric, such
as costly chintz, and applied to a plain, less expensive
background cloth.

Appliqué was popular in the 1800s, and there are
thousands of examples, from exquisite, brightly colored
Baltimore Album quilts made in and around Baltimore
between circa 1840 and 1860, to elegant four-block
quilts made later in the century. Many appliqué quilts
are pictorial with floral designs the predominant motif.

In the 20th century, appliqué again enjoyed an upswing, especially during the Colonial Revival period, and thousands were made from patterns or appliqué kits that were marketed and sold from 1900 through the 1950s.

Pieced or patchwork quilts are made by cutting fabric into shapes and sewing them together to make a larger piece of cloth. The patterns are usually geometric, and their effectiveness depends heavily on the contrast of not just the colors themselves, but of color value as well. Patchwork became popular in the United States in the early 1800s.

Colonial clothing was almost always made using cloth cut into squares or rectangles, but after the Revolutionary War, when fabric became more widely available, shaped garments were made, and these garments left scraps. Frugal housewives, especially among the westward-bound pioneers, began to use these cutoffs to put together blocks that could then be made into quilts. Patchwork quilts are by far the most numerous of all vintage-quilt categories, and the diversity of style, construction and effect that can be found is a study all its own.

Dating a quilt is tricky unless the maker included the date on the finished item, and unfortunately for historians and collectors, few did. The value of a particular example is affected by its age, of course, and educating yourself about dating methods is invaluable. There are several aspects that can offer guidelines for establishing a date. These include fabrics; patterns; technique; borders; binding; batting; backing; quilting method; and colors and dyes.

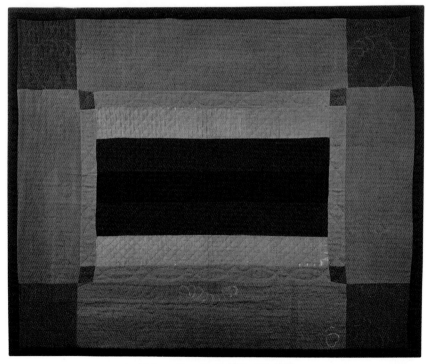

Amish bar crib quilt, 49 1/2" x 39". **$652**

Courtesy of Pook & Pook, Inc., pookandpook.com

Broderie perse friendship quilt, inscribed Sarah V. C. Quick 1844 on central panel, surrounded by 116 floral and bird appliqué chintz blocks, 97" x 87". $15,405

Courtesy of Pook & Pook, Inc., pookandpook.com

Pieced crib quilt, late 19th century, mounted, 33" x 34". $356

Courtesy of Pook & Pook, Inc., pookandpook.com

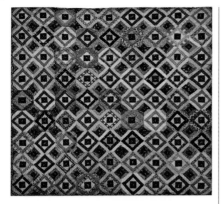

Abolitionist quilt attributed to Rowena Pingree, Maine, circa 1870, registered with Maine Quilt Heritage, July 13, 2003, 68" x 67". Accompanying documents cite the black-bordered squares as a code underground railroad travelers could read when the quilt was hung outside on a clothesline. **$3,456**

Courtesy of Rago Arts and Auctions, www.ragoarts.com

New York Beauty chintz and pieced quilt, circa 1860, six full blocks and three half blocks, divided by sawtooth sashing with star blocks, wide chintz border on all sides with green binding, hand-stitched floral, outline, and straight-line quilting, plain back, excellent condition, 83" x 93". **$3,159**

Courtesy of Jeffrey S. Evans & Associates, www.jeffreysevans.com

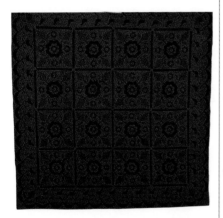

Lancaster County appliqué quilt with folk art bird on branch border, 19th century, 16-panel block with floral and leaf insert, very good condition, 81 3/4" x 82 1/2". **$4,538**

Courtesy of Conestoga Auction Co., www.conestogaauction.com

Women's Christian Temperance Union (WCTU), Capital T for Temperance quilt, late 19th century, 84" x 86". The WCTU was founded in 1874 and by 1907 had 350,000 members. Many Capital T quilts were made to earn money for the temperance movement or were made by quilters to represent their belief in temperance or abstention from alcohol. **$738**

Courtesy of Slotin Folk Art, www.slotin.com

Elaborate pieced and embroidered quilt, early 20th century, titled "The Homestead," signed F. Cochran, depicting busy farm scene with animals and figures and Illinois Central Railroad in background, 73" x 90". **$7,703**

Courtesy of Pook & Pook, Inc., pookandpook.com

Pieced crib quilt, early 20th century, mounted, 37"x 36". **$122**

Courtesy of Pook & Pook, Inc., pookandpook.com

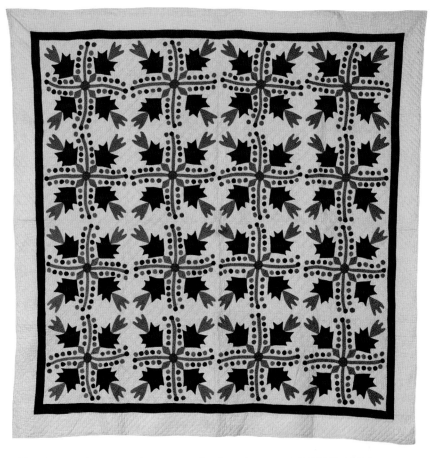

▲ Pieced and appliqued cotton Oak Leaf and Berries pattern quilt, American, late 19th/early 20th century, 16 blocks of Oak Leaf and Berry pattern, each with four red and green stylized oak leaves with intersecting stylized berry branches in red, green and orange solid colored fabrics, approximately 78" x 76". **$510**

Skinner, Inc., www.skinnerinc.com

▶ Pennsylvania pieced Star of Bethlehem quilt, inscribed Clarence J Spohn 1907 born in Oley July 25 1901, 75" x 77". **$152**

Courtesy of Pook & Pook, Inc., pookandpook.com

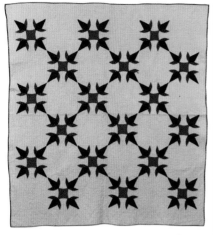

Pieced cotton Turkey Tracks pattern quilt, American, late 19th/early 20th century, hand-stitched quilt with 18 blocks of four green and maroon solid-color Turkey Track motifs and gold squares, approximately 83" x 76". **$240**

Skinner, Inc., www.skinnerinc.com

Trip Around the World quilt, early 20th century, 80" x 80". **$540**

Courtesy of Pook & Pook, Inc., pookandpook.com

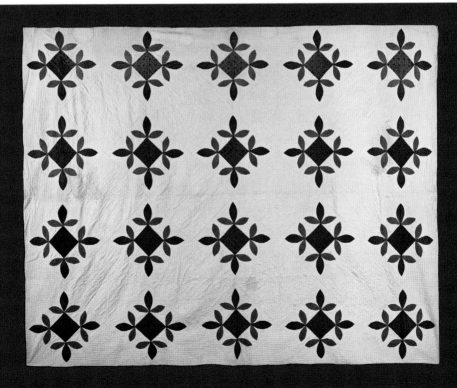

Pennsylvania appliqué quilt, 19th century, 77" x 100". **$456**

Courtesy of Pook & Pook, Inc., pookandpook.com

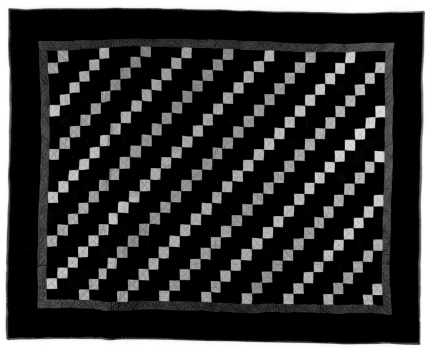

Amish Stepping Stone quilt, 20th century, 87" x 67". **$415**

Courtesy of Pook & Pook, Inc., pookandpook.com

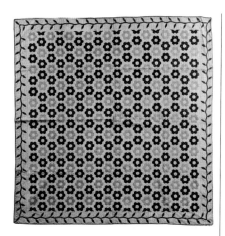

Pieced quilt with honeycomb pattern and vine border, 87" x 85". **$474**

Courtesy of Pook & Pook, Inc., pookandpook.com

Appliqué Eagle and Star quilt, late 19th century, 84" x 82". **$2,133**

Courtesy of Pook & Pook, Inc., pookandpook.com

Pieced pinwheel quilt, late 19th century,
90" x 94". **$2,252**

Courtesy of Pook & Pook, Inc., pookandpook.com

Pieced and appliqued cotton Cherry Baskets
pattern quilt, American, late 19th century,
with 44 baskets and 22 partial baskets
composed of multicolored printed and woven
cotton triangular and square segments on
off-white ground separated by red diamond
grid intersecting with light blue printed
squares, approximately 94" x 82". **$960**

Skinner, Inc., www.skinnerinc.com

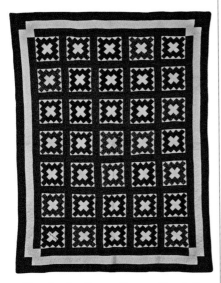

Pieced cotton Roman Cross pattern quilt,
American, hand-stitched with 35 blocks of
red calico printed squares and rectangles
arranged in zigzag design around central
white cross on off-white ground, one cross
embroidered with name Mary Buckley Nutting,
one corner of reverse stitched "ARK 1836,"
quilted with outline, chain and shell designs,
approximately 104" x 82". **$420**

Skinner, Inc., www.skinnerinc.com

Pennsylvania jacquard coverlet, dated 1836,
inscribed Emanuel Ettinger Aaronsburg Centre
Co Penna, 93" x 77", together with another,
inscribed "JH March Manufacturer Salona
Centre Co Penna 1838," 91" x 77". **$711**

Courtesy of Pook & Pook, Inc., pookandpook.com

Records

By Dave Thompson

In terms of modern record collecting, Elvis Presley is Year One. People collected records before Elvis came along and a lot of earlier records (and artists) are very collectible: Frank Sinatra, for example; Bing Crosby; Roy Rogers, et al. But Elvis was different.

In terms of legend, rarity and (more subjectively) quality, Elvis Presley tops the rock 'n' roll 45s chart. Starting in 1954, Elvis released five singles for Sam Phillips' Sun Records. After Phillips sold Elvis' contract to RCA in late 1955, RCA turned around and reissued the original Elvis Sun recordings with the RCA label in place. And while those RCA reissues have collector value, it is the Sun originals that are coveted.

Nonetheless, Elvis became a superstar at RCA. In 1959 RCA released an album titled "For LP Fans Only," at a time when singles (and extended play EPs) were the pocket-money purchase of choice. For a lot of people, that was the first LP they ever bought, but it would not be the last.

Bearing in mind the sheer number of Elvis Presley records sold over the years—almost 140 million in the U.S. alone, including 90 gold albums, 53 platinum and 25 multi-platinum—collecting Elvis does not need to be an especially costly pursuit.

Of course Elvis has more than his share of solid-gold rarities, with that first run of Sun label 45s close to the top of every fan's wants list. For both the specialist and the general collector, Elvis' career is most easily broken down into four basic categories. His early years with Sun, and the first with RCA devour the bulk of his 1950s output, and it is here that we hear (and see him) at his most incendiary, churning out the hits that remain most people's first thought when considering his work – "Heartbreak Hotel," "Jailhouse Rock," "Love Me Tender," "Baby, Let's Play House" and so forth.

The 1960s were largely devoured by his movie

DAVE THOMPSON is the author of *Goldmine's Essential Guide to Record Collecting*. He is the research and pricing expert for an array of vinyl record guides, including *Goldmine Record Album Price Guide*.

soundtrack recordings, a corpus of 15 albums that it is very easy to mock, but which nevertheless includes some fabulous, and very successful, recordings; and then there is the sudden reappearance of Elvis the rootsy rocker, first broadcast on the 1968 NBC TV special, and extending through the last years of the sixties and across such subsequent albums as *From Memphis to Vegas / From Vegas to Memphis* and *Elvis Country*. And finally, there is Elvis the icon, the jumpsuit-and-rhinestones bedecked showman born onstage in Las Vegas and spread across the last years of his life.

These eras are not inclusive. Among the soundtracks can be found the late fifties showpieces *Loving You* and *King Creole*, both of which are essential to any appreciation of that period; throughout his career, there were the gospel and Christmas albums that did so much to broaden his appeal beyond the rock and pop audience he originally courted.

Live recordings, dating back to his formative days performing at the Louisiana Hayride, offer an entirely different view on Elvis' career—it seems incredible today to consider that his first official live album (the aforementioned *From Memphis to Vegas / From Vegas to Memphis*) did not appear until 1969, but the archives have opened many times since then, to offer us glimpses into any number of shows.

Indeed, we are fortunate that the tapes were rolling at any number of key concerts—the Hayride tapes represent many people's first exposure to Elvis in concert; a recording made aboard the USS Arizona in 1961 marked his last show for seven years (find it on the Elvis Aron Presley box set). 1968 saw him back in action for the benefit of the NBC cameras, and the epochal Elvis TV special; 1969 brought his Las Vegas debut; 1972 saw him headline Madison Square; 1973 brought a worldwide satellite broadcast from Hawaii; and on June 27, 1977, he was recorded live at the Market Square Arena, Indianapolis, at the last concert he would ever play.

All of these, and many more besides, have now been released, some by RCA and its subsequent owners; some through less official channels; and some by Follow That Dream, established in 1999 as the Official Elvis Presley Collectors label, and responsible now for some of the most laudably curated compilations and collections that any artist's catalog can boast. That these are all largely confined to CD-only is a drawback that every vinyl collector must learn to live with. But Elvis collectors in general have never had it so good.

The most valuable of all Elvis records is, in fact, his very first recording. In January, 2015, Third Man Records founder Jack White paid $300,000 for the only existing copy of "My Happiness" and "That's When Your Heartaches Begin," a 10-inch acetate recorded by Elvis in July 1953, as a gift for his friend Ed Leek. (It was Leek's daughter who placed the disc on sale.)

Top Ten Elvis Rarities on RCA

1

6

7

8

9

1. "Elvis Christmas Album" (RCA LOC 1035; mono LP red vinyl, 1957). **$20,000**

2. "That's All Right"/"Blue Moon of Kentucky" (RCA Gold Standard 447-0601; red label, misspelled "Preseley"). **$6,000**

3. "Elvis Presley... the Most Talked-About New Personality in the Last Ten Years of Recorded Music" (RCA EPB 1254; with picture sleeve, 1956). **$6,000**

4. "Good Luck Charm"/"Anything That's Part Of You" (RCA 37-7992; 33 rpm 7-inch with picture sleeve, 1962). **$5,000**

5. "Elvis Presley" (RCA SPD 23; Triple EP with picture sleeve, 1956). **$5,000**

6. "Aloha from Hawaii" (RCA VPSX-6089; promo quadradisc w/Chicken of The Sea sticker on cover, 1973). **$3,500**

7. "This Is His Life: Elvis Presley" ("Mystery Train"/"I Forgot To Remember") (RCA 47-6357; promo 45 with picture sleeve, 1955). **$3,000**

8. "Elvis Gold Records Vol. 4" (RCA LPM-3921; mono promo LP, Indianapolis pressing, 1968). **$3,000**

9. "Speedway" (RCA LPM-3989, 1968), original soundtrack, mono, bonus color photograph inside. **$3,000**

10. "His Latest Flame"/"Little Sister" (RCA 37-7908; 33 rpm 7-inch with picture sleeve, 1961). **$3,000**

Famously, this is the recording that first alerted Sun Records founder Sam Philips to Presley's talent (Philips owned the studio where the acetate was recorded); and, of course, for more than 60 years, it was one that would escape every collector's clutches. Just months after his purchase, however, White reissued the disc for Record Store Day, a limited edition "so close to the historic original as to almost be indistinguishable from one other." Prices for the reissue are themselves steadily rising (copies currently sell for around $125), but at least it is now attainable.

There are other treasures, however, that are considerably less instantly recognizable—copies of 1973's *Aloha from Hawaii via Satellite* bearing a sticker advertising sponsor Van Camp's Chicken of the Sea tuna, for example; or, staying with the same album, it's 7-inch "jukebox album" counterpart. A copy of the "That's All Right"/"Blue Moon Of Kentucky" single on RCA Gold Standard label, with the artist's name misspelled "Preseley"—one copy sold on ebay for $6,000 in 2011; a copy of the *Speedway* album with the original bonus color photograph still inside is valued at $3,000.

Rare10-inch acetate record of Elvis' first recording, "My Happiness/"That's When Your Heartaches Begin," 1953. **$300,000**

And so many more. Indeed, with more than sixty years worth of recordings and releases to pursue, the fact that so many millions of records were sold is, perhaps, the last consideration that a collector needs to consider. The music is immortal. And its possibilities are infinite.

Goldmine's Record Grading Guide

Record grading uses both objective and subjective factors. Our advice: Look at everything about a record – its playing surface, the label, the record's edges, the cover and/or sleeve – under a strong light. If you're in doubt, assign the record a lower grade. Many dealers grade records, sleeves, or covers and sometimes even labels separately. The grades listed below are common to vinyl records, including EPs, 45s, LPs and 12" singles.

MINT (M): Perfect in every way. Often rumored but rarely seen. Never played and often still factory sealed. Never use Mint as a grade unless more than one person agrees that a record or sleeve truly is in this condition. Mint price is best negotiated between buyer and seller.

NEAR MINT (NM OR M-): Nearly perfect. Looks and sounds like it just came from a retail store and was opened for the first time. Jackets and sleeves are free of creases, folds, markings, or seam splits. Records are glossy and free of imperfections. Many dealers won't use a grade higher than NM, implying that no record or sleeve is ever truly perfect.

VERY GOOD-PLUS (VG+) or EXCELLENT (E): Except for a few minor things – slight warps, scuffs, or scratches that don't affect playback, ring wear on the labels, a turned up corner, cut-out hole, or seam split on the sleeve or cover – this record would be NM. Most collectors, especially those who want to play their records, are

Elvis Sun Records

"That's All Right"/"Blue Moon of Kentucky" (Sun 209, 1954). **$10,000**

"Good Rockin' Tonight"/"I Don't Care if the Sun Don't Shine" (Sun 210, 1954). **$3,500**

Elvis Sun Records

"Milkcow Blues Boogie"/"You're a Heartbreaker" (Sun 215, 1955). **$5,000**

"Baby Let's Play House"/"I'm Left, You're Right, She's Gone" (Sun 217, 1955). **$3,000**

"I Forgot to Remember to Forget"/"Mystery Train" (Sun 223, 1955). **$2,500**

happy with a VG+ record, especially if it's toward the high end of the grade (VG++ or E+). Worth 50 percent of NM value.

VERY GOOD (VG): Many of the imperfections found on a VG+ record are more obvious on a VG record. Surface noise, groove wear, and light scratches can be found on VG records. You may find stickers, tape or writing on labels, sleeves, and covers, but no more than two of those three problems. VG records are among the biggest bargains in record collecting. Worth 25 percent of a NM record.

GOOD (G), GOOD-PLUS (G+), or VERY GOOD-MINUS (VG-): Expect a lot of surface noise, visible groove wear and scratches on the vinyl, as well as more defects and repairs to labels, sleeves, and covers. Unless the record is unusually rare, G/G+ or VG- records are worth 10 percent to 15 percent of the NM value.

POOR (P) and FAIR (F): Records are cracked, impossibly warped, or skip and/ or repeat when an attempt is made to play them. Covers and sleeves are heavily damaged, if they even exist. Unless they are incredibly rare, P and F records sell for 0 percent to 5 percent of the NM value (if they sell at all).

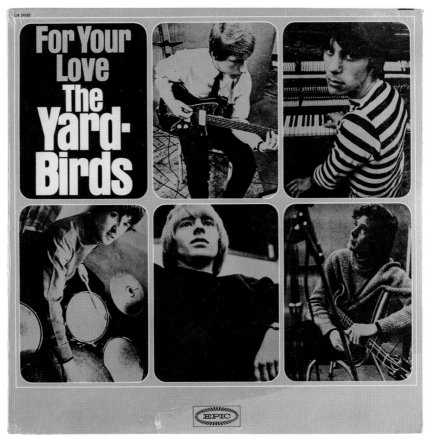

The Yardbirds, "For Your Love" sealed mono LP (Epic 24167, 1965), near mint 8/mint 10 condition, shrinkwrap with tear across right bottom, break in shrinkwrap on left corner, wear on both bottom corners. **$500**

Courtesy of Heritage Auctions, ha.com

Ricky Nelson, "More Songs By Ricky" blue vinyl stereo LP (Imperial 12059, 1960), rare, with original 17" x 23" full-color poster detached from album cover, cover in near mint, disc in excellent, and poster in very good-excellent condition, poster with tear on left side, small piece missing. **$450**

Rare Decca pressing of Tony Sheridan and The Beat Brothers (better known as The Beatles), "My Bonnie"/"The Saints" 45 RPM record (Decca 31382, 1962). Rarest of U.S. Beatles singles, including pink label promotional version of record. "My Bonnie" attracted few takers in the United States when it originally was released and most copies pressed were trashed, explaining why promotional copies outnumber the stock commercial version. Once Beatlemania hit the United States in 1964, the record was re-released on the MGM label, where it reached No. 26 on the Billboard Hot 100 charts. Collecting experts estimate only 25 stock copies of Decca 31382 are still in existence. **$16,875**

Guns N' Roses band-signed "Appetite For Destruction" LP, 1987. U.K. pressing (WX 125) signed by all five members: frontman Axl Rose, lead guitarist Slash, bassist Duff McKagan, guitarist Izzy Stradlin, and drummer Steven Adler. Rarer robo/rape cover version, record is red vinyl pressing. **$812**

Pretenders debut album, "Pretenders" (Sire SRK6083, 1982) signed in various inks; includes Chrissie Hynde's signature. **$656**

Courtesy of Heritage Auctions, ha.com

The Police ,"Zenyatta Mondatta" (RCA SP-3720) album cover signed in black and blue felt-tip ink by band members Sting, Stewart Copeland and Andy Summers. **$255**

Led Zeppelin promotional pressing of 1969 "Led Zeppelin" LP (Atlantic SD 8216). Stereo, white-label promo of legendary group's first LP. **$286**

Bruce Springsteen, "Greetings From Asbury Park" (album signed in black felt-tip pen by Bruce Springsteen and E Street Band members Clarence Clemons, Garry Tallent and Vini Lopez. **$1,465**

Sports

Sports and sports memorabilia are eternally intertwined. Since sports began, there have been mementos to draw in audiences, attract attention to the games or invite future fans to the stadiums. And because the games tend to evoke fond memories, many times those mementos are kept for a long time. Sports memorabilia is our connection to sporting events we remember and the players we loved to watch.

Today, sports memorabilia is used for more than simply waking up the memory bank or providing a connection to the past. These items are also increasingly used for home or office décor, as well as investments. Sports collectibles are more accessible than ever before through online auctions, with several auction houses that dedicate themselves solely to that segment of the hobby.

Provenance and third-party authentication is extremely important when investing in high-ticket sports collectibles. In today's market, high-quality and rare items are in most demand, with a heavy nod toward stars and Hall of Famers. Condition is everything; keep an eye toward temperature, humidity and exposure to sunlight with pieces in your collection.

◀ Grape Nuts die-cut sign with Dizzy Dean, circa 1930s, cardboard with easel back, scattered staining and general wear at edges, 40" high x 26" wide. **$2,629**

Courtesy of Heritage Auctions, www.ha.com

My best wishes to "Beans" Reardon, the greatest umpire ever lived, sincerely, Norman Rockwell

An early rendering, or original study, by Norman Rockwell of one of his best-known baseball-themed paintings sold at auction for $1,680,000. Entitled "Tough Call", the painting was featured on a 1949 cover of *The Saturday Evening Post*. Sandra Sprinkle, the granddaughter of the central umpire in the painting, Beans Reardon, owned the painting and proudly displayed it over the family fireplace for years. It was only after Sprinkle's death in 2015 that her family realized the painting was an original and not a print. Rockwell had given the painting to her grandfather, a Major League umpire from 1926 thorough 1949, signing the lower right corner: "Beans Reardon, the greatest umpire (who) ever lived." **$1,680,000**

Courtesy of Heritage Auctions, www.ha.com

Home Run Cigarettes cardboard sign, copyright 1909, stone lithographed advertisement with baseball illustration, by American Tobacco Co., very good condition, 11 1/2" wide x 17 1/2" high. **$5,750**

Courtesy of Brunk Auctions

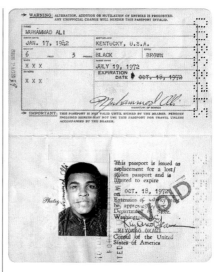

U.S. passport originally issued to Muhammad Ali in 1972 for fight with boxer Al Lewis, issued by U.S. embassy in Dublin, Ireland, likely a replacement. **$18,752**

1953 Satchel Paige Coca-Cola advertising sign, 11 3/4" x 14 3/4". **$8,295**

Robert Edward Auctions

1958-1959 Harlem Globetrotters souvenir program featuring Wilt Chamberlain. **$105**

Courtesy of Heritage Auctions, www.ha.com

1924 Lou Gehrig signed New York Yankees rookie contract, one of the most significant documents to emerge from the archives of the Yankees. $480,000

Courtesy of Heritage Auctions, www.ha.com

Lou Gehrig game-worn New York Yankees jersey, 1937. Gehrig's 1937 season was his last great season with the Yankees, batting .351 with 37 home runs and 158 runs batted in. Gehrig was diagnosed with amyotrophic lateral sclerosis (ALS) in June of 1939. He retired later that year and was soon after elected to the Baseball Hall of Fame. Gehrig, who played 2,130 consecutive games and had his number retired by the Yankees, died June 2, 1941. His life was immortalized in the classic 1942 film, The Pride of the Yankees, starring Gary Cooper. **$870,000**

Courtesy of Heritage Auctions, www.ha.com

Arnold Palmer's first golf clubs. The 1940s set features seven First Flight hickory shaft "irons" and two Louisville "woods." Carl Markwood, a schoolmate of Arnold's, purchased the clubs in 1948 from Arnold's father, Deacon Palmer, a golf pro at the Latrobe (PA) Country Club. **$45,600**

Courtesy of Heritage Auctions, www.ha.com

> ❝
>
> Arnold Palmer, who died in 2016, won seven majors, all of them from 1958 to 1964, and was the first four-time winner of the Masters. Although he won the last of his 62 PGA Tour titles in 1973, his popularity never waned.

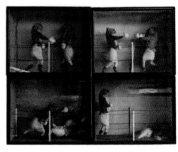

Four 19th century shadow boxes of boxing squirrels, circa 1850s, by William Hart & Sons, displayed at Great Exhibition of the Works of Industry of all Nations in 1851, each 14 3/4" x 19" x 7". **$69,000**

Courtesy of Heritage Auctions, www.ha.com

1948 Chesterfield Cigarettes ad featuring baseball greats Joe DiMaggio and Lou Boudreau, tennis player Jack Kramer, golfer Ben Hogan, and Frankie Albert. **$209**

Legendary Auctions

Honus Wagner "Eyes" original photograph, 7" x 5", circa 1915, by Charles Conlon, the foremost visual documentarian of baseball's Dead-Ball Era. Wagner played 21 seasons in the Major Leagues, winning eight battling titles. In 1936, the Baseball Hall of Fame inducted Wagner as one of the first five members. **$21,600**

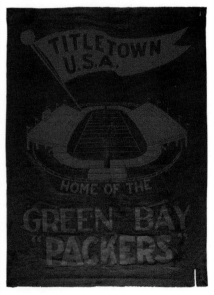

1961 Green Bay Packers New City Stadium Banner. After being defeated by the Eagles in the 1960 NFL Championship Game, Packers head coach Vince Lombardi made the claim that his team would never experience a loss in a championship game again, and he was right. Presented here is a stunning original flag that was one of numerous examples hung on downtown Green Bay buildings during Lombardi's first championship season. Measuring at 3x4', with moderate wear throughout, it displays superbly. **$2,880.**

Courtesy of Heritage Auctions, www.ha.com

Massive original artwork of Muhammad Ali by renowned impressionist LeRoy Neiman in advance of the 1971 "Fight of the Century" between Ali and Joe Frazier. The larger-than-life, 8-foot tall painting captured both the fighter and the artist at the height of their popularity. Although Frazier would beat Ali in that March 8, 1971, fight in Madison Square Garden, it was Ali who would become arguably the most famous athlete of all time. **$155,350**

Courtesy of Heritage Auctions, www.ha.com

1934 Beech-Nut Tobacco oversized die-cut advertising sign with Paul and Dizzy Dean, 28" x 42". **$14,340**

Courtesy of Heritage Auctions, ha.com

Photo by Focus on Sport/Getty Images

Paul Hornung game-worn Green Bay Packers jersey, early 1960s. Nicknamed "The Golden Boy," Hornung is the only football player to win the Heisman Trophy, be selected as the first overall pick in the NFL Draft, win the NFL Most Valuable Player award, and be inducted into both the professional and college football halls of fame. **$84,000**

Courtesy of Heritage Auctions, www.ha.com

Racing horseshoe from legendary thoroughbred Secretariat, 1973, acquired from Buck Peters, official photographer for Phillip Morris assigned to cover 1973 Marlboro Cup at Belmont Park in New York. Forty-five years ago, Secretariat galloped to victory at the Belmont Stakes, capturing the final leg of the Triple Crown and becoming the first horse in 25 years to achieve one of sport's most difficult feats. In a career that spanned just 21 races over the course of a year, the 3-year-old thoroughbred captured the hearts and minds of a nation weary from the soon-to-be-ended Vietnam War and ongoing Watergate investigations.

The week before the Belmont, Sports Illustrated, Time and Newsweek magazines featured Secretariat on their covers in the same week—an unheard of accomplishment that has never been repeated. After his victory, demand for the thoroughbred's time grew so great that his owners hired the William Morris Agency to oversee his public appearances. In 1999, the U.S. Postal Service issued a commemorative Secretariat stamp, making him the first equine to earn the honor; and ESPN named him to their list of the 100 greatest athletes of the 20th century. **$36,543**

Courtesy of Lelands, www.lelands.com

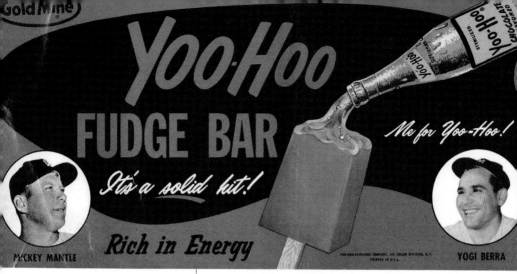

YOO-HOO FUDGE BAR

It's a solid hit!

Me for Yoo-Hoo!

Rich in Energy

MICKEY MANTLE

YOGI BERRA

▲ 1960s Yoo-Hoo Fudge Bar advertising sign with Mickey Mantle and Yogi Berra, 6 3/4" x 14". **$581**

Courtesy of SCP Auctions, scpauctions.com

▶ Lew Alcindor (Kareem Abdul-Jabbar) 1969-70 game-worn Milwaukee Bucks rookie shooting shirt. The Bucks drafted Alcindor, who changed his name to Kareem Abdul-Jabbar in 1971 after converting to Islam, with the first pick of the 1969 draft. Kareem played with Milwaukee until 1975 when he was traded to the Los Angeles Lakers. The 7-foot 2-inch center revolutionized the NBA. By the time he retired in 1989 Kareem had won six MVP awards and six NBA championships. He remains the league's all-time leading scorer with 38,387 points. **$47,800**

▼ Babe Ruth game-used bat, 1920. Ruth was baseball's greatest slugger and the most colorful figure in the game's history. Ruth hit 714 career home runs, won 12 home run titles and won four World Series championships with the New York Yankees, who retired his number in 1948. **$408,000**

Courtesy of Heritage Auctions, www.ha.com

Photo by NY Daily News Archive via Getty Images

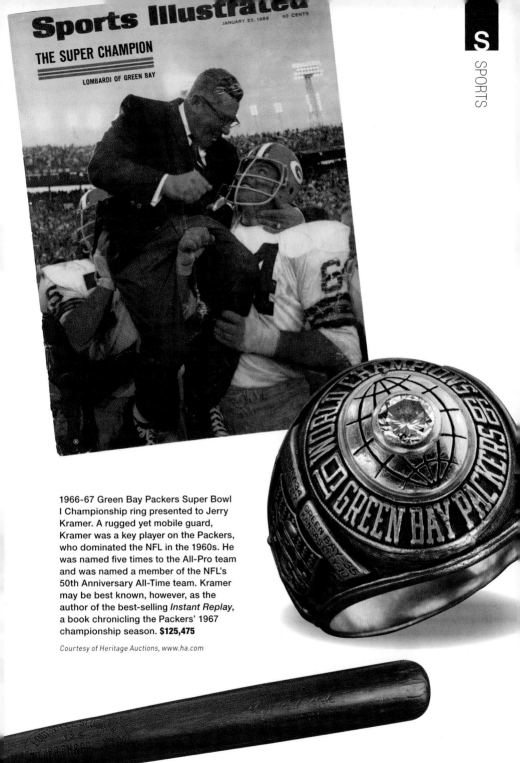

THE SUPER CHAMPION

LOMBARDI OF GREEN BAY

Sports Illustrated JANUARY 22, 1968 40 CENTS

1966-67 Green Bay Packers Super Bowl I Championship ring presented to Jerry Kramer. A rugged yet mobile guard, Kramer was a key player on the Packers, who dominated the NFL in the 1960s. He was named five times to the All-Pro team and was named a member of the NFL's 50th Anniversary All-Time team. Kramer may be best known, however, as the author of the best-selling *Instant Replay*, a book chronicling the Packers' 1967 championship season. **$125,475**

Courtesy of Heritage Auctions, www.ha.com

Toys

Toy collecting has gone through dramatic changes over the years, but the premise of collecting remains the same – holding onto something from childhood that brings a smile to your face every time you see it.

Toys are fun. There are no hidden messages when it comes to toys. They are produced for entertainment, and while they can also be quite valuable, that is not the driving force behind collecting toys.

In the following pages you will discover two new additions to our category: Hot Wheels and Star Wars. Hot Wheels cars were introduced 50 years ago this year, becoming one of the most popular toys in history. The first Star Wars movie, *Star Wars Episode IV: A New Hope,* was an epic space opera that launched one of the premiere media franchises in history. The Toys were pretty cool, as well.

Clearly, if you collect toys, you're doing it as a passion. And that's what toys are all about, a piece of nostalgia that can grow into a fascination that fills rooms in houses and provides endless stories for relatives and friends.

Over the past few years, one aspect of the hobby is becoming apparent: More people are becoming acquainted with toys and

Diamond Planet robot, made in Japan by Yonezawa, tin-litho and painted, blue variation, key is vintage replacement and works, 10 1/2" high. **$13,200**

Courtesy of Morphy Auctions

their values than at any other point in American history, thanks to the exposure the hobby has garnered from the collectible-based reality programs broadcast on television.

The best weapon in the battle for equitable prices for toys is acquiring knowledge. Education is power. Learn about the toy and its backstory, and know its manufacturer and date of production as well as its importance in the realm of popular culture.

When estimating the value of a toy, you must first evaluate its condition. Mint toys in mint packaging command higher prices than well-played-with toys whose boxes disappeared with the wrapping paper on Christmas day. Mint is a rare condition indeed as toys were meant to be played with by children. Realistic evaluation of condition is essential, as grading standards vary from class to class. Ultimately, the market is driven by buyers, and the bottom line value of a toy is often the last price at which it sold.

▲ Arcade flat top Yellow Cab, original, rubber stamped "Yellow Cab" on passenger doors, orange iron hubs and rubber tires, overall very fine-plus condition, 8" long. **$1,265**

James D. Julia, Inc., jamesdjulia.com

FOR MORE INFORMATION
on toys, see Toys & Prices, 20th edition, by Mark Bellomo.

▲ Marklin "Chicago" paddle wheeler, Germany, circa 1900-1902, No. 1080/2, hand-painted lower deck curtains, blue and brown band stacks and matching paddle wheel covers, side guns, all hanging lifeboats, with six original figures of captain and crew, 31" long. **$277,150**

Courtesy of Bertoia Auctions, www.bertoiaauctions.com

▲ Tugboat, Buddy L, circa 1928, pressed steel hull painted bluish green, gray deck with cabin and upper deck railed pilot's house, single stack, simulated searchlight on cabin roof, valve stem on deck used to fit tire pump connector and allow air motor to work rear rudder, 28" long. **$22,230**

Courtesy of Bertoia Auctions, www.bertoiaauctions.com

▼ Batman Ride-On Spring-Wound Batmobile, Marx Toys, 1966. One of four variations, car measures approximately 37" long, plastic, some losses, trunk opens, the steering wheel turns the wheels, and the spring mechanism appears to be in working order. **$179**

Courtesy of Heritage Auctions, ha.com

Little Audrey hopping toy, Linemar, Japan, from the Harvey comics list of characters, lithographed tin, key wind operated, bobbing head hopping toy, 4 1/4" high. **$ 324**

Hake's Americana & Collectibles Auctions

1929 Gendron Jordan Playboy pedal car with crisscross front bumper, two glass and metal headlamps, license plate, wood grille with hand-painted design and "Jordan" on grille, 50" long.
$3,300

James D. Julia, Inc., jamesdjulia.com

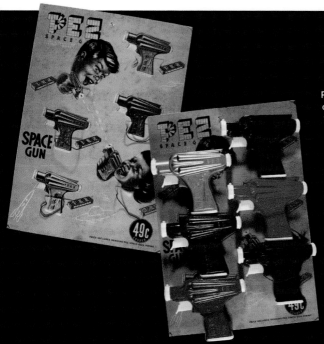

Pez Space Gun complete countertop display, circa 1950s, 9 1/2" x13 1/2" cardboard display with easel on back, images of a boy and girl using the space guns to fire Pez candy at each other, six hard plastic guns in four different colors, including rare and desirable silver plus yellow, green and three red. Each gun is 5" long with raised design on grips that includes rocket ship and planets. **$2,300**

Hake's Americana & Collectibles Auctions

Buck Rogers lithographed tin rocket ship, Louis Marx, pilot graphics at window, clockwork activated, strong sparking action, excellent condition, 11 1/2" long. **$803**

Courtesy of Bertoia Auctions, www.bertoiaauctions.com

Mother Goose tin wind-up toy, Louis Marx, Mother Goose with cat riding large goose, box, 8 3/4" long. **$680**

Courtesy of Bertoia Auctions, www.bertoiaauctions.com

German Indian skittles container with braves, polychromed in bright colors with intricate molding to facial features, original paper label on underside marked "Made in Germany" with most likely six-digit product number, stamped tin wheels, pins affixed to wooden platforms, overall very fine-plus condition, paint is largely intact with no restoration and/or repairs, 29" long. **$16,100**

James D. Julia, Inc., jamesdjulia.com

Rooster skittle set, multicolored papier maché rooster with glass eyes riding on four cast iron wheels painted gold, nine-pin set in form of chicks dressed as clowns, some minor chips on one side and old crack on left side, chicks in near excellent condition, 19 1/2" long x 15 1/2" high. **$14,950**

James D. Julia, Inc., jamesdjulia.com

German shepherd skittles with open back containing eight assorted animals pins, ninth pin is clown, aka "the king pin," original flat paint, all animals with glass eyes, overall very good condition, some animals show wear, 21" long. **$1,150**

James D. Julia, Inc., jamesdjulia.com

Lionel Donald Duck rail car, No. 1107 clockwork hand car with painted composition Donald and Pluto and full circle of track in original illustrated box, car 10 1/2" long. **$1,300**

Noel Barrett Auctions

▲ Ferris wheel tin wind-up toy, General Metal Toys, Canada, lithographed tin carnival ride with four gondolas, 12 1/2" high. **$463**

Courtesy of Bertoia Auctions, www.bertoiaauctions.com

◄ New York-San Francisco World's Fair Bus by Viktor Schreckengost (American, 1906-2008), circa 1939, Steelcraft Toy by Murray Ohio Manufacturing Co., painted metal, rubber, minor rusting, scratches throughout original paint, 7" x 6" x 20 3/4". **$4,500**

Courtesy of Heritage Auctions, ha.com

Large Japanese race car #42, late 1950s tin plate version of Troy Ruttman's Indianapolis 500-winning "Agajanian Special," chrome steering and suspension, full exhaust, radiator with "A" forming front fender, front rubber tires marked "Special Racer Gem," fine lithography with multitude of advertising, 18 1/2" long.
$1,610

Hot Wheels

By Michael Zarnock

America's love affair with the automobile was hot and heavy in 1968, and Detroit fed the affair with all the adrenaline it could. The bigger the car the better, and the more horsepower under the hood the happier car owners were. The muscle car movement was firmly entrenched as the decade's end neared.

Fifty years after their introduction it's easy to see that Mattel's Hot Wheels cars swung in at the perfect time. America's love affair with everything with four wheels was in full bloom, and with flashy Hot Wheels cars there was finally a toy car that matched the excitement of the hot cars lining car dealerships and the pages of popular car magazines. Slight rakes, opening hoods exposing V-8 engines, side-exiting exhaust pipes, hood scoops and the metallic paint colors of Hot Wheels cars brought new-found electricity to toy shelves. These features further adorned the most energetic cars on the market: Chevrolet Camaros, Ford Mustangs, Plymouth Barracudas and

MICHAEL ZARNOCK is one of the leading Hot Wheels cars authorities in the world. He has written numerous books and has twice been selected a Guinness world record holder for his Hot Wheels collection. Mattel created a Hot Wheels car in 2009 based on a hot rod Zarnock built and raced throughout the Northeast.

This ultra-rare 1969 pink, rear-loading Volkswagen Beach Bomb is a pre-production Hot Wheels model that sold for **$72,000.**

Courtesy of Bruce Pascal

Ford Thunderbirds. The sparkling paint also dressed some of the most famous custom cars of the day, such as Ed "Bid Daddy" Roth's Beatnik Bandit and Bill Cushenbery's Silhouette.

Mattel introduced 16 cars in 1968. Often referred to as The Sweet Sixteen, the cars were set off by red-striped tires, emulating performance cars of the day. These wheels were developed to roll faster and more smoothly than any other non-motorized toy vehicle of the day, particularly the well-establish Matchbox cars. Known as "Redlines," these first releases quickly caught on.

Although the look of Hot Wheels cars were the direct result of Mattel designer Harry Bentley Bradley's Detroit-built 1964 El Camino, the combination of bright colors and hot subject vehicles gave Hot Wheels cars a "California cool" image. This West Coast image helped the cars ride a wave of popularity that has not wavered for 50 years. Some of the more desirable colors of these cars are Pink, Purple and Magenta with Pink being the most valuable of colors.

Once introduced, Hot Wheels were instantly popular, so much so that a second

manufacturing facility was opened in Hong Kong. There are early Redline Hot Wheels cars with both USA and Hong Kong countries of production on their base, so pay attention to those bases. By 1972 all Hot Wheels cars were made in Hong Kong. Before Hot Wheels entered the scene, Matchbox cars ruled the toy-car world. But the English toy cars instantly became second choices among children as soon as Hot Wheels cars rolled into town. While there remains today a healthy collector base for Matchbox cars, there is no comparison to Hot Wheels cars in terms of popularity or demand.

From 1968 through 1972, Mattel used vibrant paint on Hot Wheels cars. Called Spectraflame, the paint process consisted of polishing the zinc-plated, die-cast metal bodies and then painting them with a thin layer of transparent, candy-colored paint. Some of the most desirable Redline cars feature the Spectraflame treatment. Mattel discontinued the process in 1973, and until the end of the Redline era in 1977 cars were painted in enamel colors, with the exceptions being the chrome 1976 "Super Chromes" and gold chrome 1977 "Super Chromes."

What to Look For and Where!

There are many places you can find Hot Wheels cars: online, flea markets, yard sales, antique shops, thrift stores and auction houses. Truth is, you can find them just about anywhere if you look hard enough.

When looking for Hot Wheels there are a few key things that you always need to consider.

- Condition
- Age
- Price
- What are you going to do with it?

Condition has to be the most crucial when it comes to buying and selling.

Actually, condition is everything when it comes to buying and selling. The words new in package (NIP) and mint (M) are words that get thrown around a lot by those who buy and sell. Even if a car is still in the original package, that doesn't automatically mean that it's "mint" in the package. Mint means no chips, no roof or side rubs from the plastic blister that it comes in, no base tarnish, nothing! "Mint" means perfect! Cars do get damaged and even have the paint flake off in the package, so be aware.

Packages are also graded. The abbreviation (MIMP) Mint In Mint Package means the car is perfect and so is the package. No dents in the plastic blister, no bends or creases in the card,

THE SWEET SIXTEEN

Mattel introduced 16 cars in 1968. Often referred to as The Sweet Sixteen, the cars were set off by red-striped tires, emulating performance cars of the day. These wheels were developed to roll faster and more smoothly than any other non-motorized toy vehicle of the day, particularly the well-establish Matchbox cars. Known as "Redlines," these first releases quickly caught on.

CUSTOM FLEETSIDE

Designer Harry Bradley's personal tricked-out 1964 Chevrolet El Camino is credited as inspiration for the Hot Wheels look. The Custom Fleetwood incorporates nearly all of the features of Bradley's daily ride. Made in U.S. with opening back cover. **$300**

no soft corners on the card, no stains, no nothing. It's OK to have a price sticker on the package though. That's something that does not affect the value.

Flea Markets and Antique Shops are places that you really need to be careful of. I have seen cars that are all busted up, no paint, broken windows and a missing wheel with a $20 price tag on it. The car is junk! It's not worth anything. These places think because it's old, it has value. It doesn't. Condition is everything when it comes to value and collectibility. If you think you're going to repair a car or repaint it, don't bother! Repaired or repainted cars with non-original parts have no value. Collectors do not want them. If it's something you want to do and keep for yourself, then that's a different story. You can do whatever makes you happy when it comes to your collection. But remember, if you're planning on selling it later, collectors know original from replacement.

When you're at a yard sale, look the place over. If you don't see anything in plain sight, ask if they have any old toys like Hot Wheels. Look in those big boxes on the floor that are full of small items. There are usually a lot of toy cars in the bottom of those boxes and more often than not, they are Hot Wheels. The cars in these boxes are always marked at very cheap prices.

Older cars are difficult to find and can be expensive. If anything, you may find track sets and other accessories without the cars. Accessories can be quite collectible.

When it comes to accessories, a lot of different items have been released as part of the Hot Wheels family since 1968. Things like Yo-Yo's, Frisbee's, dinnerware, birthday party supplies, anything that has the famous Hot Wheels Flame logo imprinted on it. That little flame with the words Hot Wheels within it has changed in shape many times since its first release, but it's still as recognizable today as it ever was. If you have any doubt that a piece is Hot Wheels related or not, just look for that flame logo or the word "Mattel" and a date. If neither is on the piece, it's not a Hot Wheels product.

The 1968 Hot Wheels line-up consisted of sixteen custom vehicles now called "The Sweet Sixteen" by collectors. The cars hold a significant place in Hot Wheels history and remain coveted by collectors.

PYTHON/CHEETAH

All U.S. castings and the bulk of Hong Kong castings of this car carry the best-known name Python. However, when the casting was originally built in Hong Kong it was stamped with the name "Cheetah on the base. Samples of such are extremely rare and valuable. **$120**

BEATNIK BANDIT

The famous Ed "Bid Daddy" Roth custom was immortalized in this casting. Beatnik Bandit is pictured here as a U.S. casting in olive with a clear bubble; Hong Kong versions have a blue-tinted bubble. **$90**

CUSTOM BARRACUDA

A blue U.S.-built Custom Barracuda is popular with collectors in part because the pre-1970 Barracuda has been replicated so rarely in scale – and it looks great! The hood opens to reveal a metal engine. **$550**

CUSTOM CAMARO

As one of the first castings to be released, the Custom Camaro is an icon of the Redlines offerings. There are a dizzying amount of variations but the demand for the Custom Camaro remains strong. **$600**

CUSTOM CORVETTE

The Custom Corvette, here in rose, features an opening hood. **$350**

CUSTOM COUGAR

The Custom Cougar features an opening hood and comes in an array of colors. The casting was built in both in U.S. and Hong Kong. **$475**

DEORA

With surfboards prominently displayed, the Deora was the ultimate California fantasy car. The Deora was based on a Dodge concept truck built by the Alexander Brothers. **$400**

CUSTOM T-BIRD

The Custom T-Bird was available with or without a black-painted roof and with an opening hood exposing a metal engine. **$250**

CUSTOM ELDORADO

Not every Hot Wheels casting from 1968 was based on a muscle car or a street rod, as illustrated by the Custom Eldorado. The brainchild of Harry Bradley, who worked as a designer for Cadillac before going to Mattel, is shown here in green and blue, products of the Hong Kong plant. **$250**

FORD J-CAR

The Ford J-Car, with a hinged rear engine area, was the only original Hot Wheels casting to include a sticker sheet. **$90**

CUSTOM MUSTANG

The Custom Mustang comes in assorted colors. The green car shown, with closed hood scoops and no louvers can bring **$450;** red or gold cars with open hood scoops can fetch **$2,000.** Red, yellow, orange or blue cars with louvered rear window can sell for **$1,000.**

CUSTOM FIREBIRD

In the process of adding a California touch to the 1967 Pontiac Firebird convertible, Mattel exaggerated the length, making the Custom Firebird one long-looking Hot Wheels car. **$325**

HOT HEAP

The Hot Heap features all the goodies of a fine 1960s Model T street rod. Unlike others in the line, there are no moving parts, aside from the wheels. **$130**

SILHOUETTE

The Silhouette is one of the most popular but least valuable Hot Wheels castings from 1968. Because the car's popularity made it a common car when it was new, many examples still survive. **$85**

CUSTOM VOLKSWAGEN

Custom Volkswagens were offered from 1968 to 1971 and nearly all feature an opening sunroof. **$350**

Star Wars

By Mark Bellomo

The foundation of global popular culture was shaken to its core in 1977 when George Lucas released one of the most important films in modern American history: the science fiction space opera, *Star Wars: A New Hope*.

Over the past 40 years, eager fans have popularized *Star Wars* terms that have been indelibly stamped onto our collective consciousness and even introduced into the American lexicon: words like "lightsaber," "Jedi Knight," and "droids"; expressions such as "May The Force Be With You," and the moral/psychic concept of "the dark side of the Force." Nearly 100 unique figures were produced in Kenner's vintage *Star Wars* line (discounting the company's *Droids* and *Ewoks* sub-lines released in 1985) between 1978 and 1985. Records show that the company sold almost 300 million action figures in total.

Yet little did 20th Century Fox realize the impact that the film would have on children and adult collectors everywhere, and in a brilliant stroke of prescience, Lucas may have subconsciously realized the potential of the *Star Wars* franchise. Lucas alone contracted to retain all sequel and merchandising rights for the film(s).

Kenner toys obtained the rights to produce 3-3/4-inch action figures, playsets, creatures, and vehicles based on important scenes from *Star Wars*. The smaller 3-3/4-inch scale was utilized in direct response to the oil shortages of the 1970s, scarcities that increased the cost of plastic production affecting many major toy companies such as Hasbro, Fisher Price and Mego. Little would Kenner realize the overwhelming response that their more portable *Star Wars* figures would attract on retail shelves. Soon after their release, the 3-3/4-inch action figure format became the standard in the field. At this smaller size (as opposed to Hasbro's enormous 11-1/2-inch G.I. Joe figures or Mego's interchangeable 8-inch figure body), characters were easier to produce, simpler to manufacture, and could ultimately sell higher numbers in order to allow consumers

One of the top toy experts in the country, **MARK BELLOMO** has written a number of bestselling books on toys and popular culture, including *The Ultimate Guide to Vintage Star Wars Action Figures, 1977-1985; The Ultimate Guide to Vintage Transformers Action Figures;* and *The Ultimate Guide to G.I. Joe, 1982-1994*.

Pictured clockwise, from top right (in Mint-On-Card or Mint-In-Sealed Box condition): **Stormtrooper/Imperial Stormtrooper (1978),** $375; **Patrol Dewback (1979),** $165-$190+; **Sand People (1978),** $225; **Death Squad Commander/ Star Destroyer Commander (1978),** $425-$450; **Jawa with cloth cape (1978),** $210-$225; **Darth Vader with standard lightsaber (1978):** $575-$650+; **Yoda with orange snake (1980):** $165-$185+; **Ben** Kenobi with white hair and standard lightsaber (1978), $325; **Luke Skywalker with blond hair and standard lightsaber (1978),** $650+; **Han Solo, small head variation (1978),** $750; **Princess Leia Organa (1978),** $325+; **R2-D2 (1978),** $285; **C-3PO (1978),** $315; **Chewbacca (1978),** $375+; **Luke Skywalker in Hoth Battle Gear (1980),** $145-$165; **Tauntaun (1980),** $85-$115.

Bobba Fett (with Imperial Blaster), fearsome intergalactic bounty hunter, #39250, 1979, Kenner. **$25-$32 (Mint Loose Condition)**

to purchase many more units ("collect them all") — refreshing sold-out retail pegs much more quickly.

Star Wars figures became a sensation — a phenomenon — in the late 1970s/early 1980s, and the items sold briskly throughout the release of the original trilogy, producing a bevy of toys for each of the three films: *A New Hope (Episode IV)*, *The Empire Strikes Back (Episode V)*, and *The Return of the Jedi (Episode VI)*. A total of 96 figures were available in the original "vintage" line (1977-1985), not including myriad figure variations (telescoping light sabers, vinyl-caped Jawas, etc.), or the Sy Snootles and the Rebo Band three-pack set. The most popular and valuable of these carded figures are the earliest *Star Wars* releases, those figures found on original "12-back cards" — those card backs that showed only the first 12 *Star Wars* action figures in 1977. Other pricey figures can be found within the final run of the line, 1984/85's "Power of the Force" collection, where figures (both new sculpts and previously released characters) were carded along with a collector's coin. A few of these carded samples are worth thousands of dollars in Mint on Card (MOC) condition.

Along with the standard 3-3/4-inch figures was a collection of deluxe 12-inch Large Size figures based on more popular characters from the films — these

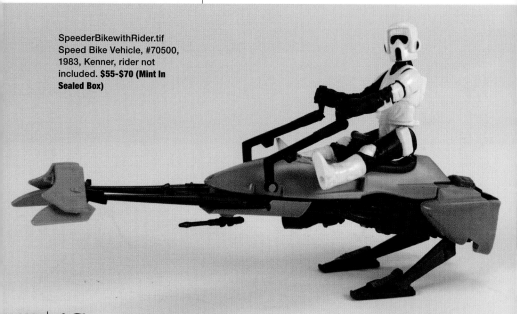

SpeederBikewithRider.tif
Speed Bike Vehicle, #70500, 1983, Kenner, rider not included. **$55-$70 (Mint In Sealed Box)**

Millennium Falcon, the galaxy's most
famous modified light freighter owned
by Han Salo, #391101, 1979, Kenner.
$2,800-$3,200 (Mint In Sealed Box)

were the first deluxe 12-inch action figures
made in the likenesses of the most popular
characters from the original *Star Wars*
trilogy, and are held in high regard by *Star
Wars* aficionados.

Apart from releasing nearly one
hundred *Star Wars* action figures, Kenner
crafted 5 creatures, 31 vehicles (including
store exclusives), 13 playsets (again,
including exclusives), a few assorted
accessories, and 7 action figure storage
cases. Also adding to the collecting fun
were assorted ephemera: proof of-purchase
mail-away items, a Collector's Action Stand,
an Action Figure Survival Kit, a Display
Arena, myriad Power of the Force coins,
pack-in posters, and special bagged figures
solicited before their official retail carded
release. These special offers added an air of
anticipation to the hobby of collecting, and
most kids couldn't wait for these packages
to arrive in the mail: Kenner always treated
kids as truly special customers.

Regardless of all of this, the vintage
Star Wars line was cancelled in 1985
due to poor sales and a shrinking sci-fi
marketplace. Sadly, it would be ten long
years before *Star Wars* collectors would be
treated to any new toys.

To much fanfare, Kenner released a
new series of *Star Wars* action figures in
1995, and the "Power of the Force" line (or,
as fans dubbed it, the "POTF II" line) was
born. Although initially criticized for their
bulky statures and poor facial sculpts, the
POTF II action figure line lasted five years
and yielded many excellent new figures, a
slew of unproduced characters, and even
improved paint applications, intricate
figure sculpts, and added articulation.

Today, *Star Wars* toys are some of
the most desirable action figures on the
secondary market, and the people who
collect them are often the most devoted
in the hobby. Vintage figures and vehicles
still sealed in their packages command
outrageous prices on online auction sites
such as eBay and in collectible stores.

The Star Wars toy universe is immense.
For a complete look, please see The
Ultimate Guide to Vintage Star Wars
Action Figures, 1977-1985.

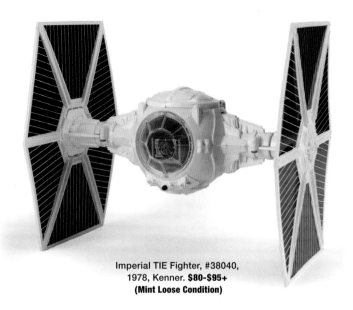

Imperial TIE Fighter, #38040,
1978, Kenner. **$80-$95+**
(Mint Loose Condition)

Jabba the Hutt Action
Playset, one of the most
popular of all Kenner Star
Wars playsets, #704901, 1983,
Kenner. **$165-$190+ (Mint In
Sealed Box)**

Star Wars Land Speeder (a.k.a. Landspeeder), #38020, 1978, Kenner. **$260-$300+** (Mint In Sealed Box; characters not included)

◄ A-Wing Fighter, #93700, 1985, Kenner. **$475-$510 (Mint In Sealed Box; character not included)**

▼ X-Wing Fighter, made famous by pilot Luke Skywalker, #38030, 1978, Kenner. **$520-$550+ (Mint In Sealed Box)**

Rebel Armored Snowspeeder, #39610, 1980, Kenner. **$650-$725+ (Mint In Box)**

▶ Scout Walker vehicle, #69800, 1982, Kenner. **$140-$175 (Mint In Sealed Box; character not included)**

Rancor Monster figure, #71060, 1984, Kenner. **$245-$275+ (Mint in Sealed Box)**

AT-AT (Imperial All Terrain Armored Transport),
Empire Strikes Back, 1981. **$825-975+**
(Mint In Sealed Box; characters not included)

Tatooine Skiff, featured in
Return of the Jedi, #715401,
1985, Kenner, characters not
included. **$225-$250+ (Mint
Loose Condition)**

World War II Collectibles

During the more than seven decades since the end of World War II, veterans, collectors, and nostalgia-seekers have eagerly bought, sold, and traded the "spoils of war." Actually, souvenir collecting began as soon as troops set foot on foreign soil. Whether Tommies from Great Britain, Doughboys from the United States, or Fritzies from Germany, soldiers eagerly looked for trinkets and remembrances that would guarantee their place in the historic events that unfolded before them. Helmets, medals, Lugers, field gear, daggers, and other pieces of war material filled parcels and duffel bags on the way back home.

As soon as hostilities ended in 1945, the populations of defeated Germany and Japan quickly realized they could make money selling souvenirs to the occupation forces. The flow of war material increased. Values became well established; a Luger was worth several packs of cigarettes, a helmet, just one. A Japanese sword was worth two boxes of K-rations, an Arisaka bayonet was worth a Hershey's chocolate bar.

Over the years, these values have remained proportionally consistent. Today, that "two-pack" Luger might be worth $5,000 and that one-pack helmet, $1,500. The Japanese sword might fetch $1,200 and the Arisaka bayonet $95. Though values have increased dramatically, demand has not dropped off. In fact, World War II collecting is the largest segment of the militaria hobby.

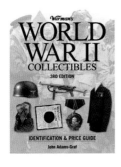

For more information on World War II collectibles, see *Warman's World War II Collectibles Identification and Price Guide*, 3rd edition, by John Adams-Graf.

"UNITED we are strong" propaganda poster, No. 64, U.S. Government Printing Office, 1943, issued by Office of War Information, near fine condition, folding creases, 28 1/2" x 40". **$188**

Courtesy of Heritage Auctions, ha.com

▲ U.S. 82nd Airborne
soldier's jump jacket
and trousers, including
paratrooper M2 knife.
$3,200-$3,865

*Courtesy of
AdvanceGuardMilitaria.com*

▲ U.S. AAF 13th Air Force
5th Bomb Group aerial
gunner's painted A2 flight
jacket. **$2,650**

*Courtesy of
AdvanceGuardMilitaria.com*

◄ German SS Judicial
Service Sturmführer
black tunic. **$10,000-
$12,000**

Courtesy of HistoryHunter.com

German Army officer's
brigade belt and buckle,
marks on buckle, with
German Red Cross officer's
belt and buckle. **$660**

*Courtesy of Morphy Auctions,
morphyauctions.com*

German M35 SS double-decal helmet.
$8,000-$11,000

Courtesy of HistoryHunter.com

USAAF flying helmet group: leather A-11 flying
helmet in excellent condition with avionics,
Type A-14 soft rubber oxygen mask with
straps, and pair of AN-6530 flying goggles
with clear lenses and soft rubber. **$435**

Courtesy of Heritage Auctions, ha.com

U.S. Army officer's summer cap
owned and used by General Joseph
W. "Vinegar Joe" Stilwell. **$3,585**

Courtesy of Heritage Auctions, ha.com

**Luftwaffe
Fallschirmjäger
helmet, 2nd Model.
$5,500-$7,000**

*Courtesy of Hermann-
Historica.de*

Kriegsmarine rear admiral's service
cap. **$8,000-$9,000**

Courtesy of Hermann-Historica.de

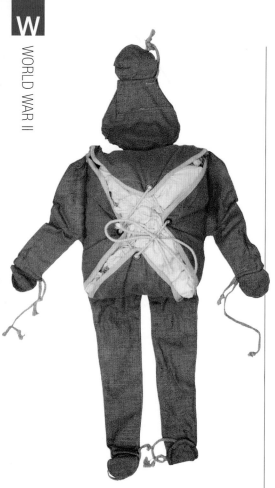

British "Rupert" D-Day dummy
paratrooper. **$3,346**

Courtesy of Heritage Auctions, ha.com

USAAF QAC A-5 parachute harness
with A-4 parachute. **$800-$1,000**

Courtesy of AdvanceGuardMilitaria.com

Large World War II airplane propeller, wood with brass tips,
marked "No. 1901 9' x 5'9," very good condition, 9' 1" x 14 1/2". **$720**

Courtesy of Morphy Auctions, morphyauctions.com

▲ German factory-cased, gold-plated and relief-engraved Walther Model PP pistol as presented to SA officer, Viktor Lutze. **$241,500**

Courtesy of Rock Island Auction Co., rockislandauction.com

▶ American World War II folding military chair along with early 20th century folding stool, Michigan, chair 19" wide x 34 1/2" high, stool 28 1/4" high. **$209**

Courtesy of Michaan's Auctions, michaans.com

▼ Winchester T3 carbine with original pattern M-2 infrared sniper scope and accessories. **$15,000-$30,000**

Courtesy of Rock Island Auction Co., rockislandauction.com

Japanese prisoners of war scroll, printed on cloth with wooden scroll bars, 25 prisoners tried in Tokyo Trials listed, scroll dedicated "To Lieutenant Herbert J. Herring/With many thanks and compliments," dated Jan. 12, 1948, three months before trial convened; 21 3/4" x 71 1/2". **$4,780**

Courtesy of Heritage Auctions, ha.com

British Bren Mk2 machine gun. $38,000-$42,000

Courtesy of James D. Julia Auctioneers, jamesdjulia.com

Nazi souvenir ladle/serving spoon, stainless steel, marked "MDA Sch.dA" with swastika and cog wheel on back ("Modell des Amtes Schönheit der Arbeit" or "Model approved by the office for pleasant work"), marked "RKW Kantinen DR RBD Augsburg" with crude eagle on front (likely from military canteen in Augsburg, Germany), marked "Rostfrei" (German rust-free stainless steel) on handle, very good condition, 10 1/2" long. $120

▲ **Japanese Type 99 4x sniper scope with case. $2,500-$3,000**

Courtesy of Chris William

Courtesy of Morphy Auctions, morphyauctions.com

▶ **A 1933-1945 Nazi officer's sword with lion head handle, manufactured in Eichorn, Germany, excellent condition, 38" long. $900**

Courtesy of Morphy Auctions, morphyauctions.com

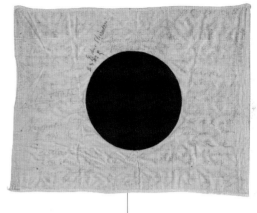

Japanese flag, cloth, autographed by 24 accused World War II criminals including Prime Minister Tojo, 13" x 10 1/2". **$16,100**

Courtesy of Heritage Auctions, ha.com

▲ German reversible lace-up camouflage smock. **$11,000-$13,000**

Courtesy of HistoryHunter.com

British MK II paratrooper helmet. **$1,250-$1,700**

Courtesy of Peter Suciu

▼ U.S. Red Cross Woman's Military Welfare Service uniform. **$385-$425**

Courtesy of AdvanceGuardMilitaria.com

Standard of III Battalion of Artillery Regiment 26, crimson silk cloth with silver fringe on three sides, both faces with hand-embroidered black army eagle on field of cream-colored silk surrounded by silver-embroidered oak leaf wreath on Iron Cross, 51 cm x 69 cm (without sleeve). The 26th artillery regiment took part in the campaign in France and the occupation of Belgium and France. On the Eastern Front, it fought at Smolensk, Moscow, Vyasma, Rzhev, Orel, the Don Bend, Kursk, Tschaussy, Mogilev and Kholm. **$41,325**

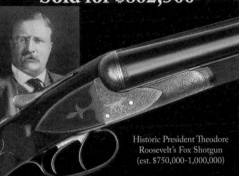